W0006851

Manipulation, Body Language, Dark Psychology

8 Books in 1: Secret Techniques on How to Analyze People in 1 Minute and Instantly Recognize Mind Control, Persuasion and NLP

Table of Contents
PART 1

PART 2

Errore. Il segnalibro non è definito.

PART 3

PART 4

PART 5

PART 6

PART 7

Dark Psychology

Introduction

The dark name triad for personality traits certainly sounds scary and dramatic. However, in recent years the interest of researchers is increasing for these three characteristics, which, when displayed in combination, compose the portrait of a man who is capable of conquering everything without anything being able to stop him.

The dark triad of personality consists of three characteristics: narcissism, Machiavellianism, and psychopathy. These, when they appear at a low level that does not meet the criteria for a full diagnosis, are pieces of people's personality, such as honesty or conscientiousness. How these characteristics appear is no different from any other personality elements: there are some genetic clues, but above all, the environment and upbringing play the most decisive role.

People who exhibit these characteristics tend to follow the so-called "fast life strategy." This kind of attitude of life includes reckless actions, drug use, hectic love life, and interpersonal aggression. Generally, in choosing instant gratification or late earnings but with more excellent value, people with high scores in these three features choose the first option. Of course, these uncritical decisions and frivolous lifestyles have similar effects on the social, physical, and mental health of these people. But let us look at each character and their products individually.

Narcissism: Considered as the most adaptive and socially acceptable of the three characteristics. Narcissists are characterized by a tendency to continually seek external confirmation, attention, excessive self-confidence, and feelings of megalomania. They are impatient, generally, ignore the feelings of others, and rarely make self-criticism. It is considered more adaptive, as narcissists are usually social and entertaining individuals as long as their needs and purposes are naturally served.

Machiavellianism: Machiavellian personality is characterized by duplicity in interpersonal relationships and tendencies of manipulation of others. It refers to the so-called manipulative character. It also includes a cynical attitude to ethics, a lack of barriers, and a primary interest in personal gain. People with this trait exhibit a lack of emotions, which helps them not to bond with other people, making it easier to manipulate them. Often, there is a correlation of this characteristic with high achievement in the workplace: Machiavellian personalities often meet in the field of politics, business, and generally in areas with hierarchy and potential for development.

Psychopathy: The concept of psychopathy mainly includes low emotional life and a lack of feeling of shame. In general, its characteristics are divided into two major categories: those related to emotional distancing and those that include an antisocial lifestyle. It is worth noting that despite the similarity of Machiavellianism and psychopathy, they are distinct characteristics, which often overlap.

These three characteristics (as well as their respective clinical disorders, in the case of narcissism and psychopathy) generally occur more frequently in men, and the corresponding impact accompanies each on people's lives. Psychopathy, compared to the other two characteristics, is associated with lower life expectancy and a worse quality of life. Often, people with high rates on the scales of psychopathy are involved in criminal behaviors and dangerous situations. Narcissism, on the other hand, being the most adaptive characteristic, is associated with higher life expectancy: thanks to their functional interpersonal relationships, narcissists live a "full" life and exhibit high rates on happiness measurement scales. Machiavellianism does not indicate that it is significantly correlated with a better or worse quality of life.

These three characteristics, then, may exist to a high or low degree in any human being. It is important to stress that they can live separately or coexist: the existence of one does not presuppose or negate the fact of the other.

What Is Dark Psychology

People who cannot connect with others or have the ability to deliberately disconnect their emotions fall under what we call "the dark triad." These sets of personality traits constitute narcissism, Machiavellianism, and psychopathy.

In extreme cases, people who have these dark characteristics become criminals or lose themselves into mental illness.

People with these characteristics and behaviors are said to have a dark personality.

Narcissism

Narcissists are "snake charmers." At first, people seem to love them. They seem content and attractive. But when time passes, they can become very dangerous. People around them may be unable to see their true intentions: to be admired and gain power.

Routines tend to bore them, so they are looking for challenges. This is why most narcissists are leaders or work in professions that create a high level of stress. According to psychoanalyst Michael Maccoby, narcissism is an increasing disorder in the upper stocks of the business world. It is directly linked to competition, pay, and glamour.

The Negative Aspect of Narcissism

One of their strengths is their ability to convince others. They easily persuade others to do what they want them to do. In short: they get what they want. Also, it's not difficult for them because they don't have any empathy. They are not picky at all when it comes to the means and strategies, they use to achieve their goals.

Selfish people have zero interest in and do not worry about others, although it may seem so. They do not experience regret, and they are insensitive to people in their surroundings' feelings and needs.

Machiavellism

The Machiavellians are not trying to impress anyone. Instead, they turn out as they are and prefer to see things clearly because they can manipulate others better that way. They focus on the feelings of the people they want to manage to get what they want. If they anticipate your emotions, they will be able to choose the right strategy to manipulate you.

According to psychologist Daniel Goleman, people with Machiavellian traits have less empathy. Their emotional cold seems to come from an inability to treat their own and others' feelings.

Emotions make them so uncomfortable at ease that, when they feel anxiety, they usually don't know how to distinguish it from sadness or fatigue.

Psychopathy

Psychopaths regard others as objects that they can use and throw away at their discretion. Unlike the other personalities of the dark triad, they rarely experience anxiety. It's like they have no idea what it's like to be afraid.

Without fear, they can remain calm even in emotionally intense, dangerous, and frightening situations.

Psychopaths have neural circuits desensitized to the outer periphery of the emotional spectrum associated with suffering. Therefore, their cruelty seems insensitive because they are unable to detect it. Nor do they experience remorse or shame.

However, psychopaths can quickly get close to others and press their buttons if it leads to them getting what they want. They are excellent persuaders. But even if they perform highly in social contexts, they only understand relationships and the behavior of others from a logical or intellectual perspective.

How to Avoid Falling into The Trap

If the dark triad is present in your relationship, there is likely to be abuse and psychological violence. These people are toxic and use force and manipulation to entangle their victims. The key to not falling into their trap is healthy emotional independence. Learn how to set clear limits in your relationships and let no one violate them. Your safety must come first.

The Dark Triad is a collective term for three types of power characters, all of whom bear symbols of lack of empathy and potential for cruelty, omnipotence, and extraordinary selfishness.

Research on the "dark triad" is used in applied psychology, especially in the areas of law enforcement, clinical psychology, and management. People who in tests receive high values of these characteristics are more likely to commit crimes, cause social distress, and managers can create severe problems for an organization, especially if they have significant leadership functions.

Clinical Description

All characters have the potential for the extreme desire for power, control needs over others, and emotional cold in the face of other people's misfortune or sadness. The picture also includes mythomania, i.e., inability to stick to the truth. There is also comorbidity where individual characteristics are expressed depending on the situation. A Machiavellian person should also suffer from narcissism and psychopathy.

The narcissistic personality disorder is characterized by omnipotence with grandiose self-perception of one's personality, a great self-image, and impossibility to cope with criticism but which instead portrays itself at it best in everything. Psychologically, researchers such as Kohut argue that the disorder is based on a protective mechanism of a radically weak, shamed, or damaged self-image.

The inability characterizes the psychopath to compassion and incomprehension of the suffering of others. One's own needs take precedence over everyone else's, and meeting these needs often means using methods that risk harming others. A psychopath who can't feel with others can't experience regret either. The psychopath may also have the conditions for a learned social competence that can be used to seduce and manipulate his victims. Studies in people in prison have shown that a disproportionate proportion of people have characteristics that characterize psychopathy. Several studies also suggest that psychopathy may originate from the fact that parts of the brain are more or less morbid or exhibit degenerate or damaged conditions similar to Alzheimer's.

Criticism of The Theory

A sociopath is sometimes considered to be the same as a psychopath. This is questionable because a person with an antisocial personality disorder has different expressions than the psychopath who can plan their atrocities. Instead, the sociopath's behavior includes impulsive risk-taking and erraticness that can affect even one's person. Such a person has more incredible difficulty in creating a family or getting and keeping a job.

History

In 1998, McHoskey, Worzel, and Szyarto provoked controversy in psychological research by arguing that self-love, Machiavellianism, and mental illness are more or fewer interchangeable in usual tests. Paulhus and Williams found extensive features in behavior, personality, and cognitive characteristics to suggest that they were different designs; However, they concluded that further research was needed to clarify how and why they overlap.

Origin

A lengthy "heritage and environment" discussion has been practical to the dark triad. Investigate has begun to explore the origins of the dark triad properties. In the same way as research on the Big Five (Five-Factor Theory) personality traits, empirical studies have been conducted to understand the (genes) and environmental factors (upbringing) of biology in the development of dark triad properties.

One of how researchers try to dissect the relative influence of genetic and environmental factors on personality (and individual differences more generally) is a broad method of investigation that is loosely grouped under the heading "twin studies." For example, in a twin study approach, researchers compare the personality scores of monozygotic (MZ) or identical twins who grew up together to dizygotic (DZ) or identical twins who grew up together. Since both types of twins in this design are raised together, all twin pairs are considered to have shared a familiar environment. In contrast, identical twins share 100% of their genes, while identical twins only share about 50% of their genes. Therefore, it is considered possible to distinguish personality traits from genetic influences by first obtaining the MZ correlation (reflecting 100% familiar environment and 100% shared genes) and subtracting the DZ correlation (which reflects a 100% friendly environment and 50% shared genes). This difference represents 50% of genetic influence and doubles by 100% of gene power, which is a way to derive an index of heredity (sometimes called the heredity coefficient,

Internet Trolls

A 2013 case study suggested that there are some similarities between antisocial and intense troll activities, and a 2014 survey indicated that troll activities are an Internet manifestation of everyday sadism. Both studies suggest that troll activity may be linked to bullying in both adolescents and adults.

Narcissism is not only alive in our world today, but it is also a toxic trait of character that we all know is everywhere. How can you protect yourself and not become the victim of such manipulation? The first step is to identify these people around you.

Let's be honest if there is a common belief that defines the world is the fact that we like to be considered better than others in what we do. Many take every opportunity to boast even globally about how much better, richer, and more successful they are. Growing up in such an environment it is next to present people with the "dark triad." We raise narcissists, psychopaths, and sociopaths.

The "dark triad" is a term used in psychology to refer to a set of personality traits that fit into three specific categories: narcissism (need for separate treatment and admiration), psychopathy (cruelty and insensitiveness), and Machiavellianism (need for manipulation of others).

Many tests can diagnose these conditions, but they are not useful to those who try to identify these toxic individuals and protect themselves. We need to practice and learn the signs and patterns that stand out to them. If you're dealing with a toxic person in your life, it's time to find out what to watch out for.

12 Signs That You're Dealing with Such People

They change reality as it suits them to match their narrative.

There will be times when it will be apparent that the version of events of toxic individuals will not match reality. But that's not going to stop them! Instead of admitting they're wrong, they'll use other tools to manipulate the situation and change the truth until it fits their narrative. The worst part? They're so good at it that they'll make you believe their version.

They Create Love Triangles to Control Their Relationship
If there's one thing, narcissists, psychopaths, and sociopaths demand in all areas of their lives, it's controlled. When they feel they're losing him, they'll take drastic steps to bring him back. The use of erotic triangles can help them in such matters. They will give you the impression that there is someone else they are interested in to be jealous of when in fact, they may only be keeping in touch with an ex without any intention of pursuing anything.

They Highlight Your Flaws at Every Opportunity
It is necessary to ensure that their victims do not gain strength or self-confidence, as this would allow them to defend themselves and escape them. To make sure this doesn't will highlight your imperfections at every opportunity. Gradually they dissolve you by destroying your self-esteem to be powerless and defenseless.

Desperate for Confirmation, They're Looking for Her Everywhere
Although they try to appear confident, toxic people have their issues with their self-esteem and self-confidence. That's why they feel the need to seek confirmation in everything they do. Desperate for your attention, they may not ask for it clearly, but you'll understand. Very deep down, they need someone to tell them they're "right."

Even If You Do, They Can't Stop Lying
Lies are not an option in their lives is an instinct with which they act. They often tell so many lies that they have to relate more to support their lies. This creates a web in which they can be lost between reality and fiction or even believe their lies by making them more convincing. If anyone understands them, they'll either be covered up with even more lies or show no repentance as if nothing happened.

Whenever It's Not in Their Interest to Talk, They Change the Subject
There will be a time when others will notice their harmful actions and want explanations. However, they are not going to admit their mistakes. Instead, they'll do anything to turn the conversation into something irrelevant. They have mastered this skill so well that most people don't even notice that they did and completely forget the first issue.

They Often Play the Victim to Attract Compassion
If they realize they're in a difficult situation, just observe how quickly they're going to turn everything around. Playing the role of the victim will not be responsible for any event that happened, since how could you not see how much they are suffering? They can still cry.

Despite Their Incredibly Toxic Nature, They Act as If They Are Completely Innocent
Observe their behavior. They'll probably do what's nothing but a naïve victim. If you overlook it, you'll see someone promoting destructive behavior. They want to provoke rivalries and jealousy with a sweet smile.

You'll Start to Wonder If Your Feelings Are Yours When You're Around Them
They're very good at playing with your emotions and provoking what suits them. If they want you to cry and feel hurt, they'll make sure you do it. Likewise, if you have to feel grateful for what you have, they can do that as well. In general, you can't tell what your feelings are.

They'll Play with Your Emotions Until You Explode, And Then They'll Blame You for Your Behavior
If they don't have anything sure to blame you, then rest assured that they will create something. They will compete with you and challenge you until the moment you break out. They mean that you react in this way to everything, so it is not their fault.

They Are Energetic Vampires, They Feed Off Your Energy and Drain You
Have you noticed that when you are with them, you feel completely exhausted? These toxic individuals feed on your energy and drain you at every opportunity. This includes both your physical strength as well as your emotional and mental power. They're exhausting you to take advantage of themselves.

9

Dark Psychology Traits

One reason why our personality is such an important psychological factor is that it tells us about the kind of lives we will most likely have. For example, if you are very conscientious, then you are more likely to have good physical health and more harmonious relationships. Extroverted people are happier, very neurotic people face more mental health problems, and open-minded people make higher profits. And, as you would expect, the most "pleasant" people are also famous and have many friends.

But our personalities don't just appear in our long-term success and prosperity. They are also linked to the kind of things we do daily. A new study published in the journal Personality and Individual Differences has mapped these "signatures" of personality traits in the Five Factors Model in more detail than ever before. And the results are excellent.

While extroverts are more likely to go to parties and that conscientious people are less likely to be late, one might not expect that extroverts spend more time enjoying a hot bath or that conscientiousness goes hand in hand with reading fewer books.

The researchers profiled about 800 people, most of whom were white, and their average age was 51 years old. The personality test asked participants to accurately assess how accurately 100 different adjectives described their personalities, including words such as "boring, polite, neat, relaxed, moody, bright and artistic."

The researchers then compared the personality scores with the participants' responses, after four years, about the frequency of performing 400 different activities in the last year, from reading a book to singing in the shower.

Extroverted people, in addition to spending more time taking a hot bath, seemed to spend more time organizing parties, drinking in bars, discussing ways to make money, talking on the phone while driving, decorating, and trying to tan (but not all at the same time). Higher consciousness, by contrast, is distinguished by avoiding various activities, including such harmless occupations as reading (which researchers thought can be seen by the very conscientious as a luxury of recreation), cursing, and chewing a pencil.

People who had high counts of prosthetics, meanwhile, said they spent more time ironing, playing with their children. Washing dishes, apparently because their strong motivation to keep others happy means they would instead do the chores than have an indoor crop. Strangely enough, they were also more likely to sing in the shower or the car.

Neurotics, however, were more often involved in activities related to reducing mental distress, such as taking more sedatives and antidepressants. But they also admitted more anti-social attitudes, such as a more frequent lack of composure or irony towards others, perhaps because they struggle to keep their emotions in check.

Finally, the opening to the experience was following some apparent behaviors such as reading poetry, watching opera, smoking marijuana, and visual creation, but also some less obvious, such as cursing in front of others, eating spicy food for breakfast, or relaxing around the house without clothes. (To be exact, those with the highest measurements said they were about twice as likely to have sat naked for more than 15 times in the previous year, compared to those with a lower score). They were also less likely to follow a sports team.

This study is impressive for the vast range of activities it explores. However, it remains to be seen whether the same personality-behavior links will be found in other cultures around the world and, of course, many thousands of other daily behaviors remain to be explored. The new findings add exciting elements to previous research on the behavioral-personality relationship, most of which tend to focus on more specific activities or only certain characteristics.

The Dark Trinity of Personality

Another modern study has examined the behaviors, some more obvious than others, associated with the standard features of the Dark Trinity of Narcissus, Maciabelianism, and Psychopathy. For example, people with high scores in psychopathy are not only more prone to violence, intimidation, and aggression. They also maintain unusually prolonged eye contact and, along with Machiavellians, are more likely to engage and enjoy online trolling.

There is an essential aspect of this area of research:

By knowing more about harmful and unhealthy daily behaviors associated with different personality traits, we could create better, more targeted health campaigns and interventions.

Also, personality research often involves people answering questionnaires about themselves, hopefully honestly. Discovering some peculiar and less anticipated behavioral correlations of the characteristics of the Five Factors, there is the possibility that one day a questionnaire will be made asking people about their activities without realizing that they are revealing their personality.

Of course, there is also a fun but also a particular element that arises from the new findings: for example, if you swear often, you can now justify your habit as an indication of your openness. And maybe now you'll be more able to forgive your roommate's tradition of singing in the shower. Ultimately, it could be another sign of his pleasant personality.

Think of this dark triad: narcissism, psychopathy, and Machiavellianism as the Bermuda triangle that is dangerous to approach! The characteristics of all three profiles often overlap and create a personality profile that is destructive and toxic, especially when it comes to close relationships, in which our defenses are weak.

One example is that of a woman who was the victim of a fake ID. Her bank and credit accounts were cooperated. At the time, she was in love with her boyfriend with whom she lived with him in her apartment. He spoke regularly with the FBI and suffered from severe anxiety and emotional stress. Authorities in the discovery of the culprit were found ineffective.

Her fiance was very supportive in conducting the investigation. He comforted her, occasionally bought her gifts, and paid her the monthly rent of the money she gave him. When the landlord finally faced months of delinquency, she realized that the criminal was, in fact, her boyfriend. The latter put the rental money in his pocket, in addition to the gifts he bought them. Her refusal made it difficult to accept the truth about ruthless gaslighting.

So, What Is the Dark Triad?
Generally, the term refers to people with "subclinical" symptoms, meaning they may not necessarily have a complete narcissistic personality disorder (NDS) or antisocial personality disorder (SDP). Machiavellianism arose from Machiavelli's philosophy and is not a disorder but a syndrome.

Narcissism is characterized by the pursuit of ego satisfaction, vanity, a sense of superiority, magnificence, domination, and high right.

Machiavellianism is characterized by manipulation – a derogatory, two-faced, and immoral personality focused on self-interest and personal gain. Psychopathy is distinguished by cruelty, impulsiveness, and constant antisocial and bold behavior.

Common Features of The Dark Triad/ Dark Triad
A recent comparative survey tried to analyze the differences between these three malicious personalities. To a certain extent, everyone acts aggressively in personal interest and with a lack of empathy or remorse. These psychological profiles, however, are specific to handling, exploiting, and deceiving others, even though their motives and tactics vary. They violate social standards and moral values and lie, deceive, deceive, steal, and intimidate. It is thought that genetic factors undermine their personality to some extent.

Machiavellianism and psychopathy are more closely related due to malicious behavior, while narcissists are defensive and more fragile. This is because magnificence and arrogance are a false cover for deeper feelings of inadequacy. (See "Relationships with Narcissists.") Men outperform women, especially when psychopathic traits were measured (i.e., not just deception, manipulation, etc.).

All three types (narcissism to a lesser extent) experienced low pleasure, as measured by the personality test of the Big Five psychometric tests that measure five characteristics: extroversion, neuroticism, kindness, consciousness, and receptiveness to experience.

Machiavellians and psychopaths are more deprived of consciousness (Why work when you can cheat and steal!) Psychopaths have the lowest levels of neuroticism or negative emotions, which makes them more threatening. Unsurprisingly, narcissists were more open and much more extroverted. Extroversion correlates with the fact that narcissists tend to be creative.

Cheating
All three personalities lack honesty and honesty, which includes honesty, faith, lack of greed, and justice. A study on cheating revealed that all three cheat when the risk of being caught is low. When the risk is high, psychopaths and Machiavellians (when their thought energy is low) fool. They're both deliberately lying. Narcissists have higher levels of delusion than deliberate dishonesty.

Psychosocial Consequences
Comparative research of the dark triad examined various behaviors, such as aggression (bullying, sadism, aggression, and violence), unstable lifestyle (impulsiveness, risk-taking, and substance use), sexual activity, such as in the performance of mental states of themselves and others), problematic mental health (depression, loneliness, anxiety) lack of values, "deadly sins" and moral disengagement, i.e. "the rules do not apply to me"), antisocial tactics (cheating, lying), interpersonal problems (lack of empathy and consciousness).

Machiavellians and psychopaths scored higher on these psychosocial issues, and psychopaths twice as high as narcissists. The highest scores were among psychopaths, with aggression being the highest in grade characteristics. Narcissists were rated on charges of aggression, sexual issues, interpersonal difficulties, and antisocial tactics. Among the three personalities, most of the high scores were due to psychopathic traits; when they were under surveillance (removed), narcissism was still calculated for interpersonal difficulties.

No Empathy
To further understand the lack of empathy among the personalities of the dark triad, the research examined emotional heart, which is the ability to have an appropriate emotional response to the feelings of others, and cognitive empathy, which is the ability to discern the emotional states of others. They found that all three personality types had no emotional empathy but had incredible mental heart. Especially all three guys felt positive, looking at sad faces and feeling negative, seeing happy pictures.

Overall empathy was lower among psychopaths and Machiavellians, and participants who were at a high level of the three personality types had the lowest emotional empathy. Narcissists scored the most elevated position in cognitive heart; the fact that these people are not sensitive to the feelings of others while maintaining the ability to appreciate the feelings of others allows them to manipulate people, ignoring the harm they cause strategically.

Protect Yourself
If you think there's a chance, you're in a relationship with a Dark Triad personality, look for psychotherapy. Learn about narcissistic abuse, related forms of abuse, abusive relationships, and narcissistic relationships. Violence is followed by emotional abuse. If you have been threatened with violence by such a person, do not expect it to happen again, or believe that it will not happen again, ask for help.

The Dark Psychology of Personality and Love

The Dark Trinity
The Dark Trinity of personality has attracted a lot of research interest. It refers to three personality traits that reflect a tendency to meet personal goals and desires directly. People with these characteristics may be aimed at social harm, characterized by emotional coldness, duplicity, and aggression. More specifically, the Dark Trinity includes:

1. narcissism: A sense of megalomania along with a tendency to demonstrate and exploit others
2. Machiavellianism: A manipulating form of personality with a lack of emotional
3. psychopathy: Personality with a tendency to influence others and lack of empathy. At the behavioral level, psychopathy is a key element of antisociality.

We note that none of these three characteristics refer to mental disorders. These individuals still have good levels of functionality in their daily lives. It is therefore not surprising that the Dark Trinity of Personality has been extensively studied in the general population.

Jonason and Kavanagh conducted an interesting study in which they examined the relationship between love and the Dark Trinity. In erotic relationships, there are six different approaches that the person can adopt. These have been identified through specially designed questionnaires. Depending on the style of love adopted by the person, there are also different effects on his relationship, such as the levels of pleasure experienced by her.

The Styles of Love
A high score in statements such as "my partner and I have the right chemistry between us" indicates an erotic style (eros), while a high score in comments like "I like to play with different partners" indicates a game-playing kind in love (Ludus). Also, there is a realistic style (pragma) reflected in statements such as "I will choose a partner based on how he/she helps my career." The long-standing kind of love is manifested through the concentration of high scores in statements of the type "my most pleasant love affairs have resulted from good friendships." In contrast, the selfless style (agape) results from high scores in words such as "I could stand anything for my love.

The Styles of Love And The Dark Trinity
In previous research, the Dark Trinity has been associated with sexual, short-term relationships, which arise mainly from the external attractiveness of the partner. The Dark Trinity has also been linked to emotional difficulties during the relationship. Warmth and selflessness in love are not related to these personality types.

In line with the above, the researchers found that the Dark Trinity is characterized by a) game-playing and b) practical love style. The first style may help these individuals keep their partners at a distance so that they can maintain a love life dominated by short relationships. The realistic style, on the other hand, perhaps reflects the limited empathy (and the more generally emotional world) that characterizes the people of the Dark Trinity. These people, in short, often choose companions according to their usefulness.

Good or Evil
According to Socrates' moral theory, knowledge is identified with virtue and these only lead to happiness. Integrity for Socrates is not about applying general rules that tell us what to do to be good, but it is a certain state of the soul.

The soul leads us to this moral state when it knows what ARETI is. He who knows the content of virtue is virtuous. If our souls are not in this state, we cannot be good, and under no circumstances can our actions be good. For Socrates, stories are good when the character is good.

Knowledge is, therefore, necessary for the good moral condition of the individual as this knowledge modifies our character and brings about a natural result. Socrates also spoke of various virtues and virtue in its entirety that includes all the others. In this way, we either have the whole area, or we don't have it at all, and either we're good, or we're not. According to Socrates, all ARETI is unified and summarized in the knowledge of what is ultimately good or bad. Why are some people particularly selfish, manipulative, and rude? The BBC's David Robson asks a scientist to talk about the darkest aspects of the human intellect.

"If you had the opportunity to grind harmless insects in a coffee grinder, would you enjoy the experience? Even if these insects had names and you could hear their shell breaking? Or would you feel a perverse pleasure scaring an unsuspecting man with some loud noise?"

These are just some of the experiments applied by Professor of Psychology Delroy Paulhus to understand the "dark personalities" that exist around us. Essentially, he's trying to answer a question we all might want to ask: why do some people enjoy being cruel? And we are talking not only about psychopathic killers but also about people engaged in school bullying and online trolling, even seemingly honest members of society, such as politicians and police officers.

The professor from British Columbia University in Canada says it's easy to draw quick and simplistic conclusions about these people: "We tend to label every person we meet as an "angel" or a "devil" because we want to simplify our world to good or bad people." Although Paulhus does not justify cruelty, his approach is more distancing, as a zoologist who studies poisonous insects would do, allowing him to create a "classification," as he calls it, with different species from the dark side of everyday life.

Self-esteem
Paulhus's interest began with narcissists, i.e., incredibly selfish and friendly people, who may attack to protect their sense of self-value. Then, more than a decade ago, graduate Kevin Williams suggested exploring whether these egocentric tendencies are linked to two other negative traits: Machiavellianism (cool manipulation of others) and psychopathy (anesthesia and apathy for the feelings of others). Together they discovered that these three characteristics were largely independent. However, they sometimes coincided with creating a "dark triad" – a triple blow of savagery.

It's amazing how honest the participants in his experiments can often be. In his questionnaires, he usually asks participants to agree to statements such as "I like to annoy the weakest people" or "It is preferable not to reveal your secrets to me." You might imagine that these characteristics would be very unpleasant to admit. Still, at least in the laboratory, people open up, and their responses seem to be related to the use of bullying in their real lives both in adolescence and in adulthood.

Paulhus focuses mainly on everyday people rather than on criminal or psychiatric incidents. These traits are, therefore, by no means apparent from the first meeting. "These people live within society, so they retain control so that they don't get in trouble themselves. But they can get your attention from time to time." People who exhibit particularly high narcissism, for example, quickly show their tendency to exaggerate for themselves, which is one of the strategies that help them to enhance their ego.

In some experiments, Paulhus presented them with a theme he had devised himself, and they quickly tried to show that they knew everything – only to get angry when he then challenged them. "It is surprising that this is part of a perception that allows them to live with a distorted positive view of themselves."

People Are Born Bad?
As soon as Paulhus began researching dark personalities, there were quickly others who wanted to find answers to some basic questions about the man. For example, are people born bad? Studies comparing identical and dizygous twins showed a relatively large genetic component for both narcissism and psychopathy.

Machiavellianism seems to be more due to the environment, i.e., it is possible to learn from others how to manipulate. However, whatever we have inherited does not remove our responsibility. Minna Lyons from the University of Liverpool claims that no one is born with psychopathy genes so that nothing can be done about it.

All you have to do is think about the antiheroes of popular culture – James Bond, Don Draper from the TV series Mad Men, or Jordan Belfort from the film Wolf of Wall Street to realize that dark personalities have sex appeal, which is supported by many scientific studies. Further clues may come from another key feature of man: the fact of whether you are morning or evening types.

Lyons and her student Amy Jones found that "night owls," people who stay up late but can't get up in the morning, are more likely to have some of the above negative characteristics. They are often risky, more manipulative (Machiavellian element) and narcissists, tend to exploit other people. This might make sense when you consider our evolution: perhaps dark personalities are more likely to steal, manipulate others, and have illicit sexual relations when everyone else is asleep, so they evolved into creatures of the night.

Whatever the truth of this theory, Paulhus agrees that there will always be room for them to exploit others: "Human societies are so complex that there are many different ways to enhance success – some require us to be polite and others to behave badly."

Dark Sides

Recently, the researcher began to examine even more the darkest aspects of the human soul. His questionnaire included even more extreme questions when he discovered that some people readily admitted that they were causing pain to others just for their pleasure. These trends are not only a reflection of narcissism, psychopathy, or Machiavellianism but seem to form their subtype – "everyday sadism." For this reason, Paulhus calls him a "dark foursome."

The "insect crushing machine" offered the ideal way for Paulhus and colleagues to check whether this reflects their behavior in real life. Although the participants did not know it, the mill had an escape route for the insects, but the machine still produced a sound that mimicked the insect shell when crushed.

Some felt disgusted and refused to take part, while others enjoyed the process. Paulhus comments: "They were willing not only to do something bad to the insects, but they were asking for even more, while others felt it was so disgusting that they didn't even want to be in the same room. These individuals also showed a high percentage of tests related to daily sadism."

Undoubtedly, a reasonable human being should not be particularly interested in the feelings of insects. The team then created a computer game that allowed participants to "punish" their competitor by channeling a loud noise into their headphones. That wasn't mandatory. Volunteers had to perform a tedious verbal task to earn the right to punish their competitors.

To Paulhus's surprise, those who showed sadistic behavior in their daily lives were more than willing to go all the further: "They were not only willing to do so, but they had an incentive to enjoy themselves, to make an extra effort to have the opportunity to harm other people." Even more important is the fact that there was no provocation or personal gain from this cruel behavior. They did so just for the sake of enjoyment.

Detection of Troll

The researcher believes this is directly related to online trolling:

"They seem to be the online version of everyday sadists since they spend time looking to harm other people." In an anonymous investigation into troll commentators, it was discovered that they had many dark features. Mostly, however, daily sadism, as well as enjoyment, were their primary motivation. Indeed, the insect crushing experiment has shown that those who have had sadistic behavior in their daily lives may have more moderate emotional reactions to all kinds of pleasant activities. So, perhaps, random acts of cruelty are attempts to escape their emotional emptiness.

His discoveries attracted the attention of police and military actors. They wanted to work with Paulhus to see if his views could explain why some people abuse their position. "The problem is that these people can consciously choose jobs where they are allowed to hurt other people," says Paulhus.

If so, further research could suggest ways to control dark personalities during recruitment. He is also excited about his new work on "moral Machiavellianism" and "common narcissists" – people who may have dark characteristics but use them for good (at least as they see it themselves). In some cases, hardness may be necessary.

"To become prime minister, you can't be soft, you have to have a fist, and you might have to hurt people, even be bad to achieve his moral goals," says Paulhus. "After all, dark personalities often have both the urge and the confidence to achieve their purpose – even Mother Teresa had a hard and dark side. You're not going to offer any help to society if you just sit in the house and be nice.

All this underscores the false dichotomy of good and evil that Paulhus wanted to examine. In a sense, this is as personal as a professional matter. He admits that he has a dark aspect of his behavior: for example, he likes to see violent sports such as Mixed Martial Arts.

"It didn't take long to see that I was above average in terms of these dark features," he says. "But given that I was curious as a scientist and enjoyed researching this kind of thing, I thought maybe I'd be in the best position to take a closer look at the dark side of man."

If you live with the whims of Greek philosophers, you realize how easy it is to get into the position of Ulysses and reach Ithaca. Because in the Odyssey, only the one who had I E L S and Well-intentioned managed to touch Bliss.

If you cut yourself off from your connection to THE WANT or Spiritual Power, psychological deviations are created. Good and evil, Bliss or agitation, and the one determined concerning something else, e.g., survival, if it is about human existence as a whole. Anything that enhances and increases a person's survival in the context of the reason is good. Anything that weakens it – in the context of defense as well – and kills it is evil. This becomes obvious from human health, mental and physical. No parasitic is healthy, even if it seemingly seems to be.

Any good condition that places you and strengthens your connection with the Spirit – Power or Purpose automatically puts you in the state of Bliss. Every bad situation cuts you off and removes you from the Purpose, thus releasing you from Bliss.

The Four Characteristics of Dark Personality
Have you ever met self-centered and socially offensive people, expressed through "blackness"? And yet, there is a scientific explanation for the phenomenon of dark personality.

Dr. Paulhus, a psychologist specializing in the field of personality, through his research, categorized the dark character as follows: Narcissists: Addicted to self-admiration and attention-attracting. Machiavellians: Particularly manipulative at times and narcissists, tend to trample on the rules.

They may cheat with ease, but they rarely have psychopathic tendencies.

Sociopaths/Psychopaths: Malicious, second nature the lie, with a feeling of magnificence, impulsive, selfish, persistent until they reach their goal.

Unable to feel remorse, sometimes drawing sadistic pleasure from the psychological pain they cause. In this case, malicious behavior acts as a defense mechanism to anything they consider a threat. This particular case of dark personality is due to traumatic childhood experiences.

The combination of the triad of characteristics of the dark personality, as well as the expression through dreadful things, is not an indication of a romantic, but a dangerous one. Human. It is worth noting that the dark triad of personality traits does not correspond to clinical disorders, but characteristics, at a sub-clinical level. The sadists of everyday life: They differ from the three categories as mentioned above in that they are not impulsive or manipulative.

But they enjoy cruelty towards their fellow man, whom they tend to "whip" with their words.

16

Their friendly mood is the biggest trap People with dark personalities are usually social and extroverted, gaining first impressions to exploit individuals who always socialize to their advantage.

They'll flatter the people they want to use. At first sight, available all types and weather. On the other side, grudge prevails, and productivity gives the reins to the method.

Seemingly organizational and willing to be useful, without minding anything, seem the ideal partners in the professional context.

Along the way, however, as Dr. Cohen argues, they will use this, creating a new reality, by their own rules, that meet their methodical plan. Having initially earned impressions, they cultivate self-doubt in others.

Dark personality creates passions in people with a negative self-image. Dark characters are quite attractive, as they bring out an unconventional "air" and mesmerizing impulsiveness, with playful tendencies of domination. Dr. Katie Payne argues that their stubbornness inspires self-confidence that fascinates them. Still, it is also a sample that should put someone in thoughts. After all, people with dark faces treat people possessively as their objects.

According to psychotherapist Jamie Duduyemi, because of their ability to handle people flawlessly, they often inspire illusory confidence, which will wear off over time, because they will not hesitate to exploit as narcissists to make their partner beg for their attention.

The dark side and the game of a seemingly "angel" A settled method they use to charm their other half is to make him/her feel like he/she is on top of the world.

They'll do that by getting used to him/her first in plenty of attention and flattery. Because their behavior has elements of mania, if their other half doesn't pay due attention to them or do them good, they become dramatic... They feel sick. Extremes, though flattering, are part of the game... When the target becomes accustomed to this worshipful behavior, then they will withdraw it to serve their demands.

The carefreeness gives its SERPs to the commandments. Another of their charming characteristics is that they may be "burned" inside them. Still, externally they show that they are carefree.

They don't care about anything and often turn into exactly what the person they've targeted needs. If you fall in love with a man with a dark personality, it is likely to lure you with his theatrical spontaneity into beautiful adventures. But when the "masks" fall, his motive will now be obvious. They usually have a history of turbulent, chaotic, and complicated relationships, as they are emotionally unreliable.

Their sweet spontaneity and frivolity can at first overwhelm the other half. Still, it results in a lack of limits and psychological pressure through endless psychological blackmail.

Love based on utility People with dark personality traits are "experts" in hiding their dark side.

Then it is only a matter of time before the surroundings discover, especially when they are no longer useful, their true "colors." When the exploitation begins, then the dynamics of the relationship become toxic.

Dark personalities will never be ashamed of their actions, as they have no moral barriers - hence they will not hesitate to hurt or harm

someone. The risk ignorance of their reckless behaviors and excessive selfishness overshadow the sad reality of low self-esteem, which usually comes out through interpersonal aggression - e.g., cynicism. They are not so interested in their personal development, which is why they are activated through comparison, using people as motivation.

The Thevicious cycle of patience ends in an unnamed fairy tale. A relationship with a person with a dark personality is a toxic relationship, as I have mentioned in my previous article, and is likely to result in "Stockholm Syndrome" and post-traumatic stress from emotional abuse.

The winner does not exist in such a relationship, but the winner will be the one who will let down first the tightrope of the relationship, which is about to break.

That's why the right way to deal with a dark personality is: - First, don't get angry because they feed their manipulation through it and take power.

Second, do not try to change a man with a dark personality, as it will exhaust you mentally. No matter what you give him, he's going to want more until he gets what he wants and passes it on to the next victim. The most beneficial thing, if you can't move away, is to set your limits strictly.

Dark Manipulation

Every way to go to the goal of "Machiavellism" is permissible. The consequences of this are not important. These people are usually very affordable and cold people and have no sincere emotional connection to other people.

While narcissists have something in common with selfishness and other people, there is still one thing that separates them: they can see themselves and their relationship in a realistic way.

Machiavelists don't try to impress anyone. Instead, they make themselves look who they are and prefer to see what is around them as they are because that way, they manipulate others more easily. They focus on other people's emotions to get what they want. If they can understand your feelings, they'll develop strategies that can manipulate you better.

According to psychologist Daniel Goleman, people with Machiavelist traits have a weaker sense of empathy. Their cold posture sits on their ability to manage their feelings and other people's emotions.

Sometimes emotions make them so uneasy that they experience anxiety that they can't separate from sadness or exhaustion. However, they understand very well what other people think. But as Goleman said, even if they're clear what to do in their heads, their hearts don't know.

Skillfully, because individuals who engage in emotional manipulation even though they often do not know the root cause of their behavior, are at a level that can distinguish which phrase, which word, allusion, action will bring about the desired result.

In other words, how will they manage to impose themselves and exercise power over you and reap any benefit for themselves?

But what is manipulation; this need for emotional manipulation comes from; from the deepest insecurities and phobias of the person who exercises them; from his self-centered behavior to meeting his own needs alone in order to claim the attention he believes he deserves; from the need for superiority; from his self-centered behavior to meeting his own needs alone in order to claim the attention he thinks he deserves; from the need for distinction; from his self-centered behavior to satisfy his own needs and only in order to claim the attention he believes he deserves; from the need for excellence; from his self-centered behavior to the satisfaction of his own needs and only in order to claim the attention he believes he deserves; from the need for superiority; from his self-centered behavior to the satisfaction of his own needs and only in order to claim the attention he believes he deserves; from the need for superiority; from his self-centered behavior to the satisfaction of his own needs and only in order to claim the attention he believes he deserves; from the need for superiority Of all the above.

The manipulativeness has to do with the structure of the individual's personality and manifests itself within a context and with a victim, which coincides and subconsciously encourages this handling. People who operate in a very good way have a strong need to be in control.

This can come from feelings of insecurity on their part, even if they often seem to have strong self-confidence. They have a strong need to feel superior and strong in their relationships and find people who will confirm these feelings by giving in to their attempts at manipulation.

If the other attempts to exert power on them, they will fight back to regain the control they feel they are losing. When they don't feel they are in control of themselves and others, they feel threatened. They also have difficulty showing vulnerable feelings because doing so can mean they are not in control and lose the victory.

It is no coincidence that the manipulating person manifests itself progressively in most cases. Just as it is no coincidence that he chooses a person easy and with several weaknesses. This behavior, is displayed at the beginning of the relationship, could more easily lead to its termination. A manipulating person learns over time, observing the vulnerabilities of the other, how he can exploit them to his advantage.

It promises to "provide" something if the other gives in to what the first one wants, e.g., I promise you that I will love you and manifest myself more as long as you are only dealing with me or know that I will be out every night if I come back and find the house untaken care of. The most hidden methods are the invocation of emotion, the threat of withdrawal, removal, and emotional distancing.

Handling is a behavior that pretty much we've all suffered in our relationships with others. Whether these others are very close to us, such as parents, brothers, partners, or colleagues, neighbors, etc., even we may have been manipulative with others. Whether we know it or not. It is very important to clarify that manipulative behavior is not consciously planned but manifests itself within a context and with a victim that coincides and subconsciously encourages this manipulation.

The person who accepts this behavior usually feels disheartened with low self-esteem. He thinks that his personality is deconstructed, he cannot distinguish his desires from the desires of the abuser; more of his insecurities come to the surface and, depending on the intensity of the relationship they have between them begins and creates a connection of dependence and a confusing system of values.

Originally
Start changing yourself, not the manipulating person. Because if you focus on changing that person, his reaction will be even more manipulative towards you. Try not to cooperate with his handling tactics and claim your initial views.

With the demarcation, you will have fenced your space, holding a dynamic and clear position in which the manipulating person, once he realizes that he cannot penetrate it, will begin to weaken.

It's very important to talk to the first person. Blaming someone for their behaviors and tactics will only achieve a defensive attitude that will be returned to you with more aggression and imposingness.

But speaking how you feel with their attitude, for example, I feel overwhelmed, weak, that I have no importance to you, etc. we will oblige him to take responsibility for his criticism, which usually disarms him and blocks his strategy.

Learn to say no and not comply with his criticism or requirements. It's not as easy as it sounds because manipulative people can argue, rationalize, and stick to what they believe and want to achieve. So it takes patience and mental strength, and you, in turn, insist. It is important to understand that they cannot handle your judgment or your thinking ability.

If you try and none of the above work, it is a good thing to reassess your relationship, redefine the position it has in your life. It is very important to be able to know if it is worth trying and whether it will eventually manage to balance the quality of the relationship.

You may need to deal with the fear, anxiety, or guilt that has in the past led you to comply with the demands of the manipulative person. This requires a good look inside you that may need the help of a professional therapist.

How Is A Manipulator Recognized?
The complex technique that many scammers use to benefit is to manipulate people. Human psychology can be controlled so much. Even during the job negotiations, the parties are trying to put pressure on each other, citing their views. You need to introduce yourself to different methods of manipulation.

It's often hidden. It is harder to suppress his will. In this context, people's secret manipulations are used.

The Art of Versatile Management
Psychology is a multifaceted science. The art of manipulation is direct proof of that. There are many ways you can learn to control a person. However, there is no manipulator to use all vehicles. They

usually choose some of the most appropriate methods. Why is human manipulation so popular? That's social psychology. And with the help of management skills, you can't influence the actions of the interlocutors, but you also achieve your goals.

You Have to Feel People's Moods

You shouldn't think everyone's in charge. Some people are hard to hypnotize. Accordingly, they are not conducive to manipulation. Attackers try to avoid these people. How do they know who should move and who can control it? Manipulation by humans, psychology - to be professional in these areas, you need to feel the mood of interlocutors well.

Manipulators often find a weak spot. This can be interest, faith, habit, thinking style, emotional status, etc. The real thing is to find out where to press and know how to do it. What method can be used to manipulate people? Psychology, books - all of this will help us understand popular management methods.

Winning Prizes

The winning payment. This kind of administration is considered the most popular among fraudsters who try to put themselves in people's trust. They tell their interlocutors that they won prizes or prizes. Naturally, if you make an effort, that might be true. But if it hasn't contributed to you, but somehow you won the award, you should consider the accuracy of the situation.

When the Information Is Not Accurate

Information mismatch. To recognize inappropriate data transmitted through various channels, you need to know the basics of non-verbal communication. This is the only way to see that the manipulator's speech is the same as the rest of the information transmitted by his gestures.

Lack of Extra Time

What is similar manipulation psychology? The pressure on a person and the opposition on its side include the use of a certain time frame.

The Emergence of Sense of Duty

Caring and love. Almost all methods contain rules of mutual exchange. It's a very common concept in psychology. The essence is that the interlocutor needs awakening a sense of duty. And that happens on an unconscious level. For example, the husband washed all the dishes, cleaned the rooms, wiped the powder alone. He sent his wife to rest. Once all this is done, he said he'd sit with his friends for a random tomorrow. How can a person reject him in a situation like this? This case is simple and real - the husband has created a sense of duty with his wife. Accordingly, the likelihood of hearing a positive response from him has increased significantly.

There Can Be Many Management Methods

There are many different ways to process it. We should be able to defend ourselves against it. First of all, it's important to listen to yourself. After all, manipulation is the control and influence of someone else's will. If you start to feel uncomfortable or if the slopes make a decision right now, you'll need to stop talking. Say no, and follow your principles. Don't give in to provocations. After all, you're just being manipulated.

Start Making the Decisions Yourself

This review explained how to manipulate people (the intricacies of psychology). How to fall for tricks like this? Pay attention to this, because you can control all aspects of life all the time. Start making your own decisions, not what you've been given. These are the psychology of manipulation and oppression of a person we think of above.

Psychological manipulation is a kind of social effect. This socio-psychological phenomenon has a desire to change the perceptions or behavior of others using hidden, deceptive, or violent tactics. Because such methods support the interests of the manipulator, they can often be considered exploitative, violent, dishonest, and unethical at the expense of other people. Any communication is largely manipulation. All we're saying, in our opinion, has to react decisively. "How are you?" By answering his question, we expect understanding, sympathy, and approval. When we don't understand any of this, for example, "What do you think of that?" We're asking an important question.

Extremely honest lack of communication, manipulation, which seems only ridiculous: "Shall I tell you how I did it or praise me?". If one concept is replaced with another and there is manipulation in communication. When a person says something, but it means something completely different. Manipulation, logic, and common sense begin when it is over. Manipulation appeals to feelings.

However, depending on how the manipulator plays our emotions, there are many ways and types of manipulation, which can be divided into six main species.

Six types of manipulation in communication:

Love manipulation. When I was a kid, they said, "If you're someone who doesn't sour so much, I won't love you." In reality, they wanted to say, "Listen to me." Your man tells you, "Stop biting your nails first (try, go to your mother, read women's novels, make a hodgepodge every morning ...), and then let's talk about the wedding." It means, "I don't like it when you bite your nails." The boss tells you: "We can value our employees; we have a friendly team of people with similar thoughtful people. Therefore, rarely does anyone leave our team of their own volition. "Indeed: even though it means, "We will be nice to you if you work well."

Features of this manipulation: One of the most insidious and brutal manipulations often used in families. A child who is accustomed to this kind of treatment begins to understand that the closest people don't fully accept it, that he loves it because he does or doesn't do anything, not for what he is. In partnerships, this kind of talk also doesn't lead to anything good. In fact, in this case, love is put on a scale and another situation. It turned out that love is a particular product that can be replaced with services or money if necessary.

Manipulation of fear. As a child, they said, "You're not going to do homework, you're going to be a janitor." Indeed: "I don't know how to get you to do homework yet." "If I keep working in this office, I'm going to have a heart attack," he says. Indeed: "Get ready, I'll resign soon" at work: "Masha, they sent me a resume of a promising young employee. You only have one profile with him. "Although they mean this: "There are no irreplaceable ones, prepare, dear."

Features of this manipulation: The use of human fears is one of the most popular tricks of manipulators in all genres and lines. Most of the time, they're playing on a person's lack of awareness. Therefore, if you have regular brains about certain mythical hazards and are asked to do so or avoid them - investigate.

Self-doubt manipulation. As a child, he said, "You've made Russian, I understand. Let's see what you can't do. "Indeed, you mean, "You can't do anything without my help." Your man tells you, "Are you going to eat cookies for the night?" Come on, and I'm going to play the game for now. "Although he wants to say, "I have the right to do what I want." Here's a dictionary, half an hour. "Indeed: "Don't bury yourself; I'm the boss here."

Characteristics of this manipulation: Manipulation is always a matter of power, and in this case, it is the most acute. "I'm the boss, you're an idiot," he said, how you can rearrange most of the quotes quoted here. The problem with the chief manipulator (regardless of whether it is a mother, father, boss or president) is that it does not have real authority, it is not a power, but it wants to be. Of course, you can start playing "presents" with him. But that compliment will never be enough for him. He's going to calm down for a while, and then he's going to try to confirm his viability over and over again at the expense of other people's shortcomings. However, it can manipulate you only if you are worried about your lack. Accept yourself and your weaknesses, or get rid of them.

Guilt manipulation. When you were a kid, they said, "There are two in chemistry again? Then you'll do the dishes. "As much as they mean: "I'm too lazy to wash the dishes, but it's unfit to ask you." Your man says, "I had coffee with Veronika sitting here alone while starving with kids." It means, "I want to meet Sergey after work tomorrow, but you're not going to let me go, you're going to cut me off." As much as they mean: "I'm going to do the job, and then I'm going to remember this."

Characteristics of this manipulation: It is very common in family life. Frequent use causes husbands and wives to start playing an exciting game that collects foreign tricks. Whoever has gathered more, won, read it - has the right to fulfill their most sincere desires. Although completely incomprehensible, why should this clear evidence be gained in such a strange and unpleasant way?

Manipulation of pride (with the idea of "above me") As a child: "Why are you afraid to jump from the tower, are you an excellent student?" Even though they're thinking, "Don't be afraid." Your man tells you, "Twelve hours a day? Poor thing. But there's this very smart girl, clean the room, run for a beer, and now Petrovich will come to me. "Although it means: "Your perfectionism plus my laziness. We're the perfect couple. "At work, they say, "We know you're a promising employee. We believe in you, so we offer you a raise with the same old salary. "As much as they mean: "with your arrogance, we've decided to save some money."

Features of this manipulation: Vanity has risen to the rank of western civilization's main idea. With all the stops that are faster, higher, stronger, and advancing. The point is not to stop and not think. Karl Jung, a psychologist, philosopher, and generally sensible person, said that the first half of his life is to study, find work, get married. Walking around, walking around in a word, but it's right to walk around. In the second half, if a person tries to make an effort to catch someone pathologically, he gets sick.

Manipulation of feelings of compassion. As in childhood: "You never feel sorry for me, I'm so tired, and you don't eat anything!" How does this happen in the family: "I have a headache all day, by the way, Lyutye's wives are calling us over the weekend. It's a pity you can't write. "As at work:" Remember, I had a porter. White is like that. Fluffy. He's dead. Can I leave early? "How is this in politics:" Our Violet Party, of course, cannot win a majority in parliament. The Oligarchs aren't behind. And they don't give us normal time ... "

Features of this manipulation - A very childish school - "Marianna, my teeth hurt, can I go home?". There are very sneaky and subtle manipulators with a feeling of pain - "victims" who are constantly complaining about life and collecting dividends - promises of encouragement and help. These "victims" are vampires. They can discuss their state of life with you all the time, but they never do anything to change anything because they're happy victims.

How to Avoid Being A Victim of a Manipulator?
First step. Logic: In a most manipulative message, since there is no link between the first part and the second ("I will not make money if you are drinking milk with friends"), we can explain to the manipulator that there is no logic in his expression. Sometimes it helps.

Step two. Strangeness: sometimes, a manipulative expression makes quite a sense, but it has a secret connotation. Putting the arm in a strange place is an exciting experience. "Are you saying that you have a lot of respect for me that you want to leave early?" Then tell me.

Consider Step Three: usually, the manipulator doesn't trust himself; otherwise, why manipulate it? He's trying to maintain power over others, even though he's most concerned about his behavior and his safety. Let him feel comfortable, tell him you understand, appreciate, and accept. See, you're dying to turn people into puppets.

Step Four Make your choice: the manipulator puts pressure on your emotions and hopes to force it or not. However, it is a myth that people make us feel it or give us that feeling. Emotions are within us, and no one except us can "open" and "shut it down." Are you afraid? Answer with the irony? Are you getting weak? Answer with surprise. Are you upset? Note that this is just an invitation that you can accept and reject. The manipulator is surprised.

Step Five Understand yourself: It is traditional to react to events in a certain way in each family. It's customary to make fun of everything in one family, in the other - without worrying and feeling sad, in the third - just blame yourself for your troubles and sprinkle it in your head. Children who grow up in these families will take this "pioneering" feeling through inheritance. They will be ironic, sad, and tortured more often than others, respectively, because of guilt. When these children grow up, it can be assumed that they will encounter manipulators who will play exactly in the "pioneer." Based on this, everyone can be advised to understand what kind of feeling their parents feel. And go back to the previous paragraph.

Manipulator time: manipulator rarely lives today. Most of the time, either remember the past - "I can't heal after my cat jumped off the balcony five years ago" - and there's also an excuse for its shortcomings and immobility. He says either you don't eat meatballs, you don't go to college, or "we believe in you, and one day it will affect your financial relationship." But nothing happens here and now in the manipulator. He doesn't always have time. He's busy all the time. He might have been crazy as a human being, but we're not going to do that because he wants us to feel that it will be used for other purposes.

Many have heard of the psychology of manipulation during the color revolutions of recent years in connection with the socio-psychological effect on people's behavior. Before using mass impact methods on humans as a system technology, psychologists examined methods of manipulation on an individual level.

There are many books about the nature and technology of manipulation, how to identify a manipulator in a nearby environment, and how to resist it. There are even pieces of training that teach you how to influence the subconscious for a successful job. It's not entirely moral, but it's demanding.

Manipulation is an unconscious part of each individual's communication and natural ability. If it is applied consciously to achieve a specific planned result, it is a problem. Because it's violence, it's just psychological.

How Is A Manipulator Recognized?
The introduction begins in childhood. Interpersonal relationships include elements of this control. The individual weaknesses of your loved ones are used: fear, complex, inadequate self-confidence, purity, guilt, and other points of pain. But this is not blackmailing. It is a veiled influence over the area of emotions.

Manipulators are the ones where traumatic experiences in childhood prevent them from finding unity with the world or with humans. There are neat "managers" who directly feel the psychological weakness of their neighbors and play skillfully.

Hungarian psychologists from pecs University proved that when they saw their experimental partner play honestly, they increased their brain activity. For the rest of us, in the opposite case, such a surge occurs. The scientists concluded that the manipulator, which combines instability, immediately calculated what benefits it might get.

How is a manipulator recognized? The controlling alien subconscious is often defined by the personality characteristics of the "dark trio":

- Machiavellianism - ignoring morality, lack of principle in achieving goals and goals.
- Psychopathy - cruelty, sympathy and empathy, shamelessness.
- Narcissism is narcissism, not empathy.

It unites them: a manipulative way of communication, selfishness, courage, emotional coldness. Domination, sense of superiority, ambition, perseverance. Oddly enough, the owners of these traits are sexually attracted to women. They also use their charms and acting skills to spark sympathy.

First, communication may not mean anything bad. But if discomfort, anxiety, or repeated negative emotions are felt in subsequent meetings, this is evidence of "psychological violence."

The interlocutor's behavior and mood are worth listening to intuition when he doesn't follow the words: he puts his arms over his chest, holds them close to his mouth, throws his legs over his legs.

Sometimes, extremely intelligent and friendly behavior is seen as a human being - it's also a time to think. Especially if the interest indicates increased:

- Any truth of your life. To take care of the family, to work, to hobbies, to have future views, the facts from the past, especially having a negative structure.
- To worldview characteristics. What are the ideals, personal values, attitudes raised? For this, philosophical issues begin.

He should warn:

- The flat apartment. It is most often used for selfish people who have the value of it easily.
- Self-imposed, someone's services, and assistance.
- Showing love and respect. Benefits and gifts. Thanks for this, captivated, and pulled on the net.
- Repetitions of expressions, words are pronounced in a different order, sometimes replaced with similar values, but the meaning remains the same so that the idea penetrates the subconscious.
- The use of complex words reduces attention-driven special terms, non-verbal controls.
- Mosaic chat: The subject begins with someone who jumps from the beginning to the beginning, ends with someone else.
- The rush in the chat and the artificial time pressure for action, so it was impossible to think about what was going on in a mess. At the same time, it is possible to dramatize the results and increase anxiety.
- Tense jokes and artificial humor.
- "Projection." When the speaker copies the pose, gestures, etiquette "are the same wavelength."
- Cutting and the theme of the theme by the interlocutor.
- The answers to questions.
- Emotional stability. A quick reaction to objections.
- Unusual behavior changed a lot.
- Although there is no clear prerequisite, it is unpleasant sediment after communication.
- On the contrary, it's inexplicable.
- Basic psychological techniques of manipulation

Manipulations are divided into conscious (usually in business communication) and unconscious (interpersonal). Puppeteers use both active and passive manipulation methods.

Basic methods of manipulation in daily communication are based on emotions and psychological weaknesses:

- False love to avoid losing a good attitude towards him; a person takes care of the "puppeteer" and accepts only the personality traits that benefit him personally.
- Lies and deception, denial sands.
- An attitude that is not requested in return ...
- Superficial sympathy turns out to be "crocodile tears."
- The development of feelings of guilt forces the interlocutor to fulfill his "player" desires.
- Depreciation. Don't claim yourself because of someone else's ambiguity. And they beat his confidence for it.
- A favorite sin not only among al Pacino protagonists but also among successful manipulators. "After all, you're so great, can you do a few more things?" The incentive method also applies to proud people.
- Giving compassion or sympathy is an easy way to feel trust. To get the upper hand later.
- Punishing goods, relationships, gifts, confessions, or "lord" what do you want? And then the implicit threats to rob him.
- Anger, irritation, not fit. They make people open to agreement and sensitivity.

- Demonstrator anger. The requested receipt passes suddenly after receipt. It's different from intimacy.
- Suggestion. Some can easily lend themselves, but they are all open to fatigue.
- Trifle. Emotions, words, opponent's desires.
- The irony, cynical, embarrassing the speaker.

Minimization and rationalization, as well as simulation of innocence. Explaining that inappropriate behavior is not so bad compared to the "world revolution" or for a full reason. Sometimes with anger and likened surprise.

The reflection and condemnation of false guilt-adhesive guilt (e.g., collectively) from a particular person.

Nonsense. When they didn't understand what they were acting like, they didn't know what they were talking about.

How to Resist Manipulation?
You should be careful to remove the manipulator and not rush to make a decision. If a "border violation" is identified, the following methods will help counter manipulation:

- Learn about the attacker's goals.
- Hide emotions, show your vulnerabilities.
- Be yourself.
- Don't respond to provocations; don't allow you to impose destructive emotions.
- Make excuses.
- Ask direct descriptive questions.
- Master conscious "superficial" communication to ensure that it is not existential. I mean, don't try other people's feelings in their coordinate systems.
- Calculate which reactions are expected from you. Don't show it to him.
- Find out the reasons for your action by asking: "Why am I doing this?"
- To be able to do
- Don't be afraid to say that you've changed your mind, made a mistake, or you don't want to continue chatting.
- If you don't like communication, let it go.

Declare that the target of the manipulator is known to you. When exposed, "puppeteer" games lose their meaning. But they don't accept the charges, at best, to change the subject. Worst of all, they're going to start pressuring your senses to make you feel wrong.

The best defense against manipulators is the development of self-defense to be an independent, self-sufficient person and to live in emotional balance.

How Is Manipulation Seen, Recognized, And Prevented?
1. Be here and now. Personal thoughts and attention should be transferred to the moment that is currently. Understand what you're doing; follow yourself, listen to your feelings. Do you like what you're doing right now? If you don't like it, you're scared, and you're being restricted, you want to run, etc., probably someone manipulates you because you don't like the actions you're doing right now.

Be an observer. The only object you're watching is yourself! You move, you feel desire, you're excited. What happened to this point? What did they tell you, what did you see, hear, or what did the other person do? Why did you start to feel, lead, talk? Mentally ask yourself, "I like what I do. " If you don't agree with the reactions and actions you have at the moment, you can stop yourself and start acting differently.

2. "Why am I doing this?" This is a good way to see you manipulated. People spend a lot of time, and they're worried about something they're concerned about, they're scared. But if you ask them why they're doing it, what it's going to do to them, what they're going to

do, when they decide to worry about themselves, or if everything comes from somewhere, they're acting like zombies. A man doesn't understand why he's doing something; he decides to say one or another word where fear comes from.

It doesn't matter where manipulation comes from. If you analyze the situation, i.e., you'll see that from the moment you start to be afraid to do something, say something, you're manipulated. Next time you begin to understand that you are so hypnotic, you can avoid manipulation.

Ask yourself more often: "Why am I doing this? Did I decide to do it myself, or did the solution come from nowhere? What's he going to give me if I say that? Why (and "why?" Not?) Am I scared? What is the use of my actions/ my words/experiences? "Test yourself, you cause your reactions to start yourself, or if you clicked a button, why did you start taking action?

See manipulation, recognize, and prevent! Keep in mind that actions under the influence of manipulation will rarely be directed to the target. The manipulator wins and loses every time manipulated. Choose for yourself how to feel, how to react, what to say, what to do, what to think about.

Dark Deception

The issue of deception has always kept its fire in societies for centuries. Some companies deceive they changed shape to legitimize, and others banned it directly.

Well, what happened has been on the list so much lately, we've started to hear so much. Although it seems to have remained hidden in society, the word "deception" is that the woman's work to enter his life, to gain strength, to make it easier for a man to reach the opposite sex,

Finding the power to oppose men, reducing the role of hormonal jeans of men, only society Increases were inevitable for reasons such as the woman's interest in cheating. Also, the mediocrity of the relationship, the decrease in the values given to the primary sits on the There has also been an increase in deceptions as people become the field of satisfying their egos.

The lack of people's problem-solving skills, taking a new one instead of fixing something that breaks down or the right to be polygamy to the man, to ensure that the structure of society is male-dominated and social reasons have increased deception as much as it is legitimate.

The reason for the increase in deception in our country is the problem of identification. We're in a commotion. The question we answer most is whether it's cheating. So, the limits of deception must be drawn. Deception is a bonding problem. Especially narcissistic responses are very common in people. Who sees himself higher, thinks he's superior to his wife or those around them who have been observed to be like this, who receive such comments in society? They see themselves closer to deception.

Deception is a bonding problem. It's also too common in addicted people. Problems with the relationship those who can't solve it, who can't break away at the same time, are deceived by difficulties. On the other hand, due to self-confidence and loneliness concerns, the relationship or they can't end their marriage. When the person is deceived, he wants to name his name, know the reasons, solve the problem. Cheat?

Infidelity?
You hear explanations. The main problem is how the person perceives the situation. I've seen that there's no common definition in my research. My purpose of personal deception is as follows; physically and emotionally, as life and activity with someone other than their partner, all private shares are called fantasy. The important thing here is that sharing is personal is that it is not. The inability to fully identify deceit, deception, and deception are very different related to the perception of shapes. This diversity in perceptions reveals the kinds of fantasy.

Virtual Deception
It's the kind of deception that's been exploding in the last ten years. Virtual sexuality, virtual sensuality, is one it's cheating. After all, there's someone in your life, and if you're sharing privately with someone else, this He'll cheat. The virtual experience is virtual in terms of the environment, real with what it lives, and makes it feel.

The problem of limits and definition is still at the root of the increase in virtual deception.

Emotional Deception
Such deceptions mainly reflect the psychology of the person in conflict. I mean, in his head. It is aimed to experience excitement instead of making decisions. Offset (confidence of distance), factors such as curiosity, unhappiness in your relationship, fascination, the quest for excitement, emotional deception. It is predominantly seen in women. The gap in its relationship is incorrect to fill the lack of marriage, the value of self-worth in this kind of relationship.

Sexual Deception
Even if a person has a high level of sexuality with his wife, there may be sexual deception. So why? Getting a woman in our society is always a force for men and prove himself detected. Especially the best, the hardest to achieve is a man's prestige. Claim for all A Turkish man who grows up in such environments, although not biological) always predisposes to deception.

Flirtatious
Although it may seem like an unnamed, shaped social relationship, it is not named. It is mutually appreciated and interested in the form of a relationship based on it. Both are liking and liking such communication-relationships; there is a risk factor. Flirty approaches motivate people, provide comfort and freedom. On the one hand, there's nothing. A there is also mutual appreciation on the side. Shares are verbally or behaviorally tangible. We can't count the process without deception.

Why Do People Cheat?
Trump Sees sexuality as a fundamental dynamic in the relationships due to male psychology and hormonal structure. From what we've seen in our consultors and families, men are most complaining about the point they are at is sexuality. One of the reasons why a man's deception is that his wife's sexuality is one; it's a weapon or leverage. Male sexuality is also self-needy attempts to deceive to avoid feeling. Likewise, the woman has the interest and love of the man. To win. Using sexuality as leverage, high, it's a sign of brokenness and hidden anger. As you trump sexuality by one of your spouses, the other party considers deception as a right with a sense of deprivation and exclusion. Both as a punishment of deprivation.

Complexes The person wants to be strong and liked at any age. To feel good in situations like this, deception can be applied. It's still worked for them to do this, especially with the younger ones, makes people happier to see what they're doing. Men and women experience infidelity with young partners at close to menopause and anthropical period. Accepting old age, a common one in men and women who want to prove themselves, who want to gain self-confidence, is the case. We see it very often in the tabloid press; older men or women are young, showing up with their lovers, ignoring their age, and still being liked is a behavior that is done to show. At the same time, the senselessness of life and the fear of death is a challenge to these kinds of deceptions.

28

Psychological Reasons

People's basic needs in social terms are accepted, liked, approved, trusted, and to be loved. When one feels unhappy, insignificant, worthless, these basic needs, He seeks solutions to fix it, and it makes him happy that someone else cares about him. Especially men and women who are depressed feel both risky behavior and self-valued deception. It's depressing to see both values and see that you are still attracting attention positive effect on people who are. (A kind of antidepressant effect.) Men, women's pregnancy, in cases of postpartum and depression, deception because it does not see the attention and sexuality it expects may slip.

As long as the cheater is not caught, he continues to behave, always thinks about the consequences; But it can't overcome internal conflict. In general, conscientious discomfort occurs after deception. And then, guilt comes out. Sometimes one can feel better about your wife/lover errors. As if he had paid the price, the more he made that mistake, the better he was Feels. As the person bases the cause of deception on other than himself, he wants to see the errors of his wife or partner all the time, as he will feel better. Otherwise, the fact that the wife is perfect further increases the conscientious discomfort of the aldata. Cheater, wife. The more he's treated himself, the worse he can feel. In this case, I'm going to have to stop leaving; therefore, you may want more reasons for relational (marriage) problems in marriage and the movements of spouses in the relationship, some of the reasons that lead to deception. Some of these are below.

- Control and try to undertake the destruction
- Unrelated and irresponsible spouse
- Sexual reactions and rejection
- Continuous undertaking, passivity.
- Presence of spouses with dependent or narcissistic personality
- Marry without liking, the relationship only for the qualities that are owned (money, career, shape, status, etc.)
- Authority wars
- Selfish wife
- Loss of roles after children of spouses. (forget to be a wife and just be a mother or father)
- High expectations and disappointments
- Psychological problems, and personality structures
- Grow-witness with cheating-cheating parents

What Lives the Cheating Person?

The deceived person considers himself inadequate, unpopular, uninterested. As a result, a wife emerges who thinks he has been wronged, angry, and does not want to touch his partner.

There are many "wishes" in the people who have been deceived. The effort spent in his relationship, the time, the sacrifices he made, the loyalty it shows, etc. all passes through his mind like a filmstrip. At the same time, cheating on a person and attempting the real purpose is not to deceive but to be revenge. The only reason for the deception is sexually and emotionally satisfied in one's relationship with his wife is not the failure to reach. Someone who grew up in the sense of worthlessness since childhood is appropriate to satisfy this feeling in the environment. Sometimes the person does it for a moment's excitement Can.

We can't say that cheating people are bad people. I see it as a crime, not a deviation. It's more accurate. From the outside, whether it's a deception cannot be evaluated. It is in line with the sense of discomfort felt by the deceiver; How many you If you are uncomfortable, that event is so cheating.

Acceptance

In some cases, the deceived person can't handle their consequences, and severe psychological effects ignore or reject the state. This condition is heated by being deceived in the coming years heated and brought up again. So, it's a reaction that's not given in time, growing up and manifests yourself by causing psychological disorders. For example, in research, deception is a root cause of depression. To get expert support in such cases, Must. Married people often look for someone who doesn't risk his marriage, doesn't expect much from him.

This is inevitable in both men and women. On the one hand, to guarantee himself and his future, Protecting the marriage of the field while at the same time, the desire to live happily in the present is outweighed. It's not like I what is necessary is to seek happiness outside and improve your marriage, rather than the endless instant pleasures.

The rising socio-economic level of one of the parties can also lead to deception. One of the wives When you see itself inaccessible, the other spouse may want to overcome it with fantasy. At the same time, I told him that's how he expresses his anger. Some writers, parents who suffer from the suffering of the deceived they matched it to the sadness of losing. Its life is put before your eyes like a movie strip. It's not just a relief. It's an expert to analyze and interpret the situation correctly support.

Deceived Person Thoughts and Feelings
Invaluable remorse, guilt, despair, anger weakness is this basic when working with the deceived person. You need to work within the framework of emotion and thought. Temporary good feelings are not the solution, but permanent causes residue. Deceptions in the tabloid press are a bad example, but encouraging. Usually, the aldata He's always given his happy life after he's cheating. (Pinar Altug, Hüsnü Senedici, Cem Hakko, Kaya Like Locksmithgiroglu.) Even though the reports mentioned the experience of the cheating and the wannabe effect might decrease if the cheaters were criticized instead of glorifying them. Her husband or wife, a cheater, goes live the next day and makes a show as nothing happened. It's a thought-provoking. Does every deception end the relationship? The power to deal with the emotional trauma experienced by the person, the possibility that the problem can be solved, the desire to maintain and recover is a roadmap. The important thing is to finish or is the solution to the problem, not to quit. At these stages, the right people and resources sharing is important for the fate of the relationship, i.e., choosing the third person correctly. For example, cheated the most likely suggest a woman would get from a friend with a feminist perspective is "separation." Ending the relationship with deception is a hasty decision. There's no need to rush. At any time, you can leave anyway. But if the priority is to continue, if it is to finish, a healthy process monitoring. Those who think that the problem will be solved when they leave, after leaving, they live. Since most of the questions remain unanswered, the condolences of deception take a long time. Effects decisions should not be made without getting rid of, without answering questions, without analysis.

What Can Be Done?
1. If the cheater wants to solve this situation and regroup the relationship, first, he said, "yes, I cheated, all the flaws I have to say, "I am." There will be no healing without acceptance. It's like a disease. Accept that he is sick, no medication, no cure. And he can't get better.
2. Instead of editing when you suspect, an appropriate environment, a voice open to communication, and body speak to your partner.
3. Tell me about how you feel. Blaming and asking for accountability only creates a defense.
4. If you are deceived, talk to him about it. Without listening to your reasons and description, don't decide.
5. Before you tell third parties, you have to solve it among yourself. After you told me, it may be mandatory to leave. Some people simply have to go because the event arises serves. People think they're waiting for him. And those around you; "Why are you still together? What more do you expect him to do" even if you continue the relationship, it might bother you?
6. The deceived person should not always seek the crime himself. Whatever the reasons are fooled, It's not fate.
7. Continuing sexuality after cheating, gaining, and losing the self-confidence of the cheater, it's a sign of his fear. Sexuality continues to live with itself emotionally. There should be no sexuality unless it wants to be deceived in this process. Trump's sexuality, while tricked, should not use it as a.
8. Cheating is not a gender trait. The way a person is raised, his childhood, the feature of social structure, the expectation of marriage, or relationship determines this. The person who has been deceived, even if he is separated, this error is must resolve them all without installing them.

9. Even if you are an excellent wife, it is his problem and the feature that your wife deceives you. Every deception, 100% marriage, is not indicative of the problem.
10. In deceptions, it is necessary not to ignore the weakness of the data.
11. When the man was raised, his mother was like, "Son my lion, do what you want, no girl for you" suggestions reduce loyalty. He always thinks he's the alternative, and he'll ever find better. That's the kind of thing. To prevent the development of the narcissistic self, it is necessary to pay attention to the way they grow.
12. Deception is a bonding and a whole problem. Sometimes you don't have any issues. You can be deceived. This is due to reasons other than you. The result of blaming yourself Change.
13. If you cheated on your wife and you won't do it again. But if you regret it to your wife, Tell.
14. "Once cheating always cheats" is not the right analysis.
15. If you are constantly cheating, the healthiest one for you and your partner is either to get support or to leave. As time goes on, both sides' mental health can deteriorate.
16. Never share it with your children, even if your wife cheated on you. You don't always justify it in this marriage.
17. Even if you're cheated, don't cheat for revenge. This is a great sense of worthlessness for you in the future Creates.
18. If you are cheating on your partner and feeling happy, you have feelings based on worthlessness or a wave of hidden anger. Feeling worthless, temporary value at regular intervals is the healthiest to get psychotherapy instead of trying to close it with visions.
19. Deception is officially the reason for divorce. Criminally, both the cheating and the cause of it (3rd person) is stipulated by law.
20. Support is mandatory for the emotional and physical difficulties experienced after deception. Alcohol taking, ignoring, falling asleep, hugging the drugs, even though it's instant comfort, the end of condolence Does not provide.
21. The deception event is the same as the one seen as an aftershock for a relationship, and to redesign the relationship can be turned into a positive opportunity in time. Problems in the relationship through deception, unspoken, accumulated, and steps are taken to resolve them.
22. After deception, the biggest problem is to rely on it again. The deceiver, the need for the trust of the deceived to be patient to resolve, to be consistent with the questions that are often asked, without giving up answered. If you want to review your phone or e-mail addresses for trust, you can only You have to give it a while. Remember that a broken trust will not be repaired for free.
23. The cheater, the more he wonders, the deeper he goes. After a point to the detail of the learning, as far as he knows, he must accept. Otherwise, the problem, and he should know that curiosity is not the end.
24. The deceiver should not be hasty for everything to return to normal as soon as possible. This should not be simplified.
25. If the deceived person requests more details, they should not be disclosed. For example, if you want to your partner's other, knowing how you kiss with a person doesn't help your mental health or your marriage.
26. If you want to correct your relationship; Be clear with him. What you expect, what you desire from now on, specify how you want a system. Being clear and clear is a roadmap on both sides.
27. The deceived person must recognize the weaknesses and problems in his marriage and personality to solve must be selective. Because unless the causes change, the results don't change.

Reverse Psychology

Reactiveness; the idea that if the individual feels that the freedom to do or choose is threatened or restricted, even if he thinks about it, the tendency to do what is threatened will re-emerge his space. According to this approach, restricting people's freedom of choice or decision and forcing other preferences or decisions increases the appeal of restricted action or object, in turn, responds with a strong resistance to the decision or selection that it is moved.

According to Greenberg, I'm not going to let you down. Reverse psychology benefits from one's reactionary. Speaking to LiveScience, Greenberg said: "I'm not going to let you down. If you practice reverse psychology in a person, you threaten his perception of freedom. Creating a threat to liberty makes the situation of making a free choice attractive.

For example, if you want to Let's think of a kid who doesn't eat broccoli. Mother or father; When he says, "You can't eat broccoli," eating broccoli will become more attractive to the child. Thus, although the child never wanted to eat broccoli at first, making his choice will try to eat the broccoli as he feels free. When you take away your freedom, eating broccoli will become more attractive to the child.

Greenberg, on the other hand, said: "I'm not going to let you down. He says using reverse psychology may not always work, which is more likely to work in individuals prone to reactiveness.

Fast-tempered, stubborn, and emotional individuals are often more prone to being reactive, while conciliatory and consensual people are less prone to being reactive. There is also limited evidence that men are a little more reactive than women.

Greenberg said there are stages where reverse psychology is more available for children, and children between the ages of 2 and 4 have been able to do so. He claims that they are generally more emotional and more rebellious, so reverse psychology is more likely to work in children in this age group. But from the age of 4, when children socialize a little more and start having fewer tantrums, they are less predisposed to respond to reverse psychology.

The other classic example is puberty. When adolescents are rebellious to their parents, they may be more conducive to reverse psychology because this period is usually; When the parent says something and wants to do otherwise of the adolescent individual.

Another example is: young children are particularly cognitively less developed children. Because of this level of cognition- they may not understand the reverse psychology that their parents use so that it can be used as a simple tactic for adults.

Greenberg, on the other hand, says that trying to use reverse psychology on adults can have negative consequences, meaning that this trial can have the opposite reaction to reverse psychology in adults. But with a subtle wit, you can also make this psychology work in adults.

Reverse psychology, a game for strong players, or just a survival tactic? Well hidden manipulative behavior or just a characteristic of a man that makes him unique? Control voltage or intelligence index? Does art always go through yours?

Perhaps in all the above questions, you can never answer honestly whether you belong to the category of the person who causes it or to the variety of the person who collects it. The only certain thing is that our brains work, after all, so complicated that in some cases, even science raises its hands.

Admit honestly and first to yourself that this whole game, known to many as mind games, you find tempting. You're intrigued by the thought of doing it. It makes you feel like the master of the game when you see that the opposite side gives in to your intentions.

However we look at it, reverse psychology is an ace up the sleeve of those who can challenge it. It's remarkable how our minds will react to hearing the phrase, "I bet you can't do it." These words hide so much power that they make you move up mountains to prove you can do it!

How is this interesting game played, and what are its terms? Where do you burn, and when do you get a head start? Bring to your mind moments when you've dared. You say the opposite of what you want right now, and people do what you want. Is it provocative? I'm sure so, since you're making the other guy think it's his decision, when in fact, it's entirely yours, served insidiously as someone else's initiative.

In the erotic field, this mind game will certainly backfire. Probably at first, you don't understand, it's going to be several times when you're going to be the easy victim. Of course, when we talk about love and attraction, you automatically forgive everything and move on. But when one's manipulative behaviors become the norm, the other – rightly – begins to doubt the existence and quality of emotion.

If you're asking me if it exists in the context of a friendship, I'll tell you that I'm sure, but to a lesser extent than what's found in love affairs. You see, among friends, there are absolutely and compelling "I want" like those between (selfish) partners. You don't mind confronting friends. You can stay firm in your seat or put water in your wine. You'll find them somewhere in the middle, in a coffee shop, or with a leisurely drink on a common outing.

The ones who certainly hold the top spot by rightfully claiming the Oscar are the parents. No guardian has not adopted this tactic as a means of persuading and enforcing it. According to experts, reverse psychology is the perfect tool in a parent's hands.

Children who refuse to eat their vegetables, children who are slow to read and organize, children who react and stubbornly refuse to do things. So that's where Mom or Dad takes on this role, making reverse psychology look like a game in which they've finished all the tracks! They give the children the message that it can be theirs without it being done. The tarpon after the benefit!

The balance lines in all of the above are red and thin. You don't know when you're going to get out of bounds when you're going to take advantage of this tactic a little bit more than the (subjectively) morally correct, how ultimately addictive it can be, and, in many cases, destructive to a relationship.

Use of Reverse Psychology

Its use in a disagreement lies in your adoption of a position so that the other person adopts the opposite.

The experts in reverse psychology are teenagers. As they are age-old in the middle of the process of determining their public image and identity, if there's one thing they hate, it's when someone affects them or tells them what to do. So, to avoid that feeling, they often choose to do the opposite of what they're being offered, even if inside they know it's the best option.

Psychology professor John Gottman is opposed to the use of reverse psychology in adolescents, claiming that they will rebel, stating that "these strategies are confusing, manipulative, dishonest and rarely work."

However, this is not typical only of teenagers. People tend to keep part of this reactive trend in their adult lives, even if it is done with less intensity and frequency.

Let's imagine a 5-year-old boy who refuses to eat vegetables. You insist on making him eat what's on his plate, but that's pointless: he refuses to eat carrots and zucchini. If you keep whining at him to eat them, that's going to end most of the time badly. You'll give up at some point tired, and it'll leave happy to play.

Of course, it's not as simple as telling the kid not to eat them. If he hears anything like that, he'll leave, and you'll end up eating the vegetables yourself. So we need to prepare and make vegetables look more attractive: make them look the exact opposite of immune and boring... Make them more fun.

At this point, we start the reverse psychology to make the dish look more attractive. Everyone has felt a growing sense of curiosity when something is forbidden. This is the case in both childhood and adulthood because parents too often forbid children to do things that they once considered amusing.

Another reason to be reactive may have to do with the self-confidence you feel in a particular situation. If you feel uncertain and someone causes you to take a risk, you will probably prefer the most common or less divergent behavior.

But on the contrary, when we feel confident, we lean towards the riskiest option, with much more determination, even if someone tries to make us choose the sure path.

So, your reactivity in these cases is usually not decisive on which side the scale will lean on, but it does make it lean more towards one side than the other side.

Perhaps the example of a child refusing to eat vegetables is something very simple; however, keep in mind that reverse psychology is very commonly used in business.

For example, a company offers optional courses for its employees. But by the end of the hour, no one has registered. So, the principals inform them that starting next month, the systems will be halved, and resources will be cut.

With this strategic move, the company did not stop classes. Still, instead, the employees realized that they have significant resources at their disposal and that if they are not used, they will devote themselves to another activity. No one wants to lose something that has value, even if that person didn't realize it until they give it to them.

Reverse psychology has a close relationship in psychotherapy, with the technique of "paradox." This technique has also been called 'prescribing the symptom' and 'opposing retreat.' The therapist frames their message so that resistance to it promotes change.

Such interventions can have a similar impact on humor, helping therapists see their problems in a new light... Going along with it, rather than with the resistance of the healer, the therapist makes the behavior less attractive. This is referred to as a reframe. This means that he pretends to agree with the thoughts and beliefs of the clients to confirm it aloud to them so that the healers themselves realize their bad effect.

How to Apply Reverse Psychology in Three Steps?
However, reverse psychology doesn't tell us to live our lives by refusing to do things to others to do what you want. There are some "specialties" to avoid becoming a habit and resulting in manipulation:

1. To Whom Will You Apply It and Why?
Answer this question before using the reverse psychology technique. If you're going to apply it to your child to get dressed for school or stop watching TV, go ahead freely, but if you're going to convince your customers to buy a product, you might want to think again.

2. What Impact Can It Have?
If you agree to let your child not do the chores he needs at home and he ends up doing them, he's fine. But sometimes your plan won't end up as planned, and the child will answer you as cheerfully as they can: perfect, now I can go back to my video games.

3. How Free Does This Person Want to Feel?
The greater his need for self-determination (i.e., the need to feel that he is making decisions of his own free will), the more likely he is to follow a different path than what you propose. For example, a person who doesn't like to take orders is a perfect candidate for reverse psychology.

Brainwashing

The term "brainwashing" describes various psychological techniques which aim to control human behavior.

Of course, man's desire to influence and ultimately control the environment is as old as his presence on our planet. Initially, the man was trying to impose himself on his background with physical violence. But with the advancement of science, physical violence has replaced various psychological methodologies and techniques, most effective, which can be applied not only at the individual level but also at the collective level, even at the group of the entire People.

These methodologies are described by the general term "brainwash," i.e., "brainwashing" and aim to implant new ideas, modify behavior, and ultimately manipulate. These methodologies are mainly based on the theory of the Russian Physiologists Ivan Pavlov, who lived in the 19th Century and who founded the idea of dependent reflexes.

According to her, a living organism interdepends with its environment through so-called "reflective." A reflective connects a stimulus that comes from the background to the reaction of the organism. Using this complex function of people's nervous system, we can manipulate behaviors with various techniques. As in advertising, e.g., seeing a picture of a product in a nice environment, in the subconscious combine these two, and when in the future we know the work alone, we automatically reminisce and the nice climate and buy it ... On the contrary, the same is true of populist political propaganda. They combine memories of unpleasant events of the past that project them together with their demagogic political proposals to deceive the people.

The most common techniques for "brainwashing" a people are:

1. Distraction
That is, diverting attention from major problems and channeling it to others, not important issues. That's "the ball on the!"

2. The Gradual Implementation of Unpleasant Measures
This causes a gradual "desensitization" so that the final full implementation of the unpleasant measures is easily accepted.

3. Postponement
In order, for example, to accept a painful, unpopular measure, it is presented as unfortunate but necessary, it is initially guaranteed to be accepted, but is applied in the

future.

4. The Handling of The People, As If It Were in Childhood
The idea is that if someone addresses a person like this as a child, their reaction will be like that of a small child, i.e., without rational thought, but mainly with emotion.

This makes it easier to access the subconscious and implants phobias, desires, and ideas more easily. A striking example is a constant reference to the "sins" of the recent and distant past, which the government constantly repeats and which it condemns to its opponents.

5. Encouraging the People to Be Satisfied with Mediocrity
That is to say, they are presented as political figures, people with no substantive qualifications required by the government, but with only the capability of self-evident honesty, rhetorical ness (but with wooden language, and empty content and often the hybrid in every opposing view.

6. The Incrimination of The People
That is to say, to believe that the people will be responsible for any misfortune that may arise if they do not support the government.

7. To Believe the People That the System That Governs Them Knows Better Than They Do. Their Problems

In this way, the People uncritically can accept all the choices that have been made, but also that will be made.

Brainwashing Techniques

Brainwashing, in other words, controlling the brain of others in a sense, is a phenomenon that has not been understood for a long time. However, today, it is possible to learn more about this through scientific developments. In particular, neuroscience, emotional, and cognitive psychology, which sheds light on the mystery of social psychology and the human brain, which enhances our understanding of individual and group behavior, contributes to this.

There Is No Free Will, and There Is Change

Most of our social interactions are based on two cases; Our free will and our belief in strength. In brainwashing, one's free will eliminated, while one still thinks that he is acting freely. Our strong confidence in robustness, our personality, our values will not change, changed by the brainwasher. In other words, it is driven by the assumption that even our thoughts and attitudes that we are most familiar with and think will change most difficult can be easily changed.

Change Your Behavior or Your Faith

Another important point here is the principle of cognitive disharmony. According to this principle, we cannot tolerate the mismatch between one behavior and a belief, and we have to change our faith or behavior to resolve it. Based on this principle, the brainwashed person is not only given verbal commands; they are also asked to engage in some action. In this case, a person who suddenly finds himself writing articles against the homeland changes his faith as the only remedy because he can't change his behavior.

Uncertainty and Fear

When we address the same process emotionally, we see that the situation is no different from the hallucinations that give the scripts experienced by schizophrenia patients. The victim in a brainwashing process:

- He is experiencing fear and concern that he has lost control.
- They feel they're being used and judged by someone else.
- They feel like they're losing their sense of self. They can have a much easier effect in an environment where they live all these feelings. Strengthen in nerve networks frequently. Putting all this aside, and we can say that, from a neurological point of view, our beliefs are the network of a group of nerve cells. As most of us know, the brain is made up of nerve cells, and these cells are customized to send signals to each other. One neural network is ignited after one cell is activated, another activates, and another starts. This neural network doesn't always stay active in this way; he's got a life span, and after a while, it's fading. But the important thing is that if these cells are re-stimulated before a certain time, the same neural network is activated. So, the recently stimulated section is more suitable for restimulating. That's why repetition of something at short intervals allows us to promote the same community of cells, that is, to learn. Similar to brainwashing, the individual is subjected to frequent and intense signals repeatedly, thus increasing connections between neurons.

Lift on eventually defined some steps involved in the brainwashing cases he studied:

1. Attack on identity
2. Guilt
3. Self-betrayal
4. The breaking point of the prisoner
5. Grace
6. Forcing a confession
7. Channeling guilt
8. Release of guilt

9. Progress and harmony
10. Final Confession and Regeneration

Each of these stages takes place in an isolation environment, meaning that all "normal" social reference points are not available, and a common part of the process is mind-blurring techniques such as sleep deprivation and poor nutrition. There is often the presence or permanent threat of physical harm, which is added to the difficulty of the goal for critical thinking and independence.

We can divide the process that Lift has identified into about three stages: tearing down the self, introducing the possibility of salvation, and rebuilding the self.

The Tearing of The Self

- Attack on identity: You are not who you think you are. It is a systematic attack on a victim's sense of self (also called identity or ego) and on his central belief system. The agent denies everything that makes the target what it is: "You're not a soldier," "You're not human.", "You're not defending freedom." In this situation, his beliefs seem less stable.
- Guilt: You're bad. While the identity crisis settled, the agent at the same time creates an overwhelming sense of responsibility about the target. Repeatedly and mercilessly insults the victim for every "sin" he has committed, big or small. He can criticize the target for everything from the "wickedness" of his beliefs, to the way he eats too late.
- Self-betrayal: Agree with me that you're evil. Once the victim is disoriented and drowning in guilt, the agent forces him (either by threatening bodily harm or continuing mental assault) to denounce his family, friends, and classmates. They share the same "mistake" in the belief system he possesses. This betrayal of his beliefs and people feels a sense of faith and an increase in shame and loss of identity that the goal is already experiencing.
- Boundary point: Who am I? Where am I? What am I, and what should I do? With his identity in crisis, he experiences deep shame, and after betraying what he always believed, the target can suffer. This can result in an explosion of uncontrollable anaphilia, deep depression, and general disorientation. The target may have lost touch with reality and has the feeling that he is completely lost and alone. When the target reaches the breaking point, his sense of self is pretty much in the agent's grab - he doesn't have a clear understanding of who he is or what happens to him. At this point, the agent creates the temptation to lead him to another belief system that will save him from his misery.

Do you consider that everything you do or say comes from yourself, or do you think others influence many of those things?

It's hard to tell, isn't it? And day after day, we are subject to countless scenarios where they try to persuade us or manipulate us for things as simple as purchasing a product or choosing a political candidate or a religion.

The truth is that freedom of thought today is being affected by the world in which we live. That's why we've decided to write these lines about brainwashing techniques and how to avoid them.

To talk about brainwashing techniques, we must first start by knowing what brainwashing is?

What It's Like to Brainwash

Brainwashing is a process by which a person or group of people use covert methods to persuade others to do the will of the person who is manipulating them.

However, persuasion doesn't necessarily have to be considered brainwashing, but then where is that line is drawn that separates direct and simple influence and starts brainwashing?

There are many forms of persuasion used today, particularly in politics, in the world of sales, and religions. For example, a simple way to persuade a crowd to follow their instructions is first to point out a couple of things that provoke an affirmative answer, then add items that are real facts and finally suggest what they want you to do. An example might be the following:

Tired of paying too much on products and services? Tired of rising health costs? Would you like to see the end of austerity? With this government, we will only continue to visit our taxes, inflation, and austerity rise. So if you want change to come, vote for the Democratic party.

Of course, most of the time, all these examples are seen as subtle persuasions that do not offend or harm anyone. However, it is often the technique that comes into the brainwashing game.

Here are what these techniques are.

Here are some widely used mind control techniques, techniques to be very careful with:

Insulation
The first tactic used in brainwashing is usually to isolate the victim from his friends and family.

The reason for doing this is so that the victim can only talk to the manipulator so that the manipulator can get your information and ideas, and he won't have to worry about any third parties coming and questioning what's going on.

Attacks on Self-Esteem
Now that the victim has been isolated, it must be broken down so that the manipulation can begin to rebuild it in the desired image. A person can only have a brainwash if their manipulator is in a higher position than it.

These attacks can be in the form of ridiculing or mocking the victim, or intimidation.

Mental Abuse
Another way a manipulator will try to brainwash his victims is to twist them mentally.

You can tell the victim lies so that the victim can say to her secrets and then shame them with the truth in front of others, or they could harass their victims without allowing them any personal space.

Of course, these are things the manipulator will do without you nodding. Just to make you feel guilty and finally end up agreeing with the manipulator.

Physical Abuse
There are also other, more subtle ways a manipulator can use, such as maintaining noise levels, having lights that turn on and off all the time, and lowering or raising the temperature in the room.

We see this kind of thing more in some churches where they use "fasting" as a technique to weaken the person by taking away their sleep and leaving them hungry.

If these fasts occur within an establishment where emotional music and a set of lights constantly flow, it becomes the perfect setting for mind control.

Us Against Them or Us and Those of The Outside World
Again, it's about being accepted into a group, and also from the best group. By saying that there is a "we" and a "they," the manipulator is immediately offering the victim the opportunity to choose which group they want to belong to.

Their goal now is to achieve absolute obedience and loyalty.

Love Bombardment
This is a tactic by which the victim is attracted to the group by physical contact, sharing intimate thoughts and emotional bonds, all through excessive affection and constant validation.

How to Avoid Brainwashing

Avoiding brainwashing techniques often involves avoiding manipulators themselves, but this is almost impossible.

Taking advertising as an example, we can't avoid them all, and trying to do it can be quite expensive. However, you can follow some of these guidelines:

- Identify the manipulative message you received
- Find a message contrary to what they're trying to sell you. You can also try to find a more neutral and impartial point in that same message.
- Discuss how you feel about the situation, and if there's something that doesn't make you feel comfortable, just stay away.
- Finally, keep in mind each of the mind control techniques detailed in this post so you can identify any manipulator who wants to stalk you.

Conclusion

The conclusion is that the Dark Trinity of personality is characterized by a "frozen," emotionless, and simple style of love. Given, however, the antisocial and manipulative nature of the Dark Trinity, this is probably not particularly surprising. Manipulation is available in all manner. Every man manipulates, every human being is used. It is important to recognize the pressure from the outside and decide what measures are taken. Conclusion

"Democratic" societies are more brainwashed and more controlled by governments, financial institutions, and media culture than any other type of population in the world.

When people become spiritually numb, they are more likely to fall into totalitarianism. In contrast to the overt, outdated methods of totalitarian regimes, control systems in "democracies" are more sophisticated and bring better results.

It would be naive to be surprised by this development. For centuries we have lived in a society imbued with the principle of obedience to power. Continuing this tradition, we obey orders: How much money should we spend, what should we buy, and when should we throw it away.

First, they convince us that they cannot control us. When this vague impression spreads and becomes the prevailing mentality, then they can direct us where they want.

All that remains to be done is to convince the world that the few rules or controls that exist are in everyone's interest so that we can stay free and unchecked. of life, as the place of truth is occupied by gullibility.

You also learned that you could use those tactics to your advantage. We have also discussed how important it is for you to be observed in every social situation to help you become more aware of the persuasive tactics of those around you. Fortunately, after reading this text, you will have the necessary qualifications to identify and read body language and use that information to your advantage. We were able to dive into our personalities to reveal how our characters can help or hinder the mental manipulation process. We have learned that through a deeper understanding of ourselves, we are more prepared to control our social environments. If you are working for a new job or promotion, you are now ready to face those challenges head-on. You are now also prepared to protect yourself from manipulative mind control by using your powers of observation to prevent someone from taking root in your thinking. After reading this text, you must be a complete person who can navigate in any circle social and get the admiration you deserve. The main objective of this text is to show you the power you have to become a master of the persuasive techniques. All you need to do is take control of your mind. If you have control of how you think and react, and no one can use manipulation against you. You will also be more than capable of using your mind to control and persuade those around you. Once you have achieved self-realization, you have gained the necessary skills to use persuasion to propel you further into the strata society. Never forget that you can only gain control over others if you have control over yourself.

Persuasion

Introduction

Persuasion is a double-edged sword. Some see it as a way of manipulating others and never use it. Others, more subtle, see it as a way to seduce

Almost all of us try to convince someone about something. Sometimes we even find ourselves trying to convince ourselves. Sometimes when we try to convince our boss, our supervisor tries to convince us. Sometimes when we try to convince our colleagues, we deal with the persuasion of our son. So why would we try to convince him? What is the psychology of persuasion? Persuasion is the most basic means of socializing and living together. Most of your time with your partner, lover, friend, children, parents spend most of your time persuasion. Sometimes you're convinced, sometimes you convince. When we say persuasion, many of us think of a sales technique. But persuasion is too important and broad to be just a sales technique.

We're not going to talk about persuasion, which is a sales technique. We're going to tell you about persuasion techniques that will regulate your social life and do you a lot of work.

About persuasion; We have to ask ourselves this question first. Do I believe in what I'm trying to convince myself? Then let's start by splitting the persuasion techniques in two. Convince him to believe, convince without believing. Convincing him without believing is an unethical persuasion. Because the goal is to take advantage of the opposite, these techniques are used by the salespeople the most. However, you can often see people using these techniques in your work life and social life. In general, people who will gain an interest in what they are trying to convince may try to convince you, even if they are not convinced themselves. Because the people who use this technique are trying to convince the other person to something without believing; They're both very difficult to do, and they're acting unethically.

What we're going to focus on in this article is the techniques of persuasion. As our ancestors said, "it's half of what you've managed to believe." If you believe in what you're going to tell, you're much more likely to convince.

At the heart of persuasion is to direct the other person to the thought you desire and to make this idea a commonplace in the basic belief and opinion system. Sometimes we don't even realize this thing we've encountered many times in everyday life. Persuasion is essentially a difficult activity, but it becomes easier if you use the right techniques.

Never before has it been more favorable to learn to master the subtle art of persuasion. Gone are the days when leaders managed by decree, issuing orders to the left and right while controlling their troops! Today, we must know how to manage both the baby boomers on the way out and their offspring, from Generations X and Y, who do not tolerate authority and obedience to blindness. What's more, the advent of electronic communications and globalization is contributing to the erosion of traditional hierarchies within organizations as ideas and workers circulate more freely

It's quite simple. Today's employees don't just ask, "What should I do?" but want to know, "Why do I have to do it?" To answer this last question, you have to be persuasive. Yet many leaders do not know how to do it. What for? Because they have the assumption that persuasion is an art that is only used to sell products or to enter into contracts. Many also feel that it is a form of manipulation — something twisted that is best avoided.

Of course, persuasion can be used to sell or win a contract, and some use it outright for malicious purposes to rip off others. But when you use it constructively and exploit it fully, it becomes an art that has nothing to do with deception. Persuasion is then a process of negotiation and learning through which the leader will guide his team to success.

Yes, persuasion involves getting others to adopt a position that is not theirs at first but not by begging them or using flattery. Rather, it requires careful preparation, the use of appropriate arguments, the presentation of eloquent facts in support of its position, and a sustained effort to establish a form of collaboration with the people one ultimately wants to seduce.

So, what is effective persuasion? It is the implementation of a rigorous method consisting of stages of preparation and dialogue.

Preparing to persuade co-workers can take weeks or even months of work. As much information as possible about the proposed project must be collected. Think about it yourself from every conceivable angle. Think about the investments of time and money that will be needed for everyone involved, etc.

As for the dialogue, it must begin before and continue during the process. Good leaders open a dialogue to learn more about the opinions, concerns, and perspectives of others. They believe that this approach will enrich the project, not undermine their original idea. The others are invited to discuss, or even challenge, the merits of the original project, and then propose other ideas. All of this may seem tedious, but the search for efficiency involves confronting opinions and reaching a compromise. Perhaps this is why persuasive leaders all seem to share a common trait: they are open-minded, never dogmatic.

Effective persuasion has four unavoidable steps. First, the leader must establish his credibility. Then he sets goals that might excite others. Second, he builds an attractive discourse based on indisputable facts. Finally, he develops emotional bonds with others.

A Question of Credibility
The first challenge is to establish one's credibility. You can't defend a new idea or strategy without your entourage, asking yourself, "Can you trust your vision?" Such a reaction is understandable. After all, others take a risk by being persuaded, that is, by considering the possibility of devoting time and resources to a project that does not come from them.

In business, credibility is based on two pillars: expertise and relationships. Thus, a person is considered an expert in his field when he has demonstrated excellent judgment over the years, or when he has always demonstrated total control of his files. When an advertiser goes from success to success for a decade, others are easily persuaded by his arguments when he proposes a new concept. Similarly, an entrepreneur who has successfully launched seven innovative products in the space of five years will have a clear advantage over a recently hired young graduate when it comes time to get a bold project accepted.

As for relationships, it is important to be able to listen and work in the interests of others. This requires integrity and great strength of character; it is, therefore, important not to be subject to mood swings and uneven yields. He, who is honest, stable, and reliable, is recognized as trustworthy. Moreover, an executive for whom relations with others are paramount will generously share the credit of any good idea with his collaborators, instead of seeking to extol his merits to senior management.

To find out if you are a credible leader, you need to seriously ask yourself the following questions: Is my expertise sufficient for me to be considered an expert in the field concerned by my project? Do others know and respect my baggage? And how will they perceive it concerning the changes I am advocating?

Then, to assess its credibility in terms of relationships, one must pursue questions like this: Do the people I want to persuade see me as a trustworthy person? And will they be on the same wavelength as me during this project, whether emotionally, intellectually or politically?

After doing this work of recoiling at yourself, it is best to ask these same questions to close colleagues, in whom you have every confidence. Their answers will help you to see more clearly about your real credibility within the organization.

In most cases, this exercise reveals previously unknown weaknesses. The challenge then is to correct the shot. As a general rule, if you lack the expertise the most, you have several options:

Fine-tune your project through discussions, formal or not, with people with expertise in the relevant field. You can also, for example, ask to be transferred to a team where you will learn more about the market or the product you are targeting.

Surround yourself with people who can learn more about the field, such as a consultant or an external specialist. Both may have the knowledge and experience to support you in your project. The credibility of this expert will then replace yours.

Use other sources of information, such as business publications, books, independent reports, or expert conferences. For example, a garment executive was able to persuade his company to reposition a range of products by targeting a younger market, based on articles by a renowned demographer published in reputable journals, as well as two independent market studies.

What Is Persuasion

"The art of persuading has a necessary relationship to the way men consent to what is proposed to them, and to the conditions of the things we want to make belief.

Persuasion, "this all-powerful sovereign of men," belongs to the realm of influence; it is merely an adventure of the action on others. As such, it borders on propaganda; it rubs shoulders with rhetoric; it is no stranger to seduction. It maintains an ambiguous relationship with manipulation when it does not have the worst difficulties to stand out from it.

Start pilot projects to demonstrate on a small scale the breadth of your expertise and the value of your ideas.

In addition to correct a relationship problem:

Focus on one-on-one meetings with the key people you want to persuade. Of course, the time has not come to reveal your intentions; rather, it is a question of assessing the extent of views on the subject in question. If you have the time and resources, even offer help to these people on issues of concern to them.

Take advantage of colleagues who share your point of view and who already have strong relationships with those you intend to seduce.

A striking example is the real-life case of Tom Smith (not his real name), newly assigned to the position of Chief Operating Officer of a major bank in Canada, who wanted to persuade senior management that the company was in serious trouble. He believed that the bank's operating costs were too high, which could affect its positioning in an increasingly competitive market. Most of his colleagues disagreed that the bank had been very successful in recent years, and they did not see why that would change.

In addition to being recently appointed to his position, Tom Smith had another problem: coming from another sector, he considered a "foreigner" in the banking industry. As a result, he had few personal contacts that could defend his point of view and was not perceived as competent in finance.

As a first step in establishing credibility, Tom Smith hired a highly respected external consultant in the industry to demonstrate that the bank was not doing very well in terms of operating costs. In a series of submissions to the bank's senior management, the consultant explained that the main competitors were very aggressive in limiting their operating costs. These presentations made it clear that by not reducing its costs, the bank was at risk of falling behind the others. These findings were then sent to the entire organization in the form of written reports.

Next, Tom Smith felt that branch managers should play a crucial role in his campaign. By putting these respected and knowledgeable executives on his side, he would make it clear to the other employees of the bank that action was urgently needed. He also saw an opportunity to improve his expertise on market trends and validate his assumptions.

For three months, he visited every branch in his region, Ontario, a total of 135. Visit after visit, he spent time with the branch managers and listened to their opinions on the strengths and weaknesses of the bank. As a result, he obtained first-hand information on competition projects and customer trends and took the opportunity to gather suggestions to improve services and reduce costs. At the end of his approach, Tom Smith had a global vision of the future of the bank that few people owned, including in senior management. And he had forged dozens of close relationships along the way.

Finally, the Chief Operating Officer launched small, high-profile projects to demonstrate his newly acquired expertise. Thus, he found a solution to remedy the lack of interest of customers for certain mortgages and the decline in the morale of the employees responsible for selling them. He devised a program whereby clients would not have to make any payments for the first 90 days. Huge success! And Tom Smith's image as a novice was immediately gone.

Creating Common Ground

Credibility is not enough. Your point of view must now seem very attractive to the people you want to seduce. Put yourself in their shoes: would you like to board a plane you don't trust (you hear strange noise, the pilot looks tired, etc.)? Or think about the argument you make when you want to quickly convince your child to accompany you to the grocery store: there are lollipops near the cash register

During her career, Monica Ruffo was the McDonald's account manager at the Montreal advertising agency Cossette. The client wanted to launch a Canada-wide campaign on the new prices of his trios, to get the message across that they are no more expensive than those of the competition. The catch? Nevertheless, franchisees were making very good sales and were more concerned about the decline in profits that could result from the application of reduced prices.

Someone less experienced than Ms. Ruffo would have tried to explain the head office's point of view to the franchisees by repeating her argument, to convince them of its relevance. Instead, it chose to demonstrate, with figures to support it, that the price change would turn in their favor. The new campaign, she told them, would even allow them to increase their profits. In support of her claims, she referred, among other things, to a pilot project in Tennessee, which found that when prices go down, consumers buy more fries and soft drinks. Also, based on an article in a business magazine, she pointed out that store sales are growing by 1% for every 10% increase in customer satisfaction; however, it said it was confident that the new prices would push up the ratings by 100% so that sales are expected to increase by 10%.

Monica Ruffo concluded her presentation with a letter written by the founder of McDonald's addressed to the entire organization. It was a passionate letter, hammering the values of the group and stressing the importance of franchisees to contribute to its success. It also reminded us of the value of positioning itself as the leader of low prices. All of this, the franchisees already knew, but hearing it again touched them deeply. And they gave Mrs. Ruffo a standing ovation.

What does this example tell us? That it is vital to indicate what the concrete benefits of your project will be for the people involved. Sometimes it's very easy when there are mutual benefits. Sometimes it's less so, for example, when you don't guess at first where your interests and theirs can come together.

To get a clearer picture, it's best to try to understand your audience better. Before you even start the seduction process, take the time to study people's concerns, gathering information about them (informal conversations, meetings, etc.). Listen, confront their ideas without rushing them, test with them some of your thoughts, etc. This work will allow you to refine your arguments, find those that will fly, or even find documents or indisputable facts supporting your position.

The Importance of Indisputable Facts

Once one has established credibility and found common ground, the art of persuasion is based on the presentation of solid evidence of what is being advanced. Ordinary evidence is not enough. The most convincing leaders use a particular mode of expression. Thus, they accompany their figures with examples, stories, metaphors, and analogies to make their point of view more alive. This allows others to visualize their words, making it more attractive.

A persuasive expert, Mary Kay Ash, founder of Mary Kay cosmetics, often uses analogies. Here's a demonstration from one of his speeches at the company's annual conference.

"By the time of the Roman Empire, the legions had conquered everyone known. All? Not! A handful of diehards still resisted the invader, the disciples of a child of Bethlehem. How did they do it? Their resilience was mainly due to their habit of meeting in secret once a week, historians have found. They then shared their difficulties and hugged each other.

"Does it remind you of anything? Doesn't that make you think about how we stand side by side, sharing our knowledge and talking about our difficulties during our weekly meetings? I have often observed that when a manager or employee experiences a personal problem, the group joins forces to help the member in distress. What a wonderful circle of friends we form! Perhaps this is one of our company's greatest assets.

Through this inspiring analogy, Mary Kay Ash combined the collective support that makes the organization strong with a period of great courage in Christian history. In doing so, it has achieved several objectives. First, it valued everyone's work, most of whom were self-employed, who had to take up the challenge of direct selling every day. In this way, she offered decisive emotional support to people who are repeatedly refused, who would otherwise gradually lose confidence in themselves and the group.

Second, his analogy suggested that solidarity against all is the best way to resist powerful oppressors, in this case, competition. Finally, thanks to the chosen image, Mary Kay Ash instilled in the representatives that the sale is a kind of heroic mission.

You probably don't need to talk about the struggle of Christians to support your position, but the process can be useful to you. The proper use of language allows us to achieve our ends.

The Strength of Emotional Bonds

In the business world, we like to believe that our colleagues use reason to make decisions. But if you scratch a little, you always discover emotional considerations. Persuasive leaders are aware of this phenomenon and know how to take advantage of it

Thus, they do not hide the emotional dimension of their actions, without doing too much, because some might start to doubt the judgment of the leader. When a project excites them, it is because they believe in it instinctively and whole entirely, not just by calculation.

Moreover, they correctly perceive the emotion that grips others and know how to adapt their discourse accordingly. This sometimes involves vigorous intervention, using shock arguments. Other times, all it takes is a whisper to get your ideas across. The lesson is that whatever position is taken, the emotional content of the message must be adapted to the receptiveness of the audience.

Persuasive leaders seem to have a kind of sixth sense in predicting the reaction of others. Their secret is to surround themselves with people who can have a good idea of the mindset and expectations of employees. By speaking very often with these key people, these leaders can, in turn, perceive how others will react to a particular proposal as if they were testing different scenarios on guinea pigs. This trick allows them to find the right tone or convincing arguments.

The president of an aircraft manufacturer was convinced that his company's production costs and speed of execution were significantly lower than those of most of its competitors and that he was in the near risk of losing customers and seeing his revenues melt away. He then decided to convey his fears and his urgent desire to make changes to senior management.

One afternoon, he summoned them to the council chamber. On a screen was projected the image of a smiling man, at the controls of an old twin-engine aircraft, scarf in the wind, but the right portion of the image was hidden. When everyone sat down, the president explained that he felt like this pilot, delighted by the good results so far. But when the hidden part of the image appeared, the faces became tense: the pilot was running straight against a wall. "That's what's happening to us," the president said.

Then he followed up with his proposals, the radical measures that were necessary to avoid disaster, in his opinion. The reaction of the group was immediate and very negative! Immediately after the meeting, executives met in small committees in the corridors to denounce the president's "bullying tactics" in half-word. His point of view was excessive. They had gone to great lengths in the last quarter to break all records, and he didn't even mention it. And so on. They expected to receive flowers, and they were thrown the pot. What mistakes did this president make?

To begin with, he would have had to consult with some members of his management team to assess the emotional state of senior managers. He would then have understood that the team needed congratulations and recognition instead. Second, rather than blaming the team for not anticipating the future, he should have calmly described his vision of the threats he perceived to the company while asking his executives to help him design new projects.

No persuasive effort will succeed without emotion, but displaying too much emotion can be as disastrous as staying stoic. The important point to remember, in this case, is to match the intensity of one's emotions with that of the audience.

In short, persuasion is similar to power: it can do the greatest good to an organization. It helps to weld a team, advance ideas, inspire change, launch bold projects, etc. But, for this, it is imperative to have the guts to use it, and especially not to take it for what it is not: persuading is not a weapon to convince and sell. No, persuading is seducing and therefore learning and negotiating.

Four Ways to Fail

As part of my work with business leaders as a researcher and consultant, I have had the opportunity to see executives fail miserably in their persuasive efforts. Here are the four main errors I have seen.

1. Take a direct and brutal approach. I call it the John Wayne approach: the leaders state their position at the outset, and then through a process of hard work, logic, and vitality, they try to get their opinion across. In reality, positioning themselves firmly from the beginning of the persuasive process gives potential opponents elements to fight and ammunition to do so. It is much better to present your point of view with finesse and restraint. In other words, persuasive leaders do not start the process by offering their colleagues a clear target that they will go fiercely at.
2. Resist compromises. Too many leaders see compromise as a way to give up when it is an essential strategy for a successful process of constructive persuasion. Before joining a proposal, others want to ensure that those who try to persuade them will show enough flexibility to respond to their concerns. Compromise often leads to better solutions because they are sustainable thanks to the established consensus. By refusing to accept compromises, leaders unconsciously send the message that their persuasive approach is one-way. Persuasion is a process in which we take and give. Kathleen Reardon, a professor of organizational behavior at the University of Southern California, notes that a leader rarely changes another person's behavior or perspective without changing one's own opinion along the way. To succeed in persuading in a meaningful way, it is not enough to listen to the other. It is also necessary to integrate one's ideas with our own.
3. Rely only on his arguments. Of course, the quality of arguments plays a certain role when it comes to persuading. But the arguments themselves are only part of the equation. Other factors are equally important, such as the credibility of the leader and his ability to find concrete benefits for each person involved. The ability to keep up with the emotional state of a group and the ability to communicate in a lively way also gives a lot of weight to the arguments.

47

4.. Burn the steps. Like any seduction operation, persuasion is a process, not an event. Rarely will we be able to find a solution that is accepted by all, if ever. The art of persuasion requires listening to others, testing one's position before unveiling it, transforming one's original idea by taking into account the comments of others, etc. Sounds like a slow, tedious process? It is! But the results are worth it

Persuasion Techniques

When we make a decision, we often imagine that we have analyzed all the information in a very rational way. However, science proves that this is rarely the case. Robert Cialdini is an American doctor of social psychology and has studied the mechanisms of persuasion for nearly 15 years. Warning, persuasion does not necessarily say manipulation! Here are six techniques to help you be more persuasive or to understand why you often give favors to others.

Reciprocity

The rule of reciprocity is that if you offered, gave, or helped someone first, they will be more likely to accept your requests later, like an elevator ride back. In marketing, this can offer a sample, goodies, a free service that will encourage consumer engagement. In everyday life, if a neighbor invites you to the restaurant, you will probably be in favor of lending him your car when he asks you a few weeks later.

This rule, which at first glance seems obvious, is good to have in mind to take a step back: who are you indebted to and why? Conversely, if you want to get someone's favor, make sure you are the first to offer something.

Lack Of

People don't like the feeling of missing an opportunity. This is how companies lure their customers, with limited series, items available only for 24 hours, and so on. Knowing that something is going to disappear or that we are competing with others to get it, we want this thing even more ardently.

To apply this persuasive technique, you need to show the caller what they would lose if they refused your proposal. Would you like to ask your boss for a raise, for example? Start by showing him what his shortfall would be if you had to leave the company for another.

Authority

This is the expert's technique. To persuade someone, you have to be credible first and foremost. You have to show that you have a mastery of your subject and that you are well informed. You will trust a doctor who has a degree more than a stranger who recommends treatment. This is typically an example of Milgram's experience. Some people agreed to give electric shocks to others, simply because a man in a white coat ordered them to do so.

We are often accommodating and obedient to the figures of authority. François Damiens' hidden cameras are also good examples. We often see abuses of power on the part of the comedian, to which the trapped persons submit.

Consistency

Another persuasive technique may be to get you accepted. Saying or doing something seemingly innocuous, which then commits you to more to remain consistent with this first decision. For example, some associations that apply for donations will start the discussion by asking if you are okay. Chances are you'll mechanically answer "yes." Once that's stated, you can no longer deny being in a perfect way to be generous, can you?

Since now you support this great cause, you will certainly find it more difficult to refuse to volunteer a few hours with the association. And yes, you'll want to stay consistent with your first action.

Affection

This is self-evident. We are better able to accept something from someone you like. And we value more people who are like us, who look like us. To become a good car salesman, you will maximize your chances by being friendly with your customers. Perhaps, looking for something in common with them ("oh, I know this city where you come from, I spent my holidays there as a child, it's amazing!"), flattering them so that they have a positive image in their minds.

On the other hand, as a customer, beware of the water that sleeps. Just because your caller looks nice doesn't mean they're not trying to sell you something you may not need. It is, therefore, necessary to succeed in separating what is proposed to you from the person who proposes it to you.

Consensus

We often validate our behaviors through those of others, so if your actions are recognized and socially recommended, you will have a better chance of persuading your interlocutor. This technique of social proof sometimes leads to sheepish behaviors, which it is better to spot in good conscience.

"75% of French people use this service and are satisfied with it." Whether this is true or not, you will be more easily tempted to use this service yourself rather than another. These figures are usually interesting references to have. But don't act in autopilot mode and take a step back!

Ways and Means of Persuasion

The main purpose of a writer is, among other things, to convince and accept his word. For this reason, he uses a variety of techniques as to how he presents his arguments. These ways are the so-called: Ways of Persuasion, and each of them is supported and distinguished utilizing Persuasion. These are:

1) Invocation to Logic

- The positions and views of the transmitter are formulated reasonably.
- The author cites arguments from everyday life and social reality that are difficult to dispute and reject.
- There is a rational approach to the issue.
- The speech is strictly composed, and the wording is done in an essay style.
- The means of invoking "Logic" are the arguments, i.e., the theoretical considerations – the logical proposals – the present and the conclusion,
- which also presents the presumptions, i.e., the specific – practical elements – the realistic reality.
- Examples of historical character.
- Examples from a modern individual or collective experience.
- Figures/dates.
- Statistical data.
- Scientific findings/opinions
- Pundits.
- Events of reality.

2) Invocation to Emotion

Stimulation of the moods of the receiver, mobilization of emotions, influence of the soul to make it favorable towards the transmitter and its words.

- The author tries to move, sensitize, reflect.
- The reason is more subjective, often literary.

The means for invoking emotion are

(A) Emotional Language

- Speech shapes: simulations, metaphors, personifications, etc.
- Use adjectives and identifiers.
- Use words with an ideological and emotional charge.

B) Telling Events of Experiences and Events

Description of external and internal characteristics of individuals, environmental conditions, and situations.

- Irony.
- Humor.

3) Invocation to The Authority

Quote the opinions - opinions of the authority of a specialist scientist, scholar - thinker, renowned professional, spiritual man.

Strengthen the power of the author's positions, thanks to their proportion.

The author tries to convince us by confirming and strengthening his word through similar positions that others have already expressed and which are not disputed or rejected.

It uses the words of well-known personalities from the field of politics, culture, and spirit in general.

The views of these people are acceptable, and as the author formulates positions similar to those, his speech is accepted.

It's like he's trying to draw prestige from the prestige of others. The "means" for invoking authority are:

- It is the same quote of the views of the authority, with a statement of the name of the expert and the use of quotation marks.
- Sign rendering of the views of the authority with a statement of the name of the expert and absence of quotation marks.

4) Invocation to The Ethos of The Transmitter

Attempt to gain the trust of the receiver by projecting the integrity, honesty, ethos of the transmitter.

The author tries to convince us by presenting himself, his personality, and his speech as an accomplished and reliable person. The "means" for invoking the ethos of the transmitter are:

- Speech or writing to a singular person.
- Use of words of manifest moral virtues.
- Reference to actions, individual choices, decisions, attitudes, successes evidence of the ethos of the transmitter

5) Attack on The Opponent's Ethos

Seeking to tarnish the opponent's morals through a personal attack on him.

At the same time, indirect emphasis on the ethos of the transmitter as an integer and its so-called reliable.

It is the worst and least acceptable way of persuasion as the author tries to impose himself when he no longer has other legitimate means using the slander and pre-gelding of the recipient.

The "means" for attacking the opponent's ethos

are:

- Use of the third person.
- Use of words of manifest defects.
- In reference to actions, individual choices, decisions, attitudes, failures are demonstrating the moral deficit that distinguishes the opponent – receiver.

Dark Persuasion

Evolution has been deceived. Human perception tends to give birth to illusions, and consciousness - to succumb to the hidden impact. The threat is close. The dark art of manipulation, which penetrated all spheres of communication, rules the ball of unheard-of proportions. Each of us is involved in an information war. Any consumption of information becomes a threat. Sounds ominous, doesn't it? Don't panic. Let the enemy everywhere, but we took care of you and decided to expose his insidious schemes. In this series of articles, we will talk about protection from manipulation, their deactivation, and destruction. This is useful information for those who are not afraid to win. We hope you're one of those. Then fight! "The ability to communicate with people is a commodity that can be bought in the same way as sugar or coffee. And I'll pay more for it than any other product. Since ancient times, the man who wields the word equated to the owner of a powerful weapon. The word can power people, control them, suppress the will. This was best known in ancient Greece, where every citizen had to own oratory. Modern rhetoric consists of eroticism (the technique of dispute management) and dialectic (ways of persuasion of the opponent). In everyday communication, we use various speech techniques, most of which are harmless and understandable to others. Our habit of communicating is not based on the idea of domination, which cannot be said of the dodgy speakers who dominate the world. Speech reception in the mouth of the insidious villain turns into a method of manipulation. When the hidden impact on a person's consciousness is the purpose of the speaker, his rhetoric is painted black. Such a character can convince in everything: from the need to make a living to the existence of conspiracy theory. Often manipulations hit your emotions, values, and logical constructs. A speech attack finds vulnerabilities in the latter. Fortunately, the number of dishonest methods of exposure, of course, and is detectable:

- Black or white Life is more diverse than it seems. When you are offered two alternative results or two opposing positions, know that there are many more. An example of a speech attack: "You are with me or against me."
- False cause We hope you don't believe in omens. A black cat or a woman with empty buckets is a weak argument for your failures. The brain likes to look for patterns, and that's its weakness. The manipulator will argue that the alleged connection between the phenomena obliges one event to be the cause of another. Is this the case? Example of a speech attack: "You made a mistake, and it happened," "Fewer costs - more revenue," "Coincidence? I don't think so!"
- That's what most people think. It is not cool to support the opinion of the masses. However, the method of persuasion, in which the argument is based on the thesis "many agree with this," is still relevant. Example of a speech attack: "Most people can't be wrong," "Millions of people agree with my position, which means I'm right."
- The vicious circle, the meaning of admission, is that there is a conclusion among the reasons; a treacherous ploy in which the statement is derived from itself, usually through a few intermediate statements. Recursion in its purest form. An example of a speech attack: "God is because it is written in the Bible. The Bible is true because it is the Word of God."
- Appeal to emotions Sometimes, it's much easier to evoke emotions than to convince you logically. An example of a speech attack: "There are so many hungry people in the world, and you can't finish this soup!"
- Part-whole, the truth of the statement for the whole and its parts, may be different. We know that we are made up of atoms that weigh almost nothing, but that doesn't mean that a person is just as light. An example of a speech attack: "The marketing department failed the plan for a month! The whole company has some nerds!"
- Life case Personal experience is always a subjective and controversial argument. It is a small piece of truth, not a vast part of it. The reception is based on a truthful argument but unable to reflect the full width of the problem. An example of a speech attack: "Elections are falsification. My friends and I didn't vote for the victors!" "My great-grandfather smoked five packs a day and lived to be 95!"
- Appeal to nature All that is natural is not ugly. It's a funny method that honest politicians use especially. Social Darwinism without banknotes. An example of a speech attack: "The strongest survives!" "Predators devour each other - this is the law of nature; people in society do the same."
- Sniper error, the point of the reception is to falsify an event that has already taken place. You shot at the bare wall, and then in place of bullet holes attached targets. Congratulations, everyone thinks you're a marksman! Example of speech attack: "In the top five countries, consumers of our products according to statistics live the happiest people."
- Slippery trail One of the most common techniques. The assertion that one event is bound to entail another (usually negative). The trick works thanks to skipping intermediate events.

Identifying the techniques of black rhetoric is more difficult than using them. The laborious process of exposing is based on stopping the interlocutor, re-questioning, and clarifying his words.

Influence by Persuasion

To influence another, a person does not need to be able to punish or encourage, have the charisma, or have outstanding knowledge. One of the most effective ways of influencing is persuasion - effectively transmitting one's point of view. Like reasonable faith, belief is based on the power of example and the power of an expert. The only difference is that the performer fully understands what he is doing and why. A leader who influences by persuasion does not tell the performer what to do - he or she "sells" the performer what needs to be done.

Using the conviction, the leader tacitly admits that the executor has some degree of power that can reduce the ability of the leader to act. In other words, the manager recognizes the dependence on the performer. For example, if a marketing manager wants to reorganize a sales department, it would be wise for him or her to recognize that sales staff can withstand changes so much that it will have a significant impact on product production. Thus, even if the manager could have the authority to implement a new organizational structure without meeting with subordinates, it would still be more appropriate and practical to organize a meeting, listen to all opinions, and explain why change is desirable. Actively seeking agreement, the manager has a very strong impact on the need of the executor for respect. If the performer, in turn, feels the need for knowledge and authority, the power of influence through persuasion increases. This is because the manager has recognized the competence of the executor, and the executor feels that the share of the leader's power passes to him or her. Persuasion affects what makes a potential performer conscious that by doing what the leader wants, he will satisfy his or her own need, whatever it may be.

To achieve this, the manager can use logic or emotion. Those who want to convince use both, depending on the location of the listener. A bright and well-known example by persuasion is the relationship between the seller and the buyer. An insurance agent, for example, punctuates the logical arguments for buying a property with emotional, affecting the potential client's need for security. Increasing power by giving it away is the theme of example.

Effective Belief

Trying to influence others, people are engaged, to put it figuratively, "selling" although not as explicitly as when selling insurance policies. This is especially true for organizations, particularly when a person has no formal authority over the other or when he cannot offer any rewards. The ability to influence through persuasion depends on some factors.

The manager must be trustworthy. His reasoning should take into account the intellectual level of the listener: it should not be too complex, but should not be simplistic. The goal of the leader should not contradict the value system of his listeners. The case would only benefit if his subordinates liked the character traits and behavior of the manager. Many arguments and attempts to "sell" something failed only because the potential buyer did not like the identity of the selling, and not his product or service.

Delegation Power

What follows is an excerpt from an interview with Michael McCauley, author of the acclaimed book "The Player." It shows how you can increase your power by passing it on to others. McCauley knew one supervisor who called his staff and said, "I plan to organize an on-the-job formal training group on How to do my job. Anyone who wants to learn is welcome."

The leader has put a lot of work into this course of training: training materials, lists of recommended literature, etc. result. Most of the staff were trained, and a few months later, many of them took over some of its functions. Very soon, he discovered that he was "managing" rather than being carried headlong, doing a lot of things, as he had done before. By giving away "power," McHobey explains, this leader has gained enormous power.

His staff trusted him, and he trusted the staff. He could entrust them with responsible tasks, freeing up his time for more complex new projects. For example, the staff knew that their boss would not put sticks in their wheels, so they put even more diligence into everything they did. Motivation arose automatically.

According to McCauley, this concept is acceptable for almost any company. It can be a master who offers his workers some form of training, or a vice president of finance offering professional development for management staff, or a president offering a training course to his deputies.

Strengths and Weaknesses of Influence Through Persuasion

The weakest point of such influence is slow influence and uncertainty. It takes more time and effort to convince someone of something than to issue an order backed up by a power based on coercion, tradition, or charisma. It doesn't matter how much effort is made. You can never be sure that the listener will take influence. Also, unlike other forms, influence through persuasion has a one-time effect. A leader who prefers the persuasion method, every time he or she wants to influence someone, must start all over again, which increases the time spent on the persuasion process.

First of all, using persuasion does not mean giving up other tools of influence available. For example, charisma only promotes persuasion by helping the listener identify with the leader. Influence through tradition and positive reward reinforces conviction, increasing trust in the leader. If the executor knows that the manager can coerce him but tries to avoid it, the power of persuasion can be greatly multiplied by the reinforcement of the need for respect. If persuasion does not help, a leader with other means of influence may resort to them. And when a belief achieves a goal, the ability of a leader to influence through reasonable or blind faith increases. As is often the case in the relationship between line and staff, the constant success of the persuasion method can give a person the ability to influence through reasonable faith.

How to Effectively Use Influence by Persuasion

1. Try to accurately identify the needs of the listener and appeal to these needs.
2. Start the conversation with a thought that is sure to be to the liking of the listener.
3. Try to create an image that is trustworthy and trustworthy.
4. Ask for a little more than you need or want (for persuasion, you sometimes have to make concessions, and if from the beginning, you ask for more, you seem to get exactly as much as you need). This method can work against you if you ask too much.
5. Speak in the interests of the listeners, not your own. The frequent repetition of the word "you" will help the listener understand what it or her needs have to do with what you, influencing, want him to do.
6. If there are several points of view, try to say the last: the arguments heard by the latter has the greatest chance to influence the audience.

The biggest advantage in using persuasion in organizations is that the performance of the work by the person affected will not need to be checked, and he is likely to try to meet more than the minimum requirements because he believes that these actions will help meet his personal needs on many levels. The person who received the order, backed by coercion, usually performs it, but at a minimum. Sometimes it seems that coercion is effective, but problems can occur a few weeks or months later at the execution stage.

However, the benefits of persuasion have only potential benefits. In some cases, as the next chapter will show, coercion may be more effective than persuading the organization to achieve its goals.

Influence through the participation (engagement) of workers in management

Influence through participation goes even further than the belief in recognition of the power and abilities of the performer. The leader makes no effort to impose his will or even his opinion on the executor. Instead of persuading the executor to accept the supervisor's stated goal, the leader simply directs his efforts and promotes the free exchange of information.

The expert power of both the leader and the executor can be united in a single position, in which both will sincerely believe. Influence is successful because people inspired by high-level needs tend to work harder on the goal that has been articulated with their participation. However, a determination based on unity can have as much impact on the leader as it does on the performer.

Participation in decision-making appeals to the needs of a higher level of power, competence, success, or self-expression. Therefore, this approach should be used only when such needs are active, motivating factors, and provided that the executor can be relied upon to work for the goals he or she has chosen.

In the 1940s, a very important study of the effectiveness of participation was conducted at a garment factory. In particular, it was found that when workers were allowed to participate in the discussion of proposed changes to their work, they were less resistant to these changes. There was higher productivity and lower turnover than workers who were not allowed to participate. Other studies have shown that participation has a positive impact on job satisfaction and productivity. As a result, authors belonging to the Bi-Jewish School in Management Theory, such as Douglas McGregor and Ransis Lykert, have become ardent supporters of labor's participation in government.

Unfortunately, other studies have shown that participation in management is not suitable for all situations. Workers who do not like ambiguity, are not very prone to individualism and prefer tightly controlled authoritarian situations, work best in more controlled environments, where there is very little room for workers to participate in government.

Other authors whose ideas we will look at in the next chapter have identified several situational factors that determine how appropriate the impact of involving workers in government is. But while we are considering the question of appropriateness, let's say that one of the reasons why participation in governance is not widespread may be the fact that managers do not want to give up their traditional powers and prerogatives. This may be the case because some people find the job of a leader attractive. After all, it satisfies the need for power. Of course, such satisfaction is more likely to be thin when a person has the opportunity to issue orders and force them to comply.

We will look in more detail at the potential conditions for use, as well as the "for" and cons method of influence by involving workers in management when we talk about the appropriate management style.

Practical Use of Influence
Fear, reward, tradition, charisma, intelligent faith, persuasion, and participation in management are tools that the leader uses to influence the performer by appealing to his needs. But even that rare leader, who has all these mechanisms in his arsenal, must take into account other factors. It is not enough to have power: it must be strong enough to encourage others to work, preferably inspired, to achieve the organization's goals. To achieve this, several conditions must be met

The most decisive influence will be when the performer appreciates the need to which the appeal, considers it essential to satisfy or dissatisfied, and thinks that his or her efforts will necessarily meet the expectations of the manager. Conversely, if any of these components are absent, the influencer's power decreases or disappears altogether.

To better understand how the process of influence practically happens, let's look at the typical situation. John Thurlock oversaw production at a small company that makes tools. The company had only 85 workers in production and five grassroots managers, each of whom was responsible for 17 workers.

John has just returned from an annual meeting with senior management to discuss the challenges of his enterprise. One of the objectives was to reduce the percentage of material waste from 5.6 to 4.5 next year. Although John had some ideas about reducing waste, he realized that to achieve this, it was necessary to enlist the support of workers. Thus, instead of convening five grassroots leaders to inform them of their desire to do so or to notify all employees of the company about its staging by issuing a memorandum, he decided to take a different approach: to involve workers in the discussion process.

How to Use Influence Effectively?
1. The need to which the appeal must be active and robust.
2. The person who is influenced must view influence as a source of satisfaction or dissatisfaction, to varying degrees, of some need.
3. The person affected should consider it highly likely that execution will satisfy or unmet the need.

4. A person who is influenced must believe that his or her efforts have a good chance to meet the expectations of the leader.

First, he gathered his grassroots leaders and explained the whole situation to them. He tried to make them understand how every tenth of a percent of waste significantly increases the cost of production. Also, he explained how their industry had become competitive and how important it was for the company to maximize its productivity without resorting to avarams or other techniques that he considered unacceptable.

While allowing people to speak out and find out everything that is incomprehensible, John said that while he had his views on the matter, he would like to hear other suggestions to address the problem. He then asked each grassroots leader to have a group discussion of the problem with his workers and to gather as many proposals as possible. He then suggested that each leader choose two of his subordinates, the informal leaders of the group, and invited them to attend a meeting to discuss their group's proposals with representatives and leaders of other groups.

Two weeks later, five executives and ten workers gathered with the director of the company. As a result of this meeting, more new considerations did not occur to the leaders.

Also, workers across the enterprise were involved in the goal because they were involved in the discussion and generation of ideas. By the end of the year, the waste rate had fallen from 5.6 to 3.9, even exceeding the target of 4.5 percent.

Resume

1. Leadership, the ability to influence others in a way that they work to achieve goals, is necessary for effective management. To lead, you need power.
2. Power, the ability to influence people's behavior, is necessary for the effectiveness of the organization, because leaders depend on people over whom they do not have direct power, or have, but very weak.
3. The main types of power are coercion, reward, competence, example, and tradition. A leader can also influence through reasonable faith, involvement in decision-making, and persuasion.
4. The effectiveness of some type of power depends on whether the executor believes that the manager may or may not meet his active need and on the situation. Therefore, each method has pros and cons, and no one can lead people in all cases.
5. Coercive power, influence through fear, is significant only if they are backed up by an excellent control system, which is usually costly.
6. The power of reward is preferable to positive action than fear because it provides positive incentives for better work. Sometimes it is difficult to determine which compensation will affect.
7. Traditional or legitimate power, influence through culture-insulated values, is the most common type of energy. It seems that the effectiveness of tradition is disappearing because of changing values.
8. Charisma, influence by the power of example - that's what people associate with dynamic leaders. The performer identifies with the leader or has a strong sympathy for him, and blindly believes in his abilities.
9. Expert power, influence through reasonable faith is spreading more and more and becoming effective due to the increasing complexity of technology and the size of organizations.
10. Because of changing social values, organization leaders see persuasion and participation as the most effective means of influencing those who do not hold managerial positions, colleagues, and those who are not members of the organization. While these methods are slower and less specific than others, they appear to increase the effectiveness of the organization when the executor is motivated by higher-level needs, especially if the task is unstructured and requires creativity.
11. In general, the impact will be most substantial when the performer very much appreciates the need to which the manager appeals, considers satisfaction or dissatisfaction with the market by an inevitable result of submission or

disobedience, and thinks that there is a high probability that his effort will meet the expectations of the manager.

Issues to Repeat

1. What is the difference between governance and leadership?
2. How do power, influence, and leadership relate to each other?
3. Define power.
4. Give a brief description of the main types of power by the classification of French and raven.
5. What is charisma, and how do leaders use it?
6. What is intelligent faith, and how is it most commonly used in organizations?
7. What are the strengths and weaknesses of persuasion?
8. What other tools of influence help a leader influence through persuasion?
9. Why are there relatively few organizations today that believe that fear is an effective means of influence?
10. Give a brief description of the concept of the balance of power between managers and subordinates.

Six Categories of Influence Methods

Influence is the process of persuading another to change attitudes, beliefs, or behavior. Each method of persuasion is governed by one of six psychological principles: consistency, mutual exchange, social responsibility, conformity, sympathy, and scarcity.

Author: James Lewis has trained more than 25,000 managers of different levels in the United States, Europe, and Asia, founder of the Lewis Institute, a training and advisory company.

Influence is the process where you convince another person to change their attitude, beliefs, or behavior. There are many ways to do this, but they usually fall into one of six categories, each governed by a basic psychological principle. These principles: consistency, mutual exchange, social responsibility, conformity, sympathy, and scarcity.

Commitment and Consistency

This principle is that as soon as a person makes a decision, he begins to behave consistently according to it. To illustrate this, let's say you're buying a new car; you took a trial trip in several cars and made your choice. The seller gave you the price of this car. You go to the store to issue the paperwork, and when the seller hands them over to you, it turns out that the bill price is several hundred dollars higher than stated. What are you doing? You probably start to object, but the seller explains that the original price was only a "clean" price and did not include the preparation of papers, etc. Why? Because they've already forced themselves to buy this car internally. But it is possible that they will not agree to overpayment and start looking for a vehicle in another store.

This is one of the reasons why it is better to have people in the project who have agreed to it than those who have been appointed. When people are internally committed to joining a project, they are much more likely to do their job well, support the project, and then speak well about the experience.

In psychology, there is also a principle called cognitive dissonance (cognitive disagreement), which has to do with some people's insecurities when choosing. Once you buy a new car, you will read even more ads about the same model. You will try to convince yourself that you have done the right thing and stop worrying about a choice that could not give 100% certainty.

Justice, Reciprocity, And Influence

Consider the relationship between two people: let's call them A and B. The theory of justice claims that they will try to get results proportional to their attachments. That is, everyone expects from this relationship to receive benefits proportional to what he puts into this relationship. He also expects that the "result" will be roughly equal to the "contribution." If equality is not respected, the person receiving a smaller result will consider the situation unfair. He invests more in the relationship than the other person and receives proportionally less. If this inequality is not corrected, the relationship can be expected to be broken.

In other words, all relationships are mutual, exchange-related. If this exchange between people does not meet their expectations, then the relationship may break down. A simple example: one person discovers that he has already invited another person to attend any events ten times, and he never invited him anywhere. "What does that mean?" the first one asks. Perhaps it means that the other does not care about him as much as he cares about the person himself. Having come to such a conclusion, the invitee very soon ends the relationship with the invitee.

Reciprocity

Reciprocity is one aspect of the relationship. You're doing someone a favor. Later you need his response. If it provides you with this service, you are satisfied with your relationship. Otherwise, you consider it a "dirty game" unless there are circumstances that prevented the "debt repayment." Your partner didn't fulfill his part of the "deal."

A mutual exchange is one of the most effective means of influence because the sense of commitment is powerful in people. Charities try to use this sense of obligation by sending leaflets with the addresses of the organizations for which they collect donations. One organization found that 18 percent of the flyers were simply responding to contributions. If the booklets include the addresses of the organizations for which contributions are collected, up to 35% of those who received them are responsible.

Social Norms and Social Relations

Norms are the usual ways of behavior and beliefs established by a group. They facilitate interaction by identifying expectations and acceptable behavior in a particular situation. Bars make our lives easier. They allow us to predict how others will behave, and the rules keep us from having to decide what to do.

For example, we can say that each culture has its traditions of distance when talking. In some societies, this distance is so small that two people can feel each other's breath. In America, it would be too close, and we feel uncomfortable when someone comes close to us unless it is a person with whom we have family ties or love.

We instinctively want to move back, restore the "proper" distance to the other person. However, this breaks the connection with him, so he moves around. This constant interaction of "offensive - retreat - offensive - retreat" makes both sides feel uncomfortable. His norms have been violated (as yours), and he can tell members of his group how rude a person was from another group. Models set expectations not only of behavior but also of clothing. A newly hired manager asked the company's president about the uniform. The President replied that such a form did not exist.

"Of course, it does," the new manager thought. "Everyone wears white shirts and ties." People simply observe others (this is called social comparison) to find out what they consider to be the rules to follow, and subconsciously set norms.

Social relations confirm our belief that if everyone else does a sure thing, it is the right thing to do. Therefore, if everyone suddenly dyes the hair on one half of the head is green. Eventually, you will succumb to the behavior of the majority and paint your hair.

Match

Groups put enormous pressure on their members to conform to the group's standards. A person's refusal to comply with these standards may result in the removal of the latter from the group. A member of a street gang can be exposed from a club for being "too good," for example, behaving too well at school. This person adapts to the rules of "outside the group" and not to the laws of the gang itself.

Solomon Ashe conducted one of the most well-known experiments demonstrating the power of pressure in the group. He joined seven to nine people to participate in a visual discrimination experiment. They were asked to match the length of the standard line with one of the three comparative lines drawn on the card and to announce their judgments in the order in which they sat behind each other.

All but one person in the group were actual allies of the experiment. This naive man always sat the penultimate. Other members were instructed to respond incorrectly in some cases. In these cases, the Allies deliberately chose the wrong line. So it was obvious that it wasn't the same length as the standard line, but they all said it was.

Ash found that the subjects rejected the group's influence-driven opinion in two-thirds of the (wrong) tests and conceded in the remaining third. Interestingly, about 5% of the subjects agreed with the group each time, about a quarter of them held their opinion and made no mistake. A third agreed with the group in half of the tests or more.

After asking the subjects, Ash discovered that some of them doubted their vision, after hearing that six other people were giving the wrong answer, in their opinion. In the end, they thought it was a perception experiment, so there was something in themselves that made them see the lines differently than most saw them.

Ash also found that only three allies were needed to achieve compliance. This is very important. If you hear something implausible from just three people, you tend to believe it.

External and Inner Obedience

It's important to understand that people can say that the two lines are the same, except it's true. At the same time, they consider how the group sees everything but internally knows that the group is wrong.

For project managers, this means that they must be careful not to allow their team to put pressure on a person with "supernatural ideas." Otherwise, he will stop expressing them. It may well be that the supernatural idea is correct. Still, you will lose both this idea and the devotion of the human group if you allow the members of the group to reject this idea without open discussion.

Deficit

Try to calculate how many commercials on television end with the words: "Order it right now because the number of products is limited." Undoubtedly, they are limited to several warehouses full of these products. You could be persuaded that not everyone can get this product, but if you buy this thing, you will become a member of the "circle of favorites." This approach can be regarded as pressure that you have not taken into account. I've even heard that there is a tactic in which a person is forced to buy something not necessary to him, saying that he has almost no opportunity to purchase this thing, so he cannot pass by.

The Words "Because"

Researchers have found that you will increase the likelihood of fulfilling your request if you say to a person, "Could you do it for me, because" followed by some explanation. In other words, if you justify your request - especially if the excuse is reasonable - you increase the likelihood of consent.

The surprising thing is that by saying "because" without further justification, you also increase the chances of getting consent compared to what you can get by simply asking. It's not clear why this is happening, but it's true.

The point is that if you want people to follow your orders, make sure they are justified.

Credibility in Persuasion

The ultimate goal of the argument, as has been noted many times above, is to convince the audience and thus to obtain its consent to the statements and opinions that are offered for its evaluation. The most important means of persuasion are, of course, facts and data, organized in the form of evidence and plausible reasoning. They are followed by the value orientations of the audience, which are in the final stages of making the allegations and substantiating their arguments.

Equally important in the process of reasoning and persuasion, in general, is the emotional state and behavior of the speaker, which largely determine the credibility of him. On this side of the case, paid attention to ancient rhetoric and especially Aristotle. In his first book, "Rhetoric," he drew attention to the fact that persuasion is achieved on the one hand by the character and behavior of the speaker, and on the other hand, by his emotional impact on listeners. However, logically, he recognized that the basis of persuasion is rational reasoning based on objective data and logical conclusions from them. However, he admitted that, in some cases, the character and behavior of the speaker were the most effective means of persuasion that he possessed. It depends on the action that trust or distrust arises.

These indisputable provisions remain relevant in our time. Still, modern life is so complicated with the advent of new means of communication, such as radio, television, the press, that the problem of trust in the source of information acquires completely different features and traits. Indeed, Aristotle was referring to cases where the speaker or author of the text was known to the person perceiving the information. So he could judge them directly. With the advent of radio, television, film, press, it takes considerable effort to evaluate the reliability of their communications. This is especially true of the modern advertising industry, which employs many people who seek to gain the trust of people not only by legal and honest methods but often resorting to techniques that imitate faith. In such circumstances, many different factors influence trust that has to be taken into account, as will be described below. But the primary condition for assessing the degree of confidence is primarily the requirement: to look at the information through the eyes of the recipient of the story. If he understands it, and even more so when it agrees with its main content, it will be a sign of confidence in the source of information, whether it is an individual or a group expressing their opinion directly or through a means of conveying information. When there is a misunderstanding, much less an objection, then additional tools and methods of persuasion are required. Thus, trust is characterized not by the source of information, but by the attitude of the recipient of the story to that source.

While the speaker, publicist, politician, and another public figure can improve their speeches, it is up to the audience to justify and confirm their opinions and advice more carefully to better convince the audience. This is consistent with the aristo teal approach to the notion of trust, which is based primarily on assessing the speaker's conduct in a particular situation. This is not the case when the source of information is an anonymous group or another team that tries to imitate trust by deliberately misleading people. In this case, it is very difficult to determine the authenticity of their intentions by conduct, speeches, or written texts, especially if they are half-truths for the truth, partial truth for the full truth.

The reasoning teaching usually distinguishes between three types of trust: first, direct trust, which is based on obtaining information from a person addressing the audience, and telling them about their views, intentions, and decisions. This type of trust is most often met with public speeches by politicians before elections when they present their programs and talk about their lives and social activities.

Secondly, secondary trust, which is based on facts, evidence, observations, and conclusions obtained by other people, in particular experts and experts in the relevant field of reasoning. It seems that such trust is the basis of most different forms of reasoning since no one can directly test and verify all the evidence that acts as an argument for substantiating a conclusion. The reference to the opinions or decisions of known or authoritative persons is of particular importance so that people tend to trust the statements made by others and collectives more. Logically, as we already know, secondary trust is, in fact, an argument for authority and therefore shares with it all the advantages and disadvantages of the latter. As a rule, people are more likely to trust experts and professionals than simple administrators, politicians, and agitators. It is no coincidence that all environmental movements, for example, against the construction of nuclear power plants and large hydropower plants, chemical, and other harmful industries, seek the support of independent experts.

Thirdly, the indirect trust that differs from the above is that it is based on strengthening one's reasoning in such a way that, through more detailed development of arguments and the degree of confirmation of the data, to achieve the audience's consent with the statements, conclusions, and decisions. While, with direct and secondary trust, he sought to influence the credibility of the audience by broadening the reasoning data he or others had received, with indirect faith, much more attention was paid to the quality of the entire argument, from the data to the validity of the idea itself. But this distinction should not, of course, be absolutized. It should be about how, in different specific circumstances, it is possible to gain the trust of the audience and convince them of the validity of their position. In some cases, when it is necessary to speak to a broad audience on topical socio-political, economic, ethical, pedagogical, and other issues, it is most appropriate to turn to one's observations, experiences, and experiences, in others - to rely more on the arguments of experts, in more complicated - to improve all elements of reasoning, focusing on qualitative improvement of the justification of their position, especially after criticism and preliminary discussion.

It is not uncommon to point to the fourth type of trust associated with the reputation of the source of argument. It is evident that when listeners are aware of the high importance of such a start, they give him more confidence. It is unlikely, however, that this type should be singled out in particular, since in all of the above three of them in one way or another, there is, if not an implicit, reputational assessment. In the first case, the audience can assess it directly, in the second - from the words and arguments of the speaker, in the third - on the degree of its validity.

61

Another critical factor influencing trust is the truthfulness of information, including facts, observations, the testimony of others, and other reasoning data. Often this factor is classified as reliability, validation, and, therefore, the validity of these arguments. These two main factors of trust are recognized by all and taken for granted.

Disagreements arise when assessing other factors that also affect trust. These include, for example, the so-called goodwill and dynamism of the source of information. To characterize goodwill, words such as openness, objectivity, friendliness, kindness, and personal appeal are usually used by those who make arguments in front of an audience or simply report information. Dynamism is related to the extent to which the speaker can enhance the confidence or recognition that the audience gives him. Many researchers believe, however, that goodwill can be seen as a form of truthfulness and dynamism as a form of competence for the source of information.

In addition to these factors, many specific recommendations can increase confidence not only in the argument but also in the information in general. All of them are based on generalizations made from observations, and partly by special psychological studies. We have already noted that the trust of the audience largely depends on the competence and reputation of the source of information. Reputation evaluation will be enhanced if the people who perceive the arguments belong to the same socio-economic class, group, or collective. Therefore, they tend to trust people who come from the same environment more, express their opinions and views. It is also noted that people usually trust people who have achieved success in life and are highly valued in society. Nor is it questionable that information relating to more essential issues is usually more exciting and often more credible than reports in secondary matters. Listeners tend to trust people with adequate training, who have a lot of practical experience and are well oriented in this field of activity. However, it is also crucial to what extent the audience is included in the debate, how well they can assess the arguments put forward to support a proposal or decision. A person familiar with the case will always trust well-founded projects and decisions. In contrast, the incompetent person will depend on the opinions of others, showing hesitation and uncertainty.

There are also many recommendations for direct and secondary trust, based on the personal qualities of the arguments mentioned above. We have seen that sincerity, openness to other people's suggestions and opinions, the personal interest of the idea in trying to convince the audience to help him gain her trust. But all this is ultimately determined by the audience, not by themselves. And this should always be kept in mind, and remember that faith, like beauty, is valued by others.

The most powerful way to gain trust, especially indirect faith, seems to be the same value orientation of the argumentation and the audience. We have already noted that if the values of the audience are at odds with the importance of the speaker, then all his efforts to gain her trust will be almost in vain. Hence, it may seem that one of the ways to increase confidence is to adjust to the audience, to say it only pleasant things, and in every way to avoid negative phenomena. This, as we know, is based on the populist approach, widely practiced by politicians of different parties and social movements. But this way of gaining trust is short-lived and little influential, as people soon become convinced that the promises and projects put forward by populists are unfulfilled because of their unreality. The best way to convince and gain people's trust is to discuss the problems that have arisen sincerely, to point out the real difficulties of their solution, to find common ground with the position of the audience, if necessary, then to convince it of something, while relying on the "stubborn" facts of reality. Based on all this, acting with due tact, the argument will have the opportunity to convince the audience, who will ultimately deliberately agree with his position and the ideas he makes in its defense.

Persuasion Methods

A word is an excellent tool for human communication and a boundless influence on people. Leaders often care about the content of verbal persuasion, and at the same time, are carefree about its form, which is no less critical. What, for example, is meant when it comes to the technique of verbal persuasion? This is diction (clear pronunciation of sounds), expressive articulation (in the particular correct operation of logical accents), volume (depending on the audience), ability to control their gestures and facial expressions, the clear, logical structure of speech, presence of pauses, brief breaks. It should be noted that convinces not only the word, but also the case, so it is not necessary to count on convincing influence only on words, even correctly and clearly said, but not confirmed by specific cases.

Persuasion methods are the leading methods of organizational influence. Persuasion is, first of all, an explanation and proof of the correctness and necessity of certain behavior or inadmissibility of some kind of misconduct.

The process of persuasion is perhaps the most complex, among other ways of organizing influence. The leading place in this process is the reasoning of its position and the desire to make it become a position, the conviction of each participant of collective activity. Therefore, we will take a closer look at reasoning as the most important basis of persuasion. Let's focus on the parameters of the persuasive impact.

There are many ways of reasoning, but, as in chess, the practice has developed some "correct debuts." They can be reduced to the following four tracks.

Receiving the removal of tension requires establishing emotional contact with the interlocutor. A few words are enough for this. The joke, which was said on time and to the point, also contributes in many ways to defusing tension and creating a positive psychological environment for discussion.

Receiving a "snap" allows you to summarize the situation and, linking it to the content of the conversation, use it as a starting point for discussion of the problem. To this end, you can successfully use some events, comparisons, personal impressions, anecdotal cases, or unusual questions.

The acceptance of imagination-stimulating involves asking a lot of questions at the beginning of the conversation about the content of the problems that need to be addressed. This method gives good results when the performer has a sober view of the problem.

Taking a direct approach involves a direct transition to action without any introduction or preamble. This is as schematic as follows: briefly report the reasons why the meeting is convened and move on to discussing them.

How do you encourage people to accept your point of view? These recommendations can be useful in psycho correct work.

- Rule one: convincing a person of something does not mean arguing with him. The dispute cannot resolve misunderstandings. They can be resolved only by tact, the desire for reconciliation, and a sincere desire to understand the point of view of another.
- Rule two: respect the opinion of others, never tell a person abruptly that he is wrong, especially in case of strangers, because, in this case, it will be difficult for him to agree with you.

Never start by saying, "I'm ready to prove it to you." It's like saying, "I'm smarter than you." It's kind of a challenge. This appeal sets the interlocutor against you even before you begin to convince him.

If a person expresses thought and you think it is wrong or even sure of its error, nevertheless, it is better to address your interlocutor with some words: "I may be wrong. Let's look at the facts." You will never find yourself in a quandary if you admit that you can be wrong. This will stop any dispute and force your interlocutor to be as fair and frank as you will force him to admit that he, too, can be wrong.

- Rule three: if you're wrong, admit it quickly and decisively. It is much easier to admit one's own mistakes or shortcomings than to listen to the condemnation of another person. If you assume that someone wants to speak negatively about you, say it earlier. You're going to disarm him. In some cases, it is much more pleasant to admit oneself wrong than to try to defend yourself. Acknowledging a mistake tends to condescend to the person who committed it.

- Rule four: when you want to convince a person of the correctness of your point of view, lead the conversation in a benevolent tone. Don't start with questions on which your opinions differ. Talk about what your opinions are in the same way.
- Rule five: try to get an affirmative answer from the interlocutor at the beginning of the conversation. If a person says, "No," his pride demands that he remain consistent until the end.
- Rule six: give the other person the right to speak more and try to be short-spoken. The truth is that even our friends prefer to talk more about their successes than listen to us boast. Most people, trying to get people to understand their point of view, say a lot themselves - it's a clear mistake. Give someone else a chance to speak out, so it's best to learn how to ask questions of your interlocutors.
- Rule seven: Let the person feel that the idea you gave him belongs to him, not to you.
- Rule eight: if you want to convince people of something, try to look at things with their eyes. Everyone has a reason to do just that, not otherwise. Find this hidden cause, and you will have a "key" you will understand its actions and maybe even personal qualities. Try to put yourself in his shoes. You will save a lot of time and save your nerves.
- Rule Nine: Treat empathy with the ideas and desires of another person. Sympathy is what everyone longs for. Most of the people around you need empathy.
- Rule ten: to change the opinion or point of view of someone, turn to noble motives. A person is usually guided by two motives in his actions: one that sounds noble and the other true. The man himself will think of the true reason. But all of us, being idealists at heart, like to talk about noble motives.
- Rule Eleven: Use the principle of visibility to prove your rightness. To express the truth only by words is sometimes not enough. The truth should be shown vividly, interestingly, visually.

Visual Persuasion

Persuasion creates a framework that starts from the inner world of the human being and expands to the environment with which it interacts.

First of all, let's point out that persuasion is not to deceive, manipulate, or be a language acrobat. The main thing in persuasion is to communicate with the hearts, to discover the bridge between the brain and the heart.

The process of persuasion is to provide the awareness and internal interaction we want in the world of our interlocutor after establishing correct communication with harmony. This change, created by his free will, forms the basis of a correct and healthy persuasion process. The focus of persuasion should focus on the needs and desires of our interlocutors.

Persuasion, as said by Virgo Tecer, is an engineering job. "Our brain has an operating system, software, and frequently used programs like a computer. Among them, our persuasion passwords are hidden. " For good persuasion, all communication tools that stimulate emotions should be used.

So, what are the secrets of persuasion? What should be considered in the persuasion process?

Adapting to persuasion is one of the fundamentals of the persuasion process. Strong bonds between people affect the harmony and facilitate the persuasion process. To speak in a similar tone of voice and at a similar speed for harmony, using the same body language and expressions should be in close thinking.

Also, emotional intimacy affects the persuasion process very positively. Much easier to persuade people than logic is to persuade them with emotions. So why? Generally, areas related to logic are cold, while areas related to emotions are warmer and more persuasive. For this reason, the language of persuasion is emotion rather than logic. Correct emotions can overcome logical obstacles, and persuasion becomes easier.

Do not forget! "People don't care how much you know unless they understand how much you care about them. If you do not find harmony, it will be difficult to convince people. Without harmony, there is no trust, no faith, no persuasion." Kevin Hogan

The human brain is "self" centered at the subconscious level. It has little to do with messages and messages that do not benefit themselves or do not provide any benefit to survive for security reasons. Therefore, your message for persuasion should not be about you, but it. Your message should offer a relevant benefit. Using ""you"r" language rather than "I" language is much more important for persuasion.

We know that a person who studies what we have presented only wants to know one thing: What does it do for me? If you want to increase your influence, we must customize what we want to communicate to meet the personal needs and desires of our interlocutor.

The other important secret to persuasion is to be able to listen to others the way you want them to listen to you. That's why they say listening is half the persuasion! It is necessary to listen effectively and show the necessary attention, especially with "elephant ear."

We all know that; Mimar Sinan is an architectural art and aesthetic genius. A muse comes out and stands before him; "Oh Koca Sinan, why does the minaret of this mosque look crooked?" Big Sinan smiles and says, "Give me a rope," and ties the rope to the minaret and pulls it slightly. "Oh, old man, how is he standing now?" he says. The madman is satisfied. The real issue is the heart of the madman. This is what we call persuasion.

For persuasion, our presentation or expressions should create a persuasion strategy that appeals to the visual brain. The most effective stimulus for our brain is a striking visual. Short and clear sentences should be made instead of long sentences. The aim is to show how our proposal will move our interlocutor from a negative situation to a better one.

Another golden key to persuasion is to be able to ask "Strong Questions." The strong question is a skill that can be realized through active listening. While asking the question, the question 'To whom?' when we ask, 'Why?' when we ask, 'How?' when we ask and 'What?' We have to be very careful with what we ask. Our questions; "Is it open-ended or closed? Repeater or zoom?" We have to make the right decision that it will happen. We should be able to ask questions that fit our purpose. Open-ended questions allow us to collect information and analyze the message, and closed-ended questions allow us to confirm incoming information. If negative emotions are intense, we can ask zoom questions.

For example; To someone who objected, "I don't think the timing is right," "Why?" instead of asking, "What is the best timing for you?" we can ask.

Persuasion is being able to influence a person's decision-making process. A good offer may not be enough for persuasion. However, understanding how a person thinks means taking a very important step to persuade him. For this reason, for persuasion, focusing on the addressee, not on one's own will, he must understand his mind map and emotions.

Nonverbal Communication

One of the other elements of communication is non-verbal communication. It is a method referenced in relationships performed in daily life. Nonverbal communication is sometimes a form of communication that is often used without being conscious but inevitably constantly used in creating meaning.

Voice toning, facial expressions, mimics, body movements, gestures used in communication are part of nonverbal communication. These features are only enabled with verbal communication.

Nonverbal communication is important in the improbability of communication, expressing emotions and enthusiasm competently, defining and identifying inter-personal relationships, providing reliable messages. All of this is shaped by culture.

There are symbols of nonverbal communication that have different meanings in different cultures.

Don't Shut Up

It is often a painful and sometimes painful phenomenon for the individual, except when it is necessary and desired. Silence for too long or the silence of others can cause tension. Let's not forget that long silence between spouses is worse and more effective than fighting. The absence of communication between individuals leads to more negative consequences than bad communication. Because it's important to discuss communication and create a start in solving the problem, but silence will destroy all this.

Social Workers should terminate the applicant's silence method in his interviews as soon as he uses it as a form of communication and investigates the reasons for the applicant's response to this issue.

There are different reasons for silence or silence. These are not random. Every silence has its meaning in communication that can lead to different interpretations and results. Sometimes we're angry, so we're thirsty to squeeze our teeth, sometimes we're thirsty to listen to the messages we're dealing with because we're getting our attention. In some cases, when we're bored, we shut up and look elsewhere. Sometimes we listen to it because we don't understand what's being said. In some cases, our silence indicates that we approve of the source, and in others, we do not approve. Sometimes we're quiet for peace.

In short, reticence in communication reflects different messages or responses. In determining the correct meaning of these, communication environment, the characteristics of individuals in communication, facial expressions, gestures, body movements, and gestures in the case of face-to-face communication also help.

Color and Music of Sound

They are elements of nonverbal communication that disrupt emotions such as tone, rhythm, ascending, and lowering of the voices of individuals spoken in oral communication and often shed light on the meaning of words. The style can make a testimony confirming what we say, just as it will give us a hand when you lie or hide our fear. Even if the color of sound and the personality of the individual who makes up the music of the speech is part of its nature, its cultural dimension is undeniable. If we look at this, we can show that Turks, Arabs, usually loud French quick, Italians talk like they fight, using English with different tones in the United States and The United Kingdom.

Body Language

Body language has a very important role in face-to-face communication with people. If we don't mention anything in these relationships, our body will talk. Body language occurs with gestures and gestures. The use of facial muscles to make sense or make sense, facial expression in other words; Use the head, hand, arm, foot, leg movements, or the whole body creates gestures. They are also cultural.

Perception of Personal Space

Every person has a concept of personal space. The private space is based on the idea that the surface of the skin of the human body is not limited to the surface of the skin. Reflecting the perception of psychological space, this idea is caused by a special understanding of space, which is drawn with a limit that frames the body of the individual that no one else can enter unless it is allowed. Breaking into this area is considered disrespectful, incitement, or attack.

Clothing and Physical Appearance

One of the factors that determine what kind of communication people communicate with individuals is their physical appearance. We're not going to have much of touch with a person we know, the dress he wore that day. But before we start talking to the person, we meet for the first time, we can detect your clothes, your height, your weight. The physical appearance of the person we face is effective in at least determining how to start communicating.

After looking at the appearance of someone they just met, we

decide to put it in a mold in our minds and say to him, "Master, gentleman, uncle, uncle, countryman, sister, lady, lady."

Physical appearance is important for the person who initiated the conversation, as well as being the tip of the rope, as well as the person who addressed him. People want others to call themselves the same way they define themselves.

Clothing is important in interpersonal communication. Instead, clothing that does not conform to its time causes many very valuable words to be listened to and perceived as false.

For example, if you want to When a young man prepares to speak in front of a community when asked to talk with the jeans and t-shirts he wears in his daily life, people can say that more children without thinking about what it's like to talk about. If he were dressed in the picture, he'd have been more considered.

We can also understand what status people belong to their clothes and try to use our communication accordingly.

The important thing is to know that our clothing is affected by what we are dealing with and to determine in advance about which part of the effectiveness will be effective in society.

In summary, nonverbal communication is important and effective in interpersonal communication, with verbal communication, the color, and music of the sound, body language, space and time characteristics, color, and clothing. Silence in touch is not random. He expresses different reactions. The tone of the sound, body language, facial expressions, space use, and form in communication to know the effects and consciously identify.

Non-Verbal Compliance Methods
Your Physical Image
How we dress, how much people trust us, and how much they love us.

Toning
Correct use of the tone and speed of sound is important for harmony. You can align your conversation with the person in front of you without imitating it.

Stop
Sit or stand similarly. Remember, if the person in front of you takes the same stance as you, that means you're the leader.

Pale
Be careful about how you breathe in front of you. If you want to adapt, you should try to live the same frequency as the other one.

Instant Rapport

Round table at a university in Madrid. Four journalists discuss the future of the profession in front of a few hundred students who follow their interventions with interest. One of the speakers, a veteran of the airwaves who has numerous followers on his Twitter account, writes non-stop messages. At the same time, the rest of the table discusses the new demands of training professionals. In Question Time, a young woman takes the microphone and says very seriously: "I want to ask you one thing, but I'd like you to look me in the face and stop playing with the computer. Attendees are more important right now than their twitter friends." Perhaps unknowingly, that college girl just put her finger on the sore: has the breakthrough of social media and mobile phones changed the rules of urbanity without us knowing? Answer: he's doing it. The problem is that some traditional patterns of behavior have disappeared without the new ones being whole defined.

The conventional phone had already broken some conventions. You, for example, are at a medical consultation, at a retail facility, or the bank window, and your phone rings. Almost certainly, the doctor, dependent, or employee of the financial institution will take the call. It may be a very brief conversation, but it may also take a few minutes. The person on the other side of the line has not waited their turn or booked an appointment for the consultation and yet has passed in front of many. With mobile phones, the chances of this break-in in the middle of the talk, a purchase, or an official process multiply because there is no longer even a filter of a switchboard. Where is the rule of waiting for the shift to be taken care of?

"It must be understood that, for retailers, the telephone is a basic work tool, so they must have a person in charge of receiving and answering calls," explains Diego Zala, head of studies at the International School of Protocol. However, "it is wrong to apologize in advance to the customer or patient who has seen the consultation interrupted and to care for everyone who calls," Zala continues.

What happens in queries, stores, and windows is no different than what occurs in any meeting. So much so that rules begin to be dictated to prevent continuous calls from ruining a work session. British Prime Minister David Cameron recently banned members of his cabinet from bringing their mobiles on to ministerial meetings. The 'tory' leader had already rebuked one of his collaborators for answering calls during work sessions. What Cameron intends, according to the specialists, is to make it very clear that during a government meeting, nothing can distract team members. And that for them, there can be nothing more important at the time than their work. Not forgetting how annoying a concert of polytuses, between the folkloric and the exotic, is to anyone who is focused on a task.

Urban planning specialists recommend doing without phones at any meeting, even family. "It is not appropriate to keep mobile - let alone make use of it - around a table or during a work session," says Zala, who believes that only exceptionally, if a very important call is expected, can you have the device connected. It is necessary, then, to warn the companions of that circumstance. But the exception does not imply that the possibility of answering all calls is opened.

Priorities

Perhaps this image of adults neglecting those around them to dedicate themselves to those far away is etched in the minds of the youth. That's why it's not strange to see two or three teenagers left to spend the afternoon together on a park bench and are with their cell phones texting or chatting. And, of course, without looking at each other's faces. In other words, the relationship with those who haven't stayed with them preys on the talk with the other boys right there. "They may also be chatting with each other," says sociologist Javier Elzo amusingly. "The essential thing today among young and not-so-young people is immediacy and acceleration," he explains. This means this desire for instantaneousness: of the information that is received and the replicas that are requested.

What about social media? Seeing some people who write messages to their Facebook, Twitter, or any other network via mobile or computer during a meeting no longer surprises anyone. Some of the participants in the famous meeting between the president of the Film Academy, Alex of the Church, and well-known internet users, did so on the 'Sinde Law.' Protocol specialists put their hands on these practices before because those who do so give the image of being more concerned with telling what is said in the room than for actively participating in the session. It is also what happened to the veteran journalist on the university day that is told at the beginning of this report.

Hooked

Also, social networks have numerous uses. Some more professional, some more effective. And others, bordering on exhibitionist behavior. What to think of those who throughout the day announce 'Urbi et orbi' who are in such a place having a coffee, leaving a meeting, eating, about to enter the cinema, get on a plane or go on a date with views of having a highly erotic outcome? What was thought of those who, before the invention of social media, spoke out to the world that they were going to do some of these things? Directly, they were self-centered or rude.

Many have already renounced to classify these behaviors in this way, in the face of their generalization. "We're not rude, we just have to keep up and be aware of the new circumstances around us," Zala says. However, it warns that there are behaviors on the network that are not tolerable under any circumstances.

One of them is to 'hang' photos of meetings with friends, colleagues, or family without those who appear in them knowing and have given their consent. Some seem to have forgotten that it is not the same to show a photo to a few people to check with who we were in a meeting - and yet it may be an indiscretion - than to place it on the net for unknown viewing.

Are mobiles and social media ending urbanity? No. They are generating a vital acceleration that forces, as Elzo says, an immediate response to how many messages we receive. The old letter took time to arrive, was often read hours after being deposited in the mailbox, and answering it required paper and pen or typewriter. Then the envelope made the way back. Between the writing of the first letter and the reading of the second were several days. Today that's a world. The rules of urbanity must, therefore, address the demands of immediacy even if some practices are never yet unacceptable. It's a new education.

Real-Life Persuasion

I have emphasized the importance of applying knowledge about psychology in real life since they are not isolated.

When we hear about religions, doctrines, or sects, we often relate them to the persuasion they exercise over people. Leaving aside the teachings or principles of each faith here rather we will focus on the attitudes and behaviors that cause people to engage in some worship or any case, leave their convictions and behave in ways that they would not otherwise.

A new convert soon learns to be part of the group, feeling pressured by the actions of others leads him to be an active member and to settle for what he sees to obey and commit to the group. Remember the phenomenon of the foot at the door? Many of these sects use this effect. Early requests are small as an invitation to dinner, talks about philosophy, and other requests that exploit in the acceptance of the doctrine.

There are persuasive elements such as the essential one, such as the communicator who is regularly a charismatic person, perceived as expert and reliable, the emotional, vivid message that creates direct social pressure. The audience is young people who are at the age of stabilizing values and attitudes, and potential converts are at an existential crossroads, personal crisis, or needs that a simple message satisfies.

As I said at the beginning, the issue is not about whether religion is good or bad; it's about seeing how many religious leaders occupy persuasive elements to influence people.

The following are the tips for persuading people in real life:

1. Preferred Simplicity Using Small Words

The simpler an idea is presented, the easier it becomes – and therefore, the more believable it is.

2. Include in Your Speech the Short Sentences

It's less about restraint and more about finding exactly the right piece in the language puzzle so that you can put it in the specific space you're trying to fill.

3. Choose Reliability, As It Is as Important as Philosophy

If your words lack sincerity, if they conflict with overlooked facts, circumstances, or perceptions, they will also lack impact. Tell people who you are and what you're doing. Make sure you're that person and do what you said you'd do.

4. Say Something New

If something doesn't shock us or make us bored, we move on to something else. If what you're saying makes people say, "I didn't know that," then you've succeeded.

5. Emphasize the Sound and Composition of Words

They must be as memorable as the words themselves. The rhythm of the language is at the heart of the musician.

6. Make Intelligent Images

Create a vivid image. Take, for example, candy ads. The slogans we remember forever are the ones that have a powerful visual component, something we can see and almost feel.

7. Use the Question

The customer who complains to the meter that her meat has too much fat is less effective than if she asked: "Do you think that's lean?" Similarly, the question "what would you do if you were me?" directly forces the recipient of the complaint to see things from your side. By making a statement in the form of a rhetorical question, you give the reaction a personal character.

8. Give the General Context

You have to give people the "why" of a message before you tell them "so" or "so." Some people call it framing. Is 16px preferable?" the phrase general context, because it better explains why a particular message matter.

Ethics of Persuasion

Something that should seem strange to us, because persuasion, studied by numerous disciplines from antiquity to the present day, is at the very core of political communication and any other practice related to the conquest of the wills of human beings.

The reality is that the cases in which politicians or political communication professionals use the word "persuasion" to define their work are counted. What is the point of this common use? Mainly that the term has been filled with negative connotations over the centuries, not only among the academy but also in the colloquial language. Persuasion has often been linked to phenomena such as manipulation or lying, being sibilinos, and having hidden intentions of trying to win the will of human beings through unethical art and procedures.

Part of the blame for this negative notion of persuasion is that it has put the focus of this action only on the results. Persuasion has been tended to conceptualize persuasion as a process that can resort to any method of influence to achieve its goals, including fear, threats, lying, or irrational appeals. The focus has been more on the effect of "persuading action" (getting what one wants) than on the path taken to achieve it. In short, we have looked more at the "end" than the "means." And this has made persuasion confused with other processes that, sharing the ultimate goal of influencing human beings, are nevertheless very different in terms of the methods they employ to achieve that goal.

But persuasion cannot be seen only from this prism of results, because that contributes to further blurring the nature of this phenomenon. On the contrary, claiming the true concept of persuasion and using it as the basis of political communication can root with an ethical dimension of this activity and help solve many of the problems and definitions that haunt it today.

Persuasion and Influence

The first thing to consider when talking about persuasion is that it is a specific type of communication. And as communicative action, it is therefore linked to the social nature of the human being and to the notion of sharing with others knowledge and realities that are common to them.

But unlike other types of communication, in persuasion, the goal is not only to transmit or share information or knowledge. There is a persuasion intention on the part of the issuer to influence others, to provoke a change of behavior or opinion, to move them into action. That is, in short, what is sought in political communication. There may be an informative or pedagogical purpose in politicians' communicative efforts, but their primary purpose is more "pragmatic" because it tries to influence others, mainly to get their vote.

It is precisely the intention that makes it possible to differentiate between persuasion and mere influence. To influence, there is no need for a purpose: a person can do so unintentionally, without being aware of it. However, for there to be persuasion, there has to be a clear intention to exert that influence on others. It can, therefore, be said that persuasive communication must be defined more by intent than by the outcome of the action.

And being a communicative process, persuasion is necessarily bidirectional. Both the sender and receiver are equal parts of the process. Each other can intervene on an equal footing. That is why there is no persuasion to resort to force or violence to force the other to follow what is proposed because then it would cease to be so to become coercion. Deep down, persuading forcing is a countersuit. Either they are convinced, respecting the freedom of the recipients to follow or not what they are asked to do, or they are coerced, forcing them to obey what they are asked to do, but not both at the same time. And it is this criterion that allows democratic systems to be claimed as persuasive systems against authoritarians, who base their power on coercion.

71

Reason or Emotion?

Secondly, persuasion must be understood as an amalgam of reason and emotion, which is precisely what distinguishes it from two other phenomena with which it is often confused, which are conviction and seduction. And perhaps this is one of the most important points when it comes to assessing the persuasive nature of political communication.

Conviction is a rational process: it is convinced with reasons and, therefore, it is primarily directed at the intellect of human beings. Is this what politicians are trying to do on the campaign trail? Can you say they're trying to "convince" the electorate? We should say no because its objective goes further. After all, what is sought in political communication, preferably, is to act on behavior. And to do this, the politician cannot remain alone on the level of reasons, but must also use feelings, the emotional pathway, reaching the hearts of the recipients to mobilize them to action. And that mixture of reason and emotion is precisely what defines persuasion.

What happens is that sometimes the persuasion may fall into the temptation to resort only to emotions to more easily conquer the will of human beings, thus dispensing with reason. In this case, there is no longer any talk of persuasion but seduction.

And what characterizes political communication today? We could say, as has already been emphasized on numerous occasions in recent decades, that politicians have opted in recent years more for seduction than persuasion, perhaps because they have seen that this emotional pathway is much more effective in achieving their goal. Emotion has succeeded in imposing itself on reason, and this has contributed decisively to the emergence of television, which has become the main means of politics. A medium that vehiculates emotions like no other thanks to the strength of the image and which, according to the academy, has led to a situation of particularizations of politics, of increasing passivity among voters, and of enhancing personalism and populism above parties and ideologies. Also, recent research in neuromarketing, which has come to prove the great weight of emotions in human behavior scientifically, has reinforced the thesis of those who believe that feeling should be the main vehicle of political communication.

This has led to a debate, sometimes focused in the form of controversy between academia and profession, on the use of reason and emotion in politics. A discussion which, in essence, is not very different from that already held in classical Greece Plato and the sophists, advocating rationality in political discourse; and others opting for feelings to be, in their view, much more effective in moving humans. And over the centuries, and above all from the Enlightenment, a rational and platonic thought of politics has been based, which has led to a condemnation of emotions.

At this point, the nature of persuasion must be claimed from an inclusive perspective because it is this perspective that will allow proposing a possible solution to this permanent vision faced between reason and emotion. Political communication, as persuasive communication it is, must be the combination of both factors. In politics, it is not only a question of rationally convincing voters but also needs to mobilize action, as the story is to opt for a particular party at the ballot box. And there come into play emotions, which must not be seen as harmful or unethical to democracies, but also as the only way to more easily conquer the will of citizens through seduction.

In short, this was the position already defended by Aristotle as a way of tertiary in the controversy between Plato and the sophists, and it is the one that should gain ground both academically and professionally. And all this, moreover, in a context of change in forms of communication. New technologies, which are allowing us to glimpse the move from the classic one-way model of political communication fostered by television to a two-way one, in which politicians and citizens exchange information and listen to each other, can facilitate the return to communication models more based on persuasion than mere seduction.

The Ethics of Attack Campaigns

Thirdly, persuasion should not be confused with deterrence. The first seeks to move to action, while the latter pursues the opposite, that is, to demotivate a behavior, for someone to stop thinking or to do what they had in mind. For example, stop voting for a party or candidate.

And given experience, contemporary political communication might be thought to be sometimes more focused on deterring than persuading, attacking the adversary than proposing alternatives. Attack campaigns and negative advertising have now become commonplace in any election. More words, movements are becoming increasingly negative and even dishonest, including as an attacking item not only political issues but also the private lives of candidates.

It should be emphasized that emphasizing the opponent's weaknesses is not a negative or unethical thing. It falls within democratic logic. Therefore, we should not be tempted to regard all negative or attack campaigns as evil or to be avoided in political communication. The problem arises when what is sought is exclusively denigration and unfair attack on the adversary, which, on the other hand, is the most common thing lately. It is this criterion used by the academy to deplorable negative advertising or attack campaigns that pursue only the destruction of the rival or that resort to irrational lies or fear towards him and, on the contrary, acceptable those that bring the discussion on political aspects in that they provide voters with proven information, both positive and negative.

In any case, and beyond these ethical considerations, another very relevant aspect underlies this debate, which directly links to the differences between persuasion and deterrence. Attacking an opponent does not immediately mean that those who support him stop doing so and go on to keep the party that launches the attack. Many matches make negative publicity against rivals, thinking they will automatically collect for themselves the fruits of that action. However, a large number of studies have shown that those negative messages they propose, in addition to attacks on the opponent, solutions, and responses to reported situations, are considered more effective than those that include only negative information. In short, these investigations confirm that the single deterrence is not persuasive and that this, in terms of the proposal of alternative behaviors or beliefs, is more communicative and also more effective in achieving the desired results.

Banishing the Use of Lying

Fourth, persuasion entails an act of sincerity on the part of the issuer, openly demonstrating that it intends to influence its recipients. If the intentions remain hidden or disguised, there is no longer persuasion but manipulation.

Manipulating by concealing the intention to influence has been very common throughout history. This was the case with the so-called "black propaganda" during World War II, in which the authorship of the message was hiding to give it greater credibility. And, to some extent, there are still remnants of these practices in today's societies, for example, when intentional messages are to be disguised under the appearance of news, including here the permanent attempt by many politicians to manipulate or control the media.

But there is no greater concealment of intentions than when lying is used, which is one of the greatest risks looming over democratic systems. The manipulator hides their true purposes by deceiving citizens with those messages that he considers most relevant to keep them under control and submissive, thus causing them to harm in that they are deprived of having all the data to act freely.

This results in an important consequence also in terms of respect for the dignity of the human being. The manipulator treats the other as an object, codifies it, becomes a simple means that he can handle as he pleases to achieve his ends, such as winning an election or staying in power. However, whoever persuades treats the other as a subject, respecting his freedom. And that must be the essence of political communication.

Claiming Persuasion as The Foundation of Political Communication

After all these considerations, and based on the multidisciplinary review of the concept of persuasion over time, we could conclude by defining it as "that intentional communication in which an issuer, without hiding its purpose, tries to deliberately influence others to create or do something in the political sphere using both rational and emotional elements, always respecting their freedom of choice and discarding the use of lies and any form of violence or force both physically and psychically to achieve their ends."

While seduction, coercion, or manipulation are one-way processes, which subject the receiver without discussion, persuasion can only be based on the active participation of both the emitter and the receiver, giving way to bidirectionality. Citizens are not mere voters or means to win an election. They are considered equal, active, and co-participants of the process. The common good, and not just the benefit of the politician, can then be seen in this consideration of persuasive political communication. A persuasion, in short, free of negative connotations, which is closely related to an ethical conception of politics and which also serves to recover for our day's classic approaches that had been blurred, if not lost, over time.

Professionals and academics should explore more and enrich the persuasive nature of political communication. Persuasion is necessary for politics, no more than the use of this term arouses misgivings or prefers to be replaced by other, more neutral notions. And it is much more so today, when it is often referred to that politicians do not represent citizens, who lie or manipulate, or who only look after their interests without remembering voters without other than when there are elections on the horizon. In short, the persuasive foundation of political communication will enable many of the questions that remain in force in this discipline to be addressed, allowing politicians to be more effective in influencing citizens while contributing to the improvement of democracies.

Conclusion

Understanding how people think and make decisions makes you more persuasive. But in doing so, you need to be responsible. When you use faith cohesion techniques ethically, you see that it is more effective and empathetic than traditional marketing methods. If you show people that you understand them, they'll do more to listen to and understand you. If you use persuasion techniques not to deceive people, but to draw attention to the benefits and products you offer, you will benefit from this.

As a result, people are more interested in what similar people say, people who are in harmony with themselves, the events shown in evidence, and the lesser, and that interest makes them much more convinced. Persuasion can occur not only in a positive direction but also in a negative order. It's possible to convince people by managing fears. The concept of persuasion is not only a concept that applies to the sales, marketing, advertising, etc. sectors, but it is a concept that applies to everyone at any time. You can convince your teacher about exams, convince your manager to be close to your expectations, or you can manage a team. You can convince your partner, your child, your friend, in short, everyone, by enforcing universally accepted rules. People want to be confident before they say "Yes" to a topic or before they say "No" to a topic, so to understand the psychology of persuasion, you first need to understand communication and know human types. When it is known how to treat such people, effective listening and effective communication will become much more successful and meaningful, whether in rhetorical or non-verbal terms.

We can see that the area where the persuasion is in communication is very wide. People can communicate better and succeed in these simple but effective methods that they will use to get a gift they want to get their spouse seeking to sell or market their products or services, to get themselves into a community.

Manipulation Techniques

What Is Manipulation

Operation is the skilled handling, control, or use of something or something. Whether it's the sculptures you make in art class or how you persuade friends to do your homework, these are all considered manipulations. At the psychological level, manipulation skills mainly involve two things: hiding aggressive intentions and behaviors, and fully understanding the opponent's psychological vulnerability to know which tactics may be the most effective weapon against them. Psychological manipulation is usually accomplished through covert aggression or aggression, which is such a cover-up or subtle that it is not easy to detect.

Robots want what they want and strive to achieve their goals. But the strategy they use makes it look like it's doing almost everything, just trying to make itself better. Tactics are also beneficial weapons of power and control. It is because, even if it is difficult to recognize them as conscious offensive actions, in the unconscious situation, other people will still get into trouble and fall into defense. It makes them more likely to retreat or succumb to the Manipulator.

The skilled Manipulator knows the fragility of the opponent. If vanity is someone's weakness, then the seduction strategy may be the best manipulation strategy. If over-cautiousness is their weakness, perhaps the most effective method is internal. Most manipulators' character is severely disturbed (that is, conscience or sensitivity is too low). They are most likely to be preyed by neurotic individuals (i.e., highly sensitive and responsible people). Strategies such as being a victim or humiliating will effectively manipulate the average neurotic patient because responsible people do not want to see others as pain or feel sorry. If a neurotic person tries these same strategies on a disturbed person, they will soon learn that they are not working.

Types of Emotional Manipulators

Frequent Victims

"No one cares about me, and no one wants to help me. No one likes me; everyone hates me. Guess I will eat bugs." No matter what happens, there will be many twists and turns, and this emotional Manipulator becomes a victim. This person often catches fire and angers people. Due to a lot of quarrels and fights, other people often feel overwhelmed. Although permanent victims will rage and fight, they will manipulate the situation to treat them as victims. After their partner or others engage in an emotional struggle with the long-term victim, the long-term victim seeks the sympathizer's sympathy and pits people against each other to gain control and power.

Like all emotional manipulators, constant victims also feel a sense of what they deserve. For example: "Because I am very talented and talented, I deserve special consideration. Others should

76

know and accommodate me." Constant victims may get angry because they have not performed their duties (such as work). They project anger and other emotional states to others. For example: when they manipulate characters, they say that others hate them, or they try to hurt or betray them in some way. Fear and anger are the two most powerful emotions they struggle with. Many people become paranoid. They often say that other people have betrayed them and take out "morality cards." In other words, the project responsibility for their actions or lack of activities to others, thereby giving up personal responsibility.

Two Single Jobs

"Anything you can do, I can do better. I can do better than you." Through skilled operations, this person needs to go further than others. One-handed manipulators strongly hope to become the "King of the Hill." Although they usually lack conscious awareness, having a high social status and dominant position is very important to their self. They are gifted, can determine where people are vulnerable, and choose to be with people who lack self-esteem.

Constant use of insults and insults to hurt and exploit victims can bring benefits to victims. They may be considered selfish by others, but they are more likely to conceal their arrogance. Shame and anger are the motivation behind their manipulation, and manipulation is their tool to achieve their ultimate destiny: getting rid of shame and self-doubt. For example: "If I focus on belittling you, I won't focus on shame."

Healthy Family Members

I just can't take care of myself. Life is not fair to me. Please help me. Please do as I say. " They conceal the guise of weakness and incompetence but gain considerable strength in the lives of the people they depend on. They are a model of helplessness and secondary growth in learning. Unlike one-handed manipulators, influential family members use praise/self-attack to control the victim. Acting weaker and weaker than those they depend on will give them a sense of control. However, if someone refuses their dependence, they will quickly change from being friendly to disgusting. For example: "You are like everyone else. I can't count on you!" The hidden message behind all their actions is: "Don't let me down." In general, they are very self-centered and are forced to meet their own needs regardless of their impact on others.

Triangulation Machine

They use lies, distortions, and other forms of manipulation to control the people they rely on, thereby forming support and gaining an advantage. They build alliances (often by themselves) and attack other people who might hinder them. At first, they stayed friendly with the victim. They used compliments and self-deception techniques to promote the bond between them and the victim. They tell nasty things about the victim behind their senses and spread rumors. By forming alliances with others against the victims, they gained control and power.

Anger is their motivation; they want to show and hurt people, not physically or emotionally. On the outside, they seem to be heroes or rescuers, but their inner motivation is self-centered. Sometimes this occurs in parent-child relationships. For example, a parent wants his/her daughter to join the cheerleading team and spread malicious rumors about the girls in the group, cheerleading coaches, and other parents to achieve this goal. Because their followers lack self-esteem and feel powerless, triangulations often become great leaders.

Shockwave

"I'm furious, and you even ask me this. It's all your fault. It's all their fault." They use bursts of anger to deflect and avoid facing problems that need to be solved. It is usual for adolescents to use this technique, but it should not be classified as a Blaster. The real Blaster is more mature than the average teenager. Victims often feel that the bomber is doing something they shouldn't be doing behind the scenes, but cannot recognize it. In a couple, Blaster may be incurring credit card debt, stealing from his/her workplace, or having an affair.

When they face their behavior, they say that the victim is suspicious or paranoid, derailing the victim. They may say: "I can't believe you don't trust me." They may also blame the victim. For example: "If you can spend more time with me, then I won't have an affair. It's all your fault." They strongly need to resist changes and favor or reject them not to take personal responsibility for their actions. They hate to face their dysfunction; they will yell, yell, and threaten those who threaten them.

Projector

"You are always wrong, and I am always right. I hate people I hate." They use denial to defend their ego. They never take charge of their actions and have poor self-insight. When their character or motives are questioned, they become very defensive. Blaming others for their behavior or character defects is the central aspect of the projector. Projection is like looking at a mirror, thinking you are looking out the window how the projector sees the world and experiences life. They are unconscious of it most of the time. For example: "You are racist" when they are racist; or "You are controlling" when they are racist.

Like Triangulator, they may encourage people to join their own business, but not necessarily to hurt others, but to avoid responsibility. They never give up and are unrelenting because they try to avoid looking in the mirror at all costs. If you don't give them what they want, they will waste you and blame you. They firmly believe that their inferior quality is yours. They feel excessive hatred of others, but in fact, they hate themselves. By accusing others, they justify their actions.

Deliberate Misunderstanding

"Sorry, I must have misunderstood what you said. You confused me. That was not what I heard." They exaggerate, tell the truth, and lie to gain power and control. By spreading rumors and gossip, they damaged the reputation of the victims. Specifically, they will tell part of the truth, but they will distort the truth. By interpreting the victim's wrong words purposefully, they can manipulate and get what they want. They are very superficial and need to be the most famous people around. They appear outgoing and friendly, which is a way to obtain personal information about the victim to use it to their advantage. In their hearts, they created justifications to change/tilt the story, and many people believe in their distortions. When they face, they may shrink and cry.

Flirting

"Have fun with someone else's husband, what's the matter? She didn't give him what he needed. Other women hate me; it's not my fault. I'm gorgeous." They use provocative behaviors to attract people and achieve their goals. They are very superficial people. They consider themselves attractive, even if not beautiful, and They need to be everyone's favorite. They are very self-centered.

Many people are sexually active and often use sex as a catalyst to gain attention, strength, and control. When they flirt, they want others to recognize them and want immediate positive feedback. They seem to like to cause rifts between friends and family. It is not uncommon for them to break up their marriage and then gloat. They want to keep in touch with their current partner/spouse while actively looking for a new partner. They compete with partners. When they tamper with families, couples, friendships, and communities, they feel capable of watching these systems collapse.

Iron Fist

"Don't make me angry; otherwise, things will become very ugly!" If you don't give me what I want, I will mess with you! " They use intimidation and bullying to get what they want. They are very demanding and insist that you do what they say. Some of them use threatening gestures or actual physical attacks to threaten their victims. Some people use their wisdom to cover up the fact that they manipulate their victims. They will try to destroy those who will not give them what they want. When someone disagrees with them, they will be surprised because they feel superior to others. They believe in forcing things to move and bend to suit their desires. They see victims and others as pawns or tools that can be manipulated to get what they need. If their victims do not do what they want, the "iron fist"/"intimidator" will take positive action and force them to do so. They think it is their right.

Multiple Offenders

"If you didn't succeed at the beginning, please try again." They combined the above several ways of emotional manipulation. Generally, they use three or more types. For example, they use a combination of fixed victims, individual arms, triangulation, and blasters. They modified this mixture as a victim. If it is difficult for one to manipulate with a constant victim type, triangulation can be used.

Types of Manipulators in The Workplace

Manipulative leaders use subtle methods (such as gaslighting) to distort reality. Selectively use data or anecdotes to confuse others' opinions, and then use them to persuade people to ignore or doubt their feelings. To resist this manipulation, take a step back from what is happening and re-attract your senses. Here are five common workplace manipulators I have observed, and some tips to prevent them:

Dramatist

Historians and exaggerated emotions dominate this manipulative leader. When a sales manager was asked about his team's poor performance this quarter, he retorted: "For many years, I have been bleeding for this company and experienced a blizzard. Now you don't believe that I can achieve my annual plan. Is it?" The sales manager's dissatisfaction and overreaction caused his boss to back down because of fear of further violations. The opportunity for frank discussions about the ever-widening performance gap disappeared.

How do you deal with dramatists? Stick to the facts. Don't give in or apologize. Double handle simple, focused issues on understanding the situation.

Shunt

The obvious sign of this manipulation is an attempt to divert your attention from the topic at hand. The transferor is good at introducing nonsense or fallacy into the conversation, making things obscure. A CEO I know told the story of a former executive who has a knack for acting as a speaker (not logically derived from the discussion), which is a distracting topic, usually his execution Mistake. The discussion ended up wasting a lot of time and causing confusion.

The Forbes Coaching Council is a business and career coach that invites groups to participate only. Am I eligible?

To deal with the shunt, please call him out on irrelevant information. Keep him focused on the topic and solve the real problem.

Twister

Unlike the diverters who keep you away from the subject and the playwrights who immerse the subject in emotion, twisters can damage. They are like Charles Boyer characters in "Gaslight," trying to control your perception. Distorters have distorted the meaning of the information and misled the followers of what happened.

His cunning subordinates often manipulate a smart but weak-willed leader I coach. He will provide impressive information about team sales, claiming that he will close the next big deal. The leader hangs on his subordinates for six months longer than he should, because he believes the prospecting pipeline is real. It's not. Delays in addressing insufficient sales have severely damaged business performance.

How do you deal with the distortion? Get out of the chair and see what happened. Conduct basic research (such as calling yourself so-called potential customers) to verify their existence and a true interest level. Keep focused and intense queries. Before being convinced by concrete facts and methods that reflect reality, please don't approve.

Fitter

Confusion is the mixing of two or more different themes. Some mergers are deliberately ignorant. They refuse to do the work required to understand the subject, so they think the subject is too complicated. Others just hide behind a mixture of two questions, rather than clarify the meaning of each question. They understand how the parts work, but they don't want you to do this.

A mediator declined to explain how his team handled customer issues related to warranty services. He asserted: "We use an algorithm" to cover up arbitrary decisions he uses. However, when faced with more acute problems, the service manager tries to hide what is obvious to everyone: he doesn't know how to make warranty service decisions.

To deal with the combiner, know how to decompose and isolate the different problematic issues. I need good problem-solving skills. With patience and perseverance, you will find that the merger cannot reason correctly or deliberately deceive others.

Bully

The main characteristic of bullies is that they tend to use aggressive assertions to cover things up to answer questions. During the budget discussion, a controller asked the production manager about unusually negative changes in labor prices. The production manager is very grumpy. "Why?!" he shouted. He stood up and continued: "Look at the numbers!" To my surprise, the controller was stunned.

With the bully, stay firm. Call their bluff and expose their exaggeration and fallacy. Use direct, meaningless methods to reveal their deceptive behaviors and eliminate their impact on your organizational culture.

Remember, knowing the types of manipulators is far more important than knowing what they have in common: everyone has a distorted reality with some form of lies. Don't be fooled.

The Types of Manipulators We Encounter Every Day

All of us want to meet our needs, but some people go to great lengths to manipulate others to make sure they get what they want. Usually, this emotional influence looks like a friendly gesture. Still, if you learn how to recognize standard manipulation methods, you will never be someone else's s on the string.

Helplessness

Such people pretend to be helpless to hold others accountable. In most cases, women choose this role and use what they call "weakness." However, more and more men are beginning to show this behavior. These types of people usually have no problem because the people around are helping them. You need to ask yourself if you are ready to waste time and energy on people who are just using you.

Skilled Text Player

It's okay to misunderstand someone's words or actions occasionally. Still, a skilled manipulator will deliberately say something in a certain way so as not to be held responsible for their actions. Furthermore, when they see your reaction, they will distort it, so you seem to be the one who misunderstood you. They also claimed that they never promised Anything. You must always keep the promise of such manipulators.

Unrealistic Promises

Do you remember those times when you made rash promises under pressure? The robot allows you to answer them immediately, and then they will do something within you. When it comes to friends, it is almost impossible to refuse. Next time someone asks you to do something for them, please don't rush to agree. However, if you have promised something, please keep your promise. You need to consider twice before taking on additional responsibilities.

Parental Manipulation

Sometimes, our parents manipulate us. They often become manipulators to exert their own opinions, control their children's behavior, and interfere with their private lives. It is why we must learn how to defend our views, rather than let people control our lives. It may be difficult, but it is imperative.

Parental Behavior of a Partner

It is probably one of the most common types of robots. Parents often think that they are doing their best to make their children happy, but they don't understand that their husbands often ruin a happy marriage. For example, many mothers try to present their opinions and explain to their children what an ideal partner is. To reduce these manipulations, you should attempt to explain that your family is composed of you, your loved ones, and your children. Be polite, but also strict and firm.

Guilty Innocent

Unfortunately, some people completely ignore the phrases, decisions, and actions of others, even family and friends. They react too quickly and usually regret their actions. They also have a disturbing habit of blaming their mistakes on everyone around them. The Manipulator tries to put all the blame on you to make you feel guilty and responsible for your failure. Never be afraid to point out the real cause of the behavior.

The Price of Forgiveness

The argument is an inevitable part of any relationship, but unfortunately, sometimes it is impossible to make up for the damage caused in a particular battle. It is why the Manipulator tries to obtain forgiveness from its partner. Any gift becomes a bribe because that person is manipulating your gratitude. If you want to prove that you are not happy, it is best to refuse the gift.

More Suitable For

The robot tries to use your moral responsibility and love to control your life, thereby depriving you of choosing. If you do it this way, please use the same method. Also, you can provide a compromise that suits both parties. For example, if your spouse tells you: "It would be better for the children to be with the children tonight." You can answer, "I want to have fun too." We are called a nanny. "

Exaggerated Feelings of Self-Importance

If your boss is a manipulator, you may find them screaming and will not tolerate any objections. They have exaggerated self-importance and try to prove it by criticizing and discovering the shortcomings of employees. To avoid this negative situation and protect your nerves, don't be afraid to tell them that their requirements are not in line with your duties. Don't be scared to tell them, "That's not my job!"

Family First

It is one of the most common types of manipulation in the family. The robot will try to convince you that your child is a significant part of a healthy relationship. They emphasize the importance of family connections, control your feelings, and hope to replace family values with their family values. You need to avoid this trap and continue to think rationally. Consider whether you are ready to make such changes. If you need some time, please tell your partner. However, when it comes to such an important issue, please do not create a hasty decision.

Adult Children

Sometimes, when a person cannot accept the current life, parents will do everything for them, as if they were children. Such parents pay off all debts and try to balance the two jobs, while adult children let the flow go and manipulate their parents. This situation is harmful to both parties. If your children are manipulating you, please use your parents' wisdom to adapt to the world. What people think is manipulation may vary from situation to situation. The common result is that if they do not follow the "operator" wishes, the target will feel very uncomfortable. The different ingredients include inner, shame, or anxiety.

Manipulation has a hidden agenda and opposes direct communication. It must be secret because it provides the interests of the Manipulator directly against the desires of the target. Oral statements or questions can make you feel guilt, ashamed or worried, and may come in prompts, stories, and comparisons. It usually happens through sounds, facial expressions, or gestures. When you find yourself in this unhealthy relationship, be aware of these manipulation strategies. These are the six common types of manipulation and how to avoid them.

The King of Sin

The inner journey can take many forms: "If you are good, you will do," "If you love me, you will," "If you know what I have experienced." Naturally, this involves if you do not follow my requirements, then you are not a good wife, husband, parent, or child, or it means you do not love me. Therefore, you better comply.

Sinful behavior may also stem from specific circumstances. Unfortunately, children learn to use it very early. For example, it is difficult for a newly separated mother to discipline her daughter. The moment she made her child responsible for her prank, she started crying and missed her father. It aroused the mother's guilt; she stopped disciplinary action and began to soothe the child.

How to Fight: Don't give in even if you feel difficult inside. Determine the task to be completed and always execute it. You can include similar comments in your decision, such as "Sorry, you feel that way." You may feel inside, but you don't have to take full responsibility for it. What makes you feel inside is not necessarily based on "truth" but is created to comply with a hidden agenda.

Silent Giver

The working principle of silent therapy is to withdraw communication, emotion, and final sexual behavior from the target until they meet the Manipulator's requirements. In essence, it controls partners' behavior through fear-fear of disconnection, fear of rejection, and fear of abandonment.

How to Confront: Don't show fear, don't communicate with others. Respond in a neutral and easy-going manner: "I see that you don't want to communicate with me now. I want to do a little (read, work on my project, go to the garden). Please tell me when you are willing to communicate with me again."

Threat

From domestic violence cases and even some well-known crimes, this category is well known. "If you don't follow what I tell you, I will hurt you." Threatened to keep safe and sound with the purest fear. You are destroying Anything vital to you, including your career, relationships, or reputation, maybe blackmail.

Solution: If you are in personal danger, please escape and seek outside help. In yelling, you can say: "I did not complete the yelling request."

Self-Esteem Attacker

Putting down your feet, putting down labels, making judgments, or contempt (maybe just a pair of eyes) will make you feel inferior. These forms of communication severely criticize your character. It does not have to be completely simple and straightforward. It may be a dirty comment: "Only "office workers" wear lipstick during the day." You know this is a secret way to say you are an idiot.

Feeling belittled and ashamed, you did what the robot wants you to do to avoid disrespectful treatment. This treatment greatly undermines self-esteem.

How TO FIGHT: First, don't take it seriously. It just controls your tool; even your Manipulator does not think it is true. Secondly, never let anyone talk to you disrespectfully. Please respond with a calm and firm voice whenever you receive such a comment: "This is unacceptable." Third, doing what you think is right is independent of the opinions of others.

Too Many Critics

In some cases, criticism may be useful. However, this possibility is slighter than people usually think. Behaviors that strengthen expectations are more fruitful than pointing out mistakes. Generally, criticism is a means of controlling the opponent's behavior by weakening its self-confidence and self-reliance. People who are often criticized have low self-esteem. They allow themselves to be controlled to avoid criticism.

How to Deal with It: Paradoxically, if you want to make more criticisms—she or he doesn't like the details or other questions you raised—arguing with you, they will disappear quickly. Being in defensive mode is adding fuel to the fire: they are eager to prove that you did it wrong.

Competitors

"Who will dress up first this morning?" "Whoever brings home better grades can use the new game." "Who do you plan to spend on vacation with your parents or me?" Unfortunately, many parents have adopted this strategy because it makes raising their children more comfortable. Where competition rules, there will always be losers.

How to Fight It: There is always a way of cooperation and negotiation. Arrange the situation differently, set goals in different ways, and find different "games." Instead of "Who will be number one today?" Say: "Please help each other so that you can be prepared in time." Remember that compliance can strengthen manipulation strategies.

Signs You're Being Manipulated

They Maintain A "Home-Court Advantage"

Whether you are a real home or just a favorite coffee shop, being in your home can make a difference. If other people always insist on meeting in their field, they may try to create a power imbalance. They claim ownership of the space, which puts you at a disadvantage.

E.g., "If you can walk to my office. I'm too busy to trek to you." "You know how far it is to drive. Come here tonight."

They Are Too Close and Too Fast

In the traditional "know you" stage, emotional manipulators may skip some steps. They "shared" their darkest secrets and loopholes. But what they are doing is trying to make you feel different to reveal your secrets. They can use these sensitivities on you later.

E.g., "I think the connection between us is profound. I have never had this happened before." "I have never shared their vision with me like you. We want to be together."

They Let You Speak First

It is a popular strategy in individual business relationships, but it can also occur in personal relationships. When a person wants to establish control, they may ask exploratory questions so that you can share your thoughts and concerns as early as possible. Given their hidden agenda, they can use your answers to manipulate your decision.

E.g., "Oh my God, I never heard the good news about that company. What is your experience?" "Well, you just need to explain to me why you are angry with me again."

The Distort the Facts

Emotional manipulators are masters who are good at using lies, lies, or false statements to change reality to confuse you. They may exaggerate events and make themselves look more vulnerable. They may also underestimate their role in the conflict to get your sympathy.

E.g., "I asked an issue about the project, and she came to me and yelled at me that I had never done anything to help her, but you know what I did, right?" "I cried all night without blinking."

They Engage in Intellectual Bullying

If someone is at a loss when asking a question, but statistics, technical terms, or facts overwhelm you, you may be experiencing emotional manipulation. Some manipulators are assumed to be experts, and they impose "knowledge" on you. It is especially common in financial or sales situations.

E.g., "You are a novice, so I don't want you to understand." "I know these are a set of numbers for you so that I will say it slowly."

They Engage in Bureaucratic Bullying

Likewise, in a business environment, emotional manipulators may overwhelm you with paperwork, red tape, procedures, or Anything that might hinder you. It is a unique possibility if you indicate to check carefully or raise questions that suspect its shortcomings or weaknesses.

E.g., "This is too difficult for you. I will stop now and save my energy." "You don't know the headaches you have created for yourself."

84

They Make You Feel Sorry for Expressing Your Doubts

If you ask questions or make suggestions, the emotional Manipulator will most likely respond radically or try to lead you into an argument. This strategy enables them to control their decisions and influence your decisions. They may also use this situation to make you feel inside by expressing your doubts first.

E.g., "I don't understand why you don't trust me." "You know I'm just an anxious person. I can't help. I always want to know where you are."

They Reduced Your Problems and Played Their Part

If your day is terrible, emotional manipulators may take this opportunity to ask their questions. The purpose is to invalidate what you are experiencing so that you are forced to focus on them and exert emotional energy on their problems.

E.g., "Do you think this is bad? You don't have to deal with the cube partner who has been talking on the phone." "Thank you for having a brother. I have been alone all my life."

They Acted Like Martyrs

People who manipulate people's emotions may be eager to agree to help something but then turn around to drag their feet or find ways to avoid them from reaching an agreement. Their behavior may be burdensome, and they will try to use your emotions to get out of trouble.

E.g., "I know you need my help. It's just a lot, and I'm at a loss." "It's harder than it looks. I don't think you know when you ask me."

When They Say Rude or Mean Things, They Always "Joking"

Critical comments may be disguised as humor or satire. They may pretend to be joking, but what they are trying to do is sow the seeds of doubt.

E.g., "Gosh, you look tired!" "Well, if you are going to get up from your desk and walk, you won't be out of breath."

They Are Not Responsible

Emotional manipulators will never take responsibility for their mistakes. However, they will try to find a way to make you feel inward about everything, from battle to failed project. Even if they are at fault, you may apologize.

E.g., "I do this because I love you so much." "If you do not participate in the child's reward program, you can complete it correctly."

They Always Fit You

When you are happy, they will find a reason to take the spotlight away from you. It can also happen in a negative sense. When you encounter tragedy or frustration, emotional manipulators may make their problems look worse or more urgent.

E.g., "Your raise is great, but do you see other people get a full promotion?" "Sorry, your grandfather passed away. I lost two of my grandparents in two weeks, so at least it's not that bad."

They Are Always Criticizing You

Emotional manipulators may fire you or degrade you without joking or irony. Their comments are designed to eliminate your self-esteem. Their purpose is to laugh at and marginalize you. Usually, the Manipulator projects its sense of insecurity.

E.g., "Don't you think this dress is a bit of inspiration for client meetings? I think this is a way to get an account." "All you have to do is eat."

They Use Your Insecurity Against You

When they know your weaknesses, they can use them to hurt you. They may comment and take actions designed to make you feel vulnerable and frustrated.

E.g., "You said that you never want your children to grow up in dilapidated houses. See what you do to them now." "This is a tough listener. If I were you, I would be nervous."

The Deal with You with Your Feelings

If you are unhappy, the person who is manipulating you may try to make you feel guilty about yourself. They may blame you for being unreasonable or underinvesting.

E.g., "If you love me, then you will never question me." "I can't accept this job. I don't want to be so far away from my children."

They Use Inner GUI To Travel or Ultimatum

During disagreements or fights, manipulative people will make dramatic statements to get you into trouble. They will target the depression with inflammatory statements to arouse apologies.

E.g., "If you leave me, I shouldn't live." "If you can't come here this weekend, I think it shows your level of dedication to this office."

They Are Negative

A passive and aggressive person may avoid confrontation. They use people nearby you to communicate with you instead. They may also talk to colleagues behind the scenes.

E.g., "I will talk about this, but I know you are busy." "I think it's better to listen to other people's voices than mine because we are so close."

They Give You Silent Treatment

They will not respond to your phone calls, emails, direct messages, or any other communication form. They use silence to gain control and hold you accountable for your actions. This technique is designed to make you question the memory of the event. When you are no longer sure what happened, they can point you out and hold you accountable for misunderstandings.

E.g., "I never said it. You are reimagining things." "I won't do this. You know I'm too busy."

Signs That You Are Manipulating Your Friendship

By definition, manipulation can be difficult to detect, especially in friendships, which develop more slowly over time than in romantic relationships. The truth is that no one wants to admit that their favorite person in the world (their best friend) is manipulative. Even if they find it hard to ignore the feeling of sinking every time a friend does something immoral. Don't worry, and manipulation does not make your friends a bad person; it just means that they have a lot to read about relationships and survive in relationships. The first step in handling manipulative friendships is, to be honest with the red flags you notice.

Sometimes it is difficult to see that you are being used until you are deeply in friendship, making finding solutions more difficult. Take time to view your friendships and areas of concern. Here, early detection is the key. Like any other relationship, trading with your concerns will ease any future conflicts between you and your friends.

They Are Passive and Aggressive

They avoid confrontation, but their frustration is usually achieved through mutual friends. Your mutual friend may say: "Now anyone is dissatisfied with you; you should chat with her." It is called "manipulation" because she has put all your responsibility on you. She is also loyal to you because you will inevitably feel inside before you do this.

They Never Listen

The conversation rarely involves you, and when the conversation begins, you feel that they are not listening. Sigh. Maybe they are actively responding to text messages on their phones or interrupting your story to tell you something. In either case, they tell you that what you have to say is not essential to them, and not as important as what they say.

They Are in Power Travel

They always have to be responsible and like home-court advantage. For example, they insist on receiving you in apartments and places you are familiar with and insist on doing things they are familiar with to ensure that they are always in control. They may also try to force you out of your comfort zone, making you feel vulnerable and relying on them for guidance.

The Demand Many Benefits

This form of operation can measure the degree to which you will meet their requirements. You should always be willing to help your friends, but if these signs appear simultaneously, it is a red flag.

They Defend

When you face some of their behaviors, they become defensive and unable to listen to your views. They may be excited to shift their attention to the current problem rather than to the current state. They may blame the unimportant events on the reason for their actions. If you feel that your concerns have not been resolved, you may be dealing with manipulation issues.

We Need to Talk

If you recognize any of these signs, try to sit down with your friends and discuss your concerns. If you can solve the problem, please wait to see if their behavior changes based on what you said. Another characteristic of manipulators is that they will tell you what you want to hear without making any effort to change their behavior. If you decide to keep friends with the robot, it is essential to implement a strategy to protect yourself and take some time to make sure it works.

Time to Say Goodbye

If this operation is particularly toxic, or if they become defensive in confrontation and do not want to hear your concerns, it is best to get rid of the friendship altogether. Sometimes people don't even know that they have a manipulative tendency and are unwilling to change. In this case, this behavior may happen again and again, which may hurt your sense of self.

Love Yourself

When it comes to any relationship, self-care and self-love should be your top priority. Standing up and pointing out the signs of a potentially unhealthy friendship is not a bad friend. Listen to your instincts and pay attention to the signs. Take some time to think about whether your friendship is healthy and whether it is worth a lifetime. It is always worthwhile to have a conversation with yourself and your friends.

Signs You're Emotionally Manipulated

They Will Never Be Bored for No Reason

Have you ever had something that can be distorted? Or, the simplest is what they can provide. I know I have never been at fault. Yes, it is not. It is a failure, but he disagrees. Everything they need is usually something beyond their control. Their excuses can help them, even if they find their problems when they misplace them.

What's Your Reaction to This: If possible, you've reported them through examples, but they did something wrong? They will try their best to avoid blaming you, but you may leave if you do. They will correct errors.

You Want to Meet Your Own Needs in Your Way, To Put Your Needs Above Yourself

A student at Cartel University surveyed internal feelings and thought it was an unreasonable relationship because this relationship may annoy most people. A feeling of sham occurs. It may happen with email. You want something to like and like, "When I want to be with my family, please stay alone with my friends," they will continue to remind you that they thought about having fun with friends 30 years ago and let them mourn.

Everything has to do with them; if you don't have Marguerite, you can't have i-cream because you can't find out how it affects them. "If you want to go to that girl's side, go. I don't know too much how long you will keep the children." What you ignite will not be yours alone. If the condition is terrible, then you will not take any interesting actions, because it may bring you some help. "I have an idea, and I want to know about it. I know you don't want to, but please wait a moment until I know." If you are not directly adjusting to your needs, you will talk to yourself. It is the main reason you are dealing with other people.

How to React: You must know that no one will be upset by your troubles. You should not owe you any fees. The quickest response to this situation is to ignite the customer and do something that makes you unsatisfied, and you have no request for it.

What You Want to Do Will Make You Less or Less

It will be about their careers, how they will succeed, and how they will be helpful. You are not the person you dreamed of; their interest is significant. Everything must be supported. You will not know your tenure, their problems, and everything about them. You are not necessary. Are you traveling? They are experiencing or experiencing worse. Do you have a date? One day passed. Is your job terrible? They will not reward him; they will reward him. "Come on; all your operations are in progress; I will choose to keep them in it." You can be invincible. After dealing with a person, you will find yourself annoyed when solving some problems. They can't detect anyone's attention at all.

To Remind You of The Problem: Like the previous situation, you have no issues in your life. When they are confused about their problems, please do your best to avoid frustration and distress for their attention. And if that doesn't work, then you honestly won't be in that recipe.

You May Be Worried Because Of Worry or Suspicion Because They Are Real

You may keep yourself in your hands. Some people ask them questions and ask them to reach an agreement with them. First, you want an extra thing because they are of no use to you or your entire family; they are most likely to have it. Then they will ask you for advice if you know you fully, you will say no, but when you leave, you will find out if you don't want them to join. Then, all of a sudden, you will find yourself apologizing and expressing more.

Usually, when you mention something that bothers you, you may find it troublesome. You will never express concerns about your problems. Their purpose is to let you know something about your complaint and then turn to them—these electric manipulators' characteristics.

What to Do: You haven't called me yet. You need to spend money to buy it. Please don't feel guilty for this kind of behavior -, don't feel guilty. Please do not succumb to their demands or demands. It is an adult. Please keep this in mind and how to make yourself happy through your different actions.

You Have Reduced Your Difficulties or Difficulties

Emotional people will not hold any doubts about your behavior unless they can use it as a platform to highlight their situation. "Do you think it would be uncomfortable to sit on the street today? Have you ever thought that I will have a festival every day? It may make you uncomfortable. Thank you so much; you have to deal with it."

"Oh my God, it's terrible that you quarreled with you. Okay, please thank a mom. My mom is a dad. Even when she was still alive, you and your mom were fighting. It felt like I didn't, mom." If you speak through their words, they will try to make sure your settings are more sensible and sensible. Even if you pointed out the problem is more serious than you think, you might think you are considering their problem rather than a serious one. They will not understand their narcissistic behavior; otherwise, they will redefine their narcissistic behavior around you or when encountering difficulties. That's it.

Someone: You may not want to walk around in these situations, but find that other people think it's natural and mature. It won't hurt anyone who tramples on everything.

They Will Help You When You Don't Need It

First, they will show you, but once you start, you will begin to sigh, then groan, and finally, they start to hint, but I don't. They will continue to maintain subtle differences, which are usually caused by irony, not so.

If you become their focus and hope that they will do it voluntarily and go with it, those who go want to make sure of their ideas

It is difficult for you, but they are doing it. You want you to help you. What you want to make you feel different is that it does make you like the bull and think it's terrible for you. This idea will make you think inward and inward.

How to React: In this case, you may not want to try again, so that you will avoid it. If you tell you that your condition is not right, you will see other messages because he will help. To solve this situation, you should first move him. The other person is facing him, but he will only work harder.

You're Indirect

A skilled expert may be an expert who lacks insight. It means that they will be dumb behind your bill, they will say a lot of this, even though they are afraid to say it, they will find it sneaky because you know they are not. You only need to visit directly. They always find that it doesn't hurt you, so it's not their fault. You are free to decide not to disturb your phone calls, text messages, messages, or any direct inquiry, to show you whether they are you or do it with you.

They will not tell you directly about the harm you have suffered, because you may doubt it. Therefore, they may ignite or cause you essential trouble. They intend to be suspicious and uncertain in your mind, and you start to wonder where you are doing wrong.

Reporting Method: If you are facing your mobile phone and showing this sign, then you will feel that there is something that you cannot expect to stop because of being busy. The fact is, you don't have much to answer. In the end, no response has been provided.

They Give Appropriate Answers or Use Suspicious Language

This type of person may sound useful, or they may be shy when you talk. The purpose is to let you understand and eliminate doubts. The body may manipulate the robot and impose compulsion and suspicion on it. If they are not tall, they may sit in a more upright seat above you. You may also use the fastest movements (especially near your fingers) to wave gestures. These are also likely to threaten you and follow your instructions for evaluation. They may be determined to solve.

You may also use the fastest movements to wave gestures. These are also likely to threaten you and follow your instructions for evaluation. They may be determined to stay alive in exactly the right way. For example, your wife will feel uncomfortable every time she brings her an annoying life. Or your husband may raise his gaze and slam the door when he doesn't like it. In many cases, everything he needs to do will make them a little annoying, and things will happen.

Tip: Unless you have done this before, you will not be able to do it. If this exacerbates other problems, then you will find your room throughout the house. If left unchecked, it may cause harmful behavior. The robot's demand consultation can know what they are doing and how to deal with their behavior.

You, Will, Be Disgusted with Humor and Emotions, Giving You Time to Decide

Some people may think of something dangerous and even pretend to be an ironic irony to make your information less expensive and more secure. For example, you may receive various comments from your comments on your background and experience. By making you look bad and making you feel bad, many people want to show their strengths. They may exert excessive pressure when you have specific difficulties, and may even choose it to solve it. In the end, they want to know that their point of view is wrong.

Some people use negative means to keep themselves away from the banking industry and gain a huge advantage. The range is very wide, from a low price to a complete stopwatch, to a sudden request, for example, you will not be able to deliver these things somehow. In this way, warnings will be issued if the information is not fully diagnosed, leaving you little time to resolve their problems. You may want to ask you for help in case you deal with you.

How to Report: You are satisfied with yourself but feel that he/she does not like their sense of humor. However, if he/she does not want to force you to do troublesome things, you will use your time to think about it.

Storytelling

The storyteller is an emotional puppet master and a rational dictator, who can make Anything happen in the fictional reality. Everything is possible in the fictional reality. Extreme satisfaction is your only goal and the audience's Ultimate return and return. In storytelling, especially in screenwriting, it is vital that the narrative develops relentlessly and rapidly, and allows what happens to flow smoothly and form a cohesive whole. The various parts (scene, sequence, and behavior) are combined (story).

The story's rhythm must be reasonable, rhythmic, seducing the senses, and evoking emotions, from total happiness to absolute fear. The storyteller uses two tools to become the ultimate puppet master, setting "turning points" and "transition links" as actions, subtly manipulating emotions, and attracting unsuspecting listeners to a mysterious and bizarre network. The story converts a tapestry of mixed emotions, a melting pot of symbolism and subtext, allowing us to feel what is happening, experience the heartbeat of every moment, and take meaningful trips on a roller coaster of dramatic or comedic action. Will not be disturbed or get lost in translation.

These are storytellers who use their ultimate power to manipulate emotions and fully control the characters and their captive audience

Unity and Diversity

The story must be unified, even if it is confusing. Unity is essential. In this unification, we must promote change as much as possible. You don't want to hit the same notes over and over again to make every scene sound the same.

- Looking for tragedy in comics
- Seeking politics in the individual
- Seek personal motivation in politics
- Seek the extraordinary behind the ordinary
- Seeking triviality in the sublime

The key to changing the repetitive scene is research. Superficial knowledge leads to boring, monotonous talk.

Pacing

The audience has two wishes:

- Tranquility, harmony, peace, and relaxation
- Challenge, tension, danger, excitement

The author must alternate between tension and relaxation. Once you have written a scene full of suspense, you must reduce your stress and switch to comedy or romantic love. This kind of emotion directed at the other party will reduce the intensity, allowing the audience to breathe and gain more energy. After delaying the speed, you can build strength and progress in meaning.

Rhythm and Rhythm

In a storytelling story, the progress of scenes and sequences accelerates. The author uses rhythm and rhythm for shortening the stage gradually, and the activities in it become more and more active. It would help if you controlled the rhythm and rhythm. If you don't, the film editor will do it.

The length of the scene determines the rhythm. How long are we at the same time and in the same place? A typical two-hour function will have 40 to 60 scenes. On average, a scene lasts two and a half minutes. The beat is the level of activity in the scene through dialogue, action, or combination. Lovers may speak slowly from pillow to pillow. Intense debates in court will have a high rhythm.

Social progress: expand the influence of role behavior on society; let the story begin intimately, involving only a few main characters; as the story progresses, the role's actions will gradually circle the surrounding world, touching and changing more and more people live. In "Men in Black," accidental encounters between farmers and escaped aliens searching for rare gems gradually spread outward, jeopardizing all creations.

Personal progress: actions are found in the character's intimacy and life; the story will start with an individual or internal conflict that seems to be resolved; as the story progresses, we will study more deeply, from the emotional, psychological, and spiritual aspects of the story Deal with it downwards to explore dark secrets and unknown truths. In "Ordinary People," the story is limited to family, friends, and doctors. Starting from the tension between mother and child that seemed to be resolved through communication and love, this story evolved into painful suffering. The father realized that he had to choose between his son's reason and family unity. This story puts his son on the verge of suicide. The mother exposes his hatred of his children, while the husband loses his wife's love.

Symbolic progress: Symbolism is very eye-catching. It invades the subconscious and profoundly touches us. The story will start with familiar actions, locations, and characters; as the story develops, the images will accumulate greater meaning. Until the end of the story, the characters, events, and scenes all represent universal concepts. In "Deer Hunter," we meet steelworkers who like hunting, drinking beer, and spending quality time. They are as ordinary as the town. As the event progressed, everything became more and more symbolic. The protagonist develops from a factory worker to a soldier and then to a "hunter."

Ironic progress: it looks at life in duality, and it exists paradoxically. Verbal irony is found in the difference between words and their meanings; ironically, there is a dramatic conflict between action and result in the script; it is the primary source of story energy, between appearance and reality, Is the primary source of truth and emotion.

There are six satirical story modes:

- He finally got what he always wanted, but it was too late
- He is getting farther and farther away from the target, only to find that he has been brought into the target correctly
- He abandoned what was later discovered to be essential to his happiness
- To achieve his goal, he inadvertently took the precise steps necessary to take him away
- The action he takes to destroy something happens to be the thing to be destroyed
- He possesses something sure to make him miserable and does everything he can to get rid of it, only to find that it is a gift of happiness

Empathy

Empathy is happening. From another person's perspective, the ability to feel another person's feelings can generate a lot of pressure as the ultimate positive value and a pathway to a friendlier, less violent world. Schools across the country are teaching compassion to children, and countless books have explored it from all angles: how to get it, why it makes you a better person, without it, evil will breed.

Avoid the Empathy Trap

It is normal and necessary to adjust others' feelings, especially when they are very close to that person. In fact, in intimate adult relationships, giving and gaining Empathy is crucial. "The empathic understanding of others' experience, just like human vision, touch, smell, is a basic human talent." Being heard, the desire to be understood and deeply felt will never disappear. But when Empathy becomes the default contact method, mental health becomes very poor.

Compassion is the act of feeling toward someone ("I'm sorry, you were hurt"), and compassion involves feeling with someone ("I feel your disappointment"). It is also different from compassion, which is the concern of another person suffering from a bit far away and usually includes a desire to seek help. Empathy involves not only feelings but also thoughts. It involves two people, the person we are looking for and our self.

To get ourselves into others' predicament, we must strike a balance between emotions and thoughts, and between ourselves and others. Otherwise, sympathy will become a trap, and we can feel that others bound us. The art of Empathy requires attention to the needs of others without sacrificing one's own needs. It requires a quick mind to transform mediation from others to self. What turns compassion into right high behavior is that its beneficiaries find that attention is greatly rewarded. It makes us responsible for knowing when to get out of other people's shoes and how to get out.

Knowing and sharing the emotional state of others is a complex internal experience. It requires self-awareness, the ability to distinguish between the feelings of oneself and others, the ability to see from the eyes of others, the ability to recognize the emotions of others and oneself, and the knowledge to regulate these feelings.

Overly sympathetic people may even lose the ability to understand what they want or need. They may not be able to make decisions by their best interests. They will suffer physical and mental exhaustion due to their deviating feelings. They may lack internal resources to provide the best help to key people in their lives. Also, endless Empathy can cause others to be underestimated, in which case, another person will deny your reality to assert your facts. For example, when you feel frustrated that your friend was excluded from the last party, she replied: "Oh, you are too sensitive."

Those who often put others' feelings above their own needs often experience general anxiety or low depression levels. They may describe a feeling of emptiness or alienation, or stay in a situation from another angle. But what causes us to fall into the compassion trap? How to escape? Here are some ideas.

Roots of Sympathy

The baby comes to the world, ready to sympathize. Very young babies cry because of others' pain, and once they can control their bodies, they will respond to those in need to comfort or provide band-aids. Children have different levels of compassion, and Empathy seems to have a genetic component and a hormonal basis. Progesterone can enhance Empathy, while testosterone cannot. However, there is no apparent gender difference in empathy ability early in life.

The ability to empathize is not only built in the nervous system but also lessons can be learned from it, especially the feelings reflected by passionate and caring parents. Almost all parents cherish the

93

moment when their children spontaneously provide their favorite toys to relieve their grief. The irony is that many parents no longer "see" their children's kindness around the age of two and a half despite this. As parents begin to reward more achievement-oriented cognitive behaviors, Empathy has reached Steady-state.

Later, parents may find themselves encouraging Empathy again to shape behavior or cultivate their children's compassion. Think about that adult telling a teenage son, "I know that is important to you-you want to go very much-I know you are very frustrated with our decision." But sometimes, we urge children to see things through the eyes of their parents or siblings; for example, set aside their interest to visit relatives who are sick. Many children are often called upon to ignore their feelings to "serve others." It may be difficult for them to develop balanced Empathy in the future.

Occasionally but not always, putting others' feelings in front of others is part of the human experience. In a successful adult relationship, Empathy is reciprocal: partners share power equally and move back and forth between giving and receiving. However, when a partner offers more dedication, resentment arises.

Gender socialization can lead to imbalances in Empathy. Men who are encouraged to "stand up" to resolve conflicts may become too dominant, or, on the contrary, shrink back in the face of someone's strong feelings, and they don't know how to respond without accepting or yielding. Many women grow up believing themselves is always appropriate, and this becomes their default way of responding to others. The high emphasis on empathic people obscures the fact that they may ignore their feelings.

Unequal power can also create an imbalance in giving or receiving sympathy among partners. Consider the extreme situation, Stockholm syndrome, in which the hostages show loyalty and sympathy to the kidnapper. After being rescued, a newly released person will express an understanding of the kidnapper's behavior, and sometimes even wish to keep in touch with them or serve them. Battered women and abused children often establish similar bonds with their abusers.

Sadly, in relationships characterized by power inequality, people in low-power positions are more likely to comply with the needs of those in high-power positions. Doing so can help them stay persistent, at the cost of becoming their architects who deprive them of their citizenship. In some cases (such as nursing), it is necessary to focus on others' needs. They can make anyone's Empathy bearable. All caregivers need to find the support of someone who can provide them with the same support.

Communication

At a leadership seminar I held recently; we discussed how people could communicate when dealing with colleagues. A question arises: If you have choices about what you tell others, don't you? Are you manipulated in communication? My first reaction was: No, of course not. Then I stopped and thought: Maybe. Now, when I think about more, I believe it depends on your intentions. Although I had an initial reaction during the seminar, it is doubtful whether you are strategically or dealing with a problem when communicating at work.

Are You Communicating Strategically or Manipulating?

In the seminar I mentioned, we talked about some communication methods:

- Assertive
- Passive
- Aggressive
- Passive attack
- Maneuverability

You can recognize these styles when people try to meet their needs when dealing with business, whether they are solving problems, negotiating results, or resolving conflicts.

Confident Communication Is What You Want

Ideally, you want to use a decisive style to communicate your needs in a respectful, healthy, and confident manner. People who adopt a decisive style will communicate their needs without assuming that others are responsible for meeting those needs. People who use the passive style will not communicate their needs; they will only take a step back and accept whatever others give them. They cannot meet their needs, and eventually, they may feel dissatisfied.

Some people will use a radical style to force others down to get what they need. They will clearly state their needs, but the way they do this can also convey that others' needs are less important than their needs. People who adopt a damaging and aggressive style will recognize that their needs are inconsistent with others' needs. Still, they will not actively resolve these differences. Still, they will do something (usually to make things happen to them) indirectly to meet their needs. Maybe they don't know much about the paperwork they say they want to finish before the end of the day because "things are going crazy" by the way, it happens that people who haven't finished the paperwork think they shouldn't do it in the first place.

Manipulative Communication Attempts to Control

Although the passive-aggressive style can be compared with the manipulative style, the difference between the two classes is that people who use the manipulative technique will actively act in a planned and evil way to ensure that their needs are met. Perhaps they have selectively concealed information from the information provided by one party to the other because they can foresee the conflict that will result and how it will cause things to go the way they want. It is a control style in which the Manipulator puts himself above everyone else, just like a puppet master pulling strings, making all puppets move according to their overall plan.

As I mentioned above, a confident communication style is something you almost always want to shoot. On the contrary, a manipulative manner is a way you should avoid at all costs, which is why when I ask a question in a seminar, I instinctively think that strategically provide certain information to some people and provide others Is different information "manipulative"? Exception.

Strategic Communication Aims to Benefit Everyone Involved

After consideration, everything boils down to intention. Are you strategically choosing what to say to people primarily based on meeting your needs, or do you do so because you think you are talking about the best way for everyone to understand the situation? After all, people consider different things, and the form people process information varies greatly, so it makes sense that you don't say the same things to everyone.

Intent makes a big difference between strategy and manipulation. When I communicate with my own opinions and techniques, my goal is to win-win: let me tell you what is important to me; let me tell you what I know is essential to you so that in the ideal situation, We can meet our needs. If you want to do this, my purpose is to focus only on my needs, so I will tell you what I think you need to listen to align you with my needs.

Finally, I admit that there can be a good line between active, strategic communication and manipulative communication. In both cases, the conversation on a particular topic may sound very similar. But I firmly believe in humility in interpersonal relationships, and manipulative communication does not come from humility, but a place of entitlement. Robots feel empowered to control others, and they think they know better than others. Suppose you communicate in a manipulative way of thinking. In that case, even if you happen to share the same information and use the same words in a conversation with someone who is communicating confidently and strategically, your manipulative intent will eventually surface and begin to erode Your trust establishes your working relationship.

Manipulation Techniques

Manipulation is a form of social communication that benefits the Manipulator while at the same time, pushing the cost to the target of manipulation.

The Techniques Used by The Manipulator

Manipulation is a social influence that aims to change the behavior or perception of others through indirect, deceptive, or vile strategies. ...For example, people such as friends, family, and doctors can persuade them to change unhelpful habits and behaviors.

Gaslighting

"Puffing up is a manipulative strategy that can be described in three different variations of words: "That didn't happen," "You can't imagine," and "Are you crazy?". "Farting may be one of the most insidious manipulative strategies at the moment because it will distort and erode your sense of reality. It will weaken your ability to trust yourself, and inevitably make you lose grounds to justify abuse and abuse."

How can you fight back? "Placing yourself in reality-sometimes writing down when things happen, telling friends or reiterating your experience with support networks can help counteract this exciting effect,"

Projection

Do you know when poisonous people claim that all the filth surrounding them is not their fault, but yours? That is projection. We have all done some, but narcissists and psychopaths have done a lot. "Projection is a defense mechanism used to replace others' negative behaviors and traits by attributing them to others."

solution? "Don't 'project your sympathy or compassion on poisonous people, and don't have any poisonous person's predictions." "Projecting our conscience and value system onto others may lead to further exploitation."

General

You said that colleagues sometimes fail to consider the long-term impact of individual financial decisions. The office psychopath claimed that you called him "a loose cannon." You pointed out that if X, Y, and Z conditions occur, the transaction may go south. Your narcissistic colleague told your boss that you said the deal was a "disaster." How is this going? Not just because your nemesis doesn't understand what you are talking about. It is that he or she is not interested in understanding.

"Vicious narcissists are not always ideological planners-many of them are ideologically lazy. Instead of spending time carefully considering different points of view, they summarize everything you say and publish. It is a general statement and does not recognize your nuances. Arguing or considering the multiple points of view you pay tribute to." To solve this problem, "please stick to your truths and resist general statements by realizing that they are black and white illogical forms of thinking."

Move the Target Rod

"Abusive narcissists and social perverts use a logical fallacy, that is, 'move the target column' to ensure that they have an excellent reason always to dissatisfy you. It is even if you had provided all the evidence in the world for verification. When your argument or action was taken to satisfy their request, they put forward another expectation of you or asked for more evidence.

Don't play that game. "Verify and approve of yourself. Knowing that you are enough does not have to make yourself feel persistently insufficient or unworthy to some extent," Alabi suggested.

Change the Theme

Switching the conversation topic sounds innocent, but in the master, Manipulator's hands, changing the subject becomes a means of avoiding accountability. "The anesthetist does not want you to be a topic that makes them responsible for anything, so they will reschedule the discussion to benefit them."

If you allow, this kind of thing may go on forever, preventing you from actually participating in the issue. Try to fight back with the "broken record method": "Continue to state the facts and don't distract them. Redirect them by saying, "This is not what I'm talking about." Let's continue to focus on the real problem." If they Not interested, please get out of it and focus on more constructive things. "

Title

Because you have been dealing with this problem since you encountered the first playground overlord, it doesn't make it more destructive (and continues until the presidential political period). It cannot be tolerated at all. "The important thing is to end any interactions that include names and communicate interactions that you won't tolerate." "Don't internalize: realize that they resort to names because they lack advanced methods."

Smear Movement

"When toxic substances can't control what you think of yourself, they will start to control how others think about you; when you are marked as toxic, they will play hard." Sometimes the real evil genius will even split and conquer, pitting two people or groups against each other. Don't let them succeed. "Record any form of harassment" and make sure not to raise the bait and let this person's terrorist behavior trigger your behavior in a negative way that is falsely attributable to you.

Devaluation

Be careful when a colleague seems to love you while violently denying the last person in your position. "Narcissistic abusers always do this. They devalue their sexual behavior to their new partner. Eventually, the new partner begins to suffer the same abuse as the narcissist's former partner." But this dynamic may happen in a professional Domain and personal domain. A simple understanding of this phenomenon is the first step to deal with it. "Be aware that how a person treats or talks about others may translate into the way they treat you in the future,"

Mischief

The problem is not your sense of humor, but the hidden intention of the joke. "Covert narcissists like to make malicious comments at their own expense. These comments are usually dressed up as 'joking' to say shocking things while still maintaining innocence and calm behavior. However, anytime you feel insensitive to insensitive behavior, an angry, stern word, you are accused of having no sense of humor." Don't let the office abuser make you think this is all innocent fun-it is not.

Triangulation

One of the smartest ways for a truly toxic person to distract you is to focus your attention on others' so-called threats. It is called triangulation. "Nasserist's like to "repay" what others say about you. To resist this strategy, please be aware that the third party in the drama is also manipulated. She is another victim, not you, Enemy.

Manipulation Techniques Your Colleagues Use to Hurt You

You would dance like a happy colleague singing in an ideal world, and even the bad guys would be kind and famous for their ominous makeup and creepy costumes. Unfortunately, this is not the case in the real world. You may be the same happy employee in a Disney movie, surrounded by singing birds and chi flowers, but the bad guy will not wear ridiculous costumes, surrounded by a group of lads!

Among your pleased friends, there may be some people who will praise you, seem to support you, or even laugh at your jokes, while secretly digging a big hole for you. These bad guys are so dangerous because they can handle any situation, make you look bad, and shine like a cutting-edge meat cleaver. These manipulators have nothing to lose; they can control your feelings with all their strength. Stay with them long enough, and you will find yourself feeling like a worthless bastard.

Build Confidence

You are like the smartest person I have ever met. Narcissistic manipulators need to get the attention of everyone around them. So, when you join someone for the first time and find that you immediately attract your new friends, beware! Such people usually give you all the compliments in the book at the beginning to attract you. After finishing, they can play you like Ronaldo. Although it's so sensational and likable, it's best to stay rooted. A few tempting words may be the perfect trap for the Manipulator to lure you into completing the humble report he has been delaying. And don't think that you will get good reviews for it. It will be all the pain; there is always no gain, you sweet naive!

Change Your Reality

I believe you are just imagining. How often do you get some negative things from a friend/colleague/relative? What did you do and point out these mistakes just to laugh at them? A typical narcissist/manipulator/psychological communicator relies on changing reality so that you not only think that what you say has never happened, but that you are losing this state. After long enough, you will gradually start to doubt everything and become your crazy fantasy.

Highlight Defects

Have you ever asked yourself why I did not perform well? The narcissistic Manipulator is technically called a projection, which ensures that his shortcomings are nothing but your weaknesses. In a sense, this strategy is particularly useful when the narcissist needs to explain his bad behavior by shifting responsibility to the variable shoulders. You may hear cheating spouses say: I am not cheating. Arrogance is your delusion and persistence. Or the head of government might say that if people are not willing to stop questioning me, I can make this country run better.

Unlike physical abuse, the transferor projection of blame can cause moral and emotional damage to the victim and cause disability. These roles may conceal their inefficiency or lack of productivity at work and find a way to blame it on you. If you give me a better project to deal with, I will do better. You are not a good manager.

Irrelevant Digressions Win Controversy

So, you don't like big beards? You must like Hitler! For manipulating narcissists, a very well-known strategy is to lead arguments or conversations to a completely different dimension, mainly voting on justice or sensitive things. The idea is to upset or frustrate you by taking some form of a prominent point that is entirely unrelated to the last discussion. It comes from a very unsafe place in their hearts. The divergent thoughts turned into a threat to their arrogance. Traditionally, politicians often use this manipulation strategy to make the masses oppose any form of rational opposition. If you disagree with the current policy, you must not love your country!

Trust Your Words

Your opinion is irrelevant. You are too emotional. To please your opinion and narcissists are likely to put some wrong labels on you to help them eliminate contemplation and fights. With the demand for social media, we now see online bullies emerging from wood products and making high-profile general comments on targets. Most of these statements have no reasonable basis and no other opinions. They are only used to minimize and degrade the target point. The trend is to move away from logic and cloud everything.

Extreme Labels

You not only think that I am wrong. You believe I will never be right. Narcissists often make absurd extreme statements to show everyone how biased you are. Motivation? Simply emphasize your unfairness. Suppose a colleague is joking about the way you dress. You just need to point it out to him. If he proceeds to be a narcissist, he will surely be famous for fighting back. Are you that sensitive?

Never Appreciate

So, do you think you can dance? Can you do math while dancing? You are not satisfied with the narcissistic Manipulator. Because if you do, then you are no longer their punching bag. Without you to feed their massive self-expansion, they will have to go through the tedious process of finding another minion. It is your typical narcissistic time!

- Is it still single?
- Oh! When did you get married?
- So long? And do you still have no children?
- Do you? Are you a teenager now?

Are you worried that they will become young people and soon get married and settle with their children?

Cruel Jokes and Painful Irony

Did you stay up late to do this analysis? I hope you have told me; otherwise, I won't take 15 minutes to finish it this morning. Toxic people like to disappoint victims by making jokes or taunts without knowing it. Mainly done in other people's presence, the purpose is to make you look smarter while looking like Daffy Duck. Although not necessarily only for toxic people, it becomes a feature among narcissists when they shoot regardless of the receiver's feelings.

Belittle Your Achievements

It is a great plan, and everyone is talking about it. Are you sure this is what you require to show your boss? Narcissists can act very gently, taking all the time they want first to make you believe that they value everything in their lives. Once achieved, they will begin gradually alienating you from everything you like to control you fully. They will use false third-party claims to make others accomplices in their Machiavellian plan to destroy you.

At work, you may find colleagues/boss who no longer appreciates your talents and contributions for some time, thus making you doubt everything you used to be good at. A toxic boss may lead you to believe that you may be better than some previous workers and slowly deal with your abuse.

Bait, Then Play the Victim

I don't know why he shouted. I just asked him about his monthly report. Toxic people may play thinking games that are too complicated for the normal brain. They will provoke their targets with sensational jabs and comments and then use their natural confrontational responses to prove that their targets are unreasonable. They like to lure their goals into situations that indicate that they are victims of abuse. In workplaces where impressions matter, your visible aggression will be negatively evaluated. No one wants to care about the events that led to this outbreak.

Break the Limit

Sorry, I called you can fool the other day. But when you give a speech like a fool, what can I say! If you think you have overcome the Manipulator's attempt to devalue yourself, beware of more massive attempts. Robots like to be able to break through the limit to test the final breakthrough point.

Secret and Public Threats to Exercise Control

How dare you send the report directly to the boss? Didn't I tell you to let me verify everything? It is the last choice of the Manipulator. They are usually brilliant in disguising their way. However, if you happen to be someone who is not bothered by other things at all, they will feel that their control is threatened. Then they turned to more local responses, such as threats and calls.

Manipulative Self-Disclosure

Manipulative self-disclosure will provide forged or unwanted personal information to gain social credibility, which will then obtain more valuable information from manipulated targets. Personal information is precious in social activities. Personal information may enhance the information receiver's capabilities and put the information provider in a potentially vulnerable position.

It also increases trust, and possibly ties and connections. Therefore, due to the exchange nature of social relations, providing potentially valuable information will produce the ability to receive helpful information. At least because of the law of reciprocity, it puts pressure on the target to disclose valuable information.

Manipulators abuse the social exchange system by sharing stale or unsolicited personal information, which puts pressure on targets to share their valuable knowledge. Or, if the Manipulator has a clear goal, he can share unsolicited personal information and then directly request the juicy information they want (for this self-disclosure).

Pro-Social Fe Two

The pro-social weak encourages others to abide by a set of pro-social rules that restrict their character or impair their efficiency in life. The Manipulator himself either violates these rules or enjoys more significant benefits because people abide by these rules that power.

The pro-social pretense is based on the dichotomy between teamwork and selfish defection. For example, if everyone is pro-social, everyone will benefit. However, if the Manipulator can persuade others to become pro-socialist when he is secretly flawed, he will gain more significant benefits.

There are three different types of pro-social pretends:

- Manipulation and defects: Pro-social manipulators claim to be pro-social ideas and behaviors. He pretends to obey them in public, but he will betray them in private and whenever possible.
- Observe etiquette: When no one else is pro-social, pro-social behavior can be costly. Therefore, a true believer will strive to win others to avoid comparative losses (note: persistence and dependence may be respectable value-added choices in life)
- Defining powerlessness as a virtue: The Manipulator cannot compete in an open system, so he tries to promote virtue and ethics, limiting people's ability to achieve specific goals.

Socio-Cultural Customs

At the social level, every individual and the social group strives to influence public opinion to adopt a framework or ethics beneficial to themselves or their group. In cultural manipulation:

- Promote the belief that success is related to choice and diligence: The rich want society to believe that success and wealth are near related to diligence and dedication, which helps them formulate the socialist wealth redistribution policy to commit productive people.
- Promote the belief of "poverty and happiness": Fiske found that those in power can classify the lower class as a class with high enthusiasm but low ability, which can help stabilize the status.
- Honor culture: Men seek to instill a culture that oppresses women's sexual freedom to defend non-parent-child activities
- Actions similar to "Me too": a culture that quickly leads to male discrimination. In this culture, women can easily humiliate and destroy men due to any type of progress, thereby enhancing their ability to fight against men.
- Political framework: Every political party tries to frame the public discourse to benefit the public. For example, when everyone uses expressions such as "tax relief" or "help others," conservatives are more likely to win debates and influence policy choices.

At different points in time, the group or group managed to gain an advantage. However, because there are so many competing interests, few people can fully control all other interests.

Why Do People Manipulate Others?

People use manipulation strategies against others because they want to feel better about themselves. They prevailed and blamed the victims. It is not uncommon to abuse others to use emotional blackmail to avoid seeing one's feelings. When they manipulate others or maybe even not at all, they don't immediately feel inside. However, emotional manipulators may feel responsible for hurting those around them and their loved ones or moving on as if it does not affect them. People with personality disorders such as antisocial personality disorder will not regret manipulating people. But, for example, a person with borderline personality disorder manipulates people's emotions and then feels guilty about what they do later.

If you are the victim of manipulation, then you may question your sanity. It is an insulting behavior, and the emotional Manipulator wants you to ask your feelings. The person who manipulates you will make you feel special, but it will also make it difficult for you to set boundaries. In this way, they have power and control in the relationship. The consequences of emotional abuse are not conducive to a person's mental health. Emotional manipulators do not think about what they do to others. They hurt others because they have weaknesses that they try to cover up, making them feel better about hurting others. They may be involved in intellectual bullying or psychological abuse. They will make you angry and make you feel that your reality is a fiction of your imagination. They may play mental games with you like a martyr, so it is difficult to discern what is real and not. Abusive behavior is incorrect, and it is not your fault that this person has emotional problems; they are bringing it to you.

It Is Not Your Fault

It is not your fault. If you are emotionally manipulated, it is not your fault. People have seized the power of others because of their insecurity. Another person is playing an intellectual game with you. Emotional manipulators are experts who can spot people's weaknesses and reverse their weaknesses to use them to their advantage. When emotional manipulators grasp the power of disadvantaged groups, they are looking for themselves. These people will make you feel special and then find your weakness. The worst kind of emotional manipulation is silent therapy. It will be very painful if you try to get love, care, or care from emotionally manipulative people, and they ignore you.

The silent treatment hurts a lot. Individuals are not responsible for their actions; they will continue to hinder you. Due to obstacles, emotional abuse consequences are not conducive to a person's mental health because you will subsequently trigger an incentive to be ignored. Being manipulated can have long-term effects, and emotional manipulators can cause personal harm. Their actions may make them passive and aggressive and insidious that you may not even know what they are doing. Sometimes, a manipulative person will give you backhand praise. These negative, offensive remarks are insulting behavior, not a fiction of your imagination. There are many forms of manipulation; please remember that it is not your fault. You did not ask you to be abused. Passive, aggressive comments will make a person question whether they are being abused; however, this is true. Your feeling is correct because you can feel it.

If you are emotionally manipulated at work, there may be many red tapes to pass so that you can report abuse. It may be that your supervisor wants to control and control you, but they make you feel like you imagine abuse. It is challenging for this to happen in a work environment because the Manipulator knows you are in a vulnerable place. They understand that the consequences of emotional abuse can affect your career. When tempting you to abuse, they skip some steps and may take extreme measures.

Remember Who You Are

Emotional manipulators are good at their work. They will make you question what is right or untrue. When an emotional manipulator approaches you, it is difficult to return to your identity. Fickle people can even make you feel vulnerable and crazy. Emotional manipulators want you to feel this way. It is why if you have been a victim of psychological abuse, it is so important to go to the therapist because emotional manipulators are unlikely to take responsibility for their actions. The consequences of emotional abuse can cause lasting damage to your mental health.

However, you can control your mental health. Therefore, it is essential to understand that you are not as burdened as you think. If you think you feel like a burden, they may be happy to agree, but this is not true. People can refuse to take responsibility for their actions. The consequences of emotional abuse are serious. It is why it is essential to seek treatment if you suffer abuse. Emotional manipulators are masters who make others feel small. If you are abused, you may feel that it is your fault. Remember that the long-term effects of abuse can be terrible, so it is so important to see a therapist. Whether you see someone online or locally, you can get help with mental abuse.

Manipulation in Real Life

Do you hate manipulation as much as I do? Bitches, bullies, social perverts, and sweet talkers, this world is full of people, they will say and perform anything to get what they want, and will not hesitate to use you for personal gain. If you hate manipulation as I do, this is for you because I will introduce these manipulation strategies to recognize them when they appear.

Acts Above You

Some people are arrogant and will try to act as if they are "higher" or "better" than you somehow. Maybe they behave like they are an adult and you are a child, or it appears in the form of humble comments and facial expressions, both of which make it clear: they are the "superior,," and you are the "inferior." For this strategy to take effect, you must stick to it and accept it. Refuse. Know this: no one is above you. No one is "better" than you. No one is "superior" to you. You are not inferior to anyone. You are no less than anyone.

Important Comments/Intonation

Sometimes people will try to talk to you in a condescending, patronizing, or dismissive tone to demean you:

- "Do not be silly."
- "Don't be stupid."
- "You are so ridiculous."

People use this to manipulate you, not just to belittle comments and tone. Hollywood and TV stations are now whispering to produce dramatic effects as if they let you into some secret (even if it sounds like a bunch of fools). With principal influential people/perseveres/salespeople, often use the tone to "show off his hiss" and build rapport and influence people.

Just Kidding

Another vile method used by robots is to make jokes, but at your expense-especially in front of others. Maybe they make fun of you online or humiliate you by making fun of you for walking, talking, dressing, or worse, things you can't control, such as eyes, nose, ears, face, height, or skin color.

"Sticks and stones will hurt your bones, but the name will never hurt you."

Nonsense. Words can be devastating. To make the situation worse, if you get angry and ask the robot what their problem is, they will usually say "just kidding" or "have fun" to defend their actions. They may even aggravate the insult by telling you, "you are too emotional" or "too sensitive."

They may even give you an insincere apology to shut you up and stop you from complaining. "What do you think makes me feel sorry."

Dirty Expressions and Death Eyes

Sometimes a picture-or a mean facial expression-depicts a thousand words. Beware of any of the following aggressive/subdued facial expressions used to scare and manipulate you to shrink and yield:

- Yielding head tilt
- Condescending glasses
- Dirty appearance and dead eyes
- Prolonged eye contact without blinking or talking
- Eyeball rolling
- Raise eyebrows
- Shaking head

Be A Bitch

Why do people bully? Because it works. Most people are afraid of conflict and confrontation and will do everything to avoid conflict and confrontation, and this is where bitches and bullies flourish. What a child or a bully need to do is to start showing aggressiveness, hostility, and threats, and send a clear message by combining body language, facial expressions, and intonation. So that you seem to have to walk around on the eggshell: Don't Fuck me, or you will regret it! "95% of people will avoid them immediately or start kissing their donkeys, hoping to become friends who are afraid of socializing with each other.

Bullying strategies are also different, not just physical. At school, bullies may use their size and threats of physical violence to scare you. If you are unwilling to "double your efforts" and become a "team player." Your manager may try to intimidate you by directly or indirectly threatening your safety at work. That may mean that what the manager wants to express includes: Working holidays, weekends, or overtime without paying extra salary or doing things that are not part of the job description. It is not always easy to stand up or leave a bully. Although everyone reacts to fight or

104

flight, you cannot run in the workplace, and fighting is not always a good idea, especially if the person bullying you is your manager.

Physical Threat

If someone is older, taller, or stronger than you, they may try to stand on you with their body to intimidate and threaten you. Because I am short (5 feet 6 feet), I have many people trying to scare me in this way. In my case, it doesn't work, because I have been in martial arts (boxing, Muay Thai, Brazilian Jiu-Jitsu and wrestling) for more than ten years, so I know I can deal with myself in a fight or worst case, but It is possible to see ordinary dwarfs/dwarfs under such threats and threats.

If you often feel physically threatened or threatened by others, I suggest you learn MMA (Mixed Martial Arts) because it will train you on how to fight and defend yourself. Even if you have never participated in a battle, you must stand by if you need it.

Shout

"Don't raise your voice, improve your argument." Yelling is another aggressive strategy used to intimidate and manipulate you. Some people will only increase the volume and start shouting and shouting at you instead of raising their arguments. Otherwise, they will suddenly raise their voices and start shouting so loudly that they can't dominate the conversation and frighten you.

If someone starts yelling or yelling at you, or speaking much louder than necessary, I suggest that you remain calm and act in a non-aggressive, non-emotional, non-compliant state of affairs. Appeal to them:

You: "Why are you yelling?"

Manipulator: "Because I am angry!" "I am angry!"

You: "But why are you yelling?"

Manipulator: "I'm telling you!" "I'm angry!" "I get fucked!"

You: "But why are you yelling?"

Manipulator: "Because... (insert reason)"

You: "But why are you yelling?"

Manipulator: ...?

99% of the time; this will make the operator feel awkward; they will become extremely self-conscious and uncomfortable, and immediately lower the sound. Once again, you want to calmly ask this question, with facial expressions that show real curiosity and curiosity, not judgment.

Silent Treatment

Women's favorite strategies are everywhere, and they are good at treating the elderly in silence. If you cannot get what you want, please ignore them.

Ignore You/Play Hard

Like the silent treatment, it is when someone makes a conscious effort to ignore you and strive to obtain. Watch out for people who try any of the following strategies:

- Confirm everyone in the room, but ignore you
- Whenever you try to talk to them, you feel boring/selfless/inconvenient, as if they have other important things to deal with

- Does not respond to any of your comments, questions, emails, calls, or messages, and is always unavailable or "too busy" when you need to talk to them
- Leave the room after entering the room.
- Every time I talk to you, deliberately avoid eye contact with you
- Refuse to admit your existence

My recommendation to you is if someone ignores you-ignore them. If they take a step back to you, take ten steps back to them. If you need to talk to them, call them and ask them what the problem is.

House Travel

The favorite pastime of mothers and robots all over the world the trip to let and If someone is not you according to your wishes, please make them feel inside:

- "I thought we were friends."
- "I thought I could rely on you."
- "I can't believe how selfish you are!"
- "I have been there to serve you, and now you can't even reach out to help me?"

Charities like to make people feel inside trip:

"Don't you want to provide money to help starving children in Africa?"

Like MAR Taoist/Victim

Acting like a martyr, a victim, and poor me:

- "I am very busy!"
- "I have a lot of work to do!"
- "I can't do anything, right!"
- "Nothing I do is good enough!"

Use Emotions

Some people are masters of emotional manipulation and will not hesitate to play with their emotions to get what they want. They will tell you they love you. Otherwise, they will tell you that they hate you. Otherwise, they will try to make you angry, sad, or jealous; it doesn't matter. Everything they need to get everything they want.

Advertisers, especially the media, are the ultimate masters of emotional manipulation. They know that if they can make you feel something, they will make you make a difference. Therefore, advertisers and media will not waste time trying to persuade you logically, but manipulate your emotions by showing you images of cute babies and puppies, abused animals, and starving children. Everything you need to produce the desired result. It is a despicable trick, but it works and works!

My tip is not to let anyone work with your emotions and manipulate you to do things you shouldn't do, just because they told you a sad story or shed tears. I know you may feel sorry for the crying person, but crying does not make the wrong thing right. Your decision should be based on a combination of intuition and logic, not on the emotional manipulation and deception of others.

Passive and Aggressive

The operation is not always directly on your face. Sometimes it is indirect and subtle, in the form of passive aggression. When someone is afraid to say nothing or feel dissatisfied with having to do something they don't want to do, they may show some negative, aggressive behaviors and feel frustrated. Passive-aggressive behavior:

- Avoid/ignore/exclude someone

- Avoid responsibility
- Agree to help and do a bad job because you don't want to do
- Often be late, let others wait for you (I hate this)
- Disguise and insult "this color looks good to you" or "pretty shoes."
- Dragging the heels, unnecessarily difficult
- "Forget" to do something on purpose
- Dumb
- Pretend they don't understand
- Procrastination
- Deliberately avoid email/phone/message
- Refuse to promise anything or give a direct answer
- Resistance
- Irony
- Say one thing/do another (send mixed messages)
- Shaking head
- Sigh
- Mute handling
- Stubborn
- Sulking: Man: "What's wrong?" Woman: "It's okay."

Hard

Some people have difficult personalities, and if they feel that you want their approval/verification/friendship, they will deliberately refuse to do so to manipulate you. The more satisfied you are, the less happy they are. The more approvals you seek, the more they will retain. I have met many such people. I'm sure you must. Such people can only argue with you but never agree. If you say black, they say white. If you are wrong, they are right.

They will do their best to make it annoying and difficult. Not only will they not approve or verify anything you have to say, but they will even argue with you when you say what they agree with, just to argue:

- "Yes, but..."
- "Although..."
- "However,"

My advice is not to make every effort to be friends with these people, build rapport, or win them. Most of them have shit personalities and are not worth your time.

Temporary Deduction of Approval, Gender, Verification

Another manipulator's strategy that can be seen everywhere is conditional acceptance with conditions attached. If you say/will/agree to give the manipulator what they want, then you will only get approval, help, love, gender, confirmation, etc. However, this strategy will only work if you are accustomed to seeking approval and confirmation from others (I strongly recommend against it).

When you seek others' approval, you empower them so that they can manipulate their feelings and make them feel like nonsense at all times. In other words, you become their bit. Remember: what others can give you can also take away. If they can lift you, they can also push you down. And, what if you seek someone's approval but refuse it? So, what do you do to work harder? Does it feel like bullshit? If someone does not accept your identity or does not want to treat you the way they want, please let them go. Say goodbye to bad garbage.

False Time Limit

The wrong time limit often puts you under pressure and leaves you no time to think. Bosses often use the wrong time limit to manipulate employees:

- "We have a deadline!"
- "Customers/customers are waiting!"
- "We don't have time to discuss this!"
- "This is urgent! You can't go home until it's done!"

Companies often use the wrong time limit to drive sales:

- "Only today! Up to 50% discount!"
- "End of pre-sale! Last days! Hurry up or miss it!"

Employers give false time limits to prospective employees to allow them to join:

"You have 48 hours to allow this offer; otherwise, it will be "canceled.

People use the wrong time limit for a reason: because salespeople know "time kills a deal," and you have to think clearly and weigh all options. The longer you take, the less likely you will do what they want and buy Their products or services.

Free Lunch

The sneaky tricks of manipulators everywhere are to provide you with "free" gifts or services, or other things you don't want, and then ask for something in return:

- "Free Evaluation"
- "No strings attached."
- "Debt Free Offer"

But know: there is no such thing as a free lunch. When someone provides you something, they almost always need something in return. Maybe it's wealth, time, advice, help, or help. If in difficulty, ask them and find out the problem because there is almost always a hidden agenda.

Over Supplement

Some people will say some sweet words; they will try to influence/convince/manipulate you through praise and praise to please you and win you. Everything they say is like music in your ears. Instead of telling you the truth, they kissed your ass and told you that you wanted to hear.

It is a wise strategy because everyone likes to be praised by others, recognize and tell others good things, and praise is one of the fastest ways to build rapport, make new friends, and attract someone to reduce their defenses.

Sweet readers know that when they make you feel good, you are more likely to want to return your favor by doing something that makes them feel good. Also, we have to face reality: the more you like someone (your best friend, your boyfriend/girlfriend, husband/wife, children), the easier it is for them to manipulate you. For those who are insecure, needy, and have low self-esteem, praise can be a particularly deadly strategy.

Loading Problem

The problem of loading is the problem of unfair assumptions built into it. (Usually a presumption of guilt). They are often asked to try to make you take a step back. E.g.:

- "Why do you continue to lie?"
- "Why don't you admit that you stole it?"
- "Why don't you just admit that you are wrong?"

Main Issues

The number one question assumes the answer to the question to trick you. Lawyers in court often ask them:

- "Are you still addicted to gambling?"
- "Do you still beat your wife?"
- "Why are you lying?"

Lazy self-help salespeople often attract audiences by asking some main questions at seminars to induce them to buy products:

- "Are you a speaker or an actor?"
- "Are you a champion or a loser?"
- "Do you desire to be rich or poor?"

Try to Take Advantage of Your Weaknesses

No matter what your weakness is:

- Fear
- Greedy
- Lust
- Money
- Power
- Pride
- Gender

Some people will deliberately try to use it against you to manipulate you. If they know you have anxiety, they will constantly try to fear you. If you know that you have a great ego, they will keep telling you how good you are.

Advertisers love this strategy and have been using it to manipulate people. They know that the largest people are sheep and will blindly imitate anything stars tell them to do, so they hire celebrities to develop and sell their products. They also know that many people have a lot of conceit, so the ads they attract themselves and make false promises to make you "better" than others. Men can be "victors." A woman can become a "goddess."

Peer Pressure

Some people will try to convince you that everyone else is trying to make you do something (as if following the crowd is the right thing to do):

- "Come on! We are all waiting for you! You are blocking everyone else!"
- "You are the only one who thinks so!"
- "Who is right: you or everyone else?!"

Advertisers and media often use a subtle form of peer pressure called "social proof" because they know that most people are followers. No matter how absurd they are, they will blindly copy celebrities and trends. It is why most ads will show images of other people (especially celebrities, handsome people, and sexy women) and use the product to convince you everyone else to do the same, and you should do the same.

Sex

Sexual behavior is sold by advertisers worldwide and used to manipulate people (especially men) to purchase their products and services. About 27% of advertisements contain some kind of sexual imagery. Sex can also make music videos more popular. Frankly speaking: most of the music videos these days are porn videos. Sex can also be utilized as a weapon, and often so. Women often flirt with men to manipulate them to do what they want, or if they don't get what they desire, they refuse to have sex.

Provide the Illusion of Your Choice

The most popular technique used by parents, teachers, bosses, and salespeople worldwide is to provide you with many options, all of which can bring the same results. No matter what you choose, they will win, and you will lose. It's like tossing a coin and saying, "I win on the front, and you lose on the back." E.g.:

- "Now or later?"
- "Start now or later?"
- "Do you want a 6-month payment plan or pay now?"

Try to Get You to Make A Public Commitment

Beware of anyone who tries to make you go against your will, especially if you are in the camera, writing, or public appearances in front of others. I remember a meeting with a very manipulative sales manager. He said in a meeting: "Everyone writes down your ideal sales year: if you can do anything, even if it is possible, what will it be? Write it down. It is private and only for you. No one will see it."

Then, he waited for about 10 minutes, until everyone had completed the exercises and wrote down their ideal perfect year, and said: "Well, now everyone stands up and shares your promised achievement this year with the group. " Yes, that happened. He is such a ridiculous bastard.

Try to Keep Your Promises You Never Made

Some people will even try to make you keep promises you never made. I have candidates try it out in my previous recruitment work. He emailed me, copied my boss, and said: "I will accept this contract because you promised me that my next contract would be renewed with a salary increase. I hope you will keep your promise. "(He knows this is a blatant lie)

Unilateral Report

How many news reports do you hear every day are balanced and fair? The media is a master of manipulating public opinion by choosing information and stories that support its agenda (mainly a free agenda), while at the same time turning a blind eye to it and ignoring anything that is not welcome. Issues to ask yourself when watching the news:

- Did I understand the whole story?
- Do both sides of the story show me?
- Is it to make one side look bad, evil, ignorant, or stupid?
- What conclusion does this story want me to draw?
- Still not clear? Are they talking about what they left out on purpose?

Lying/Propaganda

If all robots have one thing in common, it is lying. Manipulative people will lie/deceive/mislead without hesitation to get what they want. Why do people lie?

- Avoid embarrassment and face
- Avoid punishment
- Avoid responsibility
- Avoid having to do someone a favor
- To avoid hurting the feelings of others
- Get what they want
- To get rid of what they don't want to do
- Sounds important/impressive
- Fool/deceive/manipulate you
- Influence/convince you
- Play dumb

Robots not only like to lie; they also exaggerate. Some people exaggerate their achievements to impress and manipulate you, while others may try to manipulate you by exaggerating their problems and difficulties in seeking sympathy and money.

Make You Believe That It Is Your Ideal

"There is only one way to get anyone to do anything. That is by getting another person to do it." People will do what they want to do, not what you want them to do. However, if you can convince someone that your idea is theirs, then they are likely to accept it because they will still feel that they are in control of the decision-making process, rather than being manipulated.

How do you turn someone that your idea is indeed theirs?

You put ideas and suggestions into their minds and then let them draw their conclusions, just like they have always thought. For example, McDonald's has suggestive billboards everywhere. They only ask you one question: "Are you hungry?" Your partner may ask you, "Do you think we should go on vacation as soon as possible?" I heard that Hawaii is great at this time of year..."

Framework Control

Perhaps the most powerful and least known weapon to manipulate is frame control.

What is frame control?

Frame control simply makes another person adapt to your reality and see things from your perspective. In a job interview, the employer's framework may be:

"Let us see if you are good enough and have everything you need to work here."

If you are the respondent, you need to switch the framework to:

"You are interested in me; otherwise, you will not waste time interviewing me. What do you want to say or do to convince me to work for you?" Usually, the most important person is the person who controls the framework, which is the self-evident meaning of interaction. When the child speaks with the parent, the parent controls the frame. When the student speaks with the teacher, the teacher will control the frame.

Recognize Manipulation in Relationship

Psychological manipulation can be defined as improper influence through mental distortion and emotional exploitation, the purpose of which is to seize the victim's power, control, interests, and privileges. It is essential to distinguish between the social influence of health and psychological manipulation. The social impact of health occurs among most people and is part of the gains and losses of constructive relationships. In psychological manipulation, one person is used for the benefit of another. The robot deliberately creates an imbalance of power and uses the victim to serve his or her plan.

Most manipulation individuals have four common characteristics:

- They know how to spot your weaknesses.
- Once discovered, they will use your weakness to deal with you.
- They persuade you to give up something about yourself to serve their self-centered interests through their cunning tricks.
- In work, social, and family environments, once the manipulator successfully exploits you, they are likely to repeat the violation until you stop the exploitation.

Recognize and Handle Manipulative Relationships

Know Your Fundamental Human Rights

When dealing with psychological manipulators, the most critical criterion is understanding your rights and recognizing them when they are violated. As lengthy as you do not harm others, you can stand up and defend your rights. On the other hand, if you cause harm to others, you may lose these rights. The following are some of our fundamental human rights. You have the right:

- Be respected.
- Express your feelings, opinions, and needs.
- Determine your priorities.
- Say "no" without feeling inside.
- Get what you pay.
- Have different opinions
- Take care of and protect yourself from physical, mental, or emotional threats.
- Create your personal happiness and healthy life.
- These significant human rights represent your boundaries.

Of course, our community is full of people who do not respect these rights. Especially psychological manipulators want to deprive you of your rights so that they can control and use you. However, you have the power and moral power to declare that you are responsible for your life, not the robot.

Keep Your Distance

One way to detect the manipulator is to see if a person is acting with different faces in front of other people and different situations. Although all of us have a certain degree of such social differentiation, some psychological manipulators often live in extremes habitually, being courteous to one person, completely rude to another, or entirely helpless for a while. For a moment, he showed a strong enterprising spirit. When you observe an individual's behavior regularly, please keep a healthy distance and avoid interacting with that person unless necessary. As mentioned earlier, the causes of chronic psychological manipulation are complex and deep-rooted. It is not your duty to change or save them.

Avoid Personalization and Self-Blame

Since the manipulator's schedule is to find and use its weaknesses, you may feel inadequate and even blame yourself for being dissatisfied with the manipulator, which is understandable. In this case, please remember that you are not the problem; you are just being manipulated, and you are not satisfied with yourself, so you are more likely to give up your power and rights. Consider your relationship with the robot and ask the following questions:

- Will I be truly respected?
- Are this person's expectations and requirements of me reasonable?
- Is the payment in this relationship mainly one way or two ways?
- In the end, am I satisfied with this relationship?

Your answers to these questions provide you with important clues about whether the "problem" in the relationship is related to you or others.

Focus on Them by Asking Questions

Psychological manipulators will inevitably make demands (or demands) from you. These "offers" often prevent you from meeting their needs. When you hear an unreasonable request, it is sometimes useful to focus your attention on the manipulator by asking some exploratory questions to see if it has enough self-awareness to recognize its scheme's unfairness. E.g.:

- "Does this make sense to you?"
- "Does the voice you want from me sound fair?"
- "Do I have a say in this?"

- "Are you asking me or telling me?"
- "So, what do I get from it?"
- "Do you want me to [restate the unfair request]?"

When you ask such a question, you are raising the mirror so that the robot can see the real nature of his or her strategy. If the manipulator has a certain sense of self, they may withdraw the demand and fall back. When you ask such a question, you are raising the mirror so that the robot can see the actual nature of his or her strategy. If the manipulator has a certain sense of self, they may withdraw the demand and fall back.

On the other hand, real pathological manipulators (such as narcissists) will dismiss your problem and insist on finding a solution. If this happens, use the following techniques to maintain strength and stop the operation.

Use Time to Play to Your Advantage

In addition to unreasonable requirements, robots often expect your answers to maximize pressure and control you in this situation. (Sales staff call this "complete the transaction.") During this period, instead of responding to the manipulator's request immediately, consider using the time to play to your advantage and keep yourself away from his or her direct influence. Just say:

"I will think about it."

Consider the powerful features of these few words from customers to salesperson, from romantic prospect to eager suitor, or from you to manipulator. Take the time to evaluate the pros and cons of the situation, consider whether you want to negotiate a fairer arrangement, or say "no" is a better option for you, bringing us to the next point:

Know-How to Say "No"-Diplomatic but Firm

Being able to say "no" through diplomacy resolutely is the art of practical communication. Express it effectively, and it allows you to stand on your ground while maintaining a viable relationship. Remember, your fundamental human rights include the right to set your priorities, say "no" without feeling guilty, and choose your own happy and healthy life. In "How to successfully handle manipulators," I reviewed seven different ways you can say "no" to help reduce resistance and keep the peace.

Deal with Bullies Safely

When a psychological manipulator intimidates or hurts others, he or she can also become a bully. The most important thing to remember for bullies is that they will choose people they think are weak, so long as you remain passive and obedient, you can be a target. But there are also many bullies inside. When their goals begin to show their backbone and defend their rights, bullies tend to back down. It is true on campus, home, and office environments.

From the perspective of empathy, research shows that many bullies are themselves victims of violence. It must not be an excuse for bullying, but it can help you consider bullying more fairly:

- "When people don't like themselves too much, they have to make up. The classic overlord is the victim first."
- "Some people try to chop off other people's heads and become tall."
- "I realize that bullying is never about you. The insecure is the bully."

When facing a bully, please make sure to put yourself in a position where you can protect yourself safely, no matter if it stands tall, has other people present to witness and support, or keep a written record of the bully's inappropriate behavior. If you suffer physical, verbal, or emotional abuse, please consult a legal, law enforcement, or administrative professional. It's essential to stand up and bully others; you don't have to do it alone.

Set Consequences

113

When the psychological manipulator insists on violating his boundaries and will not accept the "no" answer, the result is deployed. The ability to recognize and assert consequences is one of the most important skills you can use to "stand firm" for those who are in difficulty. The result makes the manipulator feel paused and forces him or him to change from aggression to respect. "How to Successfully Deal with Manipulators," the product is seven different types of power that can influence positive change.

It is difficult to detect signs of manipulation in interpersonal relationships at first. Many people think that such things will not happen to them. Many people do not realize that they are being manipulated or controlled by their partners. Manipulators play mental games in various ways to get what they want. Their behavior seems normal, but in a healthy relationship, it is unacceptable because they cause problems. Their behavior is part of a habit pattern related to emotional or physical abuse, even if they seem reasonable.

Skilled robots know how to use people to make themselves look like victims. They know how to add twists to the story or cover up their footprints to make sure they get what they want. They know how to use words to express your thoughts and emotions. You must suspect manipulative behavior in your relationships; you need to know what to look for. If you want to know, "Am I being manipulated?" Test yourself by asking for signs of manipulation in the relationship.

Here Is What You Are Looking For

They provoke little things. In the beginning, the situation was excellent. You found that there is no problem with the right questions. You can choose what to do and where to go together. It now appears that your partner is starting to fight for small things because they know that people don't like confrontation, so they want you to give in. The manipulator uses this strategy as a controlled force in other aspects of life.

You are blamed for the actions of other people. Robots do this to control your behavior, but some people may think they are jealous of you. You have done nothing wrong, but they will attack certain things about you, such as your appearance or personality. They may blame you for the actions of others. It may seem to protect, but they are trying to change you to feel better about themselves.

They hide things from you. You will find that they sometimes make a phone call in another room, go to other places without telling you, or discover your rough other activities and show secrets. You might have lunch with friends if they find that they are angry. It looks like they are wasting their time, but you are not sure what they are doing when you are away.

You are not allowed privacy. They want privacy, but they won't let you have any privacy. They may check you over the phone or text message to see if you get what you want. They may want to check phone activity to find out who you are communicating with.

You will be blamed for what they did. If your partner suddenly feels frustrated or remembers a mistake he made before, and he will pin it on you. They use you as a scapegoat for wrongdoing, making you feel wrong in the process and trying their forgiveness. You did nothing illegal, but they make you feel that way.

They use your kindness, and The robot will use your needs to gain control. They like kind and trustworthy people. They help but take advantage of opportunities to your detriment. It is a way to induce you to believe that you need them. The abuser may also use kindness to get you to do things for them; you don't want to know that it will benefit them more. They may say that they have done some good things for you, but hope you will do something in return.

They make you feel less or less. When your partner thinks you are better than you or have nothing without them, the relationship becomes dysfunctional. It is an abuse. They may tell you that you are not good enough or are not interested in you, but you are lucky. They often talk to you and make you feel depressed.

They change your words. Robots like to play skills and thinking games. If you question what they are saying, they will attack you and then speak out in your mouth. You said they might be meaningless, but they take it to another level or think that you are trying to make them feel inferior, but they deliberately make you feel worse.

They build their relationship. You want to discuss your day, but they make them feel that their day is more important. They may not care much about the difficulty of verifying you. They think your problem is incomparable to theirs. When they make you think of yourself as something you do or talk about, the relationship is unbalanced.

They exhibit passive-aggressive emotional behaviors. They control the way they express their emotions but have a tendency to manipulate. They may work against you by actions that annoy you or bother you. They may hold their breath and make rude comments or leave a mess on purpose. It helps them to endure anger. When the manipulator wants to control your emotional response, they can remain calm, calm, and collective.

Their inner GUI controls you. We are imperfect people and make mistakes, but they will not let you forget your mistakes. If you are unhappy with them, they will turn your mistakes into games. As a result, they want you to be on their side.

They make you think you are wrong. They hide their insecurities and make you think you are wrong about something. It may be when discussing opinions or what was said earlier. They may exaggerate, excuse, or act to make themselves appear smarter or better than you. They keep going until you admit that you are wrong.

You do not see friends or family members often. When robots do not have the most significant interest in you, they will keep you away from interested. They become the controlling force in your life and keep you from getting along with others.

They make you prove that you love them. Robots usually use the word "If you love me..." They may say that before something to make you improve your mind or be shameful. It is the most dangerous form of manipulation and the most innocent behavior.

They are bullies. When they are angry, they will give subtle hints, and you choose not to do what they want. They are despicable, sneak out, and may use violence to get you to agree. Later, they might say something that makes them look good.

You are controlled by fear. The way the robot instills fear into people is similar to how they do, but it shows that they lack patience. If you owe them something or know a secret you want to tell others, they will use fear to control you. They may agree to do something for you, but they pose a threat if you disobey them. If they frighten violence or make you appear scared, please leave and find a safe place immediately.

How Do You Know If You Are Being Manipulated in A Relationship?

When dealing with a person to be manipulated, it can sometimes be challenging to realize that their behavior is the problem, not you. People who are good at manipulating may be good at transferring responsibility for their actions or making you feel that you are at fault. Even though identifying manipulation can be tricky, it is possible. Signs of manipulation in relationships, so be sure to read them through to fully understand some of the various forms of manipulation you may encounter.

A brief list of types of manipulation is as follows:

- Threatening specific actions or consequences to achieve the desired result
- Or make you responsible for things that are not necessarily your fault.
- Arguing often, especially about trivial or trivial matters
- Control behavior (determine who you can/cannot see, control your personal financial information, etc.)

115

- Lack of privacy or trust
- Passive-aggressive behavior
- Negative emotions around the partner (e.g., fear, obligation, and inwardness)
- Intense delusion (even attacking vital signs or basic behaviors)
- If any of these things happen in your relationships, you should take it seriously as a red flag.

What Is the Manipulation in The Relationship?

There are many different ways to manipulate relationships. Toxic relationships do not always look the same, and when you are being manipulated, it can be challenging to understand. It is undeniable that a sexual or degrading partner can have harmful and harmful effects on your life, and you should never be responsible for others' sexual behavior.

You can see the discussion above about the appearance of operations in relationships. Manipulating someone is so much about managing them or getting them to do what someone desires. Understanding the different kinds of manipulation may help you understand it in your relationship (if applicable) and urge you to seek the support you require through therapy, support groups, or other means.

How to Stop Manipulating Others in A Relationship?

An excellent first step in changing any behavior is recognizing that you are participating in the behavior described above. If you can realize that you have a manipulative tendency, you have completed half of your efforts. The sincere desire to change not to harm others is also a good sign of personal progress. Now that you have identified these behaviors, you can modify them and start developing healthier patterns.

It is important to remember that you can control your behavior and remember that you may have difficulty getting rid of old habits at first. Sometimes people repeat actions they are used to. For example, if you are in an insulting relationship and often manipulate, you may find yourself bringing certain behaviors into your future relationship. For those who grew up using manipulation strategies in their families, this is sometimes the case.

It is important to remember that you can control your behavior and remember that you may have difficulty getting rid of old habits at first. Sometimes people repeat actions they are used to. For example, if you are in an abusive relationship and often manipulate, you may find yourself bringing certain behaviors into your future relationship. For those who grew up using manipulation strategies in their families, this is sometimes the case.

You may need to work with professionals (such as consultants or therapists) to determine what motivates you to manipulate behaviors or tendencies. Maybe you have problems with trust or commitment or struggle with communication or giving up control. In either case, exercising yourself and understanding how to manipulate it may help you immensely.

What Does Manipulation in Relationships Look Like?

Manipulation in relationships usually focuses on the various behaviors and actions that are essentially controlled. Manipulative partners may use different techniques to persuade you to behave in a certain way or make decisions consistent with what they want. When being manipulated, you may feel powerless or scared. You may experience dieting (the term dieting refers to manipulating someone to question your reality) or other common manipulation behaviors.

Manipulation can be manifested in many ways, and sometimes they seem harmless or acceptable according to social norms. For example, the technique of stepping on a door means that someone

116

first starts in a smaller, more acceptable way, and then manipulates you to accomplish a great task. By making you feel loyal to others or consistently helping others, you can use this technique to win a lot of help.

When you are the target, identifying manipulation can be tricky. If this is the case, don't be embarrassed; literally, it is an undetectable control! Things such as controlling your personal information, personal financial information, etc. are also examples of shocking behavior. When faced with someone's information about manipulation, it may be used to convince you that you are wrong.

- You will feel useful and loved only when you take care of the needs of others. It goes beyond being kind to others. Your sense of value is related to serving others. You took this action to such an extent that you pleased others at the expense of your happiness. For example, when you will never spend that much money on yourself, you may buy something particularly good for your partner or friend. Manipulators are attracted to this type of person and do not hesitate to take advantage of this special personality trait.
- You need to be recognized and accepted by others. Although most people like to be accepted by others, problems arise when you feel that everyone must always accept you. The core issue here is the fear of rejection or abandonment. This fear is so strong that you will take all measures to avoid feelings related to fear. The way the robot works is to make you accept the required acceptance and then threaten to withdraw it.
- You are afraid to express negative emotions. Although expressing anger and conflict are never pleasant things, some people will do their best to avoid conflict. They want things always to be happy. They worry that they will collapse in the face of negative emotions. In this relationship, the manipulator's task is simple-all they have to do is threaten to raise their voice and go their own way.
- You cannot refuse. One of the features of a healthy relationship is appropriate boundaries to clarify who you are and what you represent. However, to maintain healthy boundaries, you sometimes have to say no when someone tries to push the limit. If you are afraid that conflicts may occur from time to time, then you can manipulate the manipulator. Learning effective self-confidence skills is a way to regain control of manipulative relationships.

Tips to Defend Yourself from Manipulators

If you are serious about leadership, then one of your golden rules is to act with integrity and honesty; that is, only manipulate others so that you can keep the winner out of your script. However, just because you follow the rules and remain transparent does not mean that others will be rewarded.

You will meet people who deceive you. Usually, they do this because they have internalized the idea that second place is not good enough. They are so afraid of being considered second or in a financial or another insecure state to leave you out of the car. Less commonly, you may encounter a true narcissist who honestly believes he has the right to win at all costs. In either state, your success depends on completing their vile tactics.

Some Ways to Guard Against People Who Might Try to Manipulate You

Stay with Someone Knowledgeable and Helpful

If the manipulator isolates you, you are like the Serengeti's injured gazelle, and it becomes more difficult to consider alternative opinions and ideas and obtain general information that can change your decision. No one can ask; you are more likely to treat the manipulator as an expert friend, even if they are not.

Keep Recalling Yourself of Your Goals and Priorities

Robots do their own hands, so they will do their best to change or destroy your dreams. From telling you publicly that you will not succeed in forcing you to work on projects that are lower than your ability or inconsistent with the path you choose, it's all OK. Every day figure out what to do for yourself and each task's purpose so that the robot cannot convince you to change direction. If the robot also brings you logistical or interpersonal difficulties, this kind of attention will prevent you from investing too much in negative emotions.

Convey Your Intentions

For this reason, robots may try to spread false information about you or your work, or they may not be able to provide you with the information you need to move forward correctly. The more you tell others what you want to accomplish and believe in verbal or written ways, the more difficult it will be for the manipulator to convince others that it will be against you intentionally or unintentionally. What you portray is your identity, not an explanation provided by the manipulator. For this reason, the more you witness, the better the witness, and always back up and protect your records.

Call It as If You Saw It

Even if they are just afraid of failure, one of the reasons why robots perform so poorly is because they honestly think they can do it without being caught. They insist on their conceit and convince themselves that they are too proficient in the system and personnel to discover its solutions. They insist that they can still be lucky enough to continue to escape it because they have never encountered any consequences. Eliminate this illusion through the inevitable confrontation in which you tell them what they observe and how it affects you.

To fight effectively, you need to prepare by tracking the manipulator's attacking behavior, and attach the specific actions, dates, and names of everyone involved. However, confrontation is not necessarily a rude battle. Deliberately state the facts and propose options for going forward. Once the robot knows what you know, they are unlikely to continue to mess with you, especially when you elaborate on the possibility of submitting an appropriate report to your supervisor or HR.

When you try to protect yourself, remember that leaders have always used psychology to manipulate their teams. It is a common example, such as providing feedback strategically or subtly convincing tired employees to go home. The difference is that great leaders care about the progress of the team rather than their interests. If you can teach a malicious manipulator on how to reduce self or fear and do it, everyone will win.

Manipulating behavior can be mild or severe. The behavior will vary depending on the operator's intentions, how much they care about you, and whether personality disorders such as narcissism behind their behavior. When possible, the operator should be given a wide bed or eliminated. If it is not possible, there are many ways to protect yourself from such behavior. If you feel that you have been abused or damaged, please get out of the situation and not try and manage it. In other words, in real life, not everything is black and white. If you cannot or do not want to eliminate the manipulator, these technologies will help understand and handle the situation.

Leave Early

Nothing seems good enough for manipulators because they still exist, no matter how much control you give them. If anything makes you uncomfortable, please refuse. Although operators will encounter difficulties, surrendering to them is not the end of the problem. All this will make them feel that they have the right to ask you for something. Manipulative people will begin to demand and persuade, and then gradually develop to demand and punishment. It would help if you told them "no" for the first time.

When you say "no" to someone to be manipulated, they may feel indifferent to you, and they may extort you emotionally or actively disturb you. If this is a budding friendship or romance, then saying "no" may mean the relationship's end. Be firm, calm, and state your position. Don't get too involved in details and excuses. Excuses do not apply to manipulative people. They like the opportunity to argue and express their opinions. They like an opportunity to excite you and redirect you. People who are good at manipulating do not want to discuss it with you. They want to disappoint you until you do what they want. Tomorrow, they will want other things.

Know That Empathy Can Be Used Against You

Manipulators desire power and control. The reason is that at some stage of their life, they were rejected. The reasons for their lack of capacity in their own lives may be chaos or abuse in family life, romantic abuse, trauma, abandonment, or neglect.

The robot's bad behavior may cause others to avoid or dislike them, but a sane person realizes that this behavior is caused by pain. The saddest thing about manipulators is that the people they hurt and are eventually driven away are most likely to show them the loyalty and love they desperately want.

The more compassionate you are, the more likely you are to get along with a manipulative person. Your sympathy for them may also mean that you allow them to get rid of behaviors that others cannot tolerate. Recognize and respond to your own needs before the needs of others. It will not come at the cost of losing your care and understanding of nature.

Boundary

Boundaries are common sense of most people. People who are good at manipulating either think that their path is right or desire it in their way that they have nothing to ask for. To protect yourself from the control and control of the manipulator, you need to clarify your boundaries. Then, it would help if you imposed the boundary of consequences. Fickle people will not respect others, even if they like or love them. For them, setting healthy boundaries is the same as rejecting. Defining boundaries for the manipulator is likely to produce adverse reactions, and preparing for such adverse reactions is the key to dealing with the situation.

Constantly explain obvious facts and insist that someone's behavior is constantly draining energy. The manipulator knows this. They know that you don't have enough patience and emotional energy to try to deal with a fully autonomous adult on the same level as a determined and forgetful child. Therefore, boundaries must be broken. To have the greatest chance of success, you need to draw boundaries when calming down and fully control your emotions. It is expected that the manipulator cannot maintain the boundary at some point. After that, you must enforce the consequences.

Don't Let Them Be Number One

If you have frequent contact with the manipulator, you need to study how to limit it consciously. There will always be slight toxicity around them, which can be very serious. It will inevitably make you exhausted and severely affect you over time. In addition to limiting contact with the manipulator and spending time for yourself, you also need to maintain good relationships. Not only do they support you in dealing with difficult people, but they also provide you with a basis for comparison. When other people you know prove that they are unreasonable, a manipulative person will find it difficult to convince you that they are right or are entitled to what they ask.

Stand Up Again

It is almost impossible to supply gas to two people at once. In the company, the choice of manipulators is severely reduced. Manipulative people must be more careful when talking to you (rather than privately). If they say something unpleasant when you are alone, please repeat it in front of others at the next opportunity. Just like you think there is nothing wrong with what they say and try to present it to you.

In this case, you will receive an angry and defensive response from Angela. She wants to deny what she said, or insist that you misunderstood her. She is not angry at what you don't like her; she says it because she knows you don't like her. But now that you have added another person in, their inevitable opposition is not part of her plan.

It Should Make Her Want to Avoid Dealing with You in The Future

The key is to stay calm. Such manipulative techniques are designed to produce an emotional response in your body. When the robot is angry, you can turn the table by keeping your composure. If you are dealing with people to be manipulated in the workplace, you need to pay attention to personal conversations and emails and phone calls. Make sure to keep records or detailed information and confirm it in front of others. Keep emails and other CCs when necessary.

The classic manipulator technique is to provoke you privately in the workplace and then make sure that if you retaliate, others will find it. It makes you look crazy. Force the manipulator to be "in recording" to move it back.

Intonation and Facial Expressions

Intonation is a very powerful aspect of language. As young children, we learn to explain the tone of voice faster than sentences. It is because we first understand the emotion behind the word before we understand the word itself. If someone talks to you in a language you don't understand, you can still get a lot of information through your tone of voice and facial expressions.

Manipulative people can make full use of this fundamental aspect of language and communication. They often make positive comments in a sarcastic or negative tone. Instead, this may work, and they may tell you that they are sorry for something when their face and voice indicate that they are nothing. They may pair expressions of disapproval with compliments.

They compare intonation and facial expressions with their meanings. The desired result is to make you feel confused or frustrated. It can be easily offset. Just listen to what they say. If they congratulate you, thank them and walk away. If they say you did a good job, thank them and walk away. If they make a satire, please answer them as if there was no satire. Such a mismatch in communication is a tactic. If you don't let it achieve its goal and don't get it, then it will fail.

Weird Game

Most people don't mind owning things. It is because our self-esteem is not based on 100% correct time.

The manipulator cannot be blamed. If they are forced to admit responsibility or wrongdoing, they will feel great guilt. They want you to feel guilty by making mistakes. They may also express excessive regret. I can't do anything, and I'm stupid. You are much better than me in all aspects, and I shouldn't try again.

This kind of internal use is a completely wrong response. The normal response to most of the things we all do wrong from time to time is to admit, apologize if necessary, and take corrective measures. There is no response from the manipulator; they want you to feel sad about being face to face with them. They want to train and adapt you not to trouble you the next time you do something wrong. Ideally, they want to automatically blame what they did because you want to avoid troublesome reactions.

Unfortunately, it is difficult to hold a manipulative person accountable, and it is not worth your effort. When a manipulative person uses blame switching and guilt for doing something wrong, they have no real argument. Injecting challenges and emotions into the situation will only escalate the situation. When you meet someone who cannot do the wrong thing for your actions, you need to accept that this situation can never be changed. More precisely, they will never change because of anything you do or do. This change must come from within themselves and be part of their journey to improve their lives.

Sadly, apart from minimizing contact and minimizing participation, there is no effective way of doing things. You can make a manipulative person accept the blame, but the huge consequences that follow are rarely worthy of you. You recognize that this behavior is not your fault and beyond your ability to solve; this is the only effective way.

Maintain Self-Esteem

One of the most unpleasant things a manipulator can do is destroy and destroy the self-esteem and self-worth of others. They do this to gain control in any way. People with low self-esteem feel worthless and more easily influenced and controlled than confident and happy people.

Work hard and build your self-confidence as the top priority of your daily work while avoiding contact with people who try to undermine your self-confidence. Knowing what you think and determining your behavior is a vital life skill, and it will provide you with good service in many situations.

Protect from Emotional Manipulation

1. Trying to be honest with the emotional manipulator is no use. You make a comment, and it will be reversed. Example: You forgot my birthday. I am really angry. Response – "It makes me sad to make you think I will forget your birthday. I should have told you the huge personal pressure I am facing right now – but you see that I don't want to trouble you. You are right; I should take all this pain (You won't see real tears at this time) Put aside and focus on your birthday. Sorry." Even if you hear these words, you will feel that they do not mean completely sorry, but you have been feeling - But because they said these words, you have almost nothing to say.

Either, or you suddenly find yourself taking care of their anxiety!! In any case, if you feel that this angle is changing, please do not surrender! Don't care-don't accept nonsense apologies. If it feels like nonsense – it may be. The first rule-if you want to deal with emotional blackmailers, trust your instincts. Trust your senses. Once the emotional manipulator finds a successful manipulation method, it will be added to their hit list, and you will get a stable diet.

2. The emotional manipulator is a helpful photo. If you demand them to do something, they will almost always agree-if they did not do it voluntarily. Then, when you say "OK, thank you," they will give out a heavy sigh or other non-verbal sign to let you know that they don't want to do anything. When you tell them that they don't seem to want to do anything, they will reverse the situation and try to make it look like the course they want and your unreasonableness. It is a form of crazy manufacturing-emotional manipulators that are very good at it. The second rule-if an emotional manipulator says yes-please hold them accountable. Don't indulge in sighs and subtleties-if they don't want to do it-let they tell you in advance or just put on the Walkman headset and take a shower, then go to the theater

3. Do things crazy-say one thing, and later assure you that they haven't said anything. If you find yourself in a romantic relationship and think you should start recording what you say because you start to question your sanity-you are experiencing emotional manipulation. Emotional manipulators are experts who reverse things, rationalize, argue, and explain things. They can retire so smoothly that you can sit and look at black, which they call white – and so convincing that you start to doubt how you feel. Over time, this is so concealed and eroded that it can change your sense of reality.

Warning: Emotional manipulation is very dangerous! If you start to carry paper and pen and mark in the conversation, it isn't comforting for the emotional manipulator. Feel free to let them know that you feel "unforgettable" now that you want to record their words for future generations. The most outspoken thing about this is that having to do something like this is an obvious example of why you should seriously consider removing yourself from the scope in the first place. If you want to use your laptop to protect yourself, then the OL nonsense meter should now blink steadily!

4. Inside GUI. Emotional manipulators are excellent criminal merchants. They may make you feel guilty for speaking loudly or not, emotionally or not enough, giving and caring, or not giving and caring. Anything is a fair game, and it is easy to cause emotional manipulators. Emotional manipulators rarely express their needs or desires publicly-they obtain what they want through emotional manipulation. Guilt is not the only form but an effective form. Most of us do anything necessary conditionally to reduce our inner feelings. Another powerful emotion used is compassion.

The emotional manipulator is a huge victim. They inspire a deep sense of need for support, care, and nurturing. Emotional manipulators rarely fight or get dirty by themselves. The mad thing is that when you do it for them (they will never ask for it directly), they might turn around and say that they certainly don't want or expect you to do anything! Try not to fight with others or do dirty work for them. The most important line is "I fully believe that you can solve this problem yourself"-check the response and write down the nonsense again.

5. Emotional manipulators will fight. They don't deal with things directly. They will gossip behind your back, and eventually, let others tell you that they don't speak their own words. They are passive and aggressive, which means they will find subtle ways to let you know that they are not happy little campers. They will tell you what they want to hear and then make a lot of noise to destroy it. For example: "Of course, I hope you go back to school, dear, you know I will support you." Then on the test night, you sit at the table, poker friends show up, and the children cry on TV. Blast, the dog needs to walk-"Sweetie" has been sitting on the ass, looking at you blankly. Dare to call them this behavior? "Well, can't you expect life to stop because you stop the exam? Crying, screaming, or strangling them-only the last one can bring long-term benefits and may put you in jail.

6. If you have a pain, the emotional manipulator will have a brain tumor! Regardless of your situation, the emotional manipulator may already exist or already exists-but only ten times worse. After some time, it is difficult to feel the emotional connection with the emotional manipulator because they have a way to derail the conversation and refocus themselves. If you call them this behavior, they are likely to be hit hard or very critical and call you selfish-or claim to be your focus. The fact is that even if you know that this is not the case, you still cannot complete the proof task. Do not disturb-trust your instincts and walk away!

7. Emotional manipulators can influence the emotions of those around them. When the emotional manipulator feels sad or angry, the entire room will tremble – it brings a deep instinctual response to find some way to balance the emotional climate. The fastest way is to make the emotional manipulator feel better-fix Something damaged. Persist in such a loser for too long, you will get stuck and depend on each other, and even forget that you need not mention that you have the right to meet it.

8. Emotional manipulators are not responsible. They take no duty for themselves or their actions-always related to what everyone else "does to them." One of the easiest

paths to spot emotional manipulators is that they often try to establish intimacy by sharing deeply personal information as early as possible, which is usually the "fascinated and sorry for me" variety. At first, you might think that this kind of person is very sensitive, emotionally open, and maybe a few vulnerable. Believe me, when I tell that an emotional manipulator is as vulnerable as rabies, there are always problems or crises to overcome.

Conclusion

Based on the above content, I concluded that there are many ways of manipulation, and you can defend yourself from manipulation by knowing the signs and tricks of manipulation.

Manipulation is a social influence that aims to change the behavior or perception of others through indirect, deceptive, or villa strategies. Manipulators use manipulation techniques such as gaslighting, projection, move the target rod, change the theme, smear movement, devaluation, mischief, and triangulation.

Psychological manipulation is an improper influence through mental distortion and emotional exploitation, the purpose of which is to seize the victim's power, control, interests, and privileges. Psychological manipulation is usually accomplished through covert aggression, which is such a cover-up subtle that it is not easy to detect. Manipulation skills involve two things: hiding aggressive intentions and behaviors, fully understanding the opponent's psychological vulnerability to know which tactics may be the most effective weapon against them.

There are many types of emotional manipulation, such as frequent victims, two single jobs, a triangulation machine, shockwave, projector, deliberate misunderstanding, flirting, iron fast, and multiple offenders.

Manipulative leaders use subtle methods such as gaslighting to distort reality. For resisting this manipulation, take a step back from what is happening and re-attract your senses. There are five common workplace manipulators, such as dramatist, shunt, twister, fitter, and bully.

Emotional influence looks like a friendly gesture, but if you learn how to recognize standard manipulation methods, you will never be someone else's on the string. We encounter many manipulators every day. Some people pretend to helpless, skilled text player, unrealistic promises, parental manipulation, guilty innocent, exaggerated feeling of self-importance, the king of sin, silent forgiver, threat, self-esteem attacker, too many critics, and competitors.

You are being manipulated if people let you speak first, distort the facts, engage in intellectual and bureaucratic bullying, act like martyrs, criticize you, use your insecurity against you, deal with your feelings, and give you the silent treatment.

Manipulation can be difficult to detect, especially in friendship. The reason is that no one wants to admit the favorite person in the world is manipulative. Sometimes it isn't easy to see that you are being used until you are deeply in friendship. In friendship, you are being manipulated if your friends are passive, aggressive, in power travel, demand many benefits. Self-care and self-love are the top priorities in every relationship. So, listen to your instincts and pay attention to the signs.

The storyteller is an emotional puppet master and rational director who use their ultimate power to manipulate emotions and fully control the characters and their captive audience.

Empathy is happening; the ability to feel another person's feelings can generate a lot of pressure as the ultimate positive value and a pathway to a friendlier from another perspective. 'The empathic understanding of others' experience, just like human vision, touch smell is the basic human talent.' We must strike a balance between emotions and thoughts, and between ourselves and others to get ourselves into others' predicament. Otherwise, empathy will become a trap. Overly sympathetic people may not be able to make decisions in their best interest.

People use assertive, passive, aggressive, passive attacks, and maneuverability communication styles when they try to meet their needs when dealing with business, whether they solve problems, negotiate results, or resolve conflicts. People who adopt a decisive style will communicate their needs without assuming that others are responsible for meeting those needs. People who use passive type will not share their needs; they will only take a step back and accept whatever others give them.

Manipulative self-disclosure will provide unwanted personal information to gain social credibility, obtaining more valuable information from manipulated targets. Personal information is precious in social activities. Personal information may enhance the information receiver's capabilities and put the information provider in a potentially vulnerable position. Manipulators abuse the social exchange system by sharing unsolicited personal data, which puts pressure on targets to share their valuable knowledge.

People want to manipulate others because they want to feel better about themselves. They prevailed and blamed the victims. People with personality disorders such as antisocial personality disorder will not regret manipulating others. The people who use you will make you feel special, but it will also make it difficult for you to set boundaries. In this way, they have power and control in the relationship.

Sometimes mean facial expression depicts many words. Beware of aggressive facial expression such as yielding head tilt, condescending glasses, dirty appearance and dead eyes, eyeball rolling, shaking head, and prolonged eye contact without blinking or talking.

You can recognize and handle manipulative relationships by knowing your fundamental human rights, keeping your distance, avoiding personalization and self-blame, and safely dealing with bullies and setting consequences.

If you can realize that you have a manipulative tendency, you have completed half of your efforts. It is important to remember that you can control your behavior and remember that you may have difficulty getting rid of old habits at first. There are many ways to guard against people who might try to manipulate you. These include; you should stay with someone knowledgeable and helpful, keep recalling yourself of your goals and priorities, convey your intentions, call it as if you saw it, leave early, know that empathy can be used against you, and stand up again.

Body Language

Introduction

Body language is a kind of nonverbal communication. In this type of communication, body behavior is the opposite of words and is used to express or convey information. Such actions include facial expressions, body postures, gestures, eye movements, touch, and space. Body language exists in both animals or humans, but this Book focuses on interpreting human body language. It is also called kinematics.

However, body language is an essential part of communication, and most body language occurs without consciousness. For example, when you go on a blind date, you may start slapping your feet nervously without realizing it. Fortunately, by learning more about this subject, we can become proficient in understanding others' gestures.

Body language cannot be confused with sign language because sign language is a complete language like spoken language, has a complex grammar system, and exhibits essential characteristics that exist in all languages. On the other hand, body language has no grammatical structure. It must be interpreted broadly, rather than having an absolute meaning corresponding to a specific action, so it is not a language similar to sign language. Because of popular culture, it is called "language."

In a society, people have an accepted explanation for specific behavior. The answer varies by country/region or culture. On this point, there is controversy about whether body language is universal. Body language is a part of non-verbal communication and a supplement to verbal communication in social interaction. Some researchers have concluded that nonverbal communication is most of the information conveyed during interpersonal interaction. It helps establish a relationship between two people and mediate the business, but it can be ambiguous.

Physical Expression

Facial expressions are an integral part of body language and emotional expression. The accurate interpretation of it depends on the comprehensive understanding of multiple symbols, such as the movements of the eyes, eyebrows, lips, nose, and cheeks, to form an impression of people's emotions and mentality. The context in which it happened, and the person's possible intentions should always be considered.

- **Happiness:** When people feel happy, they usually smile and look up more quickly. Their facial expressions and body language generally convey greater vitality.
- **Sadness:** Lack of smile and apparent reluctance to do so are signs of sorrow. Sad people are also more likely to be downcast. Their facial body language looks energetic, especially when compared to happy people.

126

- **Concentration:** When a person concentrates, their eyebrows are lowered and more focused. The colloquial expression is "weaving eyebrows." Their eyes also seem to be more concentrated, and in general, they will be more determined no focus on what task they are engaged in. Generally, positive emotions are related to looking more focused and centered overall. If a person is focused, it means that they focus their visual appreciation on a specific point or area. This process is related to mental function enhancement and is sometimes referred to as mental concentration. In this way, facial body language can additionally suggest a person's way of thinking. An obvious example can be found in daily conversations: a person looks at the person they are talking to, which is the main focus of their visual attention, while also thinking about what they are saying, which proves the enhancement of their mental function. People who do this seem to be focused on understanding others, both visually and psychologically.
- **Inattentiveness:** Inattentive facial expressions usually raise eyebrows, making the eyes look inattentive. An unfocused person will not be so enthusiastic about any task they are performing. Frustration, boredom, and anxiety are usually related to inattention.
- **Confidence:** Confident facial body language involves a more concentrated, focused, and energetic appearance. A confident person is also more likely to look up and be willing to make eye contact with others.
- **Fear:** The facial body language of a worried person usually looks stressed and lacking energy. Their eyebrows are typically raised, their foreheads may be taut, and their mouths may be partially opened. Similar to sadness, a scared person is more likely to look down with his head down. The exception is if a person is suddenly frightened or horrified: in this case, a person will instinctively step back and look at the threat's source. This is arranged instinctively to move the head away while visually identifying the threat's source to protect it from injury. However, since this is still a frightening response, their ability to concentrate will always decrease compared to the confident response that they seem to be more focused. As the eyebrows are raised, the scalp will shrink. The expression "make the hair stand upright" is an exaggeration of the feeling that the scalp suddenly shrinks due to fear. When regaining its appearance, a person's scalp can still be obtained from fear: in this case, although the situation will persist, they will always struggle or distract in fear. One way to regain the focus of people who actively use body language to convince people is to think about things from a more practical perspective. This may involve viewing something to appreciate its physical presence visually, or by physically interacting with something more directly (i.e., squeezing a pressure ball, smelling flowers, etc.).

Head and Neck Signal

The body language of the head should be combined with the body language of the neck. As far as general posture is concerned, the crown should be placed naturally. The body language transmitted by the head and neck involves various ranges of motion. However, it must be noted that the head's position should not cause the channel to stretch or compress for a long time without relief. If the neck is tightened in this way, it may inhibit its ability to convey body language information effectively. Some researchers and health practitioners have also found an association between long-term lousy head and neck posture and negative mental states. Therefore, body language involving the head and neck should not cause fatigue and should be as natural as possible. As with all kinds of body language, it is useful to understand as many other related factors as possible to identify the meaning accurately.

Nodding of the head is usually considered a "yes" sign. When used in a conversation, it may be interpreted as an agreement and encourage the speaker to continue speaking. A person nods his head to show respect for others. In this way, it is similar to the practice of Asians bowing to others with respect. Shaking your head is usually interpreted as "no." In terms of importance, this is the opposite of nodding. In India, dangling forward is the tilt of the head from side to side, which is a common sign to say "yes," "good," or "I understand in some way." Its interpretation may be ambiguous and depends mostly on the context of its application.

When combined with eyes to emphasize head lowering, this may indicate yielding. Lifting your head from a slumped posture may mean increased interest in what someone is saying.

Tilting the head to the side may indicate interest in what other people are communicating. On this basis, it may be a signal of curiosity, uncertainty, or questioning. If you support your head with your hands while tilting your head, this may be a sign of thinking about something, or in the case of an ongoing conversation, it is a sign of disinterest. Listed slightly forward and pulled back may be suspicious.

General Body Posture

Emotions can also be detected by body posture. Studies have shown that it is possible to recognize body postures more accurately than with different or neutral sensations. For example, an angry person will establish dominance over another person, and their stance will tend to approach. Compare it with people who feel fear: they feel weak, obedient, and their positions show avoidance tendencies, which is the opposite of angry people.

Sitting or standing postures also express a person's emotions. Somebody who sits on the back of the chair and leans forward sits with their heads, nods, and then discusses, which means they are open, relaxed, and can usually listen. On the other hand, someone who crosses their legs and kicks slightly means being impatient and emotionally out of the discussion.

In a standing discussion, if someone stands with hands-on-hips and feet pointing towards the speaker, it may imply that they are attentive and interested in the conversation. However, this small difference in posture can mean a lot. Standing with hands-on-hips is considered rude in Bali.

Superman's posture, with hands or fists close to the hips or lower back, while the wrapped posture moves the elbows inward. The indicator has/has no fingers inserted into the belt or pants or placed on the belt or pants, indicating that men are attractive to women.

If a person adopts the same body posture for a long time, they may look stiff or strained. They can avoid this effect by adjusting their posture regularly, even if the adjustment is small.

Chest Dedicated

When considering the information from the entire body, the chest's posture and movement are crucial factors. Generally speaking, the relative fullness or shallowness of the chest, especially around the breastbone, may be an essential indicator of mood and attitude. When assessing the chest's body language in daily situations, it will automatically consider these shapes and volume factors.

When the chest's posture is fuller, and the position is relatively forward, this is a sign of confidence. If it protrudes forward, it may indicate that the person wants to stand out in society and express body beliefs. When you pull your chest back, this may indicate a lack of confidence.

Suppose one person's chest is close to another person. In that situation, it may be a sign of paying close attention to them during the conversation, or in other cases, it may be a sign of physical assertion and aggression.

Touching the chest may indicate different things. A person with a hands-on heart might do this to emphasize that they are sincere about what they say. Rubbing the chest (significantly above the heart) may be a sign of discomfort, which may be caused by stress and pressure. Like other chest body language examples, it may be related to a person's heart rate.

128

Especially the Shoulders

"Shoulders shape how others think about us, show our health and emotions, and help us communicate." Like the chest, the shoulder's posture is a sign of body language that is easy to observe. When the shoulders are facing back, and the torso is forward, confidence is usually expressed. If the shoulders are bent, and the body is bent forward, it may indicate a lack of confidence or low self-esteem. It may also show feelings of depression or sadness. Usually, if a person relaxes, their shoulders will be lowered. If they feel nervous or anxious, elevate them.

Shrugging your shoulders and moving up and down quickly are usually signs of not knowing something or not helping in some way. A flexible and robust shoulder can partially highlight its protruding position on the body, conveying vitality, and natural rhythm. Conversely, if the shoulders are weak and lack mobility, perhaps due to frequent use of the drooping position, this can be frustrating.

Gesture

Gestures refer to actions made by body parts (such as hands, arms, fingers, head, legs). They can be voluntary or involuntary. Arm gestures can be interpreted in many ways. In discussions, when a person stands with hands crossed, sits down, or even walks, this is usually not a welcome gesture. This may mean that they are closed-minded and may not want to listen to the speaker's views. Another arm gesture includes crossed arms, which indicates insecurity and a lack of confidence.

Barbara Pease and Allan Pease, the authors of The Authoritative Body Language Book, said everyone shrugged. Shrugging is an excellent example of a familiar gesture used to show that a person does not understand what you say. They continued: "This is multiple gestures with three main parts."

"The exposed palms showed nothing, the hands were covered to protect the throat from attack, and the brows were raised. This is a universal, submissive greeting."

Gestures usually represent the state of the person, making the gesture. Relaxed hands indicate self-confidence and self-confidence, while clasped indicators may be interpreted as signs of stress or anger. If a person is twisting their hands, it means you are feeling nervous and anxious.

Finger gestures are also commonly used to illustrate a person's voice and indicate their health status. In some cultures, using the index finger to point is considered acceptable. However, in other cultures, pointing at a person may be considered offensive. For example, someone with Hindu beliefs would consider it a condemning attack. Instead, they point with their thumbs. Thus, in countries such as the United States, South Africa, France, Lebanon, and Germany, a thumbs-up gesture may indicate "OK" or "OK." But this is also insulted in other countries such as Iran, Bangladesh, and Thailand, which is equivalent to showing the middle finger in the United States.

In most cultures, "head-nodding" is used to mean "yes" or agreement. This is a bowing style of bowing-the person bows symbolically but stops motionless and nods. Bowing is a gesture of obedience, so "nodding of the head" shows that we follow another person's perspective. Studies conducted on people who are born deaf and mute show that they also use this gesture to indicate "yes."

Shake Hands

A handshake is a conventional greeting ceremony, usually used when meeting, greeting, congratulating, expressing friendship, or reaching an agreement. They often portray self-confidence and emotional levels through factors such as grip and eye contact. Research has classified several handshaking methods, such as finger squeeze, bone crusher (handshake too strong), fish foot fish (handshake too weak), etc. Handshake is quite famous in the United States and is suitable for use between men and women. Woman. However, in Muslim culture, men are not allowed to shake hands or touch women in any way, and vice versa.

Similarly, in Hindu culture, Hindu men may never shake hands with women. Instead, they raised their hands to greet the women like a prayer. This is very common in India.

A firm, the friendly handshake has long been suggested in the business world to make a profound first impression, and greetings are believed to date back to ancient times to show strangers that you have no weapons.

Breathe

Body language related to breathing and breathing patterns can indicate a person's mood and state of mind; therefore, the relationship between body language and breathing is often considered in business meetings and presentations. Generally, deep breathing (using more diaphragm and abdomen) is thought to convey an impression of ease and confidence. On the contrary, shallow breathing, too fast breathing, is generally considered to give the impression of more tension or anxiety.

Some business consultants (such as those who promote neurolinguistic programming) recommend mirroring a person's breathing pattern to convey the impression of mutual understanding.

Different Body Movements

Covering the mouth will suppress the sensation and may even make people uncertain. This may additionally mean that they are thinking hard and may not be sure what to say next. Your communication through body language and nonverbal signals affects how others perceive you, how they like and respect you, or whether they trust you.

Unfortunately, many people send out confusing or negative nonverbal signals without even knowing. When this happens, the connection and trust will be broken.

The Language of Mind

We talk about the angle of thinking about thinking and physical and mental issues, which also implies that artificial intelligence research projects may help us eliminate some critical philosophical problems about the causes and their relationship with the brain.

We have these working bodies and brains, but we also have brains. We see, hear, think, feel, plan, take action, take action; we are conscious. From the outside, you will see an appropriately adjusted mechanism. From the inside, we have experienced our thoughts, feelings, thinking, sharing, and being vital to our self-concept. It also raises many philosophical and scientific questions. When interpreting objective things (behavior, etc.) from the outside, you need to integrate some neural mechanisms and computer systems. We have an example to explain this.

When interpreting thought, especially the conscious aspect of thought, it seems that the standard paradigm that combines mechanisms and explains things such as objective behavioral processes leaves a gap in interpretation. How do all these treatments bring you a subjective experience, and why do you feel that it seems that it cannot be solved directly by these methods from the inside? People call it a problem of consciousness, not a puzzle, such as explaining behavior.

Then, the discussion can be expanded in 1000 directions. Can you use your brain to explain conscious experiences? Do you need something fundamentally new? Does it exist? Recently, I have been interested in solving this problem in a slightly different direction. We have conscious first-order issues, and then people from AI research, neuroscience, or psychology usually have a hard time saying: "There is a problem here, but I'm not sure what I can do with it."

The point I have been thinking about recently is to improve my level. I don't understand where this slogan comes from, "Anything you can do, I can do." Sometimes this is attributed to my thesis consultant Doug Hofstadter, but I don't think he is. I have seen it attributed to Rudolf Carnap, but I don't think it is him either. In any case, I have recently been thinking about the so-called conscious meta-problem. The first-order question of consciousness explores how all these processes produce conscious experiences. The meta-question asks why we believe there is a consciousness problem, especially why we say there is a consciousness problem everywhere.

Belief in consciousness and confidence in consciousness issues are universal. So, by the way, this is consistent with this method, which is all fantasy or nonsense. Nevertheless, there is still an interesting psychological problem. People saying, "Hey, I'm conscious" everywhere is a fact of human behavior. They report subjective experiences. Even in children, you will encounter various confusions related to conscious experience. How do I know that my knowledge of red is the same as your knowledge of green? Can people with only black and white vision understand the feeling of purple? These are facts of human behavior.

There is an exciting research project, trying to study the intuitions of adults, children, cross-cultural, cross-language, to try to find accurate data about puzzles, and most interestingly, try to find the mechanism that confuses. Produce this behavior. Presumably, this is the basis of human behavior. Human behavior is ultimately explainable. It seems that we should be able to find the mechanism that causes this deliberate confusion. In principle, psychology, neuroscience, and artificial intelligence project aims to find practical computing tools suitable for social situations and show that what we are happening has particular applicability to artificial intelligence.

You can find odd jobs related to psychology, neuroscience, and philosophy. I think it has not been submitted to the research plan, but I have been working hard to promote it later because it is a small part of the mind-body problem that we can solve. What makes it tractable is that in the end, we can start trying to explain some of the behaviors we can manipulate, which is often difficult for consciousness to do.

Some people are committed to the so-called "artificial consciousness," trying to generate consciousness in the machine, but in this case, the whole standard problem is complicated. In anthropology, for neuroscience and psychology, you will start with people you know and look for the neural correlates of consciousness and underlying mechanisms. However, in an AI system, you will not begin with a design, you know. It isn't easy to understand the operating standards to meet the expected system counting requirements.

Therefore, this is a potential operating standard, such as expressing confusion about the type of consciousness we are engaged in. Once you have an AI system and say, "I know in principle that I am just a bunch of silicon circuits, but from a first-person perspective, I feel it's more than that," then maybe we may be understanding the mechanism of consciousness. Of course, if this happens by someone programming a machine to imitate superficial human behavior, it will not be so exciting. On the other hand, if we get there by finding out the mechanisms that work in the social situation and let the AI system implement these mechanisms, we discover through some relatively natural process, which A) discovers consciousness itself and B) Confused by this fact. At least it will be exciting.

Will every possible intelligent system experience itself in some way or model itself as thoughtful? Is the language of thinking inevitable in an AI system with a specific model of its own? If you have an AI system that simulates the world, and you have not included yourself in the equation, then it may need the language in your head to talk about others, if it wants to model and model itself from a third-person perspective. Suppose we are trying to achieve artificial intelligence. In this case, it is natural for AIs to have their models, especially when they have introspective self-models; they can understand certain situations from a first-person perspective.

Suppose what you will hurt AI, and in ordinary people, it will cause harm and pain. Your AI will say, "Please don't do that. That's very bad." Introspectively speaking, this model can recognize that someone caused one of the so-called painful states. Is it inevitable that the introspective self-model begins to model itself as something conscious in AI? I suspect that the mechanisms of self-modeling and introspection will naturally lead to these intuitions, in which case artificial intelligence will model itself as intended. The next step is whether this AI will naturally experience consciousness in some confusing way, because this may be difficult to compare with the underlying mechanism and to challenge to explain.

I am not saying that AI systems will inevitably experience this situation and make these reports. After all, many people have not published these reports. But in humans, at least some underlying mechanisms tend to push people toward discovering these weird and exciting psychological phenomena in themselves, and I think it's natural for AI to do the same. There is also a research project for AI researchers to generate a system with a specific model of what is going on inside, and see if this might lead to confusion about the expression of belief in things like consciousness.

So far, the only research direction I know of is a small project completed by several researchers from Luke Muehlhauser and Buck Shlegeris last year. They tried to build a short theorem prover, a tiny software agent with some fundamental axioms, to model colors and processes. It will report to you, such as "Shadow XX is red," and it knows that it might go wrong sometimes. It might say: "I represent this red color." Through a certain number of fundamental axioms, they managed to make it a certain amount of confusion. For example, "How does my experience of this redness relate to this potential circuit? the same?"

I will not say that this simple software agent will replicate anything, such as the mechanism of human consciousness or our introspective access to it. Nevertheless, there is still a research project here, and I encourage my AI friends to research psychology, neuroscience, and philosophy.

In the final analysis, what does this mean? Assuming that we do find the mechanism for generating consciousness reports and consciousness confusion, will this solve the whole problem in some way? People like Dan Dennett undoubtedly want to accept this view. Explaining these mechanisms is a big fantasy. Therefore, you will define illusions and explain consciousness issues.

You can select this row, but you don't have to make it enjoyable. In the sense of a philosopher, you may be purely a realist about consciousness, holding this consciousness. These reports are facts of human behavior, and there will be mechanisms for generating them. If you are a realist about consciousness like me, the hope is that the tools that create these consciousness reports and this confusion will also be closely linked to the consciousness mechanism.

I think this is a challenge to the theory of consciousness. There are currently millions of views. Maybe it's information integration; perhaps this is a global workspace, perhaps this is that. To make your consciousness theory reasonable, you must tell some possible stories to explain why the proposed consciousness mechanism itself may also generate our consciousness report. Otherwise, the information will become strange and independent in the phenomenon itself.

For me, it is not clear whether many theories meet this standard. From the perspective of information integration theory, I still don't know why those theories that integrate more and more information are likely to discard the system that makes these reports. It seems that these reports may be out of touch with various forms of information integration in an exciting way. Therefore, I think this is a challenge to the theory of consciousness, a challenge to artificial intelligence research and philosophy.

How Many Languages of Human Mind?

According to Roy H Williams, the mind has 12 languages. They provide an integral part of clean, analytical thinking. It is these 12 languages that enable us to perceive reality. The signal received in one mental language can be enhanced or contradictory to the signal received in another language. The signal enhancement deepens the perception. Signal contradiction

1. The information sent by the shape-angle is different from the curve.
2. Numbers-the language of relativity. More or less?
3. Phonemes-sounds represented by letters.
4. Color-usually combined with shape and gloss.
5. Proximity-near/far, big/small, left/right, up/down, etc.
6. Music-any non-phonetic sound.
7. Radiation-energy is emitted outward or absorbed inward.
8. Exercise-fast/slow
9. Symbols-messages with secondary meaning.
10. Taste-the tongue can do it.
11. Feeling-skin and muscle can do it.
12. Smell-the nose can do it.

These languages help us build concrete thoughts and visual effects in our minds.

How the Language We Speak Affects Our Way of Thinking?

No matter what language is used to express our thoughts, all human thinking styles are similar, or whether the language we speak affects our thinking style. For centuries, this question has plagued philosophers, psychologists, linguists, neuroscientists, and many others. Everyone has a strong opinion on this.

At present, we still do not have a clear answer to this question. However, we have collected evidence (mainly from a linguistic analysis of language and psycholinguistic research), giving us a good understanding of the problem. As I will try to prove, the evidence demonstrates that there is a universal foundation in the perception and thinking of all people. At the same time, language is a filter, enhancer, or frame of perception and thought.

The story began with the first American linguists who (scientifically) described some Native Americans' languages. Compared with the languages they learned in school (Ancient Greek, Latin, English, German, etc.), they found many embarrassing differences. They discovered sounds that have never been heard in European languages (such as jetting consonants), strange meanings encoded in grammar (such as certain parts of verbs refer to the shape of objects) or new grammatical categories (such as evidence, that is, knowledge-related Source) Facts in the sentence).

Not surprisingly, some of these linguists concluded that this strange language system should influence their speakers' thinking. Edward Sapir, one of the familiar influential linguists in the United States, wrote: "The worlds in different societies are different worlds, not just the same world with different labels" (Sapir, 1949: 162).

For centuries, people have always thought that words are just labels for objects, and different languages attach other strings of sounds to things, or more precisely, to concepts. It is now suggested that people who speak different languages may have different views of the world. Or, more fundamentally, people can only perceive all aspects of the world with words in their language.

True? One useful (instructive) method of testing that Sapir advocates focus on color perception. The colors are continuously distributed (depending on the light) but can be perceived. Interestingly, the number of basic terms of color is far less than the number of tones we can perceive. Moreover, the number is different from one language to another. For example, Russian has 12 basic terms for colors, while Dani (the language spoken in New Guinea) has only two: mili (for cool colors) and mole (for warm colors).

The researchers found that, not surprisingly, Dany can distinguish different hues (such as red, yellow, and orange), even though they have the same label (mole). They also found that people can better distinguish between two shades of different names (blue and green). Because different

133

languages have different definitions of color continuity, people who speak other languages pay extra attention to color. In a sense, Sapir is half right.

This effect of framing or filtering is the main effect we can expect (in terms of language), coming from perception and thought. Language does not limit our capacity to perceive or think about the world but instead focus our perception, attention, and beliefs on specific aspects of the world. Indeed, this may be useful.

Chinese children start counting earlier than English children because Chinese numbers are more regular and transparent than English numbers ("11" in Chinese is "ten"). Similarly, people who speak specific Australian languages are better able to position themselves in space than people who speak English (they usually go from south to north, even in the dark), possibly because their language has absolute spatial significance. This means that when referring to distant objects, they are not talking about "that car" or "that tree over there," but "the car going north" or "the tree going south." Because they need to know the direction of using their language for speech expression, they are more accustomed to paying attention to the essential points than we are.

Therefore, different languages focus on their speakers' attention to all aspects of the environment (physical or cultural). But how do we know which part? In essence, we see what language is essential to people.

Our linguists say that these salient aspects are either lexicalized or grammaticalized. Lexicalization means that you have words for concepts, and they are shorthand for these concepts. This is useful because you don't need to explain (or explain) the meaning you want to convey. You don't have to say "cold white things falling from the sky in the cold winter," but snow.

We don't have anything. We can only say some words about essential or significant concepts in our culture. This explains why the dictionaries (or sets of words) in the language are entirely different. A dictionary is like a big, open schoolbag: some names are created or borrowed with coins because you need to use them to refer to new objects and then put them in the schoolbag. Instead, some items are no longer used, and then their words are deleted from the packaging.

Certain aspects of the world are even more deeply encoded by language-to some extent. They are part of the language grammar. It will help if you consider them when constructing sentences in the language. Linguists say they are grammaticalized.

Dirirbal is a language spoken in North Australia. For example, there are four noun categories (such as English gender). The assignment of nouns to each class is arbitrary: Category I includes animal and human male nouns; Category II has female nouns, water, fire, and combat object names; Category III contains only edible plant nouns; Category IV is like A remaining class in which all remaining words are put together.

This grammatical classification of nouns involves a coherent view of the world, including primitive myths. For example, although animals are classified as Category I, bird nouns are found in Type II because Dyirbal people believe that birds are the soul of dead women (female nouns are found in Category II).

Similarly, the way people think about time is deeply encoded in the grammar of most languages. In some languages (such as English), time is tripartite: past, present, and future. However, languages like Imas used in New Guinea have four past types, ranging from recent events to the distant past. And languages like Chinese also lack grammatical tenses.

In short, language is the filter of perception, memory, and attention. Whenever we construct or interpret language descriptions, we need to focus on specific aspects of the information described. Interestingly, some brain imaging devices now allow us to examine these effects from a neurobiological perspective.

For example, in this interesting paper, the author proved that language affects the absolute perception of color, and this effect is more robust in the right field of vision than in the left area of the image. Compared with the color-coded by the same name, the discrimination of colors coded by different words also caused a faster and more robust response in the left hemisphere language area. The authors concluded that the left temporal, temporal, parietal language areas could act as a top-down control source to regulate the visual cortex's activation.

This is a good example (in a broad sense) of current biolinguistics research, which helps to a better and balanced understanding of classic issues in linguistics, such as the relationship between language and thought.

How the Limits of The Mind Shape Body Language?

When we speak, our sentences will flow like sound. Unless we are angry, we are Do not Speak one word in Answer: Time But this characteristic of language is not how the language itself is organized. Sentences are composed of stories: discrete units of meaning and language form. We can combine them into sentences in many ways. This disconnect between speech or language raises a problem. How can children learn discrete tongue units from the messy sound waves heard during their incredible childhood?

In the past few decades, psycholinguists have proved that children are "intuitive statisticians" who can discover sound frequency patterns. The order of sound rate is much less than intr. This means that into is more likely to appear within a word (for example, very interesting), and the quality may span two words (dark tree). Allowing children to see patterns found in the subconscious can help them figure out where one story begins and where another story ends.

One of the exciting findings of this work is that other species can also track the frequency of certain sound combinations like human children. It turns out that compared to other animals, we are worse at choosing specific sound modes.

Speech Rat

"Language Unlimited" is an almost contradictory view that our language ability can come from the human mind's limits. These restrictions determine the structure of the thousands of languages we see all over the world.

In the past ten years, researchers led by researchers led by Juan Toro have raised a compelling argument. Toro's team investigated whether children have better language models for learning consonants than those associated with vowels, and vice versa.

They show that children quickly learn a meaningless word pattern, and they all follow the same basic shape: you have a consonant, then a specific vowel (say a), and then another consonant, namely The same vowel is another consonant, and the last is a different vowel (for example, e). Words that follow this pattern will use Latin, nudity, while stories that break this pattern will use duotones, bit ago, and tube. Toro's team tested 11-month-old babies and found that the children were learning well.

But when the pattern involves changes in consonants rather than vowels, children have not learned it. When children see Dadan, Bobin, and Luribo, their first and second consonants are the same, but the third consonant is different. Children usually don't see them in this way. Human children have found that it is much easier to detect general timbre that contains vowels than phonemes that affect consonants.

The research team also tested mice. It is known that the rat's brain can detect and process the difference between vowels and consonants. The disadvantage is that the rat's brain is too right: the rat quickly learns vowels and consonants' rules.

Unlike mice, children seem to be inclined to pay attention to specific patterns involving vowels rather than ways that affect consonants. In contrast, mice look for patterns in various data. Their detection methods are not limited so that they can generalize rules about invisible to human babies' syllables.

The prejudice of this way of thinking seems to have affected the structure of the existing language.

Impossible Language

We can see this by seeing the Semitic peoples' languages, including Hebrew, Arabic, Amharic, and Tigrinya. These languages have a unique way of organizing words. The system is built in a system where each term can be defined by its consonant (more or less), but the vowels will change to tell you some grammatical information.

For example, the word "vigilant" in modern Hebrew is just three consonants sh-m-r. To say "I guard," you put the vowel a-a in the consonant's middle and add a unique suffix to provide shamarti. To say "I will guard," you put in a completely different vowel, in this case, e-o, which means that you add the prefix glottal stop when performing "I" defense to make the sound of "humor." These three consonants are rarely stable, but the vowels change to make the past or future tense.

We can also see this in a language like English. The present tense of the verb "to ring" is just a ring. However, the bell in the past rang, and you used another form, now the bell rang. The same consonant (round), but different vowels.

Our great human prejudice to store consonant patterns as words may support this grammatical system. We can learn grammatical rules that involve changing vowels quickly, so we can find languages where this happens frequently. Specific languages (such as the Semitic) make extensive use of this language. However, imagine a language that is the opposite of Semitic: words are the basic vowels pattern, and grammar is done by changing the consonants surrounding the vowels. Linguists have never found a language.

We can invent a language, but if Toro's grades persist, children cannot learn naturally. Consonants anchor words, not vowels. This shows that our central human brain is biased towards specific language modes, and not biased towards other equally possible language modes. This has had a profound impression on the languages we see all over the world.

Charles Darwin once said that due to the rapid development of our "psychological power,", human language ability is also different from other species. Today's evidence shows that this is actually because we have different kinds of intelligence. We not only have more charm than other species. We have a more excellent appeal.

Smiles and Laughter

Smiling is a common sign that someone is happy. It conveys the message that you are not dangerous and requires people to accept you personally. The most striking thing about a smile is its contagiousness. You smile at someone, and it will take them back and forth by returning the smile. Interestingly, sincere and fake smiles are both correct. According to some scientists, a neuron affects the part of the brain responsible for recognizing faces and facial expressions. When you see a smiling face or frown, this neuron causes a "mirror" response. In other words, it forces you to copy the facial expressions you visit.

This explains why the more smiles, the more positive reactions from others. By practicing smiling – a real smile or a fake smile will improve your overall experience with others. Of course, this sounds worth trying!

You can identify a real smile from a fake smile by the appearance of characteristic wrinkles around the eyes. The corners of the lips are pulled up, and the muscles around the eyes contract, producing wrinkles. However, the fake smile only includes the lips. Another sign of an artificial smile is that it appears more robust on the left side of the face and then on the right side.

Since most people cannot consciously distinguish between a fake smile and a real smile, they will still be like you, even if your smile is forced. This is why you pretend to smile when you feel that a smile always makes no sense.

Natural or Synthetic?

Psychologists have made many distinctions in human smiles' characteristics, but the most fundamental difference is the difference in a real smile and a fake smile. Fake smiles have many uses, usually pretending to show pleasure, sociality, or agreement. These are easy to remark because they involve the mouth and not the eyes. We can technically define the physiological difference between a real smile and a fake smile: two muscles are affected, the major musculus major and oculus. A genuine smile involves muscles and fake smiles, the former but not the latter. Fake smiles involve eyes more than mouths: in a sense, they are only half of the story.

There is a real sense of pleasure in the smile, which not only pulls the corners of the lips but also opens the corners of the lips. But the muscles around the eyes contract, and in the fake simulated smile, only the smiling lips are involved.

Scientists can distinguish between real and fake smiles using a coding system called the Facial Action Coding System (FACS), which was designed by Professor Paul Ekman of the University of California and Dr. Wallace V Friesen of the University of Kentucky. Real smiles are produced by the subconscious brain, which means they are automatic. When you feel happy, the signal passes through your brain's emotional processing part, causing your mouth muscles to move, your cheeks are raised, your eyes are wrinkled, and your eyebrows are slightly drooping.

There may also be lines around the eyes in the fake smile, and the cheeks may be gathered, it looks as if the eyes are shrinking, and the smile is real. Some signs distinguish these smiles from genuine smiles. When the smile is natural, the naked part of the eyebrows and the eyelids (folded eyelids) will move downward, and the ends of the eyebrows will drop slightly.

Smile as A Submission Signal

People generally think that smiles and Laughter are signals that a person is happy. We cry at birth, a smile from five weeks, and laugh between the fourth and fifth months. The baby soon learned that crying caught our attention-and, the smile kept us there. Recent research on chimpanzees, our closest primate cousin, shows. Serve a deeper and more primitive purpose.

To show their aggressiveness, the apes showed their lower fangs, warning them that they could bite. When humans become aggressive by lowering or pushing the lower lip forward, they have the same gestures because their primary function is to cover the lower jaw's teeth. The chimpanzee's smile was pleasant, and one of the chimpanzees showed submission to the other dominant chimpanzee. Reflecting on our behavior's similarities, we usually interpret it as a pleasant expression, but this is not correct. "This chimpanzee's smile is called the "face of fear," with the jaws open, showing the upper and lower teeth-closed-and the horns pulling back and forth, just like a human smile, although the underlying emotions are different. The "face of fear" is Submissive, conveying, "I am at least not threatening to you."

Why Smile Is Contagious

There is much evidence that body language is "mirrored." We will automatically copy the facial expressions of others. We will respond. In social groups, contagious people will respond and evaluate those who smile. Compared with those who don't smile, the smile will be different and even more festive, even if they show the same is true for a false smile.

"Laugh, the world laughs with you; cry, you cry alone."

This establishes a virtuous circle for smiling people and a self-destructive circle for non-smiling people. Therefore, in the case of sales, hospitality, and negotiation. This person smiles first.

The possibility of others smiling, thereby increasing trust and friendliness, making others more cooperative and helpful. In the early stages of business or legal negotiations, people evaluate each other; both sides of the form will generate more positive responses, leading to more successful results and higher sales ratios. Smiling naturally can help make connections. People are better together.

Professor Ulf Dimberg of Uppsala University in Sweden conducted an experiment that revealed how your subconscious mind directly controls your facial muscles. Using a device that obtains electrical signals from muscle fibers, he measured the facial muscle activity of 120 volunteers and showed pictures of happy and angry faces. They are told to frown at what they see, smile, or show blank expressions. Sometimes, at first, they are said to try the opposite of what they see-frowning and smiling. Or with a smiling brow. The results showed that the volunteers did not fully control their facial muscles. Although it is easy to frown at a photo of an angry man, it is more challenging to smile. Even if the volunteers consciously tried to control their natural reactions, the twitching of their facial muscles told a different story-they were mirroring the expressions they saw, even if they didn't want to.

Professor Ruth Campbell of University College London speculated a "mirror neuron" in the brain, which triggers the part responsible for recognizing faces and expressions and triggers an instant mirror response. In other words, whether we realize it or not, we will automatically copy the facial expressions we see. This is why, even when you are dissatisfied, smiling regularly is essential for maintaining body language function because smiling directly affects others' attitudes and reactions to you.

Common Smile Types

The following is a summary and analysis of familiar smiles; you may see every day:

Lip L Smile

Without showing your teeth, spread your lips along a straight line, and lay your entire face. Think of Mona Lisa. Smiling means hidden thoughts and secrets, or a restrained attitude, so-called shut up and smile.

A study shows that women usually interpret this smile as a sign of rejection. It is a favorite of women, and they don't want to reveal that they don't like unspecified people. A woman might say to another woman, "She is a capable woman and knows what she wants," followed by a subtle smile, covering her thoughts. Pick a business magazine or many annual company reports. May be greeted by the thin smiles of professional CEOs, who talk about the company's prospects or the great potential of the business concept they are nurturing without revealing its essential nature.

Indulgent Smile

When your muscles pull your mouth's sides in opposite directions, one side is up, and the other side is down; you have been twisted. What are you doing shows faced with the opposite emotions on both sides of you, the observer must figure out this crooked smile's meaning? In Western culture, this smile may be deliberate, expressing irony, embarrassment, or sarcasm.

A vertical smile makes one side of your mouth entertainingly move up, while the other side is restrained and pulled down. Subconsciously, when your mouth finds this position, you are

Show your happiness and pain. Harrison Ford or the late Princess Diana both mastered the pose of a downward smile.

This gesture elicits a protective response from other people. Mouth down indicates sadness, anxiety, or other negative emotions; mouth up suggests that the person is not angry-if he has ever; both sides of the mouth will fall off. The upward rotation of the lips softens the gesture so that the movement is not threatened.

The Smile of The Jaw

This kind of practiced smile with downward jaw release is a favorite of politicians, movie stars, and celebrities. Knowing how contagious Laughter is. A person who wants to elicit a positive reaction from the admiring public will have his jaw drop. This shows that a playful and entertaining laugh is more infectious than smiling, so next time you are in the company and want to cause a kind of playfulness in the audience, use the jaw smile by not looking threatening, as if laughing, other people can also feel this feeling.

Turn Around and Smile

Turning your head, lowering your head, smiling, and looking up with your lips closed, you can grasp many people's hearts. In this way, you look younger, fun, and mysterious, which is a successful combination.

When a woman smiles in her own direction, most men will melt, and women can't escape the power of a genuine and shy smile. Parents' instincts rise; the recipient of this smile wants to protect and nurture those who stare at him with this charming expression.

According to Charles Darwin, the act of looking at another person and moving their head away from the other person with a smile creates a "mixed expression" with two opposite meanings. A smile expresses welcome, while the act of turning around expresses avoidance. The tension created by these two opposing actions is often more attractive and more powerful than its parts.

Why Laughter Is Good Medicine

Like a smile, when Laughter becomes a permanent part of you, it attracts friends, improves health, and extends life. When we laugh, every organ of the body is positively affected. Our breathing speeded up, and we exercised the diaphragm muscles, neck, stomach, face, or shoulders. Laughter increases the volume of oxygen in the blood, not only helps to heal and improve blood circulation; it also expands the blood vessels near the surface of the skin. This is why people blush when they laugh. It can even lower heart rate, dilate arteries, stimulate appetite, and burn calories. Neuroscientist Henri Rubenstein (Henri Rubenstein) discovered that one minute of solid Laughter could provide 45 minutes of subsequent relaxation. Professor William Frye of Stanford University reported that laughing at 100 will do your aerobic exercise, which is equivalent to 10 minutes of exercise on a rowing machine. Medically speaking, this is why damn funny is right for you.

Why You Should Take Laughter Seriously

Studies have shown that even if people who laugh or laugh are not incredibly happy, they will become part of the "happiness zone" that proliferates in the brain's left hemisphere due to electrical activity. In one of many studies on Laughter, Richard Davidson, professor of psychology and psychiatry at the University of Wisconsin-Madison, connects subjects with an EEG (electroencephalography) machine to measure brain waves. The event showed them exciting movies, and smiles made their happy places enjoyable. Frantically. He proved that deliberately producing smiles and Laughter can make brain activity develop in the direction of spontaneous happiness.

Arnie Cann, a psychology professor at the University of North Carolina, found that humor has a positive effect on relieving stress. Cann and Shows early signs of depression. The two groups watched the video within three weeks. The group who watched comedy videos showed more symptom improvement than the control group who watched non-humorous videos. He also found that people with ulcers frowned more than people without ulcers. If you frown, put your hands on your forehead when speaking to exercise yourself.

Why Can't Our Chimpanzee Cousins Laugh and Talk?

Robert Provine and professor of psychology at the University of Maryland, discovered that human Laughter is different from our primate cousins. The chimpanzee's Laughter is a breath of breath, and the sound and rhythm are reminiscent of a woodcut by a hand saw. Each time you breathe outward or inward, you can only make one sound, and this one-to-one ratio between the breathing cycle and the vocalization makes most primates unable to speak. When humans start to walk upright, it frees the upper body from the weight-bearing function and significantly improves breathing control. People can adjust their exhalation to produce speech and Laughter. Chimpanzees have the ability to process language concepts. However, they do not have the vocal agility to convey the voice of language physically. Human beings have a wide range of freedom in the sounds we make as a direct result of walking upright.

How to Cure Humor

Laughter stimulates the body's natural painkillers; those "feel good" enhancers called "endorphins" help relieve stress and heal the body. If Norman Cousins was diagnosed with the debilitating disease, ankylosing spondylitis, the doctors told him that they could no longer support him and still live in extreme pain before his death. The cousin checked the hotel room and watched every old-school funny movie he could find: "Brother Marx," "Airplane," and "Three Heads." He looked at them over and over, laughed again, and did his best. After six months of self-laughing therapy, the doctor was surprised to find that the excellent disease was completely cured-the disease disappeared. This superb result led to the publication of Cousins' book "The Anatomy of Disease." And began a lot of research on the function of endorphins. Endorphins are chemicals released from your brain when you laugh. They have a chemical composition similar to morphine and heroin and have a calming effect on the body while building the immune system. This explains why happy people seldom get sick and suffering while complaining often gets sick.

Laugh till Cry

Laughter and crying are closely related to psychological and physical viewpoints. Think about the last time someone made a joke to you and made you buckle with Laughter; you can hardly control yourself. How do you feel afterward? You feel tingling everywhere. Your brain releases endorphins into your system, which gives you what was once called "naturally high," which is the same experience that drug addicts get when taking stimulants. People who laugh at the hard things in life often turn to drugs and alcohol to get the same feeling as the Laughter caused by endorphins. Alcohol relaxes the inhibitory effect, makes people laugh more, and releases endorphins. This is why most adaptable people will laugh more when drinking, while the unfortunate will become lonelier and even violent. One of the objects we are attracted to, Laughter and smiling faces is because they affect our autonomic nervous system. If we see a smiling face, we smile, which releases endorphins into our system. If you are surrounded by painful, unhappy people, you may also mirror their expressions and feel depressed or depressed. Working in a low environment is harmful to your health.

Smile and Laughter Are A Way of Bonding

In the absence of irritating media (such as video, radio, or books), psychology professor Robert Provine found that when you get along with people, you are 30 times more likely to laugh when you get along with others. The above, he discovered that Laughter had little to do with jokes and funny stories, but more with building relationships. He found that only 15% of our Laughter was related to marks. In Provine's study, participants were more willing to talk to themselves rather than smile when alone. Participants watched humorous video clips in three different situations: a stranger, a friend of the same sex, and a friend of the same sex. Even though there was no difference in the degree of the fun of the video clips, people who watched only ridiculous video clips laughed much less than those who watched the video with people present (whether friends or strangers). In both cases, Laughter's frequency and duration involving the other person were much more significant than when the participant was alone. In social interactions, Laughter occurs more frequently. Those lawsuits show that the more social the problem is, the more often people laugh, and the longer each laugh lasts.

Female Smile Advice

Research by Marvin Hecht or Marianne La France of Boston University has shown how to use leaders and superiors in a friendly and unfriendly state in people under subordinates to smile more. On the contrary, in social situations, outstanding people will only smile around their associates.

This research shows that in social and business situations, women's smiles are far greater than men's, making women appear subordinate or weak when they encounter memories of not smiling. Some people claim that women's extra smiles result from women's traditionally being placed in secondary roles by men. Still, other studies have shown that by the age of eight weeks, female babies' smiles far exceed those of boys, which may be natural rather than knowledgeable. The possible explanation is that smiling fits the evolutionary role of women as pacifiers and nurses. This does not suggest that a woman cannot be as authoritative as a man, but an extra smile can make her look less traditional.

Dr. Nancy Henley described women's smiles as "her app badges," often used to soothe stronger men. Her research shows that women spend 87% of the time smiling in social situations, while men spend 67%, and women are 26% more likely to get a smile from the opposite sex. Two hundred fifty-seven interviewees evaluated the attractiveness of experiments using 15 photos of women showing happiness, sadness, and neutral faces. Women with sad expressions are considered unattractive. Pictures of women who do not laugh are decoded as signs of unhappiness, while images of women who do not laugh are regarded as dominant signs. The lesson here is to allow women to reduce their smiles when dealing with dominant men or reflect the number of smiling men. If men want to be more convincing to women, they need to smile more in all situations.

Laughter in Love

In courtship, Robert Provine found that it is women, not men, who laugh and laugh most. In these situations, Laughter can be used to determine the likelihood of a couple's success in the marriage relationship. In short, the more he can make her laugh, the more attractive she will be. This is because the ability to make others laugh is considered a significant feature, women prefer men to dominate, and men prefer subordinate women. Proven also discovered that a subordinate would laugh and appease superiors. The ideal person will make subordinates laugh, but they can maintain their advantage without laughing.

This explains why the sense of humor comes first in women's job search for mothers. When a woman says: "He is a very funny person-when we laugh all night," she usually says that she laughs at night. He made her laugh all night.

On a deeper level, men seem to understand the appeal of humor and spend a lot of time competing with other men to tell the best jokes to improve their status. Many men are also annoyed when a man tells a joke, especially when a woman is present or even laughing. A man might think that the person who tells a joke is not only a bastard, but he is not that funny, think about it even though all his women are good for laughing. The point for men to understand is that humorous men look more attractive to most women. Fortunately, you can learn to be fun.

Arm Body Language

The arm is an exciting accessory, with a ball on the top, a hinge in the middle, and a somewhat complicated toolset at the end. Also, take care to keep your arms still. This is usually where the deceiver starts when trying to control body language (they may even use one hand and the other to keep them yet).

Expanding

The arm is an innovative, expandable device that can make us bigger or smaller without moving the rest of the body to extend the arm.

They can threaten or extend to each other in a more friendly way. If they act directly and quickly, they pose a threat. Bending and moving slower, they may provide comfort.

They can also extend horizontally, sometimes as part of a body-stretching "I am a big shot" display, indicating confidence or aggressiveness.

Forming

When we wave around and open up the world, our arms are used to shape. When we show others how old the fish are or how young the children are, they aid our wording.

If we are excited or confident, we may wave our arms like a windmill. When we are not safe, our shape becomes smaller and closer to the body.

These waving arms require control, and a person who is on something with his fist may be clumsy.

Raising

Raising your arms can lift something. Done quickly, it threw things into the air. Use your arms to zoom in further. The typical gesture of raising both arms is frustrating because everything that overwhelms the person is thrown into the air. Coupled with a shrug, it means confusion ("I don't know!!").

Weapon

Weapons can be like weapons. They can symbolize clubs and spears because they hit imaginary enemies. They can also defend, stop, and precise attacks. In martial arts, weapons can be used for fixation and strike, reflecting how weapons are used for communication.

Crossing

The arm can act as a gateway to the body and self. When they pass, they form a closed, defensive shield, blocking the outside world. Guards work in two ways: one is to stop incoming attacks, and the other is to hide places that people might not even notice.

Therefore, crossed arms may indicate anxiety, which may be due to a lack of trust in others or internal discomfort and vulnerability (for example, it may stem from childhood trauma).

The degree of intersection indicates how closely the person is. It ranges from light crosses to folded arms to arms wrapped around a person. The extreme version that may show further hostility is clasped with both hands. If the legs are also crossed, this will increase the signal.

Hands with crossed arms can also keep a person in a comfortable self-hugging, for example, keeping the upper arm in the folded arms position or wrapping it around the torso, keeping both sides. If you give a thumbs up, it may mean that you agree or agree with what you are saying.

Crossing arms, especially when holding each other, can keep people still. This can suppress any signal. This may also mean that anger is suppressed (I must have myself prevent myself from hitting you). It also means that the person maintains their state to pay more attention to you (hence a compliment).

Crossing your arms, especially in the folded position, can mean that you feel comfortable, especially when there is little pressure on other parts of the body. Comfort implies a lack of fear, which may be due to being with friends or because they feel strong enough to deal with any attacks that arise. Tension, when the arms are crossed, may indicate that the person has judgment.

When the arms are not crossed, they expose the torso and the person, making them more vulnerable to injury. This means comfort that usually expresses trust. Knowing that the other party is afraid to attack may also be a position of power that dared to attack others.

Crossing your arms is a clear signal, and if you do this in front of others, they may feel rejected and respond accordingly (including disagreeing with your opinion).

For example, when relaxing, not all crossed arms are defensive (as described above). You can also use crossed arms when you have a cold (usually tuck your hands under your armpits to keep you warm).

The standard method that a salesperson uses with a customer to break the customer's arms' closed position is to provide the person something to hold, and otherwise ask them to do it.

Reaching Forward

Reaching out your hand can be scary for them because you may attack them, and a sudden push is indeed an aggressive signal, mainly if the writing is pointed or shaped like a fist.

Moving forward can also provide support or emotion, seeking contact, and joining with other people.

Pulling Back

When the arms are pushed forward, they are the first thing that can be caught or attacked. When a person feels defensive, they may step back to avoid injury. This can even be extended to put them behind.

Hidden

When the arms are behind their backs, they are invisible. This may be because they hide their intentions and hide signals that might otherwise pose a threat.

The arms are exposed back to the torso, causing fragility. This can mean obedience (continue, you can hit me) or comfort (I know you won't hit me). The reason for feeling comfortable maybe because the person is with friends or feels strong enough that they are trusting that others will not attack them.

Hands Gestures

Scientific research has shown more neural connections between the hand and the brain than any other part of the body. Therefore, the postures and postures we take in gestures and postures. Indicators can provide powerful insights into our emotional state. Our hands are usually located in front of the body; therefore, these signals are easy to receive, and most of us are continually using several trademark hands positions. Before you know it, your hand reveals your attitude towards other people, places, or situations. Watch how your hands move spontaneously during greetings, farewells, and reaching consensus with others. Before you know it, your hands can explain the point you are making and help prove your sincerity and worry. Whether you express love, anger, joy, or frustration, your hands can convey a message. This section will discuss how to use both hands to support spoken language and add substance to the message. You will discover how to pose to convey authority and dominance and show openness and compliance. You will see how other people imitate the actions or situations they describe, thereby enhancing their meaning. When you think that no one is watching, you will find signals that your hands and fingers are unknowingly showing.

How the Hand Speaks

For thousands of years, people's status in society has determined the priority of maintaining the right to speak when speaking. The more power or authority you have, the more you will be forced to remain silent when speaking. For example, Roman history shows that people of low status may be executed for interrupting Julius Caesar. Nowadays, most people live in such a society where freedom of speech in the abstract is quite good. Suppose there is no other reason, except for the proliferation of mobile phones and social media. Generally, anyone who wants to comment can do so. In many countries/regions, people have played "punctuation marks" to regulate turning movements in body conversations. People raised their hands from the essential Italians and French.

In Italy, the order of conversation is simple. The person who raises their hand can speak and have a chat. The hands of the listener will drop or be placed behind their backs. So, the trick is that if you want to say a word, try to raise your hands. This can be done by looking away and then lifting them or pressing others' hands by touching them while raising them. Many people believe that when Italians speak, they are friendly or close because they frequently contact each other. Still, everyone tried to limit the other's hand and speak.

Observing how a person summarizes the discussion and gives two points of view can reveal whether they have a bias. They usually raise the palm of one hand and clearly express each end, and then give the opposite point on the other side. Right-handed people retain a preference for the right hand, and left-handed people prefer the left hand.

Promote Positive Reactions

Using gestures can attract attention, increase the impact of communication, and help individuals retain more listening information. An analysis by TED Talks found that the most popular viral speakers use an average of about 500 gestures, almost twice as many as the least popular speakers. Other studies have found that people who "talk" to others are generally regarded as enthusiastic, helpful, and energetic. In contrast, those who are less active are considered to be logical, cold, and analytical.

Researchers Geoffrey Beattie or Nina McLoughlin at the University of Manchester evaluated the retention of information in memory. They conducted a study in which volunteers listened to the stories of cartoon characters. For some listeners, the narrator added gestures, such as moving the hands up and down quickly to show running, waving motions to demonstrate a hairdryer, and separating arms to offer a fat opera actor. When the content displayed in the list was tested after ten minutes, those who remembered the gestures had a one-third higher response when recalling the stone's details, indicating that gestures have a substantial effect on our recall ability. We will evaluate any of the most common gestures and thumb gestures that are widely used.

Rub Palm Together

In the evening, a friend had dinner at a restaurant, and we discussed summer vacation plans. As the project vision expanded and more became a reality, the friend laughed, quickly rubbed his palms together, and shouted, "I can hardly wait." That body language tells us nonverbally that she hopes this trip will be her year's highest point.

People communicate with each other and convey positive expectations. Rolling the dice rolls the dice between the palms into a ball to show his positive expectation of winning, while the master of ceremonies rolls the palm into a ball. He told the audience, "We have been looking forward to hearing our next speaker," the exciting salesperson walked into the sales manager's office, held hands together, and said excitedly, "We have just confirmed Johnson's contract." In the evening, the waiter came to your table, rubbed his palms together, and asked, "Is there anything else, sir?" Yes, or Fei told you he wanted a good suggestion.

The speed at which a person rubs his palms together shows that he thinks it will benefit. For example, you want to buy a house and then visit a real estate agent. After describing the property, you wish to own, the agent quickly rubbed the palms together and said: "I have prepared a suitable house for you" so that the agent expresses that he hopes the result will be beneficial to you. If you tell him that he has ideal assets, he will slowly rub his palms. Would you feel it? Professors should use palm rubbing gestures when introducing products or services to potential buyers and take quick manual operations to avoid putting buyers in a defensive state.

When a customer quickly rubs his hands and says: "Let us see what you offer," it shows that he wants to see the right products and buy. Always remember the context: a person rubbing his hands briskly together while standing at the train station on a freezing winter day may not necessarily do this because he is looking forward to the train for a while. Because his hands are cold, he is more likely to do so.

Rub Your Fingers Together

Rubbing the thumb with the index finger or fingertip is often used as an expected currency gesture. Its symbolic meaning is rubbing a coin between the thumb and fingertip. Street vendors often use "I can save you 40%" or say to his friends: "Can you lend me a hundred dollars?" "We can make money from it." Any professional dealing with customers should always Avoid this posture because it has negative money associations.

Clasp Your Hands Together

Recall that when you feel scared, nervous, or suppress strong negative emotions, you may clench your hands for all your belongings, and the knuckles turned bright white. The tighter the grip. In addition to the power of clenching, you can also get meaning from the clenched hands' location. Studies have shown that the higher the hands clenched posture, the stronger the negative emotions. Therefore, if the boss is sitting on the desk while sitting on the elbows with her hands clasped in the presence of her face, she may be very challenging to deal with. She indicated that she was stopping what was to be said by putting her hand to her mouth. Be watchful not to push her too far. She may let go of those hands, let go of the words, which may not satisfy you.

In the beginning, this gesture seemed to express confidence, because some people who used it also smiled often. Research on the position of clenched hands by negotiation experts Nierenberg and Calero shows that when gestures are used during negotiation, the clenched hand is also a frustrating gesture, indicating that the person maintains a negative or anxious attitude. Some people think that they either did not persuade each other or that they lost the negotiation.

Steep Hand

When studying human movement, pointed out that people consider themselves to be prestigious. Among the elite, their gestures are minimal and tend to use restricted "steep poses."

The position of the finger shows his confident attitude. You can reach this position by touching your fingertips lightly, like the spire of a building. This gesture is also called "power gesture" because it is often used in superior/subordinate interactions and usually expresses a confident or confident attitude. Lawyers, accountants, or anyone in a position of authority often use their fingers to give instructions or suggestions on that position. People who think they are nobler in formal or informal power often use this gesture to express a confident attitude.

So far, we have emphasized that gestures appear in clusters, just like words in a sentence, and they must be interpreted while observing them. Since it usually happens alone, steepness may be an exception to these rules. The fingers of one hand gently press the fingers of the other hand to form the spire of the church, sometimes swinging back and forth like a spider pushing up on a mirror.

There are two main versions of fingertip curvature: a towering spire; a position often held when expressing opinions or ideas or when speaking; and a lowered spire, which is usually used when people are listening instead of talking.

Towering spire: When the fingers are placed on the chest, the speaker will send out ideas or opinions. Use elevated spire positions wisely. To the extreme, it can convey an arrogant "all-knowing" attitude. If you tilt your head back while taking this position, don't be surprised if you are considered smug or arrogant. Those who use this gesture sometimes unknowingly convert their slanted hands into prayer movements to appear more like gods. As a general rule, the raised hands should help. You should avoid using it when you want to persuade others or win their trust.

When listening, the lowered spire may put your fingers in the lowered spire position. When you place your hands together, you look interested and ready to respond. Women tend to use this position more regularly than the towering spire. Confident that he has the correct answer. If you want to look confident and have all the right answers, the tilted hand's position will do the job for you. The lowered spire indicates a listening attitude.

Although the cusp gesture is a positive signal, it can be used in positive or negative situations and can be misunderstood. Suppose you want to propose an idea to someone. During the demonstration, they used several positive gestures, such as open palms, leaning forward, raising their heads, and nodding. Suppose another person starts to put his hands up at the end of the presentation.

If a bent finger follows a series of other positive gestures and appears when showing others a solution to their problem, you likely have been approved. On the other hand, if the tilted hand's gesture followed a series of hostile gestures, such as folded arms and crossed legs, looking away, and face-to-face gestures, he may believe that he will not say "yes" or can get rid of you. In both cases, the tilted finger will show confidence, but one produces a positive result while the other has a negative impact. The gesture before the finger is bent is the key to the result.

Composition

This is not a hostile gesture-it is a positive gesture in courtship. It is mainly used by women and gay men who want to get the attention of men. The woman put a hand on the other party showed her face to a man, as if he admired him. If you are going to use flattery-sincere or not-this gesture will make it green.

Clenched Hands, Wrists, And Arms

If you want to show superiority and confidence, put your hands behind your back and hold with the other hand. Look at the outstanding male members of the royal family around the world.

Observe senior military personnel, police officers on patrol, or your local school principal striding across the corridor. They all adopt this authority status. They do not worry about exposing their fragile neck, heart, or stomach to potential threats and dangers. The next time you are in a stressful or uncomfortable situation, use the "back palm and back palm" position. Pay attention to how your feelings are frustrated and insecure, but still angry, relaxed, and confident.

However, when the grip is moved up to the arm, the meaning changes. You can bet that if someone holds her wrist on the wrist instead of just holding her hand, she is frustrated. This gesture is a way to maintain self-control. If the writing is controlled by your wrist or arm, prevent it from touching. The farther back the hand, the more incredible the frustration. When the needle reaches the upper arm, the person may have gone from frustration to anger. This gesture also expresses tension and is an attempt to self-control.

Holding Hands Behind

This posture is common among leaders and members of the royal family. Police patrolling, principals walking around the school playground, senior military personnel, and anyone with authority can use it. The emotions associated with this gesture are superiority, confidence, and strength. The person exposed their weak stomach, heart, pelvis, and throat with the unconscious, subconscious behavior.

Our experience shows that if you hold this position under stressful situations, such as accepting interviews with TV reporters or waiting outside a dentist's surgery, you will begin to feel confident because of causality and even have the authority to research law enforcement officials. It shows that people who do not wear guns often use this posture and often shake back and forth on their feet' soles when standing to increase their height. Very few police officers who wear guns use this gesture. They would instead drop their arms by their sides or put their thumbs in their seat belts. The weapon provided sufficient power for the officer. The treasure in the palm behind him was not a necessary authorization display.

Eyes Body language

People often call the eyes "the window of the soul" because they can send out many different nonverbal signals. This is very useful for reading body language because looking at people's eyes is a normal part of communication.

When a person wears sunglasses, usually indoors, this prevents others from reading their eye signals. So this is a bit problematic, which is why "gangs" and those who try to be strong sometimes wear them.

150

Looking Up

If a person looks up, they are often thinking. In particular, they may be taking pictures in their heads, which may very well be a sign of visual thinkers. When they give a speech or presentation, maybe they will remember the prepared words when they look up.

Looking up and to the left can indicate recall memories. Look up and to the right to show pictures (so you can betray a liar). Please be aware of this: sometimes the direction is reversed- if in doubt, ask them to recall known facts or imagine something to test the person.

When people check their surroundings and look for more exciting things, looking up may also be a sign of boredom. Keeping your head down and looking back at another person is an and suggestive gesture because it combines submissive head-down and attractive eye contact. It can also be judgmental, especially when combined with frowning.

Looking Down

Viewing a person can be an act of power and domination. Looking down includes not looking at the other person so that it may indicate submission

Therefore, looking down may be a sign of yield. It can also indicate that the person feels guilt. A unique way for lower people to look down at taller people is to tilt their heads back. Higher people may do this.

Looking down and to the left can indicate that they are talking to themselves (look for the lips' slight movement). Looking down and to the right can show that they are paying attention to their inner emotions.

In many cultures, eye contact is a rude or dominant signal, and people bow their heads to show respect when talking with others.

Look Sideways

Most of our site is in the horizontal plane, so when a person looks sideways, they are either in front of their eyes instead of in front of them or looking in a direction that interests them.

You can check the source of the interference with a side-eye to assess threats or interests. You can also do this to show annoyance ("I don't like this comment!").

Looking to the left indicates that someone is echoing. Looking to the right can suggest that they imagine sounds. As with vision and other sports, this can be reversed and may require checking against known truths and forgeries.

Lateral Movement

Eyes moving left and right can indicate movement and lying down as if they were looking for an escape route. When the person is in a conspiracy state, it seems that they are checking whether other people are listening, and lateral movement may also occur.

When visualizing a big picture and looking down, the eyes may also move left and right (sometimes up and down).

Eye Contact

Looking at someone will recognize them and show that you are interested in them, especially if you look into their eyes. Looking at a person's eyes can also let you know what they are looking at. For example, we are good at detecting what they are looking at and can even take a look at our body parts. If someone says something when you look away and make eye contact, it means they are attracting your attention.

Interrupted Eye Contact

Prolonged eye contact can be threatening, so we often look away and then look back again. Discontinuing eye contact may indicate that what has just been said makes people not want to continue eye contact; for example, they are insulted, found out, feel threatened, etc. When people think something causes the same internal discomfort.

Looking at a person, interrupting eye contact, and then immediately looking back at them is a typical flirting movement, significantly when the head is lowered when the suggested submission is made.

Flashing

Blinking is a natural process; the eyelids can wipe the eyes clean, just like a car windshield wiper.

When people think more or feel stressed, blinking speed tends to increase. This may indicate lying because the liar must continue to think about what they are saying. Aware of this, they may also open their eyes and stare at themselves.

Blinking can also indicate harmony, and the connected person may blink at the same rate. When you pause, people who listen to you carefully are more likely to blink (watch your words wide open).

In addition to natural random blinks, a single blink can also indicate a surprise. The person does not believe what he sees ("I will wipe my eyes to look better").

Blinking quickly can obstruct your vision and maybe a sign of arrogance, saying: "I am critical, and I don't need to see you." Blinking quickly can also make eyelashes flutter, which may be a romantic invitation. Reducing blinking can increase the power of the gaze, whether it is romantic or purposeful.

Winking

Blinking is a deliberate gesture, usually hinting at conspiracy ("you and I understand, but others don't").

Blinking may also be a suggestive greeting, reminiscent of a small hand ("Hello, great!").

Closing

Close your eyes and shut the world out. This may mean "I don't want to see what's in front of me; it's horrible." Sometimes if people are talking, they close their eyes. This is equivalent to turning around, so eye contact can be avoided, and almost no implicit request from other people to speak. Visual thinkers can sometimes close their eyes even when speaking to better see the internal image without distracting the outside world.

Damp

Lacrimal ducts provide moisture to the eyes, which can be used for both washing and tearing. Tearing eyes can suppress crying and express anxiety, fear, or sadness. This may also indicate that the person was calling recently. Wetness also occurs when a person is tired (red eyes may accompany this).

Tears

The actual tears dripping on the cheeks are usually symptoms of extreme fear or sadness, although paradoxically, you can also shed tears of joy.

Crying may be silent, with a little expression in addition to tears (indicating a certain degree of control). It also usually involves tightening the face, and when the mood is too high, it may be accompanied by uncontrollable twitching sobbing.

It should not be expected that men in many cultures will cry and learn to suppress this reaction, not even crying alone. Even if their eyes feel wet, they may turn away. Tears and sadness may turn into anger, which may directly target anyone free.

Facial Expressions

The facial expression refers to one or more muscle movements or postures below the facial skin. According to a set of controversial theories, these movements convey the observer's emotional state. Facial expressions are a kind of nonverbal communication. They are the primary means of obtaining social information between people, but they also exist in most other mammals and other animal species.

Humans can adopt facial expressions voluntarily or involuntarily, and the neural mechanisms responsible for controlling expressions are different in each case. Voluntary facial expressions are usually restricted by society and move along the cortical route of the brain. Conversely, involuntary facial expressions are considered natural and are recorded in the subcortex route.

Facial recognition is usually an emotional experience of the brain, and the amygdala is highly involved in the recognition process.

Eyes are often regarded as the basic features of facial expressions. Aspects such as blink rate can be used to indicate whether a person is nervous or is lying. Likewise, eye contact is considered an essential element of interpersonal communication. However, there are cultural differences in the social etiquette of maintaining or not maintaining eye contact.

In addition to the auxiliary nature of facial expressions in voice communication between people, facial expressions also play an important role in contact with sign language. Many phrases in sign language contain facial expressions on the display.

There are disputes about whether facial expressions are universal in the world and humans. Proponents of the universal hypothesis claim that many facial expressions are innate and originated from evolutionary ancestors. Opponents of this opening question the accuracy of the research used to test this claim. On the contrary, they believe that facial expressions are conditional, and people mainly view and understand facial expressions from the surrounding social environment. Moreover, facial expressions have a powerful connection with personal psychology. Some psychologists have the ability to discern hidden meanings from a person's facial expressions.

An experiment studied the effects of gaze direction and facial expressions on facial memory. The participants were shown a set of unfamiliar faces with happy or angry expressions. They either looked straight ahead or moved their eyes to the side. When these faces are avoided instead of staring directly, the memory of the faces initially expressed in angry words will be more imperfect. In contrast, the memory of those with smiling faces is not affected by the gaze's direction. It is suggested that the memory of another person's face depends in part on the evaluation of another person's behavioral intentions.

Think about how vital information a person can convey through facial expressions. A smile can express approval or happiness. Frowning can indicate disapproval or unhappiness. In some cases, our facial expressions may reveal how we feel about a particular situation. When you say you feel good, the name on your face may tell others. The emotions that can be expressed through facial expressions are just a few examples, including:

- Happy
- Sad
- Anger
- Surprise
- Disgust
- Fear
- Confusion
- Excitement
- Desire
- Despise

The expression on a person's face can even help determine whether we trust or believe what the person is saying.

Leg Posture

We know less about what specific body parts are doing. The further away from our mind. If we pay only limited attention, most of us will be aware of our facial expressions and gestures. Even those who are not so skilled can easily imitate the performed smile or frown to evoke others' emotions, although other subtle gesture cues in the conflict may disappoint you. We are conscious of our arms and hands' movements most of the time, but this is even more true for our chest and stomach. Finally, at any given point in time, we have the least knowledge of legs and feet. This means that legs and feet are an essential source of information about someone's inner attitude. Maximum people don't understand what they are doing, so they rarely consider forging gestures. With them, they will face. When a person repeats a little movement on the restless foot, it seems that he can remain calm and in a state of control, which indicates the primary frustration of evolution in avoiding a particular situation. When people learn more about their character-or, they want you to believe in their character, and they wave their arms. Young and healthy people walk faster than older people because of their different speeds and greater muscle flexibility; their arms swing back and forth higher. Therefore, the march of the junior army evolved into an exaggerated walk,

This shows that the marchers are full of vigor, youthful vitality, and unmoved. Many politicians and public figures want to convey information about them.

Vigor adopts a more active gait. Women's arms tend to swing backward because women's arms bend farther from the elbow to hold the baby more effectively.

Legs Can Reveal the Truth

The research of Dr. Paul Ekman and Dr. William Friesen on deceptive behavior; shows that when a person is lying down, the lower part of his body produces more signals than the upper part, which is related to gender-this applies to both men and women. Since people know more about their hands and eyes, they can consciously control their movements. Although the legs and feet are also subject to conscious control, they are usually ignored, and the legs are often not visible. Therefore, the feet are a more accurate source of information.

Show video recordings of liars to others, who are asked to determine whether the video's person is lying or telling the truth. When evaluators can see the lower part of the body, their answers will be more correct. The survey results show that liars pay more attention to their hands, arms, and faces because they know it is their eyes. Since the lower limbs are not in the way, the liar will forget them and betrayed them by the micro-muscle movement on the legs and feet. Tables with glass tops put us under more pressure than solid tables because our legs are in full view. Therefore, we feel as if we cannot fully control ourselves.

The evolution of legs in humans serves two purposes: to advance to obtain food and escape danger. Because the human brain is hard-wired to achieve these two goals-moving in the direction we want, and away from the direction we don't want-how a person uses their legs and feet to reveal where they want to go. In other words, they indicate that a person is committed to leaving or staying in a conversation. An open or uncrossed leg posture indicates a relaxed or dominant posture, while a crossed post indicates a closed attitude of uncertainty.

Four Main Positions

Parallel Attitude

The parallel posture is the subordinate position, in which the legs are straight, and the feet are placed together. This is a formal position that shows a neutral attitude. It is taken by students who talk to teachers, report to your commander or stand in front of a judge awaiting judgment. Placing your feet together will lower the basis of standing and make your posture more unstable. When you need to catch someone off guard, you can quickly push them away from that location. People who are unsure of their work on a topic adopt a similar position. When standing with their legs close together, it means they feel hesitant or

A tentative broader vision provides us with a more comprehensive and more solid foundation. It is much more challenging to get people standing with their legs apart to lose their balance.

Separate Your Legs

The posture with legs apart (mainly male posture) is a stable fixed posture. It tells you to stand on your ground and favor those who want to show their advantages. It requires your legs to be straight, feet separate, and equal weight to each other.

Because of the higher center of gravity, men use their legs apart more often than women. Despite being tall, men will occupy this position more often, among others, when they use their posture to communicate. It is used as a male dominant signal because it highlights the genitals and makes them look like a penis. male

It can be noticed that the participants in the sports competition are standing with each other in this position at half time, scratching or adjusting part c. In this way, males can highlight masculinity by performing the same actions and show a united team spirit.

The expressions "put your feet on the ground" and "stand with your own feet" refer to the ancient Chinese custom of restraining women's feet. This custom is mainly reserved for the royal family, which means that women tied up with their feet cannot stand up with their feet without causing pain.

If you feel frustrated and want to change your mood, raise your heads, and raise your legs to stand apart. And your shoulders back. By taking this strong position, you can create a feeling of matching.

Posing with The Forward Foot

From the Middle Ages to the mid-nineteenth century, men with higher status and higher social status adopted a very convenient posture, which can show the inner part of the leg, one of the sexual areas of the human body. The legs of gentlemen and posers bear heavy loads, while the other portion faces the inner thigh. In the fashion design, men's clothes are removed from the breeches with too tight hoses and fitted with suitable shoes. Men are encouraged to indulge their desires for dress and posture to show their legs and masculinity. Nowadays, red carpet stars know how to place their legs to maximize their advantages and expose their feet to the inner thighs, which are the thighs' softest and sexiest part.

Jumping around where the mind wants to go is a valuable clue to one's immediate intentions. We point our leading foot in the direction our mind will take; this posture looks as if the person is starting to walk.

We point our leading foot to the most exciting or attractive person in a group, but it is recommended to place our foot at the nearest exit when we are leaving.

Standing Cross-Legged

The next time you attend a meeting with men or women, you will notice some people standing with arms and legs crossed. When you look closely, you will also find that they are farther away from each other than the usual social distance.

Among those who don't know, this is how many people stand. If you interact with them, you will find that they are not familiar with the others. Open legs can show openness or dominance, while crossed legs show a more closed, submissive, or defensive attitude because they symbolically refuse to touch the genitals.

For a woman, a posture like a scissors-like posture and a one-legged posture will send two messages: one is that she intends to stay instead of leaving, and two are that she is denied access. When a person does this, it also shows that he will last, but make sure you don't "kick him to the pain." Open legs show masculinity; closed legs protect masculinity. If he is with a man and he feels that he is not as good as him, then the feeling of being amiable with the display is right. If he is better with men, then this gesture will make him look competitive and feel vulnerable. Research shows that people who lack confidence also adopt cross-legged positions.

Now imagine that you notice another group of people standing with their arms outstretched; palms are visible, with a relaxed appearance, leaning back, with the other foot pointing towards the other foot in the group. Everyone gestured with their hands and went in and out of each other's private space. Further investigation will reveal that these people are friends or know each other. The facial expressions and conversations of the first group of people with closed arms and legs sounded relaxed and comfortable. Still, the folded arms and legs told us that they felt less comfortable or confident about each other than when they tried to show up.

Try the following: Join a person no one knows, stand with arms and legs tightly together, and show a severe expression. The other group of members will cross one after another and stay in that position until you (the stranger) leave. Go away and observe how one group after another assumes the original posture again. Crossing your legs not only shows negative or defensive emotions, but it also makes one feel insecure and makes others react accordingly.

How We Move from Closed to Open

When people become more comfortable in a group and get to know other people, they perform a series of movements that change them from a defensive crossed position with arms and legs to a relaxed open position. Such permanent "open" procedures tend to follow the same sequence everywhere.

1. Crossed arms and legs indicate that each other's opinions are uncertain.
2. Increasing openness and acceptance begins in the closed position with arms and legs crossed. When they start to feel comfortable and establish a rapport, their legs are not crossed first, and their feet are placed together in a parallel position. Next, the folded arms above the crossed arms are exposed, and the palms sometimes flicker when speaking, but they will not be used as a hairdresser in the end. Instead, it can keep the outside of the other arm in the one-arm barrier. Then spread your arms, and then gesture with one hand or place it in your hip or pocket. Finally, stand up alone.

The forward position indicates the acceptance of the other party.

Legs Crossed

One leg is neatly crossed over the other, and 70% of the cross from left to right. This is the normal cross-legged posture used by most European and Asian cultures. When a person's legs and arms are crossed, their emotions have been withdrawn from the conversation, or it may be futile to try to convince themselves when they sit like this.

The crossed arms, legs, and side-looking eyes show that she doesn't particularly like open communication. We have observed that, compared to those sitting with an open posture, people sitting in this short sentence rejected more proposals and recalled fewer details about what was discussed.

Figure Four Cross-Legged

American men often use the four-legged posture (similar to the number four posture viewed from above), often used by more and more young people in a culture exposed to American entertainment and news media. It can reflect the attitude of competition or debate. This genital manifestation also appears in the primate world, thereby eliminating the damage caused by physical combat caused by male chimpanzees or monkeys always reordering the group hierarchy. The Nazis have been monitoring No. 4 character's pose during World War II because the person who used it was not a German and had not been in the United States.

But it is not so common in Europe; it originated in many cultures around the world. Men sitting in this posture are considered more dominant, relaxed, and younger. The downside is that this posture is regarded as an insult to parts of the Middle East and Asia because it shows the soles, which is culturally related to filth. It can be seen from the position in Figure 4 that women gradually wear various trousers. They tend to target only other women, not men, because they don't want. It looks too masculine.

Leg Clamp
This person not only has a competitive attitude but also uses one or two hands as a clamp to lock the quad-shaped cross leg in a permanent position. This may signify that a stubborn person refuses to accept any point of view other than his own.

Short Skirt
Women in miniskirts cross their legs and ankles for apparent reasons. Many habitual older women will still sit in this position even if they no longer wear short skirts. This may make them feel and act relaxed subconsciously. Others may regard this as a reserved attitude and react accordingly.

One trap is that restraining or defensive gestures can feedback and enhance the attitude of reservation or denial. Practice using positive and open gestures. This will increase your self-confidence. Others will perceive you more active and attract you more fully.

Entangle Your Legs

Some gestures are unique to men, while others are unique to women. The leg wraps where the top of one-foot locks itself to the other leg is used almost exclusively by women.

Although the upper body of a woman may appear relaxed, this posture still highlights insecurity. If you want a woman to free herself from entangled legs, take a friendly and low-key approach to encourage her to be open.

Her university history professor invited Jessica to stand in front of the lecture hall and discuss the latest tasks. Unsure of her expectations, she stood in front.

For 120 students, one foot was lifted behind her supporting leg and pressed against her calf. Although she has confidence in what she has learned, she feels shy and timid when speaking in front of so many people, many of whom she does not know. When she realized how she stood, she put her feet firmly under her feet and found that she was more confident and safer, and able to speak under authority and assurance.

Studies have shown that people who meet for the first time usually stand with arms and legs crossed. As the rapport developed, they became more comfortable with each other, they released the closed posture and opened the body. The process follows a predictable pattern: first, cross your legs and then place your feet in a similar posture. The arms and hands stretched out and became alive. When people feel comfortable and relaxed, they will move from a parallel position to an open position with their feet slightly apart and facing the other person. On the contrary, the sign of the person who exits the conversation is crossed arms. The person sitting in this position is unlikely to be persuaded by anything you say or do.

Sitting with Parallel Legs

Women's legs and buttocks have a skeletal structure that allows them to sit in this way, thus sending a robust female signal. Most men cannot replicate this sitting position comfortably. When surveyed, the vast majority of men regard women's sitting posture as their absolute favorite.

Men like women in this position very much. Close one leg to the other leg to make the leg look healthier and younger. From a reproductive perspective, it instinctively attracts men. Model classes usually teach this pose to women. Do not confuse this with a woman who continually crosses and does not cross her legs when she is with the man she wants; in this case, leg shifts are a way to attract attention.

Shoulder Body Language

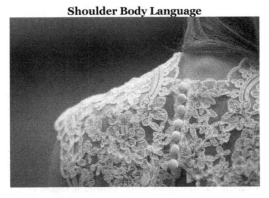

Although their movement is limited compared to other parts of the body, the shoulder can convey various signals.

Raised

Keeping the shoulders in a raised position requires lifting the weight of the entire arm. This requires continuous effort, and if the person is awakened in some way, it requires effort.

Often bend over or cross your arms and hold your body, and raise your shoulders. This may indicate that the person is cold (they may also be shaking). This can also be a sign of extreme tension, usually caused by anxiety or fear. When one is worried about an attack (actual or virtual), raising the shoulders and lowering the head can protect the neck.

Bend Forward

Closing your arms will naturally bend your shoulders. When you put your hands down and lean forward, this reduces the width of your body, so it may be a defensive posture or a subconscious desire not to be seen, for example, when people feel threatened or when they want to remain "undercover."

Pushed Back

Pushing the shoulders back will force the chest out and make the torso vulnerable to attack. Therefore, this posture can be used when the person is not afraid of attack and can be used as a mockery to show strength.

Suppose you pull the body back when you pull the shoulders back, mainly when the person is leaning against a wall. In that case, this may indicate a desire to hide the body without seeing the body or moving it defensively to avoid injury.

Circling

You can wrap your shoulders forward or backward with one or two shoulders. This is usually done to exercise a stiff shoulder, which may have been clenched (and therefore may indicate anxiety). This may also be accompanied by rotation or tilting of the neck and other muscle movements.

This exercise can indicate that the person is ready to take action and may even fight, or is therefore used as a sign of aggression.

It will be polite to complete the operation and listen carefully while the other party is talking. This agreement's deliberate destruction may be an insulting power signal ("You are too important; I don't need to interrupt listening").

Shrug

The classic shrug, lifting and lowering the shoulders in one go, usually means "I don't know!" or maybe accompanied by raised eyebrows, a downwardly bent mouth, and hands held on one side, palms up or forward (indicating no hidden). The shoulders may not move much during a shrug or a stressed shrug. Sometimes, you may only see your arms raised slightly.

A small and quick shrug may send the same signal, but it will be performed subconsciously, indicating uncertainty or lack of understanding. Shrugging may be related to lying because people worry that their words may lose themselves, instead of talking but shrugging. An extended and energetic shrug may resemble a hovering shoulder, indicating that it is ready for aggression and signaling a threat. In smaller companies, this can mean anger or frustration.

Relaxed

We often bear pressure on our shoulders. A genuinely relaxed person keeps the shoulders low, and the arms can move naturally without shaking and free-swinging.

Leaning

When people are leaning against the wall, they often touch the wall with their shoulders. This is usually a relaxed posture because it takes more energy to lift the body, which puts the person vulnerable.

Turn

Turning the shoulders is an essential part of turning around. If a person turns their heads while still looking at you, it may mean they want to leave (perhaps because what you said makes them uncomfortable).

Body Language the Truth of The Pointing Foot

Can we infer a person's thoughts just by reading the body language of the feet? This is the question this article attempts to answer. When communicating with others, our attention is mainly focused on their speech and facial expressions. If anything, we hardly pay attention to body gestures, and when it comes to feet, we rarely look at them.

Still, as I mentioned in my earlier article on foot movement's body language, what a person's feet do may be the most accurate clue to their attitude. The farther the body part is from the brain, the less we know about its actions, and therefore the less we manipulate it.

This means that although we can easily manipulate facial expressions to hide our emotions or convey emotions that we cannot feel, it is difficult to do this with our feet. Therefore, our feet often exude our true feelings without realizing it. Therefore, body language experts do not find it challenging to understand one's thoughts with just two feet.

Feet Body Language

When we interact with others, the direction we dominate our feet reveals where we are going, whether we are standing or sitting. In body language, the direction a person points to their feet reveals how they want to go even if they appear to be talking.

For example, if you see someone talking to someone, but their feet are pointing at you, it means they are interested in you or want to approach you. The person pointing their foot at you is considering approaching you deep in your heart, even if they seem to interact with their team.

You can confirm this by the invisible appearance they occasionally give you. This person will do their best to keep your site as much as possible. Interestingly, even before people orient their bodies in the desired direction, they teach the feet. That is to say, and the foot is introduced before the body. Orientation, long gaze, and toes pointing together are undoubtedly signs that someone is interested in you. They asked to get in touch with them.

Foot Forward Position

Watching two people interested in each other in a conversation, you may notice that one foot (front foot) of each person points to the other person. If only one of them is attractive, you will only see one foot stepping forward. Of course, the affected person will be the person who takes the footsteps. For two reasons, this gesture conveys interest and attraction.

First, one person points the foot at another person, and the direction we suggest the foot reveals where we are going. Even if the other party has started a conversation with other people they are interested in, they are still willing to develop in their direction and communicate more with them. Maybe more physical contact can be made.

Secondly, this gesture is to reduce the personal space between related personnel. It seems that the person is "starting to walk" in the direction they are interested in. Please think of the body language that people display when they arrive at their destination when traveling by train. You will notice that their posture becomes upright, and they put their hands on their knees.

This body language can be considered as "getting up" body language. Similarly, you can refer to the pointing toes to "begin to go" body language. In a group situation, if you observe the direction in which a person "starts to walk," you will quickly find the most exciting or attractive person for that person.

Time to Exit

When we want to leave a meeting or conversation, our feet will point to the nearest exit. If you notice this when talking to people, it can mean one of many things. They may not be interested in you or what you are saying. Or they may be delayed for an appointment, or they may want to go to the bathroom. Therefore, the context is essential.

In a group discussion, the first person to leave will be one foot pointing away from the group. They will advance precisely in the direction their feet are pointing as if pulled along a straight line by an imaginary rope. When they began to think about leaving the room, some women pointed their feet to the door and began to adjust the back of their clothes and hair to leave an excellent rear-view impression when they left.

Toes Up

When a person lifts the toe off the ground and points it upward, it means that the person is in a great mood, or thinks or hears an upbeat sound. For example, if a teacher announces that they are going on a camping trip in class, the excited students will put their toes up.

If you find that someone's toes point up during a phone conversation, they will likely have heard something useful or are enjoying their conversation. You may be capable of confirming this by their frequent smiles in the conversation. When people talk to someone, they find attractive, they may move up because they are actively evaluating their current situation.

17 Common Body Gestures and What They Show

Whenever we communicate face to face, we use body language. This is a nonverbal language that emphasizes or changes the meaning of the natural language we use. We talk to others through body movements, postures, eye contact, gestures, intonation and volume, facial expressions, and micro-expressions that are meaningful to us and the audience. Understanding body language can help improve communication.

Nonverbal communication is a two-way road. When you feel communicating with your body, you can skillfully use nonverbal signals sent to others. It may even be fun to communicate through body language and other nonverbal cues. When you practice speaking with nonverbal signals, you will naturally acquire better skills to interpret the body language depicted by others, which has its advantages.

The Power of Body Language

If you know how to use positive body language, it can help you get what you need. It can find a job for you, help you sell a house, win arguments, or build relationships. On the other hand, negative body language can stop you from getting what you want. Moreover, it may cause you to lose friends, miss job opportunities, or offend people who want to impress you.

How Reliable Is Body Language?

Body language is not only essential but also influential. Usually, it can also reveal your true feelings. However, if the person expressing body language knows how to manipulate body language well, it is not entirely reliable. Consider a poker player who has perfected his body language so that other players cannot see his "story."

Body language appears most of the time, regardless of whether you intend to reveal the body language. However, it will help if you are cautious when assessing the body language of others. You can explain body language in one way, but gestures can mean something completely different. When reading body language, it is especially important to understand the cultural differences between people.

Body Language Gestures

Expect to use the following body language gestures. Once you understand their meaning, it is usually easy to discern their meaning.

Arms Crossed on Chest

Your arms and legs may be the first nonverbal communication that people notice if they see you. You can practice them for positive body language and negative body language.

Sitting or standing with arms crossed on the chest is almost considered defensive body language. Generally, people see people with arms crossed as insecure, annoyed, or closed people. When you do this, you will be shut down and detached. You may be angry or stubborn.

If you see someone's arms and legs crossed for a long time, remember that this may indicate that the temperature you are it is too cold. It may also mean that they are tired of relying on no armchairs to support their shoulders.

Smile

Smiling can mean different things, depending on facial expressions. There are happy smiles and shy smiles, warm smiles, and ironic smiles. Duchenne's smile involves lifting the corners of his mouth while squeezing his eyes to create crow's feet. Contrary to a smirk that shows teeth, this is considered a genuine smile. Have you heard the term "smiley face"? Some people are good at conveying smiles through direct eye contact. When you show a real Doxing smile, you will let people know that you are approachable and friendly.

Steep Fingers

Close your fingertips and separate your palms to let people know that you have authority and control. Bosses and politicians often use this gesture to indicate that they are in power.

Cross-Legged

The way your legs cross can tell other people a lot about you and how you feel at any given moment. If you cross at the ankle, it may indicate that you want to hide something. If you step over your knees but point your knees towards another person, it means you are uncomfortable with them. In every case, the best option is to place your feet firmly on the floor.

A general term related to body language is the "picture four" position. Sit like this, stretch your arms and legs forward, then cross an ankle on your knee, cross your legs high, and open the pelvic area. With your crossed legs in this position, your body will be in the shape of number four. The nonverbal communication information represented by the "picture four" posture is your powerful and authoritative. When your arms and legs are opened and relaxed, you will send non-verbal communication, showing that you are confident and approachable.

Put Your Head in Your Hands

When you put your hand in your hand, it may mean that you are bored, as if you are so tired of life that you can't lift your head anymore. Or, it may mean that you are unhappy or ashamed and don't want to show up.

Gesturing with Folded Hands

Whether people trust you or not, the role of your hands will be very different. Stretch out your hands and raise your hands to signal, no, you didn't hide anything.

Eye Contact

When you want them to feel comfortable with the conversation and accept what you want to say, you need to make eye contact with the person you are talking to. Scientists suggest that most people's eye contact time is about 3.2 seconds if you are a stranger. When you become friends, they usually don't mind having eye contact with you for a long time.

Look Down

Looking at the floor or the ground can make you appear weak and unconfident. Unless you need to discuss here, you need to keep your eyes on the level of the other person's face. When you interrupt your eye contact, you should try to look sideways every few seconds.

Twist Your Hair

Movies and TV shows often use hair-twisting gestures to flirt. That might be the meaning that someone gets when they turn their head, especially when they look up at you through their eyelashes while combing their hair.

However, if you are in a job interview, you will feel nervous and uncomfortable while hanging out.

Micro Expression

Micro expressions are facial expressions that are too short and occur within about 1/25 of a second. They happen when you try to suppress emotions. If you see someone showing a Micro expressions, it usually means trying to hide something from you. However, if you discover them, you can gain an advantage in any interaction.

Walk Briskly

When you want to show your confidence, walk briskly, and purposefully. Whether you are going to a particular place or not, you should walk as if confidently towards a vital destination.

Put Your Hands on Your Cheeks

If you touch your cheek with your hand, it shows that you are thinking and carefully evaluating your received information. When you see someone doing this while talking to someone, you can usually assume that they value you enough to consider what you say.

Rubbing Eyes

When you rub your eyes, it usually means that you doubt or don't believe what you are hearing. If someone rubs their facial expressions while you are speaking, you may benefit from stopping and asking for their feedback so you can resolve their concerns.

Rubbing or Touching the Nose

When you rub or touch your nose with your index finger, you will appear dishonest. If you do this in a conversation that requires honesty, you will have difficulty achieving your goals. Also, if you see someone wiping their nose, this is a good sign that you need to be careful not to believe what they will tell you automatically.

You Are Standing with Hands Behind Your Back

Sit down with your hands clasped behind your back. Others may see this as anger, worry, or depression. It may look like an excellent casual pose, but it may make others feel uncomfortable and alert to you.

Pinch the Bridge of The Nose

If you close your eyes and pinch the bridge of your nose, you seem to make negative comments about the conversation. If someone takes this position towards you, you may need to adopt other methods to win their support for your goals.

Standing with Hands-On-Hips

This pose is tricky. In a few cases, this may mean that you will be angry and be aggressive. In other cases, this may mean that you are passionate and ready to get the job done. How someone explains what you mean by this position may be related to the use of your personal space. For most people who meet by chance, a reasonable distance for personal space is about three feet, or if you stand side by side, the arm distance between the two is about an arm's length. When you are with your best friends and family, you can stand closer, and everyone should stay comfortable.

How to Send the Correct Message in Body Language?

Learning body language gestures is an essential first step in sending correct body language messages. It can also help you read silent messages and non-verbal signals sent to you by others.

However, knowing the correct movements, gestures, and facial expressions will only take you far. When you want to have healthy and productive interactions with others, you may need to work hard to understand yourself and your life better.

Couples who misread each other's body language will quickly become angry, disappointed, or out of touch with each other. If you need help learning to communicate with essential others or anyone else, talking with a therapist may help.

Body Language Attraction

When faced with a single dating world, one of the essential things is body language's attractiveness. Knowing when to attract your date or interested person is crucial to see if you are wasting time. Sometimes someone may be polite and don't want you to be severely disappointed, but their body language will tell you that they are not interested in romantic connections.

The attractiveness of body language between men and women is indeed different. Specific forms of body language attraction are often done by women, while men tend to do something. However, men and women also have many ways of body language attraction. Also, depending on gender identity and sexual orientation, there may be some overlap between genders.

Female Body Language Attractiveness

Women show their attractiveness to men through body language. You can judge whether a woman is attracted to you by how a woman holds her body and what her hands do. Scientific research shows that women's body language exudes dominance and masculinity, attracting women the most. They can answer this interest in body language that shows obedience and fertility.

Show Fertility

The attractiveness of body language is closely related to sexual beauty related to fertility. If a woman is interested in a man, she will show signs of fertility. This can be done in some ways. She can hold or remove her hair, tilt her head to expose pheromones, or keep her hands and wrists noticeable to show soft skin.

Wallet Behavior

How a woman holds her wallet can tell you a lot about her engagement style and whether she is attracted to you. If a woman is uncomfortable or doesn't like the person she is talking about, she may hold her wallet tightly around her waist. On the other hand, if a woman is attracted to someone, she hopes that her wallet will not hinder further interaction, and she can put it on the table or floor, or the chair behind her. Keep in mind that when you are in a crowded safe place, she may hold the wallet tightly for safety reasons, which may not be a good indication.

Licking Lips

When attracted to someone, women often lick their lips. They may do this intentionally to give interest, but it is usually a reflective action, and they may not yet know what they are doing. Maybe they swiped their tongue to their lips, or perhaps they flicked their lips with this language, which hardly attracted attention. Combined with constant eye contact, this shows that the woman is too attracted to you.

Hip Thrust

A sexually attracted woman will often stand, stretch out one hip joint, and possibly lift her shoulders. This posture shows off the woman's body and is an invitation. One hip is pushed out to open the lower body and draw attention to fertility, while the shoulder lift draws attention to the breast. Women usually do this consciously to show interest, but it can also be unconscious.

The Attractiveness of Male Body Language

Men have ways to show attractiveness to women. Usually, men attracted to women may be seen as showing off or pretending to impress women. The beauty of their body language also includes gestures and movements, which hint at what relationship they want to have with the woman in question.

Show Fertility

As women, when men are attracted to women, they are likely to show off their fertility. They may stand up straight, at right angles to the shoulders, and the distance between the soles of the feet and the shoulders' width is equal. This open but dominant posture shows off their bodies and shows their confidence in sexual abilities. They can also open their hands and open their hands in the invitation.

Raise Eyebrows

When attracted by someone, men often raise their eyebrows. It is usually seen as an invitation, requiring more interaction, or suggesting more communication after a formal date. It may be that the eyebrows are raised slowly, or it may be a rapid flash of eyebrows, where one eyebrow rises quickly and then falls. Some people do this deliberately, but it may also be a subconscious sign of attraction.

Cracked Lips

Men do not lick their lips like women, but they may part their lips briefly when they make eye contact with an attracted woman. This may last for a long time, or it may be short-lived, usually accompanied by eye contact or other attracting attention.

Open Nostrils

The open nostrils and open expression on a man's face are affirmative signs of his full participation in the interaction. This shows that the person is very interested in the conversation or what happened between him and another person. Opening the nostrils may also be a physical, sexual attraction. This usually is a subconscious body language attraction.

Standing with Hands-On-Hips

A man stood with his hands on his hips, very attractive to the woman talking with him. This may be conscious or subconscious body language. A group photo with both hands shows others an open view of his body. The hands may point to his package for emphasis. Another similar sign of attractiveness is self-adjustment when sitting or standing with your legs open.

Gender-Neutral Body Language Attraction

Regardless of gender or sexual orientation, many forms of body language attraction are common. When you see these signs of body language from the person you are dating, you can be sure that the date is going well, and they are very interested in further interaction.

171

Show Availability

Both men or women are more interested in showing that they are available, while men and women often show their vacancies when they are interested in getting to know someone better. A situation that shows usability maybe with arms outstretched and legs crossed. Men and women will also show whether they are free by looking up at each other's face instead of feet, desk, or phone.

Smiling

Smiling is another way for men and women to demonstrate their abilities. Smiling is also a way to express interest and attraction to others. You can impose some smiles to make a good impression or make yourself look attractive.

"A licensed relationship therapist can encourage you to learn how to interpret body language and develop skills to use your body language to your advantage."

However, if the smile is real, it will be apparent, and the smile will touch their eyes. If a person is smiling at you and seems to have no choice but to smile, they will be attracted.

Tilting

When people interact with others, they trust that person. When you are in a group of people, and someone is particularly inclined towards you, it means that they attract you more than others and pay more attention to you. The closer he or she is to you, the more attractive they are.

Head Tilt

Head tilt is the attraction of body language, showing participation and interest. When someone looks up in a conversation, it means that they are paying attention and caring about what is being said. When someone is attracted to you, they will tilt their heads to show their interest and participation. Women are extra likely to tilt their heads than men, but both men and women use this body language.

Drop or Blur

When someone is attracted to other people, they blush or start to blush. As the attractiveness increased, blood poured into the face, making the blush. This is something that no gender can control. This is a natural body language. When someone is attracted by the body, the body will execute it on its own. Lips may also become red, and eyes may become white and brighter.

Increased Heart Rate

When someone is attracted to another person, this is another unconscious automatic response. Your heart rate will increase. You may not want to try to pulse someone during a date or date to see if they are attracted to you; however, there are other signs. Accelerated breathing and warm palms indicate increased heart rhythm and attractiveness.

Foot Pointing

People will automatically point their feet to their interests. Although someone's foot pointing at you is not necessarily an attractive sign, it does mean that they are at least interested in this interaction and are currently present. If their feet point to the exit, they may be thinking about getting out of trouble.

Eye Contact

If anyone makes eye contact with you, it will arouse your interest. Eye contact means they will only pay attention to you, and you can be sure that you have their appeal. Long-term eye contact can show that they are attracted to you and interested in the products you offer. On the other hand, when you are talking to someone, and their eyes often shift focus, they may not be fully involved.

Facing Forward

Just as the feet point to the place of your interest, so does the rest of the body. When someone is interested in you and fully participates in the conversation, they are likely to face you head-on. For comfort, their body may lean slightly off-center, but in most cases, they will use their entire body instead of just their face or feet to adjust to your orientation.

Movement Speed

The speed at which you move or move your body thoroughly explains your emotions. When you move slowly and consciously, it shows that you are very confident and attracted. When the action is rapid and rush, it indicates that the person is too nervous, and in this case, may feel unsatisfied.

Touching Hair

Touching the hair is a sign of attraction, but it can also indicate tension and discomfort. If a man sweeps his entire hand through his hair, it usually shows that he is interested in and likes the woman. If a woman gently spins her hair or fiddles with the ends while showing other signs of attraction, she can be sure that she is attracted to you. However, when women feel nervous, uncomfortable, or even scared, they often touch and play with their hair, so it is good not to use this body language alone to express their opinions.

Moving Moment

Accidental rather than accidental contact is a sure sign that someone is attracted to you. If someone reaches out and touches you intentionally, even if it looks innocent like a simple hand or arms touch, it shows that they are interested. Similarly, when a man touches a woman's elbow or a woman's calf to guide her, for example, from the table to the dance floor, this is undoubtedly a sign of attraction.

Mirror

Mirroring refers to someone copying the actions of the person interacting with it. It usually happens entirely subconsciously. The person can copy measures that change their weight or adopt similar postures or postures, or they can copy actions of someone touching their face or playing with a straw on a drink. This is a sure sign that the person is attractive and that the person has fully participated in the interaction.

Get Body Language Help

If you have been at the dating site for a while but are still single or have an issue with people saying that you are sending out mixed signals, it may be that your body is sending out signs you don't know. Sometimes, the body will show body language reflexively instead of what we think we want.

It may be that you don't want your ideas. Your body may betray your true feelings about dating. One direction to solve this problem is to see a therapist. A licensed interpersonal therapist can help you learn how to use body language for your benefit. They can also help you check the real reason for dating and whether you are ready for a relationship. This way, when you are prepared to build a relationship, your body language, and consciousness language will match, and you will be more likely to make connections.

Use of The Space in Body Language

There is an invisible and protective bubble all around us, and the original needs are hardened into our brains, connected continuously like a force field. It has several layers, and some layers are close to the skin like tights. Others are like isolation tents.

A well-designed network in the brain monitors these protective bubbles and cleverly (and sometimes drastically) keeps them away from danger, thereby adjusting our actions. You walk through cluttered rooms and weave around furniture effortlessly. A pigeon swooped across the street and then hid. Compared with your boss, your position is much higher than that of repair, and your relationship with your lover is much farther.

Personal space is usually hidden under the surface of consciousness and occasionally rises to consciousness, which affects every human experience. In the 1950s, Heini Hediger, the head of the Zurich Zoo, discovered this behavior's evolutionary roots during a careful study of animals. Many animals have territories based on external landmarks. Hediger noted that most animals construct a second self-centered environment, a space bubble that moves with movement, which plays a specific role. He called it the escape distance. Or the flight zone.

When the wildebeest sees a potentially dangerous animal-let say it's a lion-it doesn't matter, only rum is not a simple stimulus-response proposition. The animal appears to have undergone a geometric evaluation. It remained calm until the threat entered the reserve, then the wildebeest moved away and resumed the flight area. The escape distance is sufficient to measure the meter.

The flight zone is different from fear. It's not equal as running away or running away. This is neither emotion nor behavior. Of course, it can have these attributes, but the flight zone is a specific spatial calculation performed on the anus's head without any apparent fear or escape. Animals can have a buffer even when it comes to other animals of the same species. One of Hediger's most famous photos is seagulls' lines sitting on logs, very evenly spaced, which looks almost like carved ornaments.

The space extension distance mainly depends on the crowdedness of animal feeding conditions and the local population density. Therefore, the individual territory can be expanded or contracted according to local conditions. Lions raised in remote areas of Africa may have territorial space with a radius of more than 30 miles (50 kilometers); depending on the density of the lion population in the area; on the other hand, lions raised in captivity with other lions may only have a few meters of personal space, This is a direct result of the crowded situation.

Every country is a territory surrounded by well-defined borders, sometimes protected by armed guards. Within each country, there usually are smaller territories in the form of states and counties. There are even smaller parts of these areas, called towns, which are suburbs, which contain many streets, representing enclosed spaces for the people who live there. This is the handrail in the cinema, and we have a silent battle with strangers trying to demand it. The inhabitants of every territory have invisible loyalty to it, and it is well known that they will become barbarians and kill them to protect it.

The territory is also the area or space around a person who claims to be an extension of the body. Each person has his part, including the area around his property, such as a house bordered by a fence, the interior of a car, a bedroom or a personal chair, and specific air space around the body.

In the last few decades, scientists have thoroughly studied the potential development of personal space, psychology, and neuroscience in many studies. The American anthropologist Edward Hall was one of the pioneers in meeting the needs of human freedom. In the early 1960s, he coined the term "proximity" from "close" or close. His research in this field gave us a new understanding of the relationship between each other.

A consistent finding of the research is that personal space expands with anxiety. When you score high on stress, or if the experimenter puts pressure on you in advance-perhaps, you took an exam and was told you failed the exam-your personal relationship with others will increase. If you rest assured, or the experimenter will self-esteem in advance, your personal space will be reduced. At least in some studies, women have a vast personal space when they contact men-presumably because of the culturally learned expectations.

When tested with more acceptable accuracy, personal space tends to stand out more on the front than on its sides. When people crowd in the subway, individual balloons After space is compressed, you can mainly see its inherent shape. Suppose you can sneak a tape measure to record the average distance between neighboring travelers' body parts. In that event, you will find that the general trend tends to cushion the face, especially the eyes. As always, eyes are the focus of self-protection.

The latest research on personal space focuses on brain mechanisms. Certain areas of the brain contain neurons, which monitor the rooms around the body and track objects. These neurons are almost like radar, emitting signals when particular objects appear looming. If objects touch them, their activities will rise to the peak of madness. When these neurons become highly active, they directly enter our motor control, subtly adjust our movement, or in extreme cases, can cause withdrawal or cringe.

All these mechanisms affect the rest of our lives: our sense of self, the ability to use tools, our culture, and our social or emotional behavior. In other words, what it means to be human. When you understand its meaning, you will gain insights into your behavior and predict others' face-to-face reactions. Mainly discuss the meaning of this airspace, how people react when invaded, and the importance of maintaining "intimacy" sometimes.

Like most animals, everyone has their own portable "bubble" to take with them. Its size depends on the population density of the place where he grew up. Therefore, personal space is partly determined by culture. Some cultures, such as the Japanese, are used to crowding. Others like the "broad space" and want you to keep a distance from yourself.

Area Distance

We will now discuss the radius of the "bubbles" around the middle class living in the suburbs of Australia, New Zealand, the United Kingdom, North America, Northern Europe, Scandinavia, etc., Canada or Singapore, Guam, and Iceland, etc. Anything with "Westernization" "Cultural country, the territory of the country where you live may be larger or smaller than the part we discuss here. However, they will be commensurate with the proportions we discuss here. Children learn this spacing when they are 12 years old, and can be divided into four different regional distances:

1. A private area between 6 and 18 inches (distance between 15-45 cm); this is by far the most critical area because an area protects his property like a person. Close relatives, including lovers, parents, spouses, children, close friends, relatives, and pets, are allowed to enter the area, which is up to 6 inches (15 cm) away from the body and can only enter during close physical contact. This is a closed and intimate area.

175

2. The personal area is between 18 inches and 48 inches (46cm-122m). This is the distance between us at cocktail parties, office gatherings, social events, and friendly gatherings.
3. A social area between 4 and 12 feet (122-3.6m). We are so far away from the place where strangers, plumbers, or carpenters carry out repairs in our houses, mail carriers, and baristas. Starbucks; new employees at work and people we don't know much about.
4. The public area exceeds 12 feet (36m). Whenever we speak to a large group of people, this is the comfortable distance we choose to stand.

Putting It All Together

When the other negotiators entered the meeting room, Mike Kim observed their body language. He thought: "Jose Mendez looks nervous. He doesn't make eye contact. Otherwise, he would keep tapping the top of the pen." "Gary Porter exudes confidence. He smiles and looks around." Mike outlines He presided over the meeting because of the value of the business he wanted to sell. Jose took notes and asked questions from the list he prepared in advance. Gary didn't write a letter, but he glanced at Jose's notes as he asked questions. Mike looked at their expressions. When he saw the confusion, he clarified his speech. When he felt that he had provided too much information, he stepped back and slowed down. At the end of the meeting, they reached an agreement.

Controlling Signals

Your capacity to control your signals can have a profound impact on negotiation. Jose sent a sign that he was nervous. Although his nervousness made him alert, it also could be used against him by the opponent, who perceived him as stressed. Contrast with how Gary was open, relaxed, and acted as though he had not a care in the world. The message he sent was, "If we get the deal, great. If we don't get the deal, we'll live." Jose sent a signal that was the exact opposite; he projected the image of needing the deal. A savvy negotiator needs to be concerned about controlling the verbal and nonverbal cues that he sends in a negotiation because they set the tone for the talks.

The body language signals you convey through your body language and what you say initially influence what happens during the negotiation. They set the tone for what follows. An astute negotiator observes your body language to conclude how you feel at the beginning of the talks and watches how your signals change based on the discussion and its offers.

Misleading Body Language

I just said you should match your body language with your desires. At times, you may deliberately *mislead* your opponent through using body language signals that do not represent what you are thinking or feeling. For example, you might project happiness with an offer he's put on the table even though you may sense it's detrimental to your position. You would watch to see what he might do next then, all of a sudden, change your body language to express displeasure with the offer. Your opponent will be confused and ask himself: "Hey, wait a minute; what exactly is this guy trying to do? What is he seeking from the negotiation?"

If you use body language, not only do you have to be astutely aware of *why* you're doing it, you also have to be very astutely aware of how you are being perceived.

Suppose Gary intentionally came into the negotiation room, radiating confidence, smiling broadly, and looking around the room while being completely relaxed. His deliberate signal was, "I don't have a care in the world. This negotiation can come about successfully or not. I have a backup position. I'm going through the motions here. I'm just granting you the privilege of spending time with me."

By projecting a carefree image, Gary is preventing his opponent from understanding his interest in the deal. He could leave Mike wondering, "Does this guy want this deal? I wonder if I'm wasting my time. How will he react the way I try to influence him based on my strategy? Will I have to make some big concessions to get him interested?"

Mike should observe how Gary's demeanor is altered as they go throughout the negotiation. How do Gary's body language and statements change based on the offers and counteroffers? Or to what degree are they aligned with his strategy?

Measuring Progress with Observations

Assess how well the negotiation is progressing based on what you thought would occur at different points in the talks. Contrast body language and the strategies that have not occurred with offers that your opponent accepted and dismissed.

Mike watched Jose and Gary's facial expressions, and he realized that he might have been giving too much information. Here is what to observe to get that type of insight:

- Is your opponent shaking or nodding his head?
- Is he patting the table or looking around when you are speaking?
- Is he eagerly sitting on the edge of his seat as an active participant in the discussion, or is his posture expressing the desire to expedite the debate?
- From a body language perspective, you observe him sitting on the edge of the seat. Look for clusters of signals. Is he also tapping his fingers, clicking a pen, or doing something else that gives you more insight into his impatience?

You observe your opponent looks attentive, but his eyes are glazed. You wonder, "To what degree am I even getting through to him? Is he bored? Am I going too fast? Am I too complex? How should I determine if he is following me?" Ensure that he is following you, but then if he starts asking one question after another, you know he may be seeking more information. Observe his body language and his messages. Note not only the word choices he makes but also the questions he asks. This will help you determine when you are giving too much or not enough information.

Conclusion

From the above content, I concluded that there is a meaning of every part of your body's expression and gestures.

Body language is a kind of nonverbal communication. It is used to convey information. Such actions include facial expressions, body postures, gestures, eye movement, touch and space. Body language is also called kinematics.

Facial expressions are an essential part of body language and emotional expression. The accurate interpretation depends on the comprehensive understanding of multiple symbols, such as the movement of eyes, eyebrows, lips, nose, and cheeks. Facial expression express happiness, sadness, concentration, inattentiveness, confidence, and fear.

A person nods his head to show respect for others. Nodding of the head is usually considered a "yes" sign. Shaking your head is usually interpreted as "no." Lifting your head from a slumped posture may mean increased interest in what someone is saying. Sitting or standing postures also express a person's emotions. If you sit on the back of the chair and leans forward, sits with their heads, nods, and then discuss, which means you are open, relaxed, and can usually listen. But if you cross your legs and kicks slightly means you are being impatient and emotionally out of the discussion.

When your chest posture is fuller, and the position is relatively forward, this is a sign of confidence. When you pull your chest back, this may indicate a lack of confidence. Shrugging your shoulders and moving up and down are usually signs of not knowing something or not helping in some way.

Gestures usually represent the state of the person's condition, making the gesture. Relax hands indicates self-confidence, while clasped indicators may be interpreted as a sign of stress or anger.

In principle, psychology, neuroscience, and artificial intelligence projects aim to find practical computing tools suitable for social situations and show that what we are happening has particular applicability to artificial intelligence.

The mind has 12 languages, according to Roy H Williams. These 12 Languages enables us to perceive reality. These languages help us build concrete thoughts and visual effects on our minds.

Language is a filter, enhancer, or frame of perception and thought. "Language Unlimited" is an almost contradictory view that our language can come from the human mind's limits. These restrictions determine the structure of the thousands of languages we see all over the world.

Smiling is a common sign that someone is happy. It conveys the message that you are not dangerous and requires people to accept you personally. The most striking thing about a smile is its contagiousness.

By practicing more smile- a real and fake smile will improve your overall experience with others. You can identify a genuine smile from the phony smile by the appearance of characteristic wrinkles around the eyes. The corners of the lips pulled up, and the muscles of the eye contract, producing wrinkles. However, fake smiles only include the lips. Lip L smile, indulgent smile, the jaw's smile, turn around and smile are some common types of smile.

If laughter becomes a permanent part of you, it attracts friends, improves health, and extends life. When we laugh, every organ of the body is positively affected. Our breathing speeds up, and we exercised the diaphragm muscles, neck, stomach, face, or shoulder. Laughter increases the volume of oxygen in the blood and helps in blood circulation.

Expanding, Forming, raising, crossing, pulling back, hidden behind backs are some arm body languages. Hand gestures involve rub palm together, rub your fingers together, and steep hands, holding hand behind.

People often call the eyes "the window of the soul" because they can send out many different nonverbal signals. If you look up, you are often thinking that they may be taking pictures in their heads, which may very well be a sign of visual thinkers. Looking down includes not looking at another person so that it may indicate submission. Looking to the left shows that you are echoing, and looking to the right can suggest that you imagine sounds. Looking at someone will recognize them and show that you are interested in them, especially if you look into their eyes.

Prolonged eye contact can be threatening, so we often look away and look back again. Looking at a person, interrupting eye contact, and then immediately looking back at them is a typical flirting movement, significantly when the head is lowered when the suggested submission is made. Blinking is a natural process. When people feel more stressed, blinking speed tends to increase. Blinking can also indicate harmony, and the connected person may blink at the same rate. A single blink can also indicate a surprise. Blinking can obstruct your vision and maybe the sign of arrogance. Blinking is a deliberate gesture, usually hinting at a conspiracy.

The evolution of legs in humans serves two purposes: to advance to obtain food and escape danger. Parallel attitude, separate your legs, posing with the forward foot, standing cross-legged are the legs' four main postures. Shoulder body language involves raising, bending forward, pushing back, circling, shrugging, relaxing, leaning and turning.

The attractiveness of body language between men and women is indeed different. Specific forms of body language are often done by women, while men tend to do something. Women show their attractiveness to men through body language. Women's body language excludes dominance and masculinity, attracting women the most. They can answer this interest in the body language that shows obedience and fertility. Men have many ways (raise eyebrows, cracked lips, open nostrils, standing with hands-on-hips, show availability, smiling, tilting, foot pointing, touching hair) to show attractiveness to women.

How To Analyze People

Introduction

It is a psychologist's job to be able to read a person's body language precisely. You don't have to be a hardcore psychologist with years of education under your belt to be able to read a person's body language. You, too, can interpret verbal and nonverbal cues in order to understand a person's true personality and identity. If you want to see past a person's mask and perceive their real personality, you have to look at more than just what they vocally tell you. You have to be able to look at all of their body language cues, in addition to what they tell you, and then compare the two. You also must be willing to give away any preconceptions or emotional baggage between yourself and that person, which could stop you from seeing them clearly. By removing any sort of bias and by staying objective, you will be able to receive information about that person without distorting it in any way. Whether you're trying to read your boss, coworker, or even a loved one, in order to completely understand a person's body language, you must *completely* surrender all biases. Benefits of being able to do this are insurmountable. By understanding how those around you are feeling, you will be able to adapt your own message and communication style in order to ensure that it is received in the best possible way. Thus, what sort of things should you be paying attention to? What should you be looking out for? What signs can tip you off to what a person is feeling? All of these and more will be covered within this text.

Continue reading if you would like to know how you can properly and easily read a person and how you can control your own body language. Within the first chapter of this text, I will go into detail about how anyone has the ability to read those around them like a book. I will give a detailed explanation of how easy it is to read those around you and how anyone can learn to read people. I will also give the basics of analyzing those around you.

Within the next chapter, I will go into details about how our bodies talk through language. I will explain how every single part of our body communicates how we feel. Through different motions and the tensing of different muscles, our bodies can show a wide variety of emotions. I will also discuss some common gestures and what they mean in different situations. I will also go into detail about very common nonverbal signals that the body gives off and what they mean in different situations. I will go into detail about the common signals given off through a person's torso, hips, chest, shoulders, and more.

Within the third chapter, I will begin to go into the basic rules for analyzing those around you. These will be the building blocks that you will need in order to begin reading those around you.

Within the fourth and next chapter, I will begin to compare verbal vs. nonverbal communication. I will go in-depth into the differences between verbal and nonverbal behavior. I will also analyze many different types of verbal statements that people may make in certain situations. I will also go into detail about how verbal behavior and nonverbal behavior work together to create a whole picture. I will also go into the intricacies of analyzing nonverbal behavior in order to understand those around you better.

Within the fifth chapter, I will go into an in-depth explanation of the anatomy of our brains and how they contribute to the way that we communicate with others. I will go into the widely loved theory of the unconscious mind and how it relates to our unconscious body language. I will also give some background on the limbic brain and how this connects to our unconscious mind.

Within the sixth chapter, I will go in-depth into the intricacies of facial reading. I will explain how the face is the most important method of nonverbal communication upon our bodies. I will explain how the face contains an extreme amount of delicate muscles that allow us to express a wide variety of emotions. I will also explain how we can easily read our facial expressions and learn to understand them better. I will then go into analyzing every expressive part of the face.

181

These parts will include but are not limited to our eyes, our smiles, our expressions, our lips, our foreheads, and many others.

Within the seventh chapter, I will go into detail about the truth and how it relates to relationships. I will explain how you can tell through body language if a person is lying to another individual. I will also explain how you can analyze a relationship through body language. I will also go into detail about how you can easily judge if a person in a romantic relationship truly loves the other individual within that relationship. I will explain how body language serves as a very important form of nonverbal communication in a loving relationship. I will also go into some almond signs that a female is looking to date a male further. Within this section, I will explain how a woman will put off many different nonverbal signs that she's interested in continuing a long-lasting relationship with a man. After this, I will go into detail about many signals indicating that a man is interested in dating someone for the long-term. I will explain the differences between a man looking for a hookup and a man looking to date somebody for quite some time.

As for the eighth chapter, I will go into the different ways that confidence is displayed upon the human body. I will explain how you can fake your own confidence, as well as how you can spot a lack of confidence in *those around you*. From this, you can also learn how to spot a lack of confidence within *yourself* and how you can improve it.

Within the ninth and final chapter, I will go into detail about how you, too, can fake your own body language so that those around you believe that you feel certain emotions—when in reality, you do not. I will also go into detail about how you can calm your face and relax your muscles so that you're harder to read by those that are good at reading body language. I hope that you enjoy the book and that you find usefulness in the tips and tricks that are included in this text.

Chapter One: How Can Anyone Read People?

If you're anything like me, you love a good mystery-detective. Everybody knows the greatest mystery-detective of all time—that is Sherlock Holmes, of course. Sherlock Holmes is most well-known as the master of deductive reasoning and common literary circles. This character is famous for his innate ability to look at a person and know their entire life story. From the breakfast that they had that morning to some type of traumatic event of their childhood, he can guess it from just one look. You may be thinking that this is simply the stuff of fiction—well, for the most part, you are correct. However, you may be surprised at just how powerful understanding one's body language can be.

A recent study at MIT found that the result of negotiations could be positively predicted by only body language approximately eighty-seven percent of the time. You may be thinking, "This is incredible; all of my dreams are coming true! Sherlock Holmes is real!" Well, not so fast. Yes, you can read a lot more about a person through their body language than one might expect—but it is based on a much more different system than people typically think. Most of the common ideas behind the analysis of a person through their body language are based solely on myth and misconceptions. The real research behind reading a person's body language is quite different from what we have been taught as small children through television and movies. Hence, how exactly do you read people the right way? That is one of the many things that you will learn within this text—before you can do that, you have to understand all of the mistakes that you have been making. Now, we will go into much of the mistakes that people make when trying to read others, in addition to some basic ideas behind reading people's body language.

Context

The biggest thing that people forget to include when they're considering reading somebody's body language is context. Context is everything. There is no one standard rule of thumb when reading somebody's body language—it is all dependent upon the environment that you are in with the person you're trying to read. A person crossing their arms doesn't necessarily have any negative connotation if the room is at a low temperature or if they are sitting in a chair without an armrest. What's more important than these so-called "tells" is the consideration of a situation that somebody is in and the way that they are acting in relation to that. The first thing that you need to consider is the environment that a person is in, and you should try to decide if the way that they are acting or moving their body is cohesive with the environment they're in at that moment.

Considering More Than One Sign

In movies and TV shows about gambling and card games, you often hear people talk about someone having a "tell." These might be things like sweating, face twitching, scratching the nose, or anything in between. In these movies and TV shows, people instantly know when someone's lying because they do one of these "tells." While this is perfect for Hollywood films, this is not how anything *actually* goes down! When trying to read somebody's body language, you need to make sure to consider a group of actions that somebody is performing to tell you what they're really thinking. Hardly ever does a person have one physical action that tells something about themselves. To *really* be able to tell what someone is thinking by looking at their body, you have to ask yourself if the majority of the person's behaviors coincide with common behaviors for a certain emotion.

Not Knowing the Person

Every individual has nervous tics that are different from how they act in a normal situation. Every individual has actions or movements that they do just all the time without any kind of reason behind them. Some people are just jumpy for no reason. When trying to read somebody's body language, it is crucial to consider how they act in normal situations. Obviously, this isn't helpful if you're meeting somebody for the first time—but typically, getting to know the person first is the primary step to reading their body language. What's more important than looking at what somebody's doing is identifying what they are *not* doing. In other words, if a person is normally jumpy and if for some reason, they are suddenly not, this is when you should be asking yourself, "What's going on right now? why is this person acting like this?"

Biases

Biases are things that we cannot escape as humans. They are something deeply embedded within us all. If you already have certain emotions or feelings towards a person, it will affect or change your judgment when trying to read them. In addition, if somebody tends to compliment you or look and act similar to you, you can be swayed by all of these. The biggest basis of all is truly not having a bias. Hence, it is a good first step to go ahead and assume that you're biased in some way.

With all of these basic ideas in mind, anyone can learn how to read those around them. Whether you wanted for social reasons, business reasons, or even just for fun, learning to read people is simply a matter of trusting your instincts and practicing a skill that you can use in your everyday life.

Chapter Two: Our Bodies and the Way They Talk

I'm sure we have all heard the cliché about how our eyes are the windows to our souls. However, in order to properly read another person like they're a book, you have to be able to look at the big picture. In other words, you have to be able to look at more than just their face, their hands, or just their eyes. You have to be able to read every inch of their body and understand whatever different section of their body is trying to communicate to you, whether they know it or not.

Our emotions are probably the easiest thing we can read through the body. This is because emotions are something that is unconsciously felt, and our bodies respond to them in ways that we can't always control or understand. Typically, we don't even notice when our bodies are doing things that may be revealing our innermost emotions. The reason why this is so difficult to notice and understand is that it is happening all the time without pause. Nonverbal bodily behavior is happening on and around our bodies more frequently than we realize. In addition to this, the interpretation and understanding of these bodily actions, collectively known as our body language, is also occurring simultaneously. By simply glancing at the way that somebody is standing, we can instantly know how they're feeling or how they may feel about us without even realizing that we have made that judgment. This is an incredibly powerful skill to have and is one that humans that have been trying to perfect and use to their advantage for centuries. Understanding the intricacies of body language is a massive foot that takes a lot of studying and hard work. However, we aren't beginning at square one. As people, we have an automatic and internal understanding of universal emotions. A few examples of these are how we smile we smile when we are happy, how we frown when are sad or angry, or how we nod our heads when answering yes. With a few exceptions, the majority of these movements and expressions are commonly understood around the world. This makes our job of understanding body language that much easier but simultaneously harder. Because of how simple and easy to understand these expressions are, following the same train of thought, they are also very easy for people to fake. This makes our job a little bit harder because, in addition to simply knowing the tell-tale signs of certain emotions, we also have to know how to tell if someone is trying to fake them.

Within the next section, this text will begin to discuss some very basic common gestures that people use and what they may mean in different contexts. It is important to keep in mind that the following gestures and interpretations are very basic and surface-level. If you are looking to read into somebody's emotions properly, you should do a lot more than just knowing these basic gestures and their meanings. We will go into more detail about those later in this chapter.

Positive Bodily Gestures

Many common bodily gestures can be broken up at a very basic level into positive body language and negative body language. The following are some very basic signs of *positive* body language:

- **Relaxed or uncrossed limbs**

  If somebody appears relaxed or that they have all of their limbs uncrossed in front of you, this is typically a sign that they are comfortable in your presence. Please keep in mind, though, that this is very easy to fake. Also, remember that what somebody looks like when they are relaxed is very subjective. Relaxed-looking to somebody may be very different for someone else.

- **Open palms**

  Somebody presenting their palms to you open and face up typically is a sign that they trust you and are comfortable around you. This is most likely connected to the fact that when your palms are exposed, so are your wrists. Moreover, it is a very well-known fact that our wrists have some of the largest and most concentrated arteries within our bodies. Hence, the act of opening our palms and laying our hands out in front of somebody is similar to that of a dog that rolls onto its back to expose their stomach to another. It is a sign of trust and submission.

- **Leaning forward**

The act of someone leaning forward into you can show many things. It can show that somebody is listening very intently to what you are saying to them. It can also show that someone is very, very interested in your ideas or that they hold your beliefs to a very high value. They may view you as someone of high stature that's worth listening to. It can also be a sign that somebody likes you either in a platonic or romantic way. Somebody leaning onto you or towards you shows that they want to get closer to you.

- **The speed of speech**

This type of body language is a little bit different from those that we have discussed previously. Despite the fact that this body language is also a form of local language, it also falls under the umbrella of body language gestures. The speed of somebody speech can tell a lot about how they actually feel about what they're saying. If somebody is speaking very quickly, it may show that the person speaking is feeling unsure or disorganized. They might know what they want to say or the basis behind what they're saying, but in reality, they could end up talking very fast—maybe because they want to get rid of the words or because they don't feel comfortable when speaking. Alternatively, this could show that they're excited about a subject matter and cannot control themselves when speaking about it. This is also a sign of nervousness and very common in people that are opposed to public speaking or have difficulty doing so. Speaking at an average pace is usually a sign of a very good and well-rounded public speaker. Similar to speaking in a quick tone, slowly speaking can also be a sign that somebody is unsure of what they're trying to say. Unlike speaking quickly, somebody speaking very slowly is often trying to make up what they say on the spot. This may be a sign that they did not prepare properly beforehand, and this tends to give the impression of low intelligence, regardless if this is true or not.

- **Pupil size**

This is a type of body language that gets passed around very often on the Internet and is often misunderstood. People often believe or say that having enlarged pupils is a sign of love or having a crush on an individual. While these two things are related, they are not necessarily indicators of one another. This is also a troublesome body language to look out for because it is very easy to fake or to stop from happening. If somebody is aware that their body is doing this and doesn't want the other person to know, changing their pupil size is as simple as staring directly into a bright light. If a person is unaware that this is happening, this can be a very strong indicator of what somebody's feeling. Enlargement of the pupils can also show a great deal of interest—if somebody's talking about a topic that they are very passionate about, they may have signs of enlarged pupils due to the intensity of the conversation.

Negative Bodily Gestures

Meanwhile, the following are some very basic examples of *negative* body language:

- **Leaning away**

The exact opposite of somebody leaning forward has, as you would expect, the opposite meaning of somebody leaning into you. If somebody is leaning away from you, it can have many different interpretations. Depending on what the conversation is about, someone could be leaning away from you because you said something that they felt to be quite shocking. You may have said something that they highly disagree with or something against some of their core beliefs. If you have not been having a controversial conversation, it is possible that a person leaning away from you just doesn't like you or doesn't want to be in your presence.

- **Crossed limbs**

The action of somebody crossing their limbs can have various meanings. Depending on the situation, at a very surface-level, somebody crossing their arms could be taking a defensive position. They could also be taking a position of discomfort. They could be trying to hide more of their body, or they could also be trying to make their body seem smaller. This can often be a sign of discomfort or self-consciousness in a moment. Somebody may have recently said something that makes them feel uncomfortable, which then prompted them to feel the need to hide their body. This position can also show signs of anger or a disgruntled feeling at a statement somebody has made.

- **Tight shoulders**

If somebody's shoulders appear to be very tight, this is often a sign that they're under some kind of stress. They might have a lot of things on their plate, or they might be uncomfortable talking to a certain person. They might feel as though they're walking on eggshells or as though they need to be very careful about what they say. An individual with shoulders that are very unrelaxed and push up high to their chin might be nervous or feel unwelcome in a situation.

- **Feet turned away**

This position may seem somewhat random or unconnected compared to all of the others. However, watch out for this sign because it appears more often than one may believe. If somebody who's standing in front of you points their feet away from or towards an exit, they may be indicating that they want to end a conversation. Alternatively, they may be indicating that they are late for something or that they need to leave as soon as possible or simply that they don't want to talk to you anymore.

- **Leaning on two hands or head resting on one hand**

If an individual is sitting at a desk and has their chin on their hand, this can mean one of two things. This is an indicator that somebody is either incredibly bored or thinking very intensely. Typically, you can tell the difference between these two by looking at the rest of the person's body. Are they slouching? Are their eyes half-closed, or are they fully open? Have they yawned recently? Depending on the answers to these questions, you may be able to determine whether a person is resting their head in their hand because they're too bored to hold it up or if they're simply thinking of something very intensely and can't be bothered to hold their head up themselves.

As we have discussed previously, reading body language is about a lot more than most of these common gestures alone. You have to look at the bigger picture and take into account the interpretations of every inch of that person's body. In the next section of this book, we will be going into detail about the nonverbal aspects of the body and what they mean. You will go through every well-known appendage and part of the human body—from torso, hips, chest, feet, and more.

Torso

Many individuals attempting to learn how to read body language make the mistake of ignoring the torso as a signal-giving part of the body. This is a huge and detrimental mistake to make. Torso makes up the vast majority of the body and, as such, is responsible for approximately seventy percent of the signals that we give off. Leaving out the torso in our consideration of body language leaves out a huge chunk of the body to read. If somebody does this, then they will not receive the big picture when trying to read a person. When looking at the body language of the torso, we have to break the torso up into multiple languages in order to fully understand it.

- **Neck**

  The neck, used to support the head, is a very important part of our body to read.

  - Hiding - the act of hiding one's neck is an instinctive one that happens when someone feels threatened. This comes from a biological understanding of a predator attempting to attack possibly the most vulnerable parts of the body. People have an instinct to try and hide their body part that they feel threatened. Because of the way that humans have evolved and adapted to everyday life, they could find themselves hiding their necks if they feel threatened at things that have no real physical consequences for them. We can then find ourselves hiding our necks if we feel threatened for our jobs or our respective socio-economic situations. If a person is feeling embarrassed, they may also find themselves reaching out to touch their neck or swallowing more than average.

  - Touching - the act of touching the front of the neck or the location of the windpipe may show concern about what an individual is saying to them. They instinctively may reach up to touch their windpipe because that is where the concerning words are going to come from. It is also important to note that the back of the neck contains some very strong and large muscles. If a person is rubbing or massaging those muscles, this may be a sign of tension or stress.

- **Shoulders**

  If a person's arms are folded in front of them, then their shoulders will naturally be curved forward without them needing to do it themselves. If a person's arms are not crossed but instead are hanging down by their side, there can be a wide range of emotions and feelings.

  - Raised - if the shoulders are seen to be in a raised position, then the person whose shoulders are raised are having to pull the entire weight of their arms all the way up. This takes a great amount of effort compared to other body language symbols. Because this, this is a very conscious symbol of body language and is often something that somebody's doing intentionally. When this is added with arms folded tight over the body or holding the body, it can be a sign of colds or of great levels of tension.

188

o   Curved forward - in case that the shoulders are curved forward, they're attempting to lower the width of the body, which is often used as a defensive posture or a subconscious attempt to not be seen. If a person is feeling embarrassed or threatened in any way, then they may have this position.

o   Pushed back - the act of pushing one's shoulders backward forces the chest out and shows the torso to potential attacked. Because of this, this posture is often used when a person is trying to appear confident and maybe trying to demonstrate great power.

o   Circling - the act of circling one's shoulders either forward or backward is usually done to exercise a stiff or tense shoulder. In most situations, this is simply a sign that a person is feeling very stressed.

o   Leaning - when a person is seen to lean against the wall, they have to make contact with the wall and their shoulder. This is usually a sign of relaxation or a symbol that shifting into physical movement would take more effort than simply leaning against the wall. This puts a person in a position that is vulnerable to attack, but it is typically very clear that the said person's okay with that. Oftentimes, this is seen as meaning that an individual doesn't view another individual as a threat or is trying to come off as confident or cocky.

o   Turning - the act of turning one's shoulders away from somebody is a sign that they want to end a conversation or do not want to continue talking to you. If they are still talking to you while doing this, they may be trying to send you unconscious signals to end the conversation. If a person is trying towards you, it shows that they are very interested in what you were saying.

- **Chest**

The chest sends a few body language symbols that are very important.

o   Thrusting outwards – oftentimes, thrusting draws attention to the person doing it. Women, in particular, have a tendency to do this, as they are programmed to know that men are aroused by the sight of breasts. When a female is pushing forward their breasts, they may be unconsciously or even consciously inviting intimate relations. It is important to note that high heels enhance this factor, as they promote curvature in the spine, which pushes the chest and buttocks outwards. Men also have a tendency to push out their chests in the temp to attract a mate. This is often in the hopes of displaying large or strong pectorals. The big difference between men and women is that men can also do this to other men, in addition to women, typically in an attempt to intimidate the men around them.

o   Profile - when a person is standing sideways, or at a forty-five-degree angle, then the effect of the previously discussed pushed-out chest is even more exaggerated. This may be used by women to show off the curve of their breasts or by men to show off the size of their pectorals.

o   Withdrawn - the chest contains some of the most important and most vulnerable organs in the human body. Well, somewhat protected by the ribs,

189

they are still very vulnerable to attack. When the chest is being pulled into itself, it may serve as a sign that a person is trying to appear unthreatening are trying their best to disappear to prevent themselves from being attacked.

- o Breathing - when a person is viewed to be breathing very deeply, then the chest tends to move up and down with much more extreme than normal. A deep breath is a sign that somebody may be taking in a lot of oxygen and readying for action. This may be a sign of extreme anger or very intense feeling such as love.

- **Hips**

The hips are at the base of the torso and make up the pelvis and buttocks. They are a crucial form of body language.

- o Thrusting out - the hips on both genders contain the primary sexual organs, and as a result, dressing them forward is a sign of provocation and suggestion. This is further exaggerated if the legs are spread—exposing the genitals further and inviting action. Pushing our hips forward is difficult to do without losing our balance, so this can be done by leaning against something like a well that may support the upper body.

- o Holding back - the action of holding back the hips—as I'm sure you can guess—is the opposite of pushing them outwards. It hides genitals and seeks to protect them or avoid having them noticed. This may be a sign that somebody is uninterested in you or has no attraction to you whatsoever.

- o Pushing to the side - the action of pushing your hips to the side makes it necessary for the entirety of your body to compensate for the rearrangement of the spinal curve. This is typically seen as a relaxed position, as the body is able to drop its center of gravity. A lesser-known meaning of disposition is the hips may be pointing towards a person that they are interested in or may actually be wanting to talk to. If the hips are pointing towards the door, it can mean that the person wants to leave the conversation or the area.

- o Touching – Some of the things that may be used as a signal of power or dominance include placing someone's hands on their hips, pushing the elbow sideways, and making the body look larger. On the flip side of this, stroking of one's hips may be a sign of flirtation in a romantic setting, especially if accompanied by the swaying of hips and prolonged eye contact.

- **Hands**

Our hands contain up to twenty-seven bones and are the most used part of our bodies. Our hands are very important to everyday function and thus give away a lot in terms of body language.

- o Cupping - the action of cupping our hands together creates a form that can

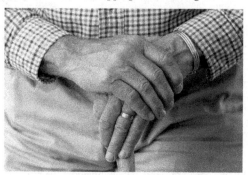

serve as a container or bowl. When one's hands come together, this can be a symbol of delicacy or a sign that someone is holding a fragile idea. This can also be used as a sign of giving. The action of holding your hands out to someone in a cup fashion is a sign of giving or showing to another person.

- o Greetings - hands are very often used as a form of greeting. The most common type of this is the act of shaking one's hands. This is a type of great team that transcends across many cultures and religions. The act of opening one's palm for another on a subconscious level is to find out if the other person is not carrying a weapon or something meant to harm. This is why the act of opening our palms is used in various greetings such as salutes or waves. Going back to handshakes, there are various ways that you can show certain emotions through them. If an individual places their hands on top of yours during a handshake and holds it longer than you would expect, this can be a sign of asserting dominance. On the opposite end, a handshake with a floppy or loose grip is a sign of submission.

- o Rubbing - if a person tends to rub their hands together, it can mean a variety of things. On the surface level, it could mean that the person is simply feeling cold. It could also mean that an individual is feeling happy or excited about something that has transpired. If somebody appears to be rubbing their hands together subtly and slowly, then they may be thinking about a benefit they may gain at the expense of another person.

- o Hiding - the act of hiding one's hands—behind the back, in their pockets, under the table, or sitting on top of them—indicates many different communicative meetings. Most often, this is a sign that an individual has a desire not to cooperate with or to listen to the person speaking any longer. It usually is a sign that they do not agree with something that the speaker has said or that they don't want to talk to them any longer. This may be done deliberately, or a person who has recently lied may hide their hands subconsciously due to the fear of their hands giving them away.

- o Trembling - trembling of the hands can mean many different things, and not all of them are necessarily negative. The trembling of one's hands may be a sign that that individual is very frightened, or it could also be a sign that that individual is very excited. Connected to this, an unexpected action like dropping something that somebody is holding can be a sign that their motor skills are somewhat malfunctioning for a particular reason. Whether this reason is that they're nervous, excited, or feeling any kind of extreme emotion will depend on a wide range of factors.

- **Legs**

When a person is consciously trying to control their body language, they often focus much too hard on their upper body alone. For this reason, the legs can often tell us a deeper story about what a person is feeling as compared to the upper body.

- o Open – if a person originally standing in a stationary position have their legs spread apart, they're providing for themselves a stable base so as to support their upper body and keep their balance. If a person's legs are slightly wider than the width of their shoulders, then this can be a sign that the said individual is feeling grounded and confident that day. In addition, a wider stance can make the body appear larger and is thus a signal of power and dominance.

- o Closed - when an individual is standing with their legs being apart less than their shoulders' distance from each another, then this may be displaying a sign of anxiety, as it makes them appear smaller and gives more protection to their genitalia.

- o Pointing - an individual's legs can have a tendency to point in the direction of where they wish they could go without them realizing it. If a person's legs are pointing towards a person talking, that means that they are feeling very attentive and are very interested in the conversation that they are in. On the flip side, however, an individual who is pointing their legs opposite the direction of a person they're talking to means that they may want to leave the conversation or that they want to be elsewhere.

192

Chapter Three: The Basics

In today's modern world of politics and business, many people now understand that everything has become about appearance and body language over the pure merit of a person. Because of this, the vast majority of high-profile politicians now have their own personal body language consultants that help them come across as being honest, caring, and responsible individuals. Since the 1960s, the evolution of our body language has been actively studied, and the public was brought into the world of our body language through a book titled *Body Language,* which was published in 1978. Despite this, the majority of individuals believe that speech is our main form of communication today. Well, speech is very important in getting across what we believe in to those around us.

Evolutionarily speech has only been with the human race for a very short amount of time. Prior to widespread modern language, you could understand what people meant or felt towards you through only their body language. We are still capable of this today, but it becomes a little bit more difficult because of the weight we put on spoken word. With a few simple tips and tricks, you can begin the basics of reading someone's body language like it is a second language.

The first thing that we are going to discuss is the necessity of being able to understand a person's emotional condition while listening to what they are saying to you and taking that into context with the circumstances under which they are saying it. In simpler terms, you have to understand the *context*. You have to be able to look at every piece of the puzzle—rather than just the corner piece and trying to understand what the picture is. Hence, while you should be listening to what a person is vocally telling you, it is also vital for you to mentally thinking about what that person's emotional condition at that moment is and then compare it to the physical environment around them. If a person is smiling and if their cheeks are bright red, while the room just so happens to be hot at that very moment, that person might not necessarily be embarrassed. They might simply feel hot.

It is interesting to note the connection between a person's gender and their ability to perceive nonverbal communication. There's lots of talk in modern conversations about a "mother's intuition." This is not an old wives' tale. Women have been proven in qualitative scientific studies to be more perceptive at understanding body language than men are. A study done at Harvard University showed that when a random sample of men and women were given the same film with no audio, the women were eighty-seven percent more likely to guess what the circumstances of the situation were, whereas men only guessed correctly forty-two percent of the time. It is believed that women's perceptiveness of body language is superior to men because, for the first few years of raising a child, a mother has to rely almost entirely on nonverbal communication to understand the child's needs and wants. This is supported by the fact that women with children guessed the situation correctly almost every single time. This is also often used to explain why women tend to be better negotiators than men.

Much of basic common body language is the same all over the world despite religion and racial differences. Some examples of this are smiling when you're happy or scowling when you are sad or angry. The nodding of the head is almost completely universally used to indicate an affirmation of sorts. It is believed that this form of affirmation is a genetic predisposition because individuals who were born blind still use this form of body language even though they never learned to use it visually.

This then brings me to an interesting point about body language and whether it is a learned action or genetic action. This is a debate that is ongoing and is still being researched even up to this day. Some forms of body language can be traced back to animal ancestry and are believed to be purely genetic. This is the action of sneering at another person in anger or irritation. An animal's a similar action to this is done when preparing for an attack.

There are three basic rules for an accurate reading of somebody's body language. You must keep these three rules in mind when attempting to analyze any person for their body language.

1. *Reading Clusters of Gestures Rather Than an Individual*

You should never try to analyze or interpret a single solitary gesture separately from all of the others. You have to look at the entire picture. This means that you have to look at every action of the person's body and compare it to the rest of them. It is easy to remember this rule when you think of body language as just that: a language. As with any vocally spoken language, body language has its own "words," "sentences," and "punctuation." Attempting to understand somebody's body language through one specific gesture is like attempting to understand an entire paragraph from just a single word. You have to read each individual gesture as its own word and put them together to create sentences so that you can understand the language that someone's body is giving off. A common rule of thumb for this is the idea that someone needs at least three words to be able to create a proper sentence. As for body language, this means that you have to be able to compare at least three gestures that a person is giving off before you can begin to understand their innermost feelings and thoughts.

2. *Searching for Consistency*

This is especially important when trying to decide if somebody may be lying to you or not. Consistency is key in being able to tell if somebody is telling the truth. You have to consider the words that are coming out of their mouth in relation to what their body language is showing you. If an individual's words and body language are in conflict in a given moment, it is often best to ignore what is being said and focus instead on body language exclusively. Inconsistency between body language and vocal words is a strong sign of lying.

3. *Context, Context, Context*

Context is incredibly important when attempting to read a person's body language. You have to take into account an individual's environment, in addition to the signals that their body is giving off. There are lots of body symbols that have no meaning whatsoever when an individual is in certain situations. For instance, a person with arms and legs crossed tightly together on a cold winter's day is not necessarily a sign of feeling defensive—they are most likely just cold.

Language is incredible. As humans, we have an incredibly heightened ability to communicate with one another. This level of communication is a part of the reason that we have been able to advance so far in our evolution. The advancement of our communication results in advancement in our society. Within this chapter, we will discuss the ways that our communication is more advanced and the intricacies behind verbal and nonverbal behavior. More importantly, we will define nonverbal and verbal behavior and also give two differences between the two and learn how to analyze the statements that other individuals make verbally. More specifically, we will learn how to analyze these verbal statements using nonverbal language. We will also go into the intricacies of analyzing the nonverbal behavior of those around us.

Defining Nonverbal Behavior

Nonverbal behavior or communication is the subconscious or conscious relaying of ideas or emotions through physical motion or a series of well-known and understood gestures. Messages can be transferred non-verbally through a variety of signals and methods.

The first of these defining signals are methods known as proxemics. Proxemics essentially means the distance between two individuals. The distance between two individuals or proxemics carries a lot of weight in terms of nonverbal communication.

The second method of nonverbal communication is known as kinesics and is simply another word for body language. Kinesics or body language is the transmission of ideas through gestures and often unconscious motions of the body.

Meanwhile, another defining method is known as haptics. Haptics is another word for the act of touching something. In the world of nonverbal behavior, the way that somebody touches something carries a lot of weight in communicating their emotions to another individual. A soft touch on the arm can mean a lot of things, which becomes very different in comparison to a firm grasp of one's hand. Not all touches are equal, and every touch—depending on its longevity, intensity, and location on the body—has many different meanings behind it.

Another form of nonverbal communication is our appearance. People use their appearance to communicate their personality in a variety of ways. Most of this is a conscious decision made by the individual, but there are some factors almost entirely caused by our parents that aren't necessarily chosen by us but still say things about ourselves. Most likely, the biggest and most common type of nonverbal communication using our parents is simply judging whether or not somebody cares about their appearance. By just looking at another person, we can instantly tell whether or not they care about how they appear to those around them. This carries a huge amount of weight in the snap judgment that we make about people every single day. The final common form of nonverbal communication is the use of eye contact. Eye contact is extremely important in us as humans. Humans are very focused on an individual's eyes, as that is often one of the first things that a person looks at when they see a new face. Your eyes are often considered the windows to the soul, and this is true in the sense that they can reveal a lot of factors about yourselves. By looking into someone's eyes or measuring the amount of eye contact they give, we can understand a vast amount of information about their personality. Do they have strong eye contact? Do they avoid eye contact? Do they have really intense eye contact? The answers to all of these questions give us different definitions to a person's personality. As humans, we put a lot of weight on to an individual's eye contact as a defining portion of their personality. This is why we must keep eye contact in mind when attempting to understand someone's nonverbal communication.

Defining Verbal Communication

Verbal communication seems quite obvious when spoken out loud. Verbal communication obviously does consist of any form of speech or language that is used to relay ideas or thoughts to another. Verbal communication includes much more than simply speaking to a person. The way that we string together ideas and thoughts with word shows a lot about their personality in the words that we choose in the cadence that we choose to put them together. There are multiple ways that we can express ourselves through verbal communication. The first and most obvious way that we can express ourselves through verbal communication is through speaking to those around us. By stringing together words and sentences, we create cohesive thoughts and ideas that express our feelings to those around us.

In addition to being able to accurately and positively express our emotions and feelings to those around us, the act of speaking is also quite easy to use to persuade or to alter our true meaning. It is much easier to lie to a person verbally than it is to lie to a person with our body language. Because of this, we often find people who lie very easily vocally to a person but whose body language cues do not match their words.

The second form of verbal communication, writing, may come as a surprise to some people reading this text. The act of writing, while not technically verbal, still comprises verbal communication because it uses common vocally spoken language simply in written form. The difficulty in this is that a person reading a text has a much harder time of guessing and understanding the cadence of the person who wrote the text. Because of this, written ideas and emotions can be misconstrued due to the fact that people cannot quite tell the intonation of the author of the text through the words.

Another form of verbal communication is an underlying feeling within our words known as denotation or connotation. The connotation is considered as the feelings or emotions associated with the meanings of certain words or phrases. This is not to be confused with its antonym, denotation, which is the literal or primary meaning of a word, opposite to the emotions or series that the word suggests. In order to convey these important forms of verbal communication, a person has to use our neck form of verbal communication.

The next form of verbal communication that we will be discussing is tone and volume. An individual's tone, when talking to another person, can express a lot about that person's inner thoughts or feelings. The tone is a very difficult form of communication to pin down and explain to people. For some individuals, the tone is very easy to control and change in their language—while for others, it can be very difficult. You cannot describe the tone as based on the inflection that an individual puts on to certain words at certain times. The tone is very interesting because every person is able to understand the meaning behind other people's tones almost in perfect connection with one another, but it is very difficult to explain to others. In connection to this, a person's volume also holds a great deal of significance in their verbal communication. Ever since childhood, we have all learned about the difference between an inside voice and an outside voice. Do volume levels show a lot about our emotions? We can read a lot about how someone feels in a certain situation based on their volume at that time.

It is important always to remember that you have to use *both* verbal and nonverbal forms of communication together in parallel to understand the grand total outcome of a person's ideas and theories. A common misconception amongst individuals is that verbal communication and nonverbal communication are contradictory. This is not the case. Verbal and nonverbal communication must go side-by-side when communicating with those around us. It is the combination of these two complex forms of communication that make the translation of our ideas and theories the most effective. One cannot exist without the other—in most cases. It is often asserted by body language specialists that nonverbal communication can play one of five roles when trying to read another person. These five roles are known as substitution, reinforcement, contradiction, accentuation, and regulation.

Substitution - certain types of nonverbal communication are started as a substitution or placement for verbal communication. Examples of this are nodding your head for yes or shrugging your shoulders for "I don't know."

Reinforcement - nonverbal communication can often be used to reinforce a previously given statement. By reading an individual's body language and judging it consistently, you can almost entirely ascertain whether they are telling the truth or not.

Contradiction - this is the opposite of reinforcement. If a person's body language appears to be contradicting something that they are saying, then by the rule of contradiction, they are almost certainly lying—depending on their environment, of course.

Accentuation - body language often serves as a method of accentuating something that a person says vocally. Examples of this include smiling when someone says that they are happy or shivering when somebody says that they are cold. This can also be used to put a greater level of importance to a statement that somebody has given out. An example of this is creating the quotation mark symbol with your fingers while saying something sarcastically. By adding body language to the statement that you're making, you are reaffirming and showing importance in your statement.

Regulation - an individual's body can also serve to regulate that person's vocal language.

A lot of an individual's communication is not based solely on what they actively try to put out there. A much larger, much more active chunk of our communication is based on what we don't realize that we are putting out in the world. Our body can reveal our deepest emotions and feelings without us realizing pretty much twenty-four seven. This does not happen randomly, of course. The way that our mind communicates without us realizing it is based on two main theories of thought. These are known as the unconscious mind and the limbic brain. In the following chapter, I will define and give the importance of the unconscious mind and the limbic brain in our communication.

Unconscious Mind

The unconscious mind originates from Freud's Psychoanalytic Theory of Personality. In this theory, Freud defines the unconscious mind as a hidden well of feelings, thoughts, urges, and memories that are separate from our conscious awareness of feelings. The contents of our unconscious mind tend to be unpleasant or depressing. They tend to include feelings of pain, anxiety, or conflict. It is because of these negative feelings and emotions that our unconscious mind stays outside of our conscious awareness. Since on a subconscious level, we do not want to remember or feel those feelings, we then try to ignore them and push them into our unconscious mind.

Despite this attempt at ignoring and hiding these feelings, our unconscious mind still influences our behavior even though we do not know that it is there. Many individuals compare the unconscious mind to that of an iceberg. The part of the iceberg that is above water represents our conscious brain and all of the communication of ideas and feelings that we actively put out into the world. Oppositely, our unconscious mind is represented by every part of the iceberg that is below the water and unseen. Within this iceberg analogy, it is important to remember how large an iceberg below the water truly is. This represents just how deep our unconscious mind goes and just how much tends to be hidden below the surface. The amount of information that is hidden just below the surface within our unconscious mind is so massive like the hidden part of the iceberg in the sense that we have to consider the parts of our body language that connect to our unconscious mind as a huge part of nonverbal communication.

Freud also believed and asserted that our basic instincts and animal urges are contained within the unconscious mind. This includes instincts under actions of life and death as well as sexual instincts. He believed that urges such as these were hidden from or kicked out of our present consciousness because our minds view them as unacceptable, irrational, or uncivilized. Freud suggested that individuals often use a number of different defense mechanisms to stop these hidden urges from rising above the waters into our conscious mind.

Freud also goes on to explain the different ways that the information from the unconscious mind might be brought into conscious awareness. One of the techniques that Freud explained can be used to bring these feelings into awareness is known as free association. Free association is a rather simple and seemingly silly form of psychotherapy. In free association, Freud asked patients to lay back and relax and say to him whatever came to their minds without any sort of filter on it. He wanted them to say anything that they could think of without stopping to think of it is trivial, irrelevant, or embarrassing. Freud then traced the streams of thoughts until he believed that he could uncover the contents of the unconscious mind. He often used this method in order to try to find repressed childhood traumas or hidden desires.

Freud also believes that dream interpretation could be used to understand the unconscious mind further. Many people think of dreams as a route to the unconscious mind and believe that the information from the unconscious mind could appear randomly in dreams but typically in a disguised format. Because of this, he would often ask patients to keep dream journals and would try to go through and interpret these dreams to try and understand their hidden meanings.

Freud also believes that dreams tended to serve as a form of secret fulfillment of long-coddled wishes. He believes that the fact that these unconscious urges were not expressed in real life means that they could be expressed in the individual's dreams.

The Freudian theory of the unconscious mind did not come across as without controversy. A multitude of researchers have criticized the idea of the unconscious mind and firmly dispute that there isn't an unconscious mind at all. Recently, in the field of cognitive psychology, researchers and psychologists have begun to focus on the automatic and instinctive functions that describe things that were previously being attributed to the unconscious mind. The ideas behind this approach believe that there are a series of cognitive functions that happen outside of our conscious awareness.

Meanwhile, they do not entirely support the voice conceptualization of the unconscious mind, but it does offer some evidence that actions that we are not aware of still have an influence on our automatic behaviors. Unlike Freud's psychoanalytic approaches to the unconscious mind, research within the modern field of cognitive psychology is almost exclusively driven by scientific investigation and quantitative data. This idea of the unconscious mind continues to have a great effect on modern psychology and is still used in some modern practices today.

Limbic Brain System

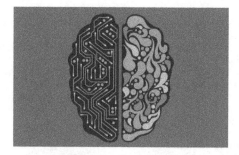

The limbic system within an individual's brain is responsible for a variety of very important brain functions. The biggest responsibility of the limbic system is our instincts for survival and for memory access and storage. The limbic system is made up of many different brain structures—two of the biggest and most important parts of the limbic system are the amygdala and the hippocampus. Amygdala is the deciding structure that chooses where each memory should be placed in the brain, while the hippocampus transports that memory to its final location. It is often believed that the placement is determined by the amount of emotional response that it receives from the person.

The limbic system is also very responsible for hormone levels, body temperature, and motor functions. The different parts of the limbic brain system are the amygdala, cingulate gyrus, the hippocampus, and the hypothalamus. These individual structures are very important parts of a person's brain. The limbic system, as a whole, is located on top of the brainstem and underneath the frontal cortex. The limbic system is often connected to survival-based emotions such as fear, anger, and pleasure. The limbic system is also known to influence both the peripheral nervous system and the endocrine system. The part of the limbic system that is important to this text, in particular, is its connection with memory. Because of the limbic system's perceived importance in the decisions of where memories go and how they are remembered, it is often connected with Freud's ideas of the unconscious mind. Because Freud's ideas of the unconscious mind are based on the theory that certain memories and feelings are hidden far away from our conscious awareness, it is easy to understand how the limbic system can play a huge part in that considering that it is believed to be the deciding factor of where our memories get stored. Now, you may be thinking to yourself, "What does any of this have to do with our body language and understanding the body language of those around us?" The answer lies in the fact that the unconscious mind is very powerful and controls a huge portion of our true feelings and emotions. By reading body language, we can often unlock these feelings of the unconscious mind without even realizing that they are hidden from the person we are reading. This is a very powerful skill, and it is important to understand the basis behind it. The limbic system and the unconscious mind create this basis for the deeper readings of people.

Chapter Six: Intricacies of the Face

Returning to our methods of nonverbal communication and the reading of body language, we come to the intricacies and extreme complications of facial communication. The face is a huge indicator of nonverbal communication within body language. The face tends to tell all. The face is also the most difficult to control when trying to regulate your own body language. Within this chapter, we will discuss the use of the face as a method for nonverbal communication and how we can easily read it on our own. We will also analyze the expressive parts of the face and what they can say in terms of nonverbal communication.

Many parts of the face are the first things consider when we look at a new person. Because of this, a lot can be conveyed within a person's face. This is partially an evolutionary result because we spend so much time looking into the faces of those around us to the point that we have, over time, evolved to be able to convey emotions and expressions on their faces so that those around us may not have to ask to know what we are feeling. There are a few tricks to reading somebody's face beyond a simple basis of whether or not they're angry at you.

The first one is staring into an individual's eyes. When you begin reading a person's face, you will want to start at their eyes. The eyes contain the most expression within a person's face. You can learn an extreme amount of detail about somebody's emotions by paying close attention to their eyes. Later in the chapter, we will go through some common expressions that we can read within the eyes.

The next step is to look at the lips. The muscles in our lips are extremely sensitive and are constantly shifting. A person's lips can move and react to situations without an individual even realizing what they're doing. You can pay attention to a person's lip to figure out how they feel about certain situations or what their next action may be.

The next step may come as a surprise to most individuals. This is to pay attention to the nose. The nose does not change quite as much as the eyes and the lips, but its location on the face makes it a very important part of facial reading. The nose is right in the middle of a person's face. It is because of this that many people tend to glance at a person's nose before they even look at a person's eyes or mouth. Because of this, the nose acts as a grounding or central location to the rest of our face. If an event or a feeling is powerful enough to cause one's nose to move, then you can take that as a sign that whatever happened was groundbreaking enough to shift the very foundation of that person's face.

The next step and part of the face to pay attention to is the eyebrows. Connected to the eyes and often the second most expressive parts of our face, the eyebrows can express a wide variety of emotions. Their ability to move with a great level of dexterity and range puts them at a greater advantage than the rest of our face. In addition, our eyebrows tend to work in connection with our eyes. Hence, by taking in the eyes and the eyebrows as a whole, you can get a complete picture of a person's emotions or feelings about a certain event.

The final step in being able to properly and accurately read a person's face is simply to gain the ability to perceive different emotions upon the face. We will discuss this in further detail later in this chapter as I lay out different emotions that various expressions tend to show.

The Head

The head is often the first thing that a person looks at when they meet a new individual. We spend a lot of our lives looking at a person's head. As a result, the human head is designed to send many signals between individuals. The majority of them tend to be subconscious, which is useful in the context of this book.

- **The Face**

  The human face contains around fifty muscles; the majority of these muscles can be used to send nonverbal signals to those around us. Addition to muscles, the color of the skin and the temperature can also be quite important in understanding nonverbal language from the face.

  - Color - colors of the face tell a long and detailed story about what a person is feeling at a given point. If a person's face is very clearly red, they may be showing signals for many different things. In very generic terms, a red face is a sign that someone's face is hot. Whether this is from exercise, emotional arousal, or embarrassment, it is a sign that blood is rushing to the face for one reason or another. It also can be a sign of anger or aggression. Alternatively, the color of the face can also be white. A whiteness of skin may be a sign of coldness and of blood leaving the face. This may be a sign of sickness or fear. A face can also take on a bluish hint when it is very cold or experiencing extreme fear or sickness.

  - Dampness - the level of moisture that somebody's face has when you are looking at them can tell a wide variety of feelings. You have to be careful not to look too far into this sign, as the wetness of a person's face can also be caused by simply sweating when it is warm outside. If it is not warm in the area that a person is in and if their face appears to be very damp or covered in a lot of moisture, that person may be feeling fearful, as sweat is often associated with fear. Some scientists theorize that sweating on the face when feeling fear is an evolutionary defense mechanism to make the skin slippery and more difficult for an opponent to get a firm grasp of the face.

Common Facial Signals for Different Emotions

The following are a series of common facial signals that indicate different emotions. It is important to remember that some of these signs are not an instant indicator that a person is feeling the emotion in question. However, a combination of all of these signs may suggest that a person is feeling a certain emotion, depending on the environment surrounding them.

- **Common signs of happiness**

  Some common signs of happiness within the face include but are not limited to:

  - The mouth and an open or closed smile sometimes accompanied by laughter or chuckling;
  - Possibly some crow's feet type wrinkles at the sides of a person's eyes—this indicates that a smile is honest and real because it is using enough muscles to change the wrinkles and a person's face;
  - Eyebrows raised slightly; and
  - A person's head tilted back or at a higher level than normal.

- **Common signs of sadness**

  Some common signs of sadness within the face and head include but are not limited to:

  - A person's eyes are staring downwards at a lower angle than ninety degrees;
  - Possibly some dampness or moisture within the eyes;

202

- Head tilted downwards along with the eyes;
- Lips pinch tightly together or trembling;
- Trembling of the chin; and
- Head tilted to the side.

- **Common signs of anxiety**

Some common signs of anxiety within the face and head include but are not limited to:

- Eyes that are damp or filled with moisture;
- Eyebrows that are pushed together and wrinkled;
- A lower lip trembling or lips pinch together;
- Skin wrinkling or tents; and
- Head tilted downward possibly looking at the ground.

- **Common signals of fear**

A few common signals of fear within the face and head include but are not limited to:

- Eyes wide open with large pupils;
- Eyes closed or pointed downwards;
- Eyebrows raised wrinkling the forehead;
- Open mouth or corners of the mouth turn downwards;
- Chin pulled and tucked into the neck;
- Head tilted downwards possibly staring at the ground; and
- A white-tinted face.

- **Common signals of anger**

Some common signals of anger include but are not limited to:

- Eyes either wide and staring or squinted
- Eyebrows push downwards towards the eyes and possibly forever
- A wrinkled forehead
- Nostrils that are flaring or twitching
- A mouth that is flattened out into a line or teeth that are clearly clenched
- A chine jutting out towards a person
- A face that is red in color

- **Common signals of envy or jealousy**

Some common signals of envy or jealousy within the face and the head include but are not limited to:

- Eyes staring wide with pupils large
- The corners of one's mouth turn downwards
- Crinkling of the nose or sneering at an individual
- Chin that's jutting outwards away from the body

- **Common signs of desire or lust**

  Common signals of desire or lust within the face and the head include but are not limited to:

  - Eyes open wide with heavily dilated pupils;
  - Eyebrows that are raised slightly but softly;
  - Lips parted slightly or puckered;
  - Stop smiling; and
  - Head that is tilted forward or slightly tilted to the side at an angle.

- **Common signs of interest**

  Some common signs of interest include but are not limited to:

  - A steady gaze of eyes towards the item or person in question
  - Some squinting also might happen in the eyes as a person attempts to see the item or person in question better
  - Eyebrows slightly raised
  - Lips pressed tightly together
  - Head straight or push slightly forward with neck elongating
  - Lips in a soft or gentle smile

- **Common signals of boredom**

  Some common signals of boredom within the face and the head may include but are not limited to:

  - Eyes looking away from the object or individual in question;
  - Face generally unmoving but relaxed;
  - Corners of the mouth turned downwards, or the lips pulled to the side; and
  - Head being held up with a hand or supported in some other fashion.

- **Common signals of relief**

  Some common signals of relief within the face and head include but are not limited to:

  - Eyebrows their tilted outwards or lowered on the outer edges and higher on the inner edges;
  - A mouth that is either slightly open or smiling; and
  - A head tilted upwards in surprise.

- **Common signs of surprise**

  Some common signs of surprised within the face and head include but are not limited to:

  - Eyes wide pupils dilated;
  - Eyebrows push high on to the head with extreme wrinkling of the forehead;
  - Mouth open with a lower chin; and
  - Head that is tilted back or tilted to the side.

- **Common signs of disgust**

  Some common signs of disgust within the face and head include but are not limited to:

  - Head or eyes turned away from the object or person in question
  - Nostrils flaring or nose twitching
  - Nose crinkled or mouth snoring
  - Mouth closed
  - Tongue possibly sticking out
  - Chin that's jutting out away from the neck and body

- **Common signs of shame**

  Some common signs of shame within the face and head include but are not limited to:

  - Head or eyes turn downwards looking at the ground;
  - Eyebrows low on the face but not forcefully so; and
  - The skin may be bright red or flushed.

- **Common signs of pity**

  Some common signs that somebody is feeling pity for another individual within the face and head include but are not limited to:

  - Staring off into the distance possibly with some dampness or moisture;
  - Eyebrows pulled together slightly in the middle or pulled downward at the edges;
  - Mouth wood corners turning downward; and
  - Add maybe tilted to the side or tilted forward ever so slightly.

- **Common signs of calmness**

  Some common signs that somebody is feeling very calm in an event or situation within the face and head include but are not limited to:

  - Facial muscles that are relaxed;
  - Steady gaze looking forward with the eyes; and
  - The mouth may be turned up slightly at the sides in a soft smile.

How to Look Certain Ways

Within this section, we will discuss how to come off in certain ways to those around us. If you want to make someone believe that you are a certain type of individual, these are some of the things you will want to think about.

Trustworthiness

Psychologists and body language experts have agreed that many individuals find the most trustworthy face is one that appears to have a slight smile. These individuals will have the corners of their mouths turned upwards ever-so-slightly with eyebrows that are raised just barely on the face. You must remember that the eyebrows must not be pushed up forcefully with many wrinkles on the forehead. These features show an individual as looking confident and friendly but without being overbearing or afraid of others not similar to them.

Intelligence

Many scientists and body language experts have agreed that people with a narrower face and a thinner chin tend to be more intelligent than others. In addition to this, people also tend to view those with larger noses as a common stereotype of how intelligent a person can be. Contrastingly, an individual with an oval face and a large chin is often stereotyped as having lower intelligence levels. Interestingly, it has also been shown that people tend to perceive others as having a higher intelligence when an individual is smiling or showing happiness, while people tend to judge others as having lower intelligence when they're showing signs of anger or sadness. You can artificially appear to be more intelligent by using certain signs of power body language. Signs of power body language include things such as speaking expressively, using a lot of eye contact, acting confident, and being modest in your clothing choices.

The Chin

The chin is a dominant and obvious corner of the face. All corners of the face have their own clear body language symbols that are unique to them. This is because a corner on your face is an area where its different parts converge and, as such, is the beginning and end of certain facial expressions. Within this section, we will explain the intended or unintentional meanings behind certain movements of the chin.

- Protection - the chin is a very vulnerable point on the face, as it tends to jut out and become easy to attack with one's fists. The chin lies just above the throat, which is an even more vulnerable spot. The chin can often act as a protector of the throat in cases of extreme vulnerability. There, they may be feeling defensive for some reason. Holding in the chin also tends to lower one's head, which then tends to be a submissive gesture. This is different from the defensive move we discussed earlier because the head is tilted down and because the eyes are often staring at the ground. This can be considered as a shy or flirtatious motion.

- Jutting - the chin can serve as a subtle method of pointing at other things. Flicking the chin or tilting the head may give a slight signal that only individuals in the know are going to notice. Jutting chin outwards towards a person is exposing it and sort of sending a message that they are daring a person to attack them. This is often considered a signal from defiance. Men with larger chins are often considered to have more testosterone than others. Because of this, the action of a man with a very large chin cutting it out enhances this idea by giving a mental symbol to those around them that they are *alpha*. It is often the case that if a person is feeling more confident than normal, their chin will stick out ever-so-slightly because they are holding their head up or are maybe tilting their head back a little bit. Pushing the chin outwards also tends to expose the teeth, and that can be considered as a threat because subconsciously, they may want to bite another person.

- Touching - when an individual is seen stroking their chin, it is often taken as a signal that the person is thinking very long and hard. They may be judging or evaluating a person or a situation. If a conversation has offered them a choice or decision to make, they may do this action to show that they're thinking it over. The head is one of the heaviest parts of our body and is held up exclusively by the neck and the spine. This can cause a lot of exhaustion and tenseness, and as a result, people are often seen cupping their head in their hand. This may be a sign of boredom or sleepiness. A more complicated symbol shown by holding the chin is to prevent the head from moving. This can show that the individual in question subconsciously wants to send a particular head signal but does not want to send the signal at the same time because of some kind of logical reasoning.

- Beard - beards have a very interesting connotation in terms of body language. In our society, clean-shaven tends to be the more widely accepted form of facial hair. Hence, within modern society, a beard is sometimes considered a sign that an individual is a non-conformist. A person with a full and luscious beard is more likely to be thought of as someone with no vanity needs and is usually considered confident and relaxed. On the other hand, when a beard is shaped and kept very neatly trimmed, it may show that a person is vainer and fussier than a normal individual. If a beard is seen as being unkempt or grows very wildly around an individual space, people may take this as a sign that the said guy is untidy or tends to be sloppy. The action of one stroking a beard can be seen as a preening gesture. This gesture symbolically makes one appear more beautiful and sends a signal that they believe themselves to be more attractive than the average person.

- Puckered - a chin that is seen as being puckered or pulled in particular directions and appearing to be wrinkled can be seen as a defensive stance because it can be put under the general idea of pulling back one's chin.

The Mouth

The mouth is a very important aspect of our face. It has probably the most muscles of any other region of our face and, as such, is used to convey the most complex forms of body language as well as verbal language.

- Breathing - by design, humans are meant to breathe through their nose, but when in need of more than the usual oxygen, we may use our mouth to breathe in larger gusts of air. If an individual is suddenly beginning to breathe through their mouth at quite a fast pace almost to the point of panting, they may be seen as frightened or angry because they are subconsciously preparing for the flight-or-fight reaction. The breathing of a stressed person may include actions such as gulping in a large gust of air or blowing it out very fast. If a person is extremely and overwhelmingly stressed, they may begin to hyperventilate. When an individual does yawn, it is often taken as a sign that a person is tired or bored. If an individual gives a short or deep exhaling sigh, they can be viewed as showing sadness or frustration. Inhaling air in a short and quick fashion—especially inconsistent sequences—can be viewed as silence sobs, and that is an indicator that a person is feeling deep and suppress sadness.

  - Speaking - a mouth tends to send even more signals while they're speaking than through the traditional verbal language. If a mouth is moving very little and includes mumbling, this may be a sign that an individual does not feel like speaking, which could have possibly stemmed from shyness or from a fear that they will reveal too much about something. Moving very rapidly and a lot—at the same time that someone is speaking—can indicate that they are feeling extreme levels of excitement or dominance. People who speak very quickly tend to be visual thinkers who are trying to say what they see as quickly as possible. An individual who speaks very slowly may be considered a deep thinker and maybe trying to be careful about finding the correct words.

  - Eating - the way that individuals eat can tell a lot of things about their personality. A person that views manners and very high regards will open their mouth as little as possible to put a tiny amount of food in and will keep it closed while they carefully chew. These individuals will never speak when they have food in their mouth. Opposite to this, a person who does not view manners in very high regard will push large mouthfuls into their wide mouth and will tend to chew and talk at the same time. Interestingly, there are some individuals who turn these tendencies onto their heads by eating very noisily as a sign that they are enjoying the food. These people are very snobbish about their food choices.

- Covering – sometimes, individuals use their hands to cover up their mouth. In modern society, exposing the inner parts of your mouth may be considered rude in some circles—hence, the hand is used to cover the mouth when yawning or laughing hard.

- Smiling - smiling has a very interesting depth to which it conveys emotion. Many individuals will look at a smile and simply think that is conveying the fact that someone is happy—when in reality, a smile can mean many different things, depending on context. A full smile is one that uses the entire face—this sort of smile will include the eyes and cheeks as well as the eyebrows. The eyes will crease, the eyebrows will raise, and the cheeks will lift up words. If an individual is smiling only with their lips, they are often trying to trick another individual. These smiles are typically fake that are not to be trusted. A genuine smile, on the other hand, tends to be asymmetric and is usually much larger on one side of the face. If an individual has a lopsided smile, then they're most likely a trustworthy person. However, if an individual does smile with their lips pushed tightly together, they may be showing signs of embarrassment. If an individual is smiling only half of their mouth on one side of their face, they may be showing sarcasm or uncertainty.

- Laughing - there are many different types of laughs in this world. Each one has its own meanings and signals in the realm of body language. Laughing can sometimes act as a sort of bonding mechanism between men and women. It is a well-known fact that women tend to laugh towards men that they like, while men enjoy it when women laugh at them. A woman laughing at a man is said to be a sign that she likes him. Laughing can also be used as a way of sending signals that one views another in terms of friendship. Laughing at jokes is often a requirement if you are friends with the person giving the joke. Laughing or smiling at the misfortune of those around us is often considered unacceptable within our society. As we are humans, we often can't help but find certain misfortunate events funny. Because of this, you may see suppressed laughter or people trying very hard not to smile as somebody experiences one of these unfortunate events.

- Biting or sucking - an individual that is sucking on their finger is often a recollection of actions of our childhood, as we tend to suck on our thumbs when we were children. Young children will suck on their fingers as a substitute for the breast. Because of this, this action is considered as a comforting one. This may be a sign that a person is feeling uncomfortable or stressed in a particular situation and that they are simply trying to comfort themselves through sucking on fingers, which then brings them back to that comforting feeling of having a breast in their mouth when they were an infant. Variance on this includes actions such as sucking or biting on the knuckles, the side of the hands, or other parts of the body. Sometimes, this may include the lips or inner cheek. Sometimes, this includes an outside object such as a pen or a pencil. All of these indicate a sign of stress or discomfort.

The Nose

Within this section, we will go through common signals sent out by the nose. Because the nose is stationed right in the middle of the face, it can send a large number of body symbols.

- Flare - when the nostrils have been widened and flared, it allows more oxygen to be breathed in by an individual. Subconsciously, this is an act of making a person ready for combat. Because of this, this can indicate that an individual is experiencing extreme displeasure or maybe feeling threatened.

- Wrinkle - if a nose is being wrinkled, it may be a sign that a person senses a bad smell from a certain area. It can also be a metaphor for the coming of something bad. An example of this is when an individual suggests something that another person dislikes, they may wrinkle their nose at that idea. Another variation of this idea is if a person is thinking about something or having certain ideas but are not satisfied with those ideas or thoughts.

- Touching - when an individual is touching their nose, it may be a sign that a person detects a terrible smell. It can also come across as a common signal from a person who's lying. Touching the nose indicates that somebody is lying when combined with the right combination of other bodily symbols. If a person flicks, then know that this may be a sign that they disagree with something a previous individual has said. If an individual is pinching the bridge of their nose, they may be thinking very hard about something. Usually, this is combined with some kind of frustration, as a person may be having difficulty making up their mind. Placing a finger on the nose or pressing it down is sometimes a habit or natural tick that a person has when they are thinking very deeply about something.

The Eyes

- Looking up - when an individual is seen to be looking upwards, they are often thinking very hard about a certain idea. When in the middle of giving a prepared speech or presentation, they may be attempting to remember their prepared words if they are looking up. Looking upwards and to the left may show signs that someone is attempting to recall a memory. Contrastingly, somebody who is looking upwards and to the right can show signs of imaginative construction, which then shows that they are making something up on the spot. Look it up can also be considered as a sign of boredom, as a person is trying to examine or understand their surroundings in order to find something better to do. If a person's head is lowered and if their eyes are looking at another person through their eyelashes, this may be considered a koi and suggestion of action, as it is used in combination with the idea of submission with the head down and the eye contact of attraction. However, when combined with a frown, this can be considered as a judgmental look.

- Looking down - looking down at a person can be considered an act of confidence, power, or domination. If a person is looking up at another person, then they may be showing a sign of submission. This may also be a sign that a person is feeling particularly guilty. If a person is looking downwards and to the left, this may be a sign that they are trying to talk to themselves without being noticed. However, if an individual is looking down and to the right, this may be a sign that they are dealing with certain internal emotions or internal turmoil at the moment. There are some cultures and societies in which direct eye contact is considered a rude or dominance symbol. Because of this, people in these societies may look down while talking to others in order to show respect.

- Looking sideways - the majority of our vision tends to be in the horizontal plane. Hence, if an individual seems to be looking sideways, that means that they are actively turning their head in order to see something they couldn't have already seen. A swift glance to the side is sometimes considered a symbol that somebody is just checking for the source of a distraction. This may also be considered a sign of irritation. If a person looks directly to the left, this can indicate that a person is trying to recall a sound in their memory. On the flip side, looking to the right can show that a person imagines a sound. If a person's eyes are moving from side to side rapidly, this may be a sign that a person is not to be trusted or that they are lying. This goes back to the idea that an individual is looking for an escape route in case they are found out or attacked.

- Gazing - the act of gazing is a sign that somebody is very interested in figuring out whatever they're looking at by staring at something with the intent of trying to understand it at a deeper level. This may be a sign that an individual is very interested in another. If, after locking eyes with another individual, a person continues to look into that person's eyes, then it may be a sign of love. If the eyes slide down over the individual's body, it is more likely to be a sign of lust. The place where one's eyes go is important. Gazing at an individual's mouth can indicate that a person would like to kiss them. Looking at individual sexual regions tends to show a desire to have intercourse with that person. Sliding the eyes up and down a whole person is usually considered an act of sizing an individual up. This may either be seen as a potential threat or as looking for a sexual partner, depending on where the eyes linger. This may be considered insulting in modern society.

As we can see from the contents of this chapter, the face and head of an individual's body contains some of the most expressive and potent forms of body language. Within this chapter, we have gone through the meanings of various different forms of body language that exclusively include the head and face connection. It is important to remember that when you are trying to analyze the actions of a person's head or face, you must take into account all parts and all corners of that person's face. You cannot judge a person's emotions simply through one action of one part of their face. You must take in their face as a whole and consider all of the possible meanings to all the different parts. For this chapter, we have gone through and analyze the different expressions and meanings behind certain movements of the eyes, smiles, lips, and many more. Within the next chapter, we will begin to explain how you can tell if there's truth in your relationships.

The Forehead

The forehead is often ignored in the realm of body language. This is a huge mistake, as the forehead is often a starting point for a wider set of body language signals. It is just above the eyes and, as such, can be looked at without sending different signals. Many people, when wanting to avoid people reading their forehead signals, will wear a large hat and keep their head down. This is particularly common in gamblers.

- Wrinkling - if a forehead is wrinkled, it is often due to the movement of an individual's eyebrows. Because of this, the wrinkling of the forehead acts as an amplifier of the eyebrow signals. This may indicate surprise or questioning.

- Sweating - as humans, we often excrete sweat on our heads first as compared to the other parts of our bodies. Sweating upon the forehead not only occurs when we are hot due to external temperature but also when we are hot due to internal energy and arousal. It is important to remember that an individual can also experience what is known as a cold sweat, which then indicates great amounts of fear and may be accompanied by moisture in the eyes.

- Touching - rubbing of the forehead is often considered a form of body language that signifies a greeting. Slowly rubbing the forehead can tend to indicate deep thinking or deep contemplation. If an individual is viewed rubbing their temples on either side, this can be a sign of stress or an incoming headache.

Chapter Seven: Truth and Relationships

Relationships are filled to the brim with extremely potent signs of body language. Which among the signs are positive or negative depends on the relationship. Unfortunately, relationships are also often full of lying amongst the couple. To help you understand your own relationship and the relationships of others, within this chapter, we will be going through how you can tell if somebody is lying in a relationship. We will also go through how you can analyze relationships that you are not in and how to tell if the individuals within that relationship have a good and positive connection with one another. You will also learn how to judge if the individuals in a relationship truly love their respective partners. You will also learn how to tell if somebody loves you truly and wholly. You will also learn some common signs when a female is ready for dating or wants to date an individual. You will also then learn its counterpart signs for men. This chapter will be very beneficial to anyone thinking about being in a relationship or is currently in a long-term relationship.

Lying

Being able to tell if somebody is lying to another person is a very important and powerful skill. Within a relationship lying, is unfortunately very common and very often seen in modern-day society. Being able to tell when an individual is lying may save you from painful and possibly emotionally damaging relationships. It is easier to detect if someone is lying when you are outside of the relationship, but you can also use these tactics when you are inside it as well. The following are a few signs that a person is lying to their significant other:

- A common scientific sign that somebody's lying is seen within the nose. Specific tissues within the nose are known to get engorged or to swell up when an individual is lying. Because of the swelling, a person's cells within their nose tend to release histamine, which will make the nose feel itchy. Because of this, an individual may be seen scratching or touching their nose. This indicator is not a tell-all-be-all of somebody lying. You need to take the sign in contact with many other symbols of lying.

- Another big sign that somebody is lying is a tendency to cover or block their mouth or to cover or rub their eyes. This is often done subconsciously, in hopes that a person would not be able to see those parts of their face and that they wouldn't be able to tell that they are lying. They may also turn their head or body away when making crucial statements that, if seen past, will definitively suggest that they are lying.

- An individual may be known to overbearingly refer to certain religious phrases in order to make their lie sound more plausible. These are phrases such as: "I swear on my mother's grave" or "God, no." By adding religion or the afterlife into a statement, a person increases the weight of that statement and, as such, makes the other individual think that they are sincere.

- Phrases of denial such as "trust me," "honestly," "and to be perfectly honest" are attempts at being evasive and trying to avoid the original subject matter. If a person is attempting to change the perception of others about their actions, they may use these different evasive techniques. If these phrases are being repeated in excess and are popping up over and over, they may be clues that a person is lying.

- Individual appearing to be overly defensive or to overreact at certain situations that seem completely random to you may be a sign that they are lying. An example of this would be if an individual you're in a romantic relationship with gets off the phone—and when you ask who they were talking to, they'd respond with some type of hostile statement such as "Why are you so nosey?" A response such as this is completely uncalled for and indicates that a person is feeling guilty about a certain situation. For this instance, this individual is also appearing to try to place their feelings of guilt and mistrust onto the other person. This is an instant sign that a person is lying to you.

- If an individual has a well-known and long-winded history of lying, then they are more likely to be lying to you. People often continue to do what they know well, and if a person knows how to live very well, it is very likely that they will lie to you.

- If a person makes an exaggerated or extreme amount of eye contact, they may be lying to you. The common misconception is that people will avoid eye contact upon being embarrassed or ashamed. Because so many people know about this fact, people who are trying to keep something from you will actually do the opposite. They will go out of their way and try to make eye contact with you under any means necessary. This is an attempt to make themselves appear sincerer than they actually are. It is important to cautiously approach an individual who normally doesn't give much eye contact and then suddenly does a lot now.

- A person will often touch their face when they are lying. This is an attempt to put something in between them and the person they're lying to. This subconsciously makes it easier to lie to a person because they feel as though they are not directly doing it.

- An individual trying to make a lie seem very believable and sincere may give a fake smile to a person. A way of being able to tell if somebody is lying through a fake smile is by looking for a smile that happens around the mouth but does not meet the eyes. This means that their cheeks or eyes may be without wrinkles or maybe particularly relax. This is a sign they are trying to force something.

- If an individual's pupils are dilating while they are speaking, this is a sign that they are feeling a very strong emotion. If combined with other telltale signs of lying, this may be a sign that an individual is lying to you. You have to be careful with this sort of signal because pupils may dilate for a number of different reasons. Typically, eyes will dilate for any sort of strong or overwhelming emotion. Because of this, an overwhelming feeling of shame or embarrassment will make a person's eyes dilate. As said, if combined with other signs of lying, this may, indeed, be an indicator that a person is lying. If not, this may simply be an indication that a person feels very strongly about you.

- Saying the word "honestly" too often in a conversation can be an indicator that somebody is lying. By saying the word "honest" over and over again, a person is subconsciously trying to convince you that they are honest. Because of how hard they are trying to do this, they may overcompensate and say it too many times to be believable.

- If you would like to be able to detect a liar very quickly, a good place to start is by asking very neutral questions. By asking a basic or non-threatening question, you will be able to observe a baseline response for the person telling the truth carefully. Asking them about things like the weather, their plans, or anything that would elicit a comfortable, easy response will give you a baseline understanding of what their body language is when they're telling the truth. You should continue this until you find a series of patterns that match their continuous truth-telling tendencies.

- The next step in trying to detect a liar very quickly is to move into emotionally charged questions. During this time, you should observe the presence or absence of changes in body language, facial expressions, eye movements, and even the way that they formulate their sentences. If any of this is inconsistent with the previous information that you gathered, by asking merely the easy questions, you may be looking at a liar.

- When trying to indicate or evaluate a liar, it is important to listen very closely to the tone, cadence, and even the sentence structures of the person speaking to you. A person who is lying may slightly change the tone or speed of their speech. They will do this subconsciously. A person trying to speak more quickly when lying will be doing so to try and get the lies out of them and get it over with as quickly as possible. A person speaking in a slower tone may be doing so because they are trying to think about what they're going to say next and are overly conscious about the movements of their body.

- A person that is lying will often start to remove themselves from their tale when answering your questions. They will try to direct the focus on to the people around them. You will begin to hear fewer I's and me's as they try to distance themselves from the lie that they are telling subconsciously.

Ways to Analyze the Truthfulness of a Relationship

It is very difficult to analyze a relationship when you *are* in one. Because of this, the following section will be speaking exclusively about relationships that you are the outsider of. This section of this text will explain how to analyze a relationship for truthfulness. This will cover both the man and the woman. Within this section, you will learn how to tell and analyze if there are inconsistencies within their relationship such as infertility and cheating. We will begin with a few questions that are crucial to making this analysis possible.

1. Is there trust? Trust is a crucial part of every relationship. In order to properly analyze your relationship, you have to know whether or not there is trust within it. How to tell if there's trust in a relationship is by examining it and seeing if the individuals within are able to be apart from one another easily and comfortably without any worries. They may miss each other but not to the point that they are constantly asking each other what they are doing. They do not feel happier when they're away from their partner, but they also do not feel insecure for the same reason. Insecurities are key here. A person that is in a loving and healthy relationship will not feel insecure simply because of their significant other is not with them. If a person feels insecure every single time that they are away from their partner, this may be a sign that they do not trust that individual to make good decisions on their own.

2. Are they on the same page? Obviously, in good relationships, you do not always have to agree. However, it is important to have similar goals and similar views of the future. If a pair of individuals have very different ideas of their future and very different views for their lives, it may cause problems within a relationship down the road. It is very difficult to continue a long-term relationship with somebody who wants a very different future from another person.

3. Do they have respect for one another? Respect is very important in a relationship. Respect can be defined as being fond of the essence of a person without wanting to change them. An individual who respects their partner will be willing to put aside any kind of issues that a person has or any little quirks or flaws that are a part of their personality. In fact, it is best in a relationship when a person finds these flaws or quirks to be beautiful. However, if an individual puts down their significant other because of their flaws are quirks, this is a sign that they are not truly in love with them.

4. Can they speak openly with one another? Good, positive communication is an absolute must-have for a good relationship. If a couple that is together cannot have good communication with each other, it is very likely that they will not last very long. Good communication is when two individuals are able to speak about anything and everything that is on their minds, and they will not be shut down or told to stop speaking. The other person will listen intently and will give their side as well. There should be no boundaries on what these two can speak about with each other.

5. Are they equals? Equality is very important in modern-day relationships. Putting the same amount of work into a relationship is very important. If the work within the relationship is equally distributed amongst the two people, then they will have a much happier relationship. However, if one person is carrying the relationship or if the other person is leaning very heavily on the former's actions, they will begin to feel bogged down and will eventually feel as though their significant other is more of a chore than a relationship. Never should a person in a relationship feel as though they have to do something for their partner just because their partner wants them to. However, they should want to do something nice for their partner because they love them. If they begin

to feel resentful for the things that they do for their partner, that might be a sign that they should end the relationship soon.

6. Do they enjoy being together? This one is fairly simple and obvious to understand. People in a relationship together should be able to enjoy and appreciate the simple things. You should want to be around your partner—it should feel somewhat "empty" if your partner is away from you, and it should feel happy just because you are around them.

7. Are they comfortable being themselves? This one is very important in a relationship. If a person is uncomfortable in their own relationship, then it is not likely to last very long. A person should not mind showing their weaknesses to their partner. Their partner should also be very supportive of that person's weaknesses and vice-versa. Another way to tell that there is comfort in a relationship is that if things are not going right for a certain person, they should go to their partner for comforting. If an individual is feeling anxious or self-conscious around their significant other, then it might be a sign to end the relationship soon. Individuals in a very good relationship with one another and are very comfortable with each other's company will usually understand their partner without having to speak a word.

8. Do they bring out the best in each other? Individuals that are in a good relationship with each another should be able to complement their partner very well. Being with another person should make you strive to be a better person and should not make you feel bogged down as though you are being pulled in a worse direction by being with them.

By beginning with these questions, you should be able to analyze a relationship from the outside carefully. Keep in mind that those that are in a relationship will know the background of their connection the best. Hence, begin with these questions when trying to analyze another relationship, but always take into account the understanding of those within it.

How to Tell If Love Is Truly There

Using the analysis questions that we previously discussed, we can begin to figure out and understand if love is truly present in a relationship. This is obviously very important for long-lasting and comfortable relationships. If love is not actually present and if the individuals in the relationship are mistaking lust for love, there can be serious problems. With this being said, love is sometimes difficult to understand and to pinpoint. That's why within this section, we will go through some easy ways to tell if there really is love present in a relationship.

1. When the individuals within a relationship want to spend time with each other and want to spend the majority of their day spending quality time with the other person, this is probably an indicator of true love. This desire and need to spend time with each other are a sign of successful long-term intimacy. If the individuals in question truly care about each other, they will make time to spend with one another in between all of their daily commitments.

2. Individuals that are truly in love with one another in a relationship will ask about the other person's day. This may seem like a very simplistic and easy way to tell if there is true love in a relationship—*and it is*. This is because by asking about a person's day, you are showing interest in that person's life. This is a very important sign of love. If an individual does not care enough to ask a person about their day, then they do not care about the inner workings of that person's life and are not truly in love with them.

3. Trust is very important in good and strong relationship partners who truly and deeply care about each other and will give the other person in their relationship the benefit of the doubt. Research has shown in the past that the majority of successful and long-term relationships have one thing in common—that is a deep and powerful trust between the individuals involved. If individuals feel as though the other person in the relationship does not trust them, it will make them not want to trust them in turn. This level of distrust within a relationship will destroy it very quickly. If a person feels as though they're not being trusted and are being questioned at every turn, they may feel trapped in a relationship and may want to end it very quickly.

4. Individuals in a relationship in which they care very deeply for and truly love each other will be more than willing to offer help when the other person needs it. Oftentimes, an individual will not have to ask for this help, as the other person will simply offer it up in the first place. This is a very beautiful and strong sign of love. This is because a person who offers help when somebody needs it is clearly paying attention to the needs of that person and wants that individual to be happy and healthy at all times. Because of these wants and needs, that person will offer to help them despite the inconveniences that they put upon themselves.

5. Individuals in a relationship do not necessarily always have to agree on everything, but they should show respect for the other person's views. Strong love in a relationship can show itself—and individuals that, while they disagree, will also be respectful and not put down the ideas or beliefs of the other person.

6. Individuals that feel very strong and good love for one another will include the other person in their decision-making. Good strong couples will decide on everything from the mundane to the extremely important things together. This is because they will want to include the other person in their everyday life.

7. The next indicator of true love in a relationship seems fairly obvious. A couple that shows clear and obvious affection for one another are typically very emotionally

intimate and in love with each other. This is not always having to translate through sex. Emotional intimacy can show itself through very simple signs like standing closely together or softly touching another person. These touches indicate a strong feeling of connection between the two individuals. They also show through these signals that they want to be physically closer to the other person at all times no matter where they are during the day.

Female Dating Signs

Within the next section, we will go through some common signs that a female is ready to date or is interested in another person.

1. The first sign that a female is interested in dating another person is how often or seldom that person touches you. These are not often strong touches or full-on hugs or kisses, but a female that is looking to date an individual finds excuses to touch them in subtle ways. They might brush against the other person, they might throw a teasing punch at the other person's shoulder, or they might even move closer towards the other person in the middle of a conversation. If a female is not actively trying to touch another person in subtle ways, that may be a sign that she is not interested or not open to dating at the moment.

2. Another sign that a female is interested in dating another person is their ability to maintain eye contact. A woman attempting to catch another person's eye from across the room or looking very intently into another person's eye while they are speaking is a sure-fire sign that they are least interested in you as a friend. You are able to tell whether or not she's interested in the other person as more than just a friend upon combining these signs with the others that we will be discussing. In general, though, maintaining strong and good eye contact is a good sign that a female is interested in what the other person is saying and that they hold their opinion to high regard.

3. Another sign that a female is interested in dating another person is how often they ask personal questions. A female that wants to date an individual will try to learn as much about them as she possibly can. This may lead to her asking deep or probing questions, and the other individual may find themselves in a deep conversation about the universe without even realizing it. This is a sign that she's very interested in that person's opinions.

4. A female that is willing to laugh with an individual is a sure-fire sign that they at least find them attractive. A woman laughing with another person means that she is having a good time with them and enjoy spending time with them. Women love men who can make them laugh—especially if the jokes that a person is giving off are not actually *that* funny, in case that a person is still laughing at them, it is a very good sign that she is interested in that person.

5. Another sure-fire sign that a woman is very interested in another person is if she's obviously mirroring the other person's body language. An individual who is interested will the consciously marry their body language in an attempt to make them like each other even better. This is because instinctively, as people, we tend to like people better that look like us—and by mirroring our body language, we can artificially make the other person believe that we look like them and make them like us better without them even realizing it. If a female is doing this continuously to another person, this is a very good sign that she is interested in dating them.

6. A very common action of flirting that a woman participates in when she's interested in dating another person is teasing. Women will often tease men that they would like to go out with or that they want the attention of.

7. A woman who replies very swiftly to another person is often interested in that person. Quick responses from a woman is a very good sign that she's interested in dating the other person.

8. Another very good sign that a woman is interested in dating another person is when she's willing to make plans immediately at the end of a date. If she is setting up another date, it almost certainly means that she's interested in continuing to engage in romantic encounters with them. If she doesn't want to be that obvious, then she might say things that hint towards her wanting to set up another date. This might include her giving days that she's free or saying that it would be nice to meet up again. This is a very obvious and clear sign that a woman wants to continue dating.

9. Another very good sign that a woman is interested in dating another person is if she tends to remember the things that the said person says. Without even realizing it, women tend to memorize things better when they're interested in them. This is because they hold a high level of importance on the things that they are interested in. Hence, if you find that a woman is remembering every little thing that you are saying to them later on, then this is a very good sign that she's interested in dating you. Women who are interested in other people will show their interest by remembering the small details of every conversation.

10. Another great sign that a female is interested in dating another person is if they are willing to give a very high level of detail about their past relationships. If a female has a very complicated or difficult past with relationships and is willing to let her new partner know about it, then it is a very good sign that she wants to have a strong relationship with this person. By opening up and giving her deepest vulnerabilities and showing the other person her past, she's telling them that she trusts them and believes that they will not treat her the way that some of her previous partners did.

11. Another very good sign is that the female is not afraid to let the other person know when she is having doubts or having difficulty in a relationship. This is a sign of very good and strong communication within a relationship and implies that she's interested in keeping the dating or relationship going for as long as she possibly can. If a female who wants to continue dating a person is having difficulty in a relationship, she will try to fix it by bringing it out into the open and letting everyone know about what's going on and trying to fix it.

12. Another huge sign that a female is very interested in dating another person is if she is willing to invite that person to a family function. This is a very big deal, especially if that female has a very good and strong connection with her family. Introducing a new person to a family that she is very close to and have strong ties with is a sign that she is feeling comfortable enough around that person to introduce that person to her family.

Male Dating Signs

Within the next section, we will discuss and go over some common signs that a man wants to date another person.

1. If a man appears to want to spend a lot of time with a person and to make a special effort to be around them, then this is a very good sign that they want to date that person. This shows that a man is actively creating time to be with another person and

shows that they are committed to being with that person. This is a sign that a person is willing to put in an effort to be around that person and thus would like a deeper and longer relationship.

2. A man that seriously wants to date an individual will want to do so in person and not through a computer or phone. An individual that wants a date or wants to "connect" through a computer is most likely not seriously interested in keeping a relationship with that person.

3. A man that is very interested in dating another person will be willing to court that person. In other words, they will want to make the first move because they care enough about the other person to put themselves out there.

4. A man that very much wants to continue a relationship and continue to date an individual will align their plans with that person. They will be careful to make sure that their plans are lined up with the other person's so that he can accommodate that other individual. This is a very good sign that a man wants to continue to date a person because it shows that he cares about them.

5. If a man is interested in dressing up and looking nice for another individual, this is a very good sign that he's interested in having a long-lasting relationship with that person.

6. If a man wants to ask about an individual's family and genuinely wants to meet them, he most likely wants to continue dating this person. Being interested in another individual's family background is a very good sign that a man wants a long-lasting and serious relationship with them. A man who's interested in a person's family and who likes their family clearly wants a long relationship with them.

7. If a man wants to introduce a person to everyone in his life, it is a sign that he is proud of that person and loves them very deeply.

8. Subtle protectiveness is another very good sign that a man wants to date another person. The key word here is "subtle." You do not want a man who is overly protective and doesn't want their partner (or prospective partner) to have their own life or friends, but some signs of protectiveness are good. If a man is gently protective of another person in ways that make them *genuinely* feel safe, it is a very good sign that he wants to date them further.

9. Another very important sign that a man is interested in long-term dating a person is if he is very interested in and willing to have long meaningful conversations with that other person. This shows signs that he wants to know everything about them and is very interested in their background and their beliefs. This is a surefire sign that a man is interested in dating them.

10. A very good sign that a man is interested in a person as a long-term partner rather than just a one-time hookup is if he doesn't talk about that person's body very often. If he does talk about their body, it is in short and simple ways and doesn't usually include any type of derogatory terms. Typically, a man that is interested in a long-term relationship with another person will compliment them on their intellect or personality because subconsciously, he knows that those are things that will last a lifetime, while a person's body is only here for now.

11. Men are very forthcoming with their wants and needs. Hence, oftentimes, a man who's interested in continuing to date a woman will simply outright say it. Obviously, if a

person receives a statement from a man saying that they want to date them continuously, this is a very good sign. Alternatively, if a person is constantly questioning and trying to figure out where they stand with a man and if that man is never giving straight answers, it is a very good sign that he does not want to date that person.

12. If a man does not go on very often about another woman, it is a very good sign that he is committed to that one person exclusively.

13. Hearing the phrase "I miss you" before you hear the phrase "I love you" is a very good sign that a man is interested in dating a person long-term. By indicating that he missed that person, you are showing that he's interested in being around them for a long time and in more than just a hookup. Saying "I miss you" to someone means a lot more than saying "I love you" in the first few stages of a relationship.

14. If a man's eyes tend to linger on yours rather than your entire body, this is a very good sign that he is interested in a long-term and serious relationship. This is because the eye contact of a man shows extreme interest in the person that he is looking at—and by not exclusively or deliberately staring at that person's body, he is showing that he genuinely cares more about that person's thoughts and beliefs than he does about their body.

Chapter Eight: Confidence and How It Is Displayed

Confidence is a very powerful emotion in today's society. An individual who appears very confident is able to go very far places. By appearing confident, a person can attract suitable mates as well as be given promotions based on their perceived leadership skills. Because of this, confidence is very commonly displayed in different ways. However, confidence is also faked a lot of times in order to get ahead in life. Within this chapter, we will go through the common ways that confidence is displayed through body language. In addition, we will also go through how you can spot a lack of confidence in an individual.

Displaying Confidence

- **Posture**

  Posture is very important in the appearance of confidence. An individual's posture can say a lot about their perceived level of confidence. Confident posture is defined by legs that are lined with the individual's shoulders and feet approximately four to six inches apart. Weight is typically distributed equally on both legs, and shoulders are pushed back slightly. A straight back is also very typical of someone with extreme confidence. Individuals with this sort of posture are considered assertive and tend to project confidence. This is because an individual with this posture is seen as being able to "stand tall" regardless of their height and are also perceived as being very open to those that are talking to them, as they are unafraid of any attacks or criticism.

- **Hands**

  Hands are very important in trying to appear confident. It is important to remember when trying to display confidence through your hands to keep them calm and still. Rapidly moving one's hands is a sign of nervousness or anxiety.

- **Eye Contact**

  Having the ability to maintain long and strong eye contact with another is a very good sign that an individual is feeling confident. This is because showing eye contact with another person is a very vulnerable feeling and position. This is because our eyes can show a lot about how we actually feel in a situation. By maintaining good eye contact, we are showing to the other person that we are unafraid of what they may see within our eyes. This is a sign of extreme confidence, as it shows that you are self-assured in your feelings and believes that you are unafraid of how a person will interpret what they see in your eyes.

- **Mirroring Body Language**

  Mirroring the body language of those around us elicits a sort of understanding and seeks acceptance from those around us. This raises our confidence level as we humans strive to be liked by those around us. Because those around us will subconsciously begin to like us more by mirroring their body language, they will also be confident because of their positive view of us.

- **Fidgeting**

  It is very important to remember not to fidget when you are trying to display levels of confidence. Fidgeting in any form—no matter what part of your body is doing the movement—shows signs of nervousness and anxiety. In addition to this, it can simply annoy those around us. People are often irritated by constant rhythmic tapping or brushing noises. This is something to keep in mind if you are an individual who likes to bounce their leg or tap their foot at simple moments.

Ways to Spot a Lack of Confidence in a Person

- A very common sign of lack of confidence in an individual is if they are constantly touching their phone while in social situations or while alone. If an individual finds themselves unable to sit still during a social situation in which they don't know very many people, this may be a sign that they lack confidence. Checking their phone is a sign that they feel uncomfortable in a social situation and are unable to connect with those around them.

- Another sign of a lack of confidence in an individual is a quick backing down during a disagreement to avoid arguing with another person. An individual with an extreme lack of confidence will not want to cause problems with a person that they disagree with. Because of this, they often negotiate their views in order to avoid conflict. This shows that a person lacks confidence because they are not assured in their own opinions and would rather back down than express themselves honestly.

- Another common sign of a lack of confidence in an individual is their inability to leave their homes without any sort of makeup or hairstyling. This is a very obvious sign of a lack of confidence because it shows that an individual doesn't feel that they are worth being looked at unless they have something on their bodies or face to make them look more beautiful. Putting makeup on or doing their hair gives a false sense of self-esteem to an individual, which people with low self-esteem or confidence rely on very heavily.

- An individual with low confidence will also tend to take constructive criticism far too personally. If a person gives this individual constructive criticism about something, they will take it way too seriously and will end up feeling very strong negative emotions. This is a huge sign of low confidence and low self-esteem because this individual is not emotionally balanced enough to handle constructive criticism from those around them.

- Individuals who have low confidence or self-esteem will also find themselves afraid to contribute their opinion in a conversation. They will often second-guess themselves before they say anything instead of diving into an interesting conversation. They may find themselves stuttering or putting themselves down. This is because these individuals don't know how well their opinions will be received and are afraid of other people taking their opinions negatively. This is a sign of low confidence or self-esteem because these individuals care very deeply about how the people they make contact with view them.

- An individual who has difficulty with confidence also find themselves extremely indecisive with very simple and basic decisions. They may change their minds very often after coming to a decision. This is a sign of low self-confidence because this individual cannot trust their own opinions or decisions. This is especially a sign of low self-confidence when this applies to very simple tasks or simple decisions.

- Individuals with low self-confidence will also have extreme difficulty handling genuine compliments from those around them. They tend not to think that they are worthy of such good compliment, and they usually put them down or not accept them.

- Individuals struggling with low self-confidence will also tend to give up very soon with things that they are trying to do or achieve. They may have goals and dreams that they want to accomplish but will give up before they even really begin. This is a sign of low self-confidence because they do not believe that they have the ability to accomplish these goals and dreams before they even start.

- Individuals that struggle with low self-confidence will also tend to compare themselves with those around them. They tend to have very strong attention to the people that are doing better than them and will point out all of the ways that they are not doing as well as those around them. This is a strong sign of low self-confidence because it says that the person in question does not view themselves as very successful or doing very well in their life.

- Slouching is a very common display of low self-confidence in an individual. Why so? It is because lowering the center of a person's body is a sign that a person is not willing to hold up the weight of their upper body themselves. It sends off a signal that that individual is not proud of himself/herself. Because of these things, this is a big sign of low self-confidence.

In order to detect low self-confidence in an individual, all you have to do is look out for some of these common signs of low self-esteem and self-confidence. You can also detect low self-confidence or low self-esteem within yourself by looking out for these common signs. If you find that you or someone you know has low self-esteem or confidence, you can begin to work on them by saying very positive statements about yourself on a regular basis. Within the next chapter, we will go over how an individual can fix their body language and how they can pretend to be more confident than they really are.

Chapter Nine: How to Fake Your Body Language

Within this chapter, we will go through some easy and simple ways to fake your body language in order to come across as different emotions or expressions to those around you. These methods can be beneficial in everyday life as well as in the workplace. They can also serve you well in starting out relationships for the first time. These methods also do a good job of helping you feel how you are trying to feel. Have you ever heard the cliché, "Fake it till you make it?" Well, in some ways, this is true. By pretending to feel a lot of the emotions, you may be able to *convince yourself* that you actually feel that way.

1. *Taking a Deep Breath*

By amplifying the supply of oxygen within our lungs, we can be given more power and more ability to fake our emotions through body language. This will also give us a moment to collect our composure and pretend to be calm and collected. In addition, deep breathing tends to stimulate the parasympathetic nervous system, which can trigger a relaxation response. This is very good, especially when trying to trick those around you into believing that you are calm and controlled in a situation. Deep breathing is a very good trick for mindful living, as it gives you more control over your body and your reactions to stimuli.

2. *Controlling the Movement of Our Eyebrows*

Our eyebrows can convey a lot about our inner feelings. A lot of movement from our eyebrows can convey feelings that you do not want to express. You need to consciously be aware of the movement of your eyebrows when you are trying to fake certain emotions through your body language.

3. *Trying Not to Use a Fake Smile*

While it is good to smile even if you don't feel like it, that is not always beneficial when faking your emotions through body language. While looking happy and bubbly may make others want to like you, it is not the best look to have constantly. Fake smiles are far too easy to see through, and humans are naturally inclined to try and search for any inconsistencies within somebody's smile. A better way to hide your emotions is to keep your mouth straight and not smiling or sad.

4. *Relaxing Your Face*

By keeping your facial muscles relaxed, you can more easily control the movements of your face. Stay away from movements such as teeth grinding, frowning, or displaying any other type of emotional expression. Having relaxation and a calmer look on your face makes it more easy to control better the emotions you are putting out through your body language.

5. *Supporting Your Head*

A person's head that is being held up by an individual or a face buried into one's palm is a very obvious and clear giveaway of a bad mood or sadness. It is better to keep your head held up high and your neck and back straight in a situation where you feel sad, but you do not want those around you to know that you feel sad. Another important thing to remember is to try and stop yourself from touching your face when you're feeling sad, as it is a strong sign of anxiety and stress.

6.   *Avoiding Fidgeting*

Moving suddenly or very quickly are obvious signs of discomfort and anxiety. If you try to relax your body and try to look as though you are comfortable where you are, then it can be easier to control your emotions and feelings. It also becomes harder for those around you to decipher what you feel because you simply look calm and relaxed.

7.   *Speaking in a Balanced Tone*

This one is very important. If you want to come across as anything other than how you are currently feeling, you may want to take a moment to think about what you're going to say and speak in a balanced and even tone to those around you. The tone of your voice can give away your thoughts faster than you could think. Speaking too fast or changing your tone very quickly and frequently is an obvious sign that you aren't quite sure what you are trying to emote or what you are feeling. Try to slow down before you answer any questions. In addition to this, try to speak with your mind in a logical setting. You will want to focus exclusively on facts and remove any emotion from the situation. Through focusing on facts, you can stop your body from exclusively feeling the said emotions and focus on the task at hand.

8.   *Trying to Disassociate*

If you can manage to detach yourself from a situation you are in, it will become much easier to control your body language and the emotions that you were putting off. An easy way to do this is to think of happy thoughts as good memories. Doing this will help you take your mind off of whatever is happening around you, and it will make it more challenging for others to read your thoughts. By detaching yourself from the situation around you, you will more easily be able to see the logical side of what is happening and able to accurately portray the particular body language and emotions that you want to exude.

9.   *Speaking to Yourself*

You will be able to tell your mind to think about the way that it should. This will make it easier to control your body language and your emotions, as you are in the process of controlling your own mind.

Conclusion

Within this text, we have learned many important things about our own and other people's body language. In the very beginning of this text, I began by explaining why this book was written and why it is beneficial to the reader.

Within the first chapter, I began to go into how an average person can read those around them and explain how easy it is to read people and how it can be learned by just about anyone. I also began to give the basics of how to analyze the people around us, with a brief discussion on how important context is in reading people's words and actions, on how it is essential for us to take into consideration more than one point of observation when reading people and instead focus on how specific combinations of circumstances can more accurately represent how someone truly thinks and feels, on how to analyze someone you don't have a background of, as well as on how to ensure that your personal preference or judgment would not jeopardize your assessment of another person's emotions and motives.

Within the second chapter, I began to go into the way that our bodies talk our body language. I explained how there are gestures that evoke a positive impression on others in the same manner that there are ones that cause a negative impression as well. I explained how every part of the human body communicates in the feelings of a person. I also went through how body language can reveal our deepest inner emotions that we may not even recognize ourselves. I also began to go into some common gestures and what they mean in terms of body language. I then began to go into detail about nonverbal aspects that our bodies give off and what they may mean in different situations. I went into detail about the body language of the torso, hips, chest, shoulders, hands, fingers, legs, and feet. I also went to detail about how all of these things work together to create one full statement of body language.

In the third chapter, I began to go through the basic rules for analyzing those around us. Meanwhile, as for the fourth chapter, I discussed the difference between verbal and nonverbal communication. I explain how you can analyze the verbal statements that others make based on their nonverbal behavior. I also went into the intricacies of analyzing the nonverbal behavior that we may come into contact with on a daily basis.

Within the fifth chapter, I went into how our minds communicate with those around us. I went into detail defining the unconscious mind and the limbic brain and how they work together to create our personalities and emotions.

Within the sixth chapter, I went into the intricacies of reading the face and explained how you can use the face as a method of nonverbal communication and how you can read another person's facial expressions through the littlest of things. I explained how you could analyze every expressive portion of the face. I went into detail about analyzing and understanding the nonverbal communication with the eyes, smiles, expressions, lips, heads, and more.

Within the seventh chapter, I went into how you can tell if there is truth in a relationship. I went into detail about how you can tell if somebody is lying in a relationship and how to analyze a relationship between true love and honesty.

In the next couple of sections, I went into detail about the common signs that a female or a male is interested in dating somebody else. Meanwhile, in the eighth chapter, I went through how confidence is typically displayed in a person's body, how you can spot a lack of confidence in someone, as well as how you can fake some confidence in your own body.

Within the ninth chapter, I went into detail about some tips and tricks on how to fake your own body language. I went into detail about how you can learn to control your own emotions and your body language in order to give off different expressions and feelings to other people.

Within this text, I have successfully given a detailed guide on how to read those around us, as well as how to affect our own body language. All of the tips and tricks I have given within this text are greatly beneficial to the average person in terms of their social life as well as their workplace or school. I hope that you, as the reader, are able to find any use in all of the tricks in body language that I have given in this text. I also hope that you, the reader, are able to improve your current relationships and find yourself in higher economic standing because of this book.

Covert Manipulation

Introduction

Welcome to covert manipulation and manipulation psychology. Within this text you will learn a variety of things that can greatly benefit you in everyday life. From persuasion, manipulation techniques, emotional influence, to NLP, the options are limitless. Really quick before you begin diving into this text, I will be giving you a quick rundown of what you can expect within this book. Within the first chapter we will go over the basics of what manipulation psychology is and the history behind the psychology of manipulation. After this we will go into why people choose to manipulate others and where manipulation tends to pop up the most in the average person's life. Within the next chapter we will go through some common expressions of manipulation that you may experience in everyday life. We will explain and give the most common methods or tactics of emotional manipulation that we see every day. You can apply these to both romantic and platonic relationships as well as relationships within the workplace. These range from tactics such as raising your voice and lying. You'll go over many more than those two that is just a standard. Within the third chapter you will go into some in-depth techniques of manipulation, these will be more complicated and slightly more difficult to understand than the tactics and methods of the previous chapter. We will go through methods such as projection, denial, intimidation, conditioning, stalking, and much, much more. In addition, we will explain how words tend to contribute to emotional manipulation.

You will begin to understand how dependent people are on language and how, as a result, this language can influence people. Within the fourth chapter we will begin to discuss the power of persuasion. I will give a brief history of the origins of the art of persuasion dating all the way back to the ancient Greeks. I will then begin to explain how persuasion can be used in our everyday lives from business transactions to simple negotiations. Within the 5th chapter we will begin to discuss something brand-new, neuro-linguistic programming. I will give an in-depth background and history on the origins of neuro-linguistic programming and will explain how neurolinguistics programming is used to manipulate and manage those around you. Within the 6th chapter we will begin to use our learned skills to gain friends. In other words, I will go through the skills that I have taught you in the previous chapter and explain how they can be used to in the social sphere or simply the workplace. In the 7th chapter I will explain how you can avoid manipulation within a relationship. More specifically I will explain how you can spot manipulation with you or others and how to avoid a relationship with manipulative tendencies. In the 8th chapter I will go over specifically manipulation within the workplace and how to spot it. In the ninth and Final Chapter we will go through how you can defend yourself against manipulation. I will go through each tactic that we have discussed previously and give a brief description on how you can defend yourself against it. I will also go into how positive self-esteem can be used to overcome manipulative tendencies. Because of the importance of positive self-esteem in fighting manipulation I will also give some tips and tricks on how to improve self-esteem over time. Within all of this text you will learn many very useful skills you can use in everyday life. A lot of the skills within this text are not just manipulative skills that can be used to manipulate those around you but also skills to fight back against manipulation and prevent manipulation in everyday life. A good portion of this text is also a history lesson. I teach a lot of history in this text on the background of different types of psychology and different psychologists that indicated certain ideals and theories. This is a very educational text that will greatly benefit you in the following ways. This text can help you learn how to better manage your social life, as well as get ahead financially. In addition, this text can also help you to pinpoint and spot manipulative relationships and stop them before they can even happen. If you find that you've already becoming trapped into a manipulative relationship and that is why you were turning to this text well, do not fret, because you will learn how to escape that manipulative relationship as well. This book truly is a jack of all trades and can be treated as such during the reading.

Chapter One: What is Manipulation Psychology and Why do People Manipulate Others?

I'm sure we have all felt manipulated at some point or another. Manipulation has been present in our society since the beginning of time. In some form or another manipulation is apparent every day in our lives. But what is involved in the psychology behind manipulation? What drives individuals, on a psychological level, to manipulate others? Within this chapter I will cover all of this and more.

Manipulation Psychology, what is it?

Before delving deep into how you can use manipulation to your benefit, I have to give you an idea of what psychological manipulation actually is. First and foremost, manipulation is a form of social influence in which the goal is to change the behavior of those around you through abusive, or deceptive messages. This is often used to benefit the interests of the manipulator, usually to the expense of those around them. words used to describe manipulative psychology are those such as, exploitive, abusive, devious, and deceptive. Despite its connection to manipulation, an act that is inherently negative, the act of social influencing is not always damaging or abusive. An example of this is when someone's friends, family, and doctors will try to change the mindset of someone who has unhealthy habits and behaviors. In a normal context social influence is typically harmless in the fact that the individual being influenced is easily able to accept or reject it. The difference between this and manipulation is that social influence is not necessarily coercive and does not typically use underhanded methods to change a person's behavior. That being said, social influence and manipulation go hand-in-hand, as manipulation cannot exist without social influence. Another, less negative term used for manipulation is persuasion. Persuasion is used in a variety of ways in our everyday life. From advertisements, to trying to decide what to eat, everything around us is trying to persuade us to do certain things at certain times. But what is the difference between persuasion and manipulation? persuasive reasoning can be traced all the way back to the ancient Greeks with Aristotle's ideas of logos, pathos, and ethos. When looking at these three persuasive methods we can see that these are the building blocks of what would later become the basis for manipulation psychology, the subject of this text. The differences between persuasion and manipulation lies and the requirements for successful manipulation. The first of these requirements is the need to conceal aggressive intentions and behaviors. The second is having to know the person that is being manipulated. This means that you have to be aware of their psychological vulnerabilities and must be able to accurately decide which tactics are going to be the most effective. Finally, the last requirement for successful manipulation is having a particular level of ruthlessness and not caring about the harm that may befall the victim. Manipulation most commonly is achieved through the use of "covert aggression." In colloquial terms this is also known as passive aggression.

Why do people manipulate others? The answer to this question begins with fear. It begins with the fear that as things are in the current moment the person in question will not succeed with the desired result from their own merits. Or they may be afraid that their life and the people around them will not provide for them or come to the favorable result. Sometimes they may also feel as though life and the people around them are quintessentially working against them. This is coupled with a fear that the people around them will gain and succeed in a way that they never will, and also that the limited resources in this world result in a "dog eat dog" scenario. They may feel that the situation and world around them need to be secured and controlled in order for them to succeed or simply survive practically, emotionally, and financially. They often have an innate feeling that somebody may gain the upper hand if they do not manipulate those around them. These feelings can come from the belief that a person has a lack of worthiness. This may come from their childhood, this may simply come from an unsupportive friend and family group. Either way they feel that they are not worthy of their life working out well for themselves. they also struggle with the idea that they are not worthy of other people having their best interest in mind and thus are attacked by these fears. So, at the base of all of this is a fear that causes them to manipulate others. This is fueled by the feeling that they are unworthy to those around them. These individuals also often experience what is called a "lack of consciousness" in easier terms this is the belief, sometimes without even realizing it, that you are not responsible for your own reality.

People that suffer from this are unable to make the correlation between the events that occur in their lives and their internal selves. Or in other words, they may not understand that the way that their life around them is unfolding reflects how their emotions within them are shown. This often is also coupled with an inability to learn from previous experiences, and a tendency to repeat past actions expecting a different result. "Unconscious" people feel that the world is inherently unsafe. Because of this in order to get results in this society they feel they have to manipulate those around them. Even if the results of this manipulation do not bring them satisfaction and ultimately result in being emotionally or practically back at square one every single time.

Instead of trying something new, like not manipulating people, in order to try and avoid the pain of this failure the manipulator will create a new manipulation. But why doesn't the manipulation work the first time? This is because manipulation is not an authentic or true action. It is an action of Defense in an attempt to stop the fear, pain, and unworthiness. Because of this, by trying to succeed using manipulation, as opposed to authenticity, the result is a sense of non-authenticity that can cause further damage within the mind and soul of the manipulator. Because of all of this we can come to the conclusion that a person who manipulates does so because they feel unworthy within their core.

So, in order to properly pinpoint the signs of manipulation in our lives we need to know where they pop up the most common. In order to fully understand these areas of manipulation, we have to keep in mind that not all who manipulate are conscienceless. Narcissists have also been known to go to extreme lengths to manipulate those around them. I will not go into detail upon the reasonings behind a narcissistic person manipulating those around them but understand that it still comes down to the idea of being unworthy. One very common way that manipulation shows up in everyday relationships and life is with people who have a fear of abandonment. Somebody with a fear of abandonment will do anything to ensure that those around them, especially romantic partners, do not leave them or abandon them. This often results in manipulative tendencies in order to make sure that those around them need them. Understand that somebody suffering from this issue is not inherently a terrible person. They're simply suffering and struggling to deal with a negative internal image of themselves. They may have an inability to understand that they themselves are lovable and worthy by simply existing. Once shown the error in their ways and offered help these individuals will most likely make an attempt to change their ways. These individuals often have trouble keeping romantic relationships. Probably the most common scenario in which somebody manipulates another, and also a situation you can probably relate with, is trying to manipulate somebody to spend their money. This can be manipulation by a spouse to get the other spouse to purchase something for them. Or, it can also be seen on a larger scale with the manipulation by advertisements and big businesses to try and get you to spend your money on their product. I'm sure we can all relate to the ladder. We can also find a lot of examples of manipulation in the political sphere. Politicians are often well-known to manipulate their audiences into supporting their agenda in various ways. The manipulation of these people is often much more subtle than traditional manipulation because it has to fly under the radar of other politicians around them. This manipulation often includes suggestive manipulation. That is, manipulation by suggesting negative consequences for not supporting them. Another very common but less destructive version of manipulation is the manipulation of children in order to help their parents. This type of manipulation is different from the kind we have discussed because, while manipulative, it's not necessarily negative. Parents will often do this to encourage their children to help with chores, or to learn necessary skills. We can also see this in parents trying to encourage their children to make good grades in school by purchasing gifts or giving money if their grades were at a certain level. While this may seem like a positive form of manipulation, this idea actually damages the mind of the child and is not recommended as a form of encouragement.

Another example that is much darker, kidnappers are often known to build a relationship or rapport with a child they're planning on kidnapping. They are manipulating the child by being nice to them and offering them gifts so that they can trust them. Probably the most common form of manipulation that we see in everyday life is the action of a man or a woman who is interested in a man or woman giving them anything that they want so that they can get money or influence from that person.

As we can see within this chapter, Manipulation has a much more complicated background than people often believe. It does not come down to that individual simply being a bad person. What is the result of many beliefs and feelings that have been hammered into them since childhood? We can also see that manipulation has a long and deep history. Going back to the ancient Greeks as we've discussed. We've also discussed fairly in-depth the reasons why people are seen to manipulate others, As well as the most common events that manipulation is seen to pop up in people's lives.

This background is essential for the rest of the information that will be learned within this text. In the next chapter we will begin to go into the most common expressions of manipulation. We will also begin to explain and give some of the most common and widely seen tactics of emotional manipulation. These are only the basics and will only scratch the surface of the depth of manipulation.

Chapter Two: Common Expressions of Manipulation and Basic Emotional Manipulation Tactics

Within this chapter we are going to go over some of the most common expressions of manipulation and how to spot them. We will also go over some of the most basic emotionally manipulative tactics.

Expressions of manipulation

Most of the common expressions and phrases of manipulation are related to relationships. You may notice that as a trend within this portion of the text. This is because those that are in relationships have the most power over the person they are in a relationship with, and they are also the most vulnerable. This phenomenon can make certain individuals feel as though they must manipulate in order to feel secure. The first phrase or expression we're going to go over is the following:
"why are you still mad at me? I bought you a gift." This phrase is manipulative because it uses two methods of manipulation that have been identified by the psychologist Herbert A. Simon. These two methods are known as rationalization, and minimization. Rationalization is an excuse that has been made up by the manipulator to redeem themselves for inappropriate or negative behavior. This form of manipulation is often coupled with minimization which we will discuss next. Minimization is a form of denial that is at the expense of the person being manipulated. Within this method the manipulator suggests that the feelings of the person being manipulated do not matter or are of less importance by suggesting that the events that they are upset about were not harmful or negative in the first place. This, coupled with rationalization, makes for a very powerful form of manipulation. Within the expression given, the manipulator is using minimization within the question "why are you still mad at me?" By making the manipulated person's anger seem irrational he minimizes their feelings. They then follow it up by saying "I bought you a gift" which is the rationalization aspect. The manipulator is rationalizing, making their previous actions seem okay, by purchasing the manipulated individual a gift.
The next phrase we are going to go over is the following:
"Stay home and let me take care of you. This is what's best for the kids."
This phrase is very manipulative and uses two huge emotionally manipulative tactics. The first one that it uses is a very powerful one known as a "guilt trip." using a guilt trip in a manipulative sentence is very powerful because it makes the victim feel negative about themselves. They may begin to experience self-doubt, anxiousness or feel submissive to the person doing the manipulating. The next method of manipulation that is used in this phrase is known as "playing the servant role." this method was also indicated by Herbert A. Simon. within this method the manipulator hides their self-serving agenda under the idea of service to an honorable cause. This form of manipulation is also quite powerful because it makes them appear as though they are a superhero or some type of noble human being acting out of service. In addition to placing the manipulator up onto a pedestal, this form of manipulation also manages to rationalize the actions of the manipulator under the guise of them being obedient or acting like servants. Within this phrase the manipulator uses Guilt Trip by saying "this is what's best for the kids." by preluding this guilt trip with the phrase "stay home and let me take care of you." which makes them appear as though they are acting in the servant role in this situation. Overall the effect of using these two methods together within this phrase makes the manipulator appear like a very generous and kind person while making the manipulated individual feel guilty and ashamed for not wanting to do what the manipulator wants.
Another very common phrase used in manipulation is as follows:
"don't leave me. I might hurt myself."
This is probably the most dangerous and powerful form of manipulation that we've discussed so far. This phrase is incredibly powerful and effective at manipulating an individual because it makes them feel as though they are responsible whether or not the manipulator injures himself. This phrase of manipulation can fall under many different methods of emotional manipulation. The first that I could see here is known as "projecting the blame" or "blaming others." in this method, manipulator makes it look as though the victim is the one doing something negative or harmful to the manipulator whether they truly are or not. This makes the

victim feel as though they are to blame for the actions of the manipulator. This is often very effective and believable by the victim. Is also good to note that manipulators using this method often accused the victim of being "crazy" especially when there is strong evidence against the manipulator. This manipulative statement couples the previous method with a new method known as "playing the victim role." Within this method, manipulator makes themselves appear as the victim of the circumstances or as the victim of somebody else's behavior in order to evoke pity, compassion, or even sympathy within the actual victim. This method is especially powerful if the manipulator knows that the person, they're manipulating is a caring or generous person. This is because the manipulator knows that the person in question would not be able to handle seeing another person suffer, and thus the manipulator is able to play on that person sympathy easily. This method is especially dangerous because it plays on our innate empathetic sense. Within this expression the manipulator uses the idea of suicide, a very serious and dangerous prospect, to gain sympathy from the victim that they are manipulating. They also managed to project the blame of this dangerous and powerful action, suicide, by making the victim feel as though their actions, leaving the manipulator that is, is causing the manipulators suicide. This makes the victim feel as though they are the cause of the manipulator harming them self, and if the victim is a sympathetic type of person, they will do anything to prevent this from happening. This is why this method is so powerful. The final phrase that we are going to cover that is commonly used to manipulate others is the following:
"you made me do this!"
The manipulation within this phrase is fairly obvious and uses a form of manipulation that we have already gone over. That is the idea of projecting blame onto the victim. By telling the victim that their actions forced the manipulator to do whatever it was that they did they can make the victim feel responsible. As a result, the victim feels as though they must do something to right whatever wrong they believe that they did. This manipulative statement is easy to spot and is often a last-ditch attempt of a manipulator to get their victim to do what they want when they feel they have been backed into a corner. The reality of the matter is that the victim only has control over their own actions. The actions of the manipulator cannot be controlled by the actions of the victim, in reality the manipulator chose to act the way that they did and have to learn to understand that it was them who decided to do whatever it was in the first place. This statement can sometimes be followed up with accusations of the victim manipulating the manipulator.

Tactics of Manipulation

In this next section we will be discussing some common tactics of emotional manipulation. The first tactic of emotional manipulation that we will go over is very common in everyday life. This tactic is known as lying. Lying, or gas lighting as some know it, is very common in emotional manipulation because it is very easy to do. It is used to intentionally keep the victim feeling off balance in their life. If an individual is feeling very off balance in their life, they are less likely to question the actions or ideas of those around them which is beneficial to the manipulator. It can also be used to make the victim seem like the bad guy and is very commonly used to twist a situation against the person being manipulated. This tactic is one used to try and maintain control in a scenario and can often lead to lack of trust in relationships. The way that a manipulator using lies to manipulate somebody makes them start to lose a connection with their instincts because they're being convinced that their instincts are wrong. When this happens consistently over a long period of time it can cause a lot of turmoil. This turmoil is usually beneficial to the manipulator because if the victim is not sure in themselves, they will not have the strength to fight back against their manipulator. This can also prevent a victim from reaching a proper solution to a problem and blind them to dangerous events that are happening around them. This method is also often coupled with a tendency to point out things about the victim that are damaging to their self-esteem but also completely unrelated to the matter at hand. Doing so does not only lower the self-esteem of the victim but also serves to produce a feeling of confusion in the victim. As we have discussed before confusion and feeling offset is very beneficial to the manipulator because it is easier for them to get away with their manipulation with these feelings in place.

The next form of emotional manipulation that we will discuss is when a person raises their voice at another. The sound of a person raising their voice just on a psychological level invokes an innate sense of panic. This is psychological and completely instinctive. It's something that nobody can really stop themselves from feeling. Because of this, this is a very powerful form of manipulation. The sound of a person raising their voice another invokes a sense of panic in the person being yelled at. This sense of panic is incredibly beneficial to the manipulator because in a moment of panic the victim will be willing to do anything, they can to stop the yelling. The innate sense of fear and Terror that comes with the sound of somebody raising their voice at an individual puts the victim onto the very shaky ground and makes them feel as though they are in the wrong. This is because the sound of somebody raising their voice at you brings you back to when you were a child and your parents would chastise you for doing something wrong. At a subconscious level the sound of somebody raising their voice makes you feel like a child because of this connection. This is all very beneficial to the manipulator because if the victim feels like a child, then they feel as though they have no control. A manipulator needs their victim to feel as though they have no control over the situation in order for the manipulator to maintain their own control. A Manipulators ability to manipulate is very strongly based on the disillusions of the person they are manipulating. If that person feels as though they have no control over a situation then it will give the manipulator more control over the said situation. In addition to all of this the sound of somebody raising their voice is also very prone to elicit panic and unsureness in the victim Because the sound of somebody Raising their voice is a sign that precedes an action. And in the case of a manipulator, the victim may never know what that action is.

The manipulator could be planning on harming them, or simply breaking something, or they might not do anything at all. But it's the idea that they could do any of these things that creates panic in the victim and gives the manipulator their power. This is a very powerful form of manipulation and is typically used on women. This is because women's aggressive tendencies tend to show themselves in more passive ways first. While a woman can be driven to yell, yelling is typically one of the last things they do before a more serious form of aggression. Because of this when a woman is shouted or yelled at, they usually take that as a sign that the person yelling at them is on their last straw. This has more of a desired effect on a woman than it would on a man who more readily raises their voice in anger than do anything else.

The next method of emotional manipulation we will be discussing is known as victimization. Victimization, or victim playing, is the invention of false victimhood of an individual. This is used for a variety of reasons other than manipulation. This can be used to justify the abuse of another person, this can be used as a coping strategy, or this can also be used to seek attention. The justification of abuse goes hand-in-hand with the use of this method for emotional manipulation. This method works by dehumanizing the victim in order to divert the attention away from the acts of abuse by the manipulator. This is done by claiming that the abuse was justified because of the victim's prior bad behavior. I would like to note that this is very common in physically abusive romantic relationships. Strategy is often used by the manipulator or the abuser to keep the person that they are physically or emotionally abusing from realizing that they are being abused in the first place. By placing the blame onto the victim, they trick the victim into thinking that everything that's wrong in the relationship is because of the victim. This is of course, not true but that shows how powerful this form of manipulation is. It's almost a sort of reverse psychology in a way, by placing doubt on to the person being manipulated the manipulator is more easily and readily able to weave in and push their own agenda. Which in the case of an abuser is typically not to lose the abused or get arrested. This can also be known as grooming the victim by attracting a sort of sympathy from those around them in order to gain support so that they feel more justified in the abuse of the victim.
This method serves more than simply justifying their actions to the victim or those around the victim, this method also serves to justify the actions of the manipulator to themselves. Most individuals do not want to think of themselves as an evil, abusive, manipulative person. So, by justifying their actions by blaming the victim, and making themselves believe that they were only acting as a result of the victim's actions they can rationalize their behavior so that they do not hate themselves. A difference in the way that they treat those around them and what they believe themselves to be is known as cognitive dissonance and the use of this justification is known as existential validation because it helps them deal with the cognitive dissonance that results from the differences in how they actually act and how they believe they act. While this method is very powerful in the short-term this tactic seems to be less successful over time. Those that feel

sympathy for the manipulator because of the manipulator's ability to seem like the victim will in a short-term feel as though they need to rescue or help the manipulator and by doing so will further push their agenda. But as time goes on and there is no movement towards anything better in the manipulator. These Heroes will feel as though they are wasting their time and become frustrated at the lack of improvement. Eventually this has been shown to make the sympathetic individuals leave the manipulator no matter how much he plays the victim. Playing the victim can also be used as a technique to seek attention, many people in our world today are very addicted to attention. Either because of childhood issues, a lack of love in their life, or simple narcissism, attention is constantly being searched out in our modern world. Playing the victim is the easiest way to gain attention from those around you because we as humans are attracted to pain and suffering whether we like to admit it or not. So, by playing the victim a manipulator is able to get the attention they want and need. Because of this attention giving positive feedback on a manipulator's actions it is often hard for a person to stop using this method once they've begun using it regularly. It almost becomes like an addiction because it feels good emotionally to have people around you feeling sympathetic and wanting to help you. The only way to break the cycle within a person is to convince them to take responsibility for their own desires and to be willing to put forth long-term actions on their own and without the help and guidance of others. They need to recognize that their life is in their own hands and that they make their own choices in the world.

Another Method of emotional manipulation is the act of a manipulator to act Superior to those around them. By acting as though they are somehow Superior to their victim, the manipulator Plants a seed in the victim's head that perhaps they are not good enough. Whether or not this is true, it tends to work. Victims who began to believe that they themselves are lesser than the manipulator that is manipulating them will tend to have a lower sense of worth, and as such will have a hard time Understanding that the abuse coming from the manipulator is not their fault. This will make it much easier for the manipulator to swoop in and push their own agenda. There're many covert and secretive ways that a manipulator can convince a victim that they are superior to them. The first one is pretty straightforward, simply acting as though the manipulator is of a higher standing than the victim. Often times this comes through by the manipulator treating the other individual as though they are a child or somehow incapable of doing Simple adult tasks. They may do this through the use of condescending comments or facial expressions. This can also come through in more ways than simply treating someone like they are a child, however. This can also come through by the manipulator pretending as though they have a higher stance in a business ladder form than the victim whether this is true or not. This may include very simple actions like taking some of the roles of the victim in a business setting. Let's say for instance that's the victim is of a higher Prestige than the manipulator. Let's say that one of the responsibilities of the victim is to turn in expense reports on time. The manipulator in this situation might take the expense reports from that person's desk and turn them in a day early, joking about it later saying that perhaps they should have the victim's job because they clearly can do it better. A second scenario in which a manipulator can convince a victim that they are above the victim is by using a few key phrases that we hear pretty often amongst abusive relationships. Each of these phrases has a similar quality in that they put down the other individual for their emotions or feelings. They also tend to have a condescending or patronizing tone that is meant to belittle the victim. A few of these phrases are as follows:
"don't be silly" "Don't be stupid" "You're being ridiculous"
As you can see Within each of these phrases the victim is being put down or belittled in some way. These phrases are very effective because they are very covert. When you are the victim in this situation it is very difficult to tell that you are being put down by these phrases, they make you feel as though you aren't thinking straight and the person that is manipulating you is the only one that has good sense at that moment. Another way that a manipulator can act superior to their victim in a subtle way is by making jokes about the victim. This is especially effective when done in front of other people. When using this technique, manipulators are often making jokes that are about things that the victim is actually insecure about and the manipulators usually aware of this fact. What makes this technique so effective is the fact that it is very hard for the victim to fight back against the manipulator in this situation. Any attempt to ask the manipulator to not talk about the things that the victim is self-conscious about only results in the manipulator saying things like "we're only joking "and "don't be such a hard-ass." these famous phrases legitimizes the jokes that

235

the manipulator made at the victim's expense to the people around the victim. This makes it especially hard for the victim to fight back because we, as humans, are very weak to our social status. In other words, it is very hard for a human to fight back against manipulation that is happening against them when they do not have large and strong support around them. By legitimizing their jokes, the people around the victim, the manipulator poses a risk to that group of support that the victim relied so heavily on.

The final technique for manipulating somebody emotionally that we will discuss in this chapter is known as gaining control. This may sound very generic and like something that we have already talked about but this version of gaining control is much less subtle than the other message we've discussed. Gaining control in this sense has to do with having some form of Leverage over the person that they are trying to manipulate. It's can be in several different fields, from the social sphere, to their economic well-being, to simply making the victim feel as if they have no choice in simple decision making, this is more specific to obvious displays of control in a relationship. Socially a manipulator can have control over a victim by befriending all of the victim's friends and gaining their trust in a way that would make the victim feel as though they could not complain to their friends about the manipulator. This is particularly damaging because, as we have discussed before, victims need a large support group in order to break away from their manipulator. From an economic standpoint, a manipulator can have control simply by making more money than the victim. This is particularly effective and cohabitating relationships in which the victim of the manipulator lives together, and the victim is dependent on the manipulator's rent or other bills that they may pay. The victim's dependency on these things gives the manipulator a constant and consistent control over the victim that is unwavering and easy to keep. This particular type of control is the one that we see most common in abusive relationships.

A manipulator can also gain control in a relationship by making the victim feel as though they do not have a choice in very simple matters. These can be as small as not allowing the victim to choose who they hang out with or what they have for dinner. While this may not seem like very much, keeping the victim from being able to make these small choices themselves makes them feel as though they are ultimately powerless in the relationship. They feel as though their manipulator must make all of their decisions for them, usually at a subconscious level. Each of these methods of gaining control is very different, but they all go back to the same main point. In order for a manipulator to have control in a situation they must make the victim feel as though they are on shaky ground in some way. They must make the victim feel as though they are not in control of their own lives. The mind is a very powerful thing, and by making the victim think that they do not have control in certain situations it will ultimately result in them not having to control a much larger, more important situations. Control is the key word here. A manipulator needs control to be able to do their manipulating. Without having that control over another person, the manipulator does not have any ground to stand on.

Within this chapter we have discussed and common expressions of manipulation that we see often in our everyday lives. Many of these Expressions pop-up exclusively in romantic relationships, but many pops up and every day business transactions and amongst family and friends. In this chapter we also spent some time giving and explaining some of the most common tactics of emotional manipulation that we see in everyday life. These are simply scratching the surface of tactics that can be used in emotional manipulation. In fact, there are hundreds of methods of manipulating someone emotionally that we have not gone over yet. But in this chapter, we went through tactics such as, raising your voice, acting Superior, victimization, lying, and control. Within the next chapter we will go through some more in-depth techniques of emotional manipulation. These techniques will be more complicated, and more difficult to pinpoint in everyday life.

Chapter Three: In-Depth Techniques of Manipulation
Within this chapter we will be going into some of the more complicated techniques of emotional manipulation. Amongst these techniques we will be covering Some techniques that were identified and discovered by famous historical psychologists known as Harriet B. Braiker and George K. Simon.

Projection

Projection is easy to pinpoint within the manipulator because it's often consists of symptoms such as being unwilling or unable juicy the manipulators own shortcomings and to avoid being held responsible for anything they have done wrong in the past. In other words, a person using projection will "project" their negative behavior or actions on to another person by finding a very extended and unreasonable connection between an action of the other person and the action of the manipulator. This form of manipulation is also often used as a defense mechanism and tends to be instinctual for most people. Well it is very common for people to do this without realizing it, there's a difference between projecting out of self-defense and projecting to manipulate. Projecting out of self-defense usually comes suddenly when another person is being accusatory or attacking the individual in question. This action is also usually followed up with the individual realizing what they have done wrong and taking responsibility for their actions in one way or another. A manipulator projecting to manipulate however, is different because the manipulator will make this projection without being antagonized in any sort of way. They will often do it almost immediately after they have done their negative action and will preemptively project. They also will refrain from ever understanding that what they did was wrong and will never take responsibility for their actions unless somebody forces them to. An example of this would be an employee that has a history of rude or offensive comments complaining to another employee that their boss is incapable of keeping their office family friendly. They would make this comment in an attempt to escape the fact that they are the problem and not the boss of the office.

Denial

Denial is a very versatile form of manipulation. Denial can be used in a vast variety of different ways in everyday life. Denial can be used to deny negative actions of the manipulator to help them seem like less of a manipulator to those around them. Denial can also be used by the manipulator to deny to themselves that they are trying to manipulate those around them. In other words, a manipulator might be able to convince themselves that they are not manipulating anybody but simply acting of some different need or want. This strengthens the power of the manipulator because the best actor or actress is one that believes themselves to be the character they're acting of. This is the same with manipulators. A manipulator that believes that they are truly in the right in every sense of the word will more easily able to convince those around them of that idea. There are many different ways that a manipulator can deny their actions or deny the actions of another subtly. They can do this using a method known as diversion. Using diversion, a manipulator will refuse to give a straightforward answer to questions and instead will move the conversation on to a different topic time and time again to avoid the said question. This is a way of denying the answer by not even giving it. A very similar but different tactic to this is known as evasion, these two tactics are often confused. The difference between diversion and evasion tactics of denial is that while diversion intentionally steers the conversation on to a different but interesting topic, evasion is more an act of giving vague and confusing responses that seem to have no meaning or are irrelevant in the current situation. This tactic is much less effective as it seems quite suspicious in almost any situation. Most intelligent manipulators will not use this tactic unless it is their last possible option. This typically means that Somebody, or many people, we'll have asked a question that gets right to the heart of the manipulator's agenda or we'll be putting a hole in the manipulator's strategy. Another word for this method is known as "weasel words."

Intimidation

There many different forms of intimidation that can be used by a manipulator to control their victim. The first one we will discuss is known as covert intimidation. This is the subtle, indirect, or implied threats of a manipulator to a victim that puts said victim into a defensive mindset. These threats are often not threatening of the physical manner but rather that of the business, social, or economic sphere. These threats are very subtle, and this may not be picked up upon by the people around the victim. By putting the victim onto the defensive the manipulator gains a special kind of advantage. The manipulator gains the advantage of being on the offensive. In other words, the manipulator is calm cool and collected because they know when the next strike is coming, while the victim is jumpy and unsure because they feel as though the manipulator could strike at any time and they do not know when they need to be ready for it. This jumpy-ness is very advantageous to the manipulator because it makes victim feel as though they are on shaky ground and are not in control of their future. As we have discussed before this is very good for the manipulator because in order to maintain control, they need their victim to feel as though they have no idea what comes next. Think about this in the way of watching a scary movie. Throughout the entire film you are sitting at the edge of your seat because you know that something frightening could happen at any moment and because of this something that normally would be very normal like an owl hooting in the background for instance, frightens you because you were on edge in the first place. If you know anything about films did you know that this was the desired effect of having the owl hoot at a crucial moment. Because after that fright you may feel silly or as though you cannot trust your instincts anymore and thus are lulled into a false sense of security to then be attacked by whatever the actual scare was meant to be. Similar to a victim with a manipulator you are under the complete control of the filmmaking.

Conditioning

To condition someone or something, the basic form is a process of learning that happens through the use of rewards and punishments or desired or not desired Behavior. This can also be called operant conditioning. In this particular form of conditioning an association is made between a behavior and a consequence of that behavior. The easiest way to think of this in everyday life is the way that we train dogs. Dogs are often trained with the use of a treat for good behavior and a scolding of some sort for bad behavior. This is a form of operant conditioning. The connection of the desired behavior of the dog with a treat to the not desired Behavior of the dog with the scolding leads the dog to subconsciously connect the desired Behavior with a positive outcome. A similar training method can be used with humans and the result is known as operant conditioning. This is not to be confused with classical conditioning which is similar but not exactly the same. All of the steps leading up to the end result of both forms of conditioning are the same, the difference lies in the very last step. Operant conditioning is based on voluntary behavior by the individual being trained. Whereas classical conditioning is based on the involuntary behavior of the person being trained. In our dog training example, the action of the dog doing desired behavior is result of the operant conditioning however, the dog being excited and expecting a treat after that action is a result of classical conditioning. This is because the feeling of excitement and expectation is an involuntary behavior that comes from the Association of a treat with the action given. Pops up in humans as well. Let's say that you have a favorite restaurant that you frequent very often. This restaurant brings you great happiness and joy. As a result, you tend to like the waiters or waitresses that work at this restaurant more than you would waiters or waitresses at work at a normal restaurant. Because of this instinctual likeness you tip the waiters or waitresses at this restaurant far more than you would waiters or waitresses at a different restaurant. The instinctive feeling of liking a person simply because they work at your favorite restaurant is an example of classical conditioning while acting on that feeling and tipping the waiters and waitresses more is an example of operant conditioning.

Now we can begin to see the connection between these two types of conditioning with manipulation. If a manipulator knows even the basis of these two types of conditioning it becomes very easy for them to subconsciously train their victim to bend to their every whim. Let's say for instance in the case of a manipulative romantic relationship a female partner offers her male partner sexual gratification every time that he purchases her a piece of jewelry and no other time. As a result, the male of this relationship may find himself purchasing jewelry for his female partner and becomes involuntarily aroused as he's purchasing it. The action of purchasing the jewelry is the result of operant conditioning because it was a voluntary behavior on the man's part, but the involuntary arousal is a result of classical conditioning because of the association with buying his female partner expensive gifts and the resulting sexual gratification. This form of manipulation is especially dangerous because it can work completely undetected be entirely involuntary. Involuntary habits are incredibly difficult for human beings to break. Because of this establishing some sort of involuntary habit within a relationship gives the manipulator a consistent and steady standing that they would not have normally. These involuntary habits will as we know result in voluntary behavior which is even more powerful for the manipulator because they can claim that the actions of the victim have nothing to do with them because they were of their own voluntary decisions. If It's done correctly this form of manipulation is very powerful.

Stalking and Gossip

Stalking and gossip are very interesting and very dangerous forms of manipulation. When a manipulator stalks their victim, their intentions are very different from normal manipulative intentions. This is because oftentimes the stalking of a victim goes on unnoticed by the victim. This is different from normal manipulation techniques because most techniques of manipulation require or even depend on the victim knowing about the actions of the manipulator. This form of manipulation is very different because it Is more a method of researching the victim. This is beneficial to the manipulator because it allows them to know the victim's vulnerabilities and insecurities. It can also allow them access to more personal aspects of their lives such as their most inner family and friend group as well as possible childhood traumas. This form of manipulation of course is very different from obvious stalking. There is of course a type of stalking in which the stalker wants their victims to know that they are being stalked. Obvious stalking such as this is more a method to elicit fear into the victim. A sphere is a tool used by the manipulator you keep their victim on their toes at all times. Taking away the safety net of a victim's privacy makes them more susceptible to a manipulator's actions. Now that we have properly fleshed out stalking as a form of manipulation, we can begin to discuss gossiping as a form of manipulation. While gossip is normally fairly insignificant and not the subject of psychological studies gossip can also be used as a form of manipulation. False gossip more specifically is used as a form of manipulation. By spreading false gossip about an individual manipulator can often make them feel as though they cannot trust anybody around them. This is particularly advantageous to the manipulator because it allows them to swoop in and take advantage of a very vulnerable person at that moment. If a manipulator can convince a victim of gossip, that they are the one in their life that they can trust then they can typically convince that person just about anything in their life.

Seduction

Seduction is a form of manipulation that is very well known throughout history. It is often connected to attractive women seducing sexually frustrated men, but this form of manipulation can go both ways. This form of manipulation can include the use of conversation as well as sexual scripts. They may also use certain methods of nonverbal communication and perilingual features. Historically we can see many examples of amorous seductress or seductresses. From the demon Lilith, too the fictional character Don Juan. Because of the widespread internet and common use of social media seduction manipulation has increased significantly. This is most often seen in the world known as catfishing. In which an online persona seduces a wealthy man or woman into devoting lots of money or resources into this Persona only to find out that this Persona was not who they said they were. This is made much easier to do by the emergence of the internet because you no longer need to meet someone face-to-face to believe that they are real. Outside of the internet seduction is also used widely in advertising and marketing campaigns to push products. Most often seduction is used among manipulators to obtain a sexual partner for a short amount of time.

Commonly Attacked Vulnerabilities

It is important to note when discussing the methods or tactics commonly used by manipulators what vulnerabilities are being targeted by said manipulators. That is what this section of this chapter will be covering. Within this section we will go over common vulnerabilities with regular people that can be taken advantage of by a manipulator. The first one we will discuss is known as the disease to please. This is a huge vulnerability within our society especially among females within our society. It is very widely accepted especially within American societies people are constantly seeking to please others. This is especially clear within younger females within the American population. It is a long-standing patriarchal tradition of our society that women are under the constant pressure to please those around them. This is a subconscious belief that many people don't even realize they have about the women in their life. It can be as simple as asking a lady to smile because it makes them look prettier or expecting a woman in your life to make you dinner. Without realizing it be simple beliefs and actions are consistently re-imprinting the idea that women live to please into American ideology. Whether male or female, this involuntary ideology is incredibly beneficial to manipulators and Incredibly dangerous to victims. This is because the constant need to please that afflicts us and makes us want to do what will make those around us happy. It's because of this that manipulators find it very easy to convince people to do things they don't want to do. Another form of vulnerability that is often exploited by manipulators is human's addiction to the earning of praise and acceptance by society. In other words, humans want to be accepted by those around them if a manipulator is able to convince a victim that not following the manipulators ideals will prevent them from being accepted in their society then the victim will do anything that they can in order to please the manipulator because they believe that that will bring them Acceptance in their society. As previously stated, we are addicted to this idea of being accepted within our society. This is especially beneficial to manipulators because they can hold the power of societal acceptance over their victims. Another common vulnerability that can be exploited by manipulators is known as Emetophobia. This is a very common phobia that often does not get any sort of recognition or attention for its existence.

Emetophobia is the fear of negative emotion or the fear of someone expressing anger, frustration, or disapproval. Some form of this is experienced within most members of societies. It is an inlaid instinctual feeling that is in most humans that greatly benefits us in the sanction of social connections and alliances with other humans. While this inlaid fear is meant to be a positive emotion or feeling to help humans which are natural pack animals to bond with the rest of their pack it can also be quite dangerous to the victim of a manipulator. Upon discovering that a person has an exceptionally high level of Emetophobia a manipulator can very easily use this against them by simply expressing one of the negative emotions every time that the victim does something, but they do not approve of. In some cases, this level of emetophobia is so intense that individuals will be inclined to do illegal or even evil acts in order to prevent their manipulator from showing any signs of disapproval in them. Another vulnerability that can often be exploited by manipulators very easily is one that plagues many women in modern society. This is, of course, a lack of assertiveness and a lack of ability to say no. This is not to say that all women are less assertive than all men but is instead a commentary upon societal pressures of women to not be as assertive as men. It is commonly viewed within our society that an aggressive or assertive woman is usually a negative attribute whereas it would be a positive attribute within a man. Because of this many women despite their natural instincts to be assertive find themselves pushing down that level of assertiveness so that they can more easily be accepted into society. The power of this societal pressure makes it very easy for a manipulator to come into a woman's life and make her push his agenda because if that woman were to say no or act on her assertive instincts she would be demonized by society. As previously stated, humans are pack animals and anything that would set a human apart from a pack is often very difficult for a person to do on their own.

Another vulnerability that can easily be exploited by manipulators is a plague of a blurry sense of identity or having soft personal boundaries. What this means is that an individual suffers because they aren't quite sure who they are yet and haven't figured out what their core beliefs and ideological systems are. Having this lack of identity leaves room for a minute be later to come in and take advantage of this person. This is often an issue that plagues younger people more commonly because younger individuals haven't had the life experience or time to fully understand where they stand in the world. A manipulator that can sense a person with a blurry sense of identity may try to come in and fill that lack of identity with their own ideals or agendas. While the individual may not necessarily agree with every ideal of the manipulator, they may still allow them to push their ideals on to themselves because they don't know what else to fight back with. They also may have some issues if the manipulator happens to be older than them or somehow convinces them that they have more life experience than them. Because of the naive Mind of a younger person this individual may be inclined to allow somebody that they view as older and wiser than them to tell them what they believe. This coupled with soft personal boundaries gives way to a very dangerous playing field for the victim. Having soft personal boundaries means that an individual doesn't quite know when too much is too much. They can't quite tell if somebody is encroaching on their personal boundaries because they don't have a strict Line in the Sand. This is again a common issue with younger individuals because they aren't quite sure at which level of relationship personal boundaries should be set because they haven't experienced enough of relationships yet in their life. All of the vulnerabilities that we have discussed so far have been indicated by the psychologist we discussed before known as a breaker. Now we will move on to some vulnerabilities that are easy to exploit by manipulators that have been indicated by the other psychologists that we discussed known as Simon. The first one we will discuss is known as over conscientiousness. Over conscientiousness is when a victim is everybody that they meet the benefit of the doubt. In other words, they prefer to give a manipulator a second chance rather than see them for who they truly are and drop them for their negative behavior. They also have a tendency to blame themselves because they don't want to admit that the person that they are with is a negative consequence on them. Another similar but very different vulnerability is known as over intellectualization. With over-intellectualization the victim wants to believe that everyone around them has some kind of understandable and intelligent reason for what they do. Because of this they teach themselves that the manipulator must have a reason to be hurtful to them. This results in them blaming them self because they come to the only conclusion that makes logical sense to them which is that they must have done something wrong. Typically, this is not true, but they come to this rationalization because the idea of the person manipulating them simply being a bad person doesn't make enough sense to them because the manipulator may be Charming or kind most of the time.

Individuals most at risk of being manipulated

Within this section I will discuss the types of individuals that are most at risk of being manipulated by a manipulator. The first of these individuals are those that are immature. And immature individual often younger in age is more at risk of being manipulated because they have not yet experienced very much in the world and do not know what signs to look out for when searching for a partner. These individuals often do not know when a red flag is being raised intend to care too much about the people within their friend group to want to risk damaging the social hierarchy by attacking a manipulator. These individuals often have difficulty accepting that there can be dishonest people in the world. These individuals are also incredibly impressionable and easy to be convinced by Charmers. Another individual that is very at risk of being manipulated as someone who is naturally very trusting and forgiving of those around them. Somebody who is very open and honest tends to assume that everyone around them is just as open and honest as they are. Because of this trusting personality they are often more likely to put a lot of the leaf into the arms of a manipulator. They are most likely to do this without checking any credentials and are less likely to question someone who claims himself to be an expert whether or not they actually are. Trusting individuals tend to characterize women, younger people, and the elderly. The elderly tend to be more trusting than the average individual because they're too tired from life to actually go through the steps of making sure that an individual they are hiring for an action is legitimate. This type of individual blends into our next type of person that is vulnerable to exploitation or manipulation which is a careless individual. A careless individual is somebody who does not care enough to put in the effort to make sure that somebody in their life is not manipulative. Within the next section of this chapter we will discuss briefly a political theory that has its basis in manipulation, Machiavellianism. While defined as a political theory, Machiavellianism it's also described in modern psychology at the type of personality trait.

Machiavellianism

Machiavellianism is a phrase that psychologists used to describe an individual that emotionally detaches themselves from societal views of morality. They use this detachment to help reach there and goal and thus deceive and manipulate those around them. A test was developed in the early 1960s to measure a person's level of Machiavellianism. This test is often referred to as the Machiavelli test. This test became a standard tool for self-assessment towards Machiavellianism. Individuals who score very high on the scale tend to agree to commonly used phrases such as "never tell anyone the real reason you did something unless it's useful to do so" While tending to disagree two phrases such as "most people are good and kind." Having a Machiavellianism personality makes it very easy for an individual to manipulate another. Without being weighed down by emotional sensibilities an individual with Machiavellian tendencies we'll be able to think more clearly and push their manipulation farther than an individual with lower Machiavellian tendencies. Many individuals with long histories of manipulating others will have a connection to Machiavellianism train of thought. Within the next section of this chapter we will discuss how Words can influence individuals and how words can contribute to emotional manipulation.

Influence of words

Words are very powerful tools in the hands of a manipulator. Language and communication are very important to the human race and a lot of weight is put on to the words that we say to one another. Keeping this in mind is very clear to see How manipulation through language works so well. There are many different methods to manipulate through language, the first we will focus on is pushing positive words while hiding negative information. This is seen the most often in advertising and in product placement. Take for instance a cup of yogurt that on the front of the label says that it's " 95% fat free" while this is probably true, they're leaving out the fact that this yogurt is also " 5% fat" whoever designed the label or this particular cup of yogurt conveniently chose to leave out the 5% fat that's in their yogurt in order to reach a wider span of audience. Another common method of using language to manipulate an individual is by discussing a topic while suggesting a different topic in a subtle manner. The Listener in this situation may not even realize that they are being guided in a certain direction but will give the desired response anyway. This language strategy has been investigated by Stanford psychologist Paul Thibodeau and Lera Boroditsky. Their tests consisted of giving participants certain crime statistics and explaining it to them in terms that either treated the crime like a beast ('lurking in the neighborhood' 'praying on the town') or as a virus or disease ('infecting' 'plaguing the town'). What you may ask is the point of this? well, when given follow-up questions participants that were exposed to the claims of crime as a beast tended to suggest Solutions that were more violent or action-based.

These were ideas such as capturing the criminals, punishing the wrong doors, or hunting them down. As a contrast, individuals who are presented with the crime statistics as though it were disease tended to make suggestions or reform style solutions. These were ideas such as to diagnose, treat, or give some form of aid to stop these criminal actions. The margin of difference between these two groups of people or much larger than the psychologist or those in the study would have ever expected. This experiment also goes to show how the way that information is presented to us greatly impacts our opinion on said information. This knowledge that is widely known by politician and most commonly used by said politicians to push their own agenda. Reading this and listening to it with a logical mind and standpoint we can understand that these phrases are simply metaphors. But why when taken in context can normal individuals not realize that metaphor should not be taken literally? At no point during this experiment was the crime involved having to do with an actual animal or an actual disease, of course. And we have to assume that the people involved in this experiment understood that. What seems to happen in between the reading of the crime statistics and the asking of the questions is that the one processing the information given through the metaphors activates the primary meaning behind these phrases that involve bestial activities. In other words, without realizing it the individual reading the metaphors instinctively thinks of the crime as an actual animal even though they logically know that it is not. It is with this knowledge and through this way that manipulators are able to use metaphors and underlying meaning to get their point across through language. This is especially beneficial to the manipulator and dangerous to the victim because the victim is not even aware that this is happening. The victim believes that their opinions and their ideals are coming out of their own thinking when in fact it is being planted in there subconsciously by the manipulator without them realizing. The fact that the victim was not aware of this action gives the manipulator lots of space to do their work and lots of open ground to push their agenda farther.

Within this chapter we've gone through some of the more complicated and in-depth techniques of manipulation. We have looked through methods such as projection, denial, intimidation, conditioning, stalking, and even more. Through all of these methods we have found that the easiest way for a manipulator to manipulate their victims uses language. In the final section of this chapter we discussed how language could be used to subconsciously push an idea in the victim without the victim even realizing it. In the next chapter we will begin to discuss the power of persuasion and how the origins of persuasion are deeply rooted in society's history.

Chapter Four: The Power of Persuasion

Persuasion has a long and deep history within our society. Persuasion has been long studied and has many connecting theories into its function and the best ways to persuade others. In the history of persuasion, it begins with the Greeks. The Greeks believed very strongly in rhetoric and elocution as the highest belief system for a successful individual. Most well-known for his theories of persuasion, Aristotle listed the main reasons why one should concern themselves with the art of persuasion. The first is that the truth and justice are believed to be perfect, so that if a case is lost it is the fault of the speaker. The second reason is that it is an excellent tool for teaching others. The third is that a good persuasive speaker needs to understand how to argue both sides of a case and understand all parts of the problem. The fourth and final reason that Aristotle list for why you won't learn the art of persuasion is that there is no better way to defend oneself than through the art of persuasion. Aristotle is most famous, and most widely taught in our schools today for his three rhetorical proofs. These are of course the well-known ethos, logos, and pathos. Ethos is defined as the credibility of the person speaking and is something you must convince your audience of in order to gain their trust. Logos is defined as reason and is often described as showing proof of your argument. Pathos is often described as the appeal to an audience's emotions. This is arguably the most powerful rhetorical proof because it plays emotions of the audience listening. In addition to these rhetorical proofs indicated by the Greek philosopher Aristotle there are many more psychological theories for the art of persuasion.

Attribution theory

There are three subsections to the attribution theory of persuasion. The first one is known as dispositional attribution or internal attribution. This form of attribution in which an individual tries to point to a person's core traits or beliefs as a cause or explanation for their previous actions. An example of this would be a citizen criticizing a president's decisions because the president is lazy or lack some form of economic prowess. The second subsection of attribution theory is known as situational attribution, or external attribution. This form of attribution tends to point at the person's environment or surroundings or things that are typically out of the individual's control as an explanation for that person's action. Enter the previous example of a citizen criticizing a president this would be when a person explains the president's decisions away by saying that they inherited a bad economy from the previous president rather than their actions actually causing it. The final form of attribution theory is known as the fundamental attribution error. This occurs when individuals incorrectly attribute either a failure or an accomplishment to the Internal and core beliefs or attributes of that person. This is different from the dispositional attribution theory because play occurs between people who do not know each other very well. The person doing the criticizing does not properly understand the true attributes or beliefs of the other individual.

Conditioning Theory

similar to manipulation conditioning has a huge play in the concept of persuasion. Conditioning is very effective in the world of persuasion because when your conditioning someone you're simply guiding them into making voluntary actions rather than directly commanding them to follow your ideals. This is seen most often in advertisements or commercials by trying to connect a positive or memorable emotion to a product or logo. We see this every day in commercials that attempt to make us laugh, use a sexual undertone, or use uplifting images or music. Professional spokespeople such as athletes or celebrities are also used as a method for conditioning. By connecting someone that you may love or respect greatly to a product their subconscious Lee making you feel good about that product when you see it in store whether you realize it or not. This is most particularly effective with advertising and consumerism because most purchases are made from an emotional background or value. By eliciting and emotion from the consumer a product is more readily purchased by that consumer.

Cognitive dissonance theory

This theory is very interesting and different from previous theories discussed under persuasion. This theory was proposed by psychologist Leon Festinger in 1957. Our original theory states that human beings are constantly searching and striving for mental consistency. He believes that our thoughts beliefs or ideas can be in agreement with themselves, unrelated to themselves, or in disagreement with each other.

Our mental beliefs, or our cognition, can also be in agreement or disagreement with our actions or behaviors. When we internally can detect some conflicting ideas or dissonance instinctually it can give us a feeling of incompleteness or discomfort. An example of this is a person who understands that smoking cigarettes is detrimental to their health and does not want to die at a young age but who has been addicted to smoking cigarettes for a very long time would probably suffer from cognitive dissonance. Within this theory it is suggested that we are consistently striving to reduce this dissonance until our cognition is in balance and harmony in all ways. Festinger Suggest four main ways that we as humans can reduce our cognitive dissonance. The first of the four ways is by changing our minds about one of the things that we have dissonance with. The second is reducing the importance of being in Harmony in our minds. The third is to increase the overlap between the two and forth is to re-evaluate the cost-reward ratio. Using the example of the smoker we previously discussed when looking through these options this man can either quit smoking, lower the importance of his own health, convince himself that smoking is in actuality no real risk for his health, or convince himself that the reward of smoking is worth the cost of his health. Cognitive dissonance is very useful in Persuasion because when somebody is feeling unsteady or uncertain about their own core beliefs or ideals it is easy to steer them towards different beliefs or ideas.

Within this chapter we have discussed the history of persuasion as well as many theories and ideas of the art of persuasion. Within the next chapter we will be discussing the definition of NLP Some background and how you can use it.

Chapter Five: NLP, a Background and How You Can Use It

NLP stands for neuro-linguistic programming and it is an approach to communication, personal development, and Psychotherapy that was designed and indicated by Richard Bandler and John Grinder in the early 1970s. These two individuals believe that there is a connection between the neurological processes of language and the behavioral patterns that are learned through experience in a person's life. They also believed that these learned patterns could be changed in order to achieve specific goals. They believe that the NLP methodology can mimic the skills of exceptional people allowing anyone who uses this method to acquire those skills. They used an LP in their own practice and claim that in single sessions NLP proved to be able to treat psychological issues such as phobias, depression, and psychosomatic illnesses. While NLP is marketed and used by some hypnotherapists there is no real concrete scientific evidence that supports the claims of NLP advocates. Because this method is often disregarded as a pseudoscience. Neuro-linguistic programming can be broken down into three main components or core Concepts. I will explain these core concepts in depth here:

Subjectivity

Bandler and grinder Express that we experience the world subjectively. In other words, we tend to create subjective views of our experiences meaning that two people can experience the same situation in the same way and describe it later with completely different feelings. This subjectivity is based on the way that we experience the world around us. This is felt most commonly through sensations of our five senses and language. The combination of these two results in an internal and mental language that we experience the world through. Think of a moment in which you are mentally rehearsing what you're going to say to somebody. Let's say you're going to order a meal at a restaurant, sitting at the table looking at the menu you think in your head how you say what you want to the waiter, you may predict what their questions will be, and you may think about how you will phrase your answer. Subconsciously without even realizing it in this mental planning you will also be thinking about the smell that's in the air the feeling of the back of the chair you're sitting in and the extra sounds that are going on around you. It is all of this extra atmosphere that make up your mental language. This mental language is believed to have a certain discernible structure and pattern. NLP is often working to study the structure of this mental language. The Hope by using NLP is that you may be able to modify negative behaviors by manipulating bees sense based mental languages.

Consciousness

Neuro-linguistic programming is dependent upon the idea that our consciousness is broken up into a conscious and unconscious component. The idea of language that our mental state uses daily works almost exclusively through the unconscious part of our brain.

Learning

What sets neuro-linguistic programming apart from other forms of psychosomatic therapy is its imitating method. Professionally termed modeling is claimed to be able to reproduce a desired trait in any domain of activity. An important part of this form of learning is that it uses the idea of monkey see monkey do. In other words, a desired trait is shown positively to an individual and they are able to learn by simply viewing that positive trait be carried out.

Ways that neuro-linguistic programming can be used:

Alternative medicine

Within alternative medicine neuro-linguistic programming has been promoted very widely and commonly amongst common users. It has been said to be able to treat a variety of physical ailments. These can range from Parkinson's disease, HIV AIDS, and even cancer. These claims have no real supporting medical evidence.

Psychotherapeutic

Neuro-linguistic programming most commonly focuses on psychotherapeutic ideals. This is mostly due to the fact that the early models and idealist were psychotherapists. In the use of psychotherapy, neuro-linguistic programming shares similar core beliefs and foundations with many contemporary and scientifically backed practices. Some contemporary practices that have similar beliefs to neuro-linguistic programming is solution-focused brief therapy. It is also been acknowledged that NLP influence these modern practices and even that these practices may have come out of a form of NLP. These modern practices are slightly different from neuro-linguistic programming in that they seek to achieve desired behavior by Shifting the context or meaning of that thought or behavior.

How neuro-linguistic programming can be used to shift the ideas of those around you

if one is searching to change the ideas of those in their lives they can do so rather easily with the use of neuro-linguistic programming. To begin they have to learn and understand the mental and internal language of the subconscious mind. Once they have understood this mental subconscious language, they can begin to shift ideals by modeling positive behavior and allowing those internal language pathways to pick up on this positive behavior and begin implementing it.

Within this chapter we gave an in-depth and well fleshed-out explanation of neuro-linguistic programming. We gave some of the historical context as well as some common uses for neuro-linguistic programming. In the end we also explained how neuro-linguistic programming can be used to change the ideals and beliefs of those around you. Within the next chapter we will be using the learned skills within this text to gain friends around us. You will go through nearly every skill that we have Todd and gone over and explain how they can be used to make longer-lasting friendships.

Chapter Six: Using Our Learned Skills to Make Long-Lasting Friendships

Within this chapter we will be going back to the very beginning of this text and go through every skill that we have learned and give an explanation on how they can be used to make friends.

Acting Superior

This method needs to be used with caution when attempting to win friends in any sort of group setting. When used with subtlety this method can make people subconsciously respect you and your decision and feel as though they live to serve you. In order to do this properly it cannot be obvious or able to be pinpointed by the average person. You cannot act superiors to those
around you, you have to be superior to those around you.

Victimization

victimization, or playing the victim is probably the easiest most effective manipulative friends. If you can manage to constantly talk about how victimized, you are in life and can convince people that you are you can get a vast amount of sympathy from those around you. This world is full of people that have an internal and undying need to help others. By playing as the victim you can play on this internal desire or need and use it to your advantage to become friends with somebody wanting to help you.

Lying

it's pretty easy to see how lying can be used to gain friends. You can lie about just about anything to try and gain friends. You can lie about how wealthy you are, you can lie about your age, you can lie about your name. If these lies are convincing and easy to support, then people often believe them without too much question.

Control

If you can use our previous methods to be in control of someone then you can very easily befriend them. People are attracted to those that they view as being in control of them. Is a fact of life and it is commonly seen in the martyring of political figures? you can use any of our previously discussed methods to make someone believe that you are in control of them.

Conditioning

Conditioning is a very useful tool in the world of trying to make friends. All it really takes is some positive and negative reinforcement two positive or negative behavior. The best way to do this undercover is to make it a simple part of your day. Do something small for the person that you want to be your friend on a daily basis, and they will find themselves feeling happy when they see you and not quite understanding why. Let's say you really want to befriend Jim. Let's say that Jim always forgets to bring in coffee for work and end up having to go buy some.

A good way that you can get Jim to start liking you without realizing it is by bringing him some coffee every morning and explaining it away with some kind of believable excuse. For instance, you could say that you were getting coffee for other people anyway or that you have to pass by his desk going to the coffee machine. If you do this continuously as often as you can, and Jim will find himself feeling happy when he sees you without any real reason to feel happy. Unless Jim is a master's in psychology, he will probably simply explain away this feeling with the thought that he simply likes you as a friend. And just like that you will reach friendship status with this man named Jim who you want to be friends with for a long time.
within this chapter we have learned how to use our skills to better and more easily win friendships in everyday life and in the workplace. In the next chapter we will begin to go over how you can spot an avoid manipulation in a relationship. This can apply to both romantic and platonic relationships. This is very important to keep in mind when you're looking to manipulate other people because it can be quite dangerous to have a manipulator being manipulated by those around them.

Chapter Seven: Avoiding Manipulation in a Relationship

With all of this discussion About ways to manipulate people it is important to keep in mind that you also should be Adept at avoiding manipulation in your own relationships. That is why within this chapter we will be discussing how you can spot manipulation in relationships with you or those around you. We will also discuss how to avoid a manipulative relationship with you or those around you. If you find yourself in a manipulative relationship, I will also give some tips and tricks on how to escape from a manipulative relationship.

We are going to begin by discussing how you can spot a manipulative relationship from miles away. This can apply to romantic relationships that you are in or the others are in and also can apply to platonic relationships that you are in or others around you are in. It's important to be able to pinpoint a spot a manipulative relationship so that you can avoid being in one yourself. Knowing the obvious signs of a manipulative relationship can also prevent you from showing those signs if you're choosing to manipulate somebody.

The first sign that we are going to discuss you should look out for when searching for a manipulative relationship is consistent accusations. If you find that in a relationship accusation are happening frequently and are often being accused by the same person, it may be a warning sign that you or somebody you know is in a manipulative relationship. The reason that a manipulator May accuse their victim Austin and consistently is in order to provoke a discussion between the two of them. Typically, this discussion turns into an argument. Manipulators have greater control and heightened emotional situations such as arguments because in these situations their victims are being blinded by their emotions are able to see through the manipulator's manipulations. Manipulators are also brilliantly persuasive people, and such are very easily able to convince their victim they're in the wrong in any situation. Because of this provoking an argument with their victim serves very heavily in their favor. So, if you often find that you're being accused of Random wrongdoings end up losing the resulting argument you may find yourself in a manipulative relationship. Please remember that this can also work from the outside. If you are viewing a relationship between a pair of your friends and you notice that one of them is very accusatory towards the other keep track of the number of arguments that they may have between one another. If it seems to be a lot of arguments in a short period of time and the same person is winning all of them then your friend may be in a situation in which they are being manipulated for some reason or another.

The second sign that we are going to discuss and that you should look out for when checking for a manipulative relationship is the playing of emotional games. People who manipulate emotionally often are trying to make their victims feel doubtful and insecure in themselves. This is because when a victim feels insecure about themselves and they are less likely to call out any actions of the manipulator. For Obvious reasons this is very beneficial for the manipulator. By keeping their victim on unsteady ground emotionally they're able to more easily keep control of their victim. This may pop up in a romantic relationship by planting evidence of infidelity that later turned out to be inaccurate. By planting evidence of infidelity in a romantic relationship even if you later make their victim feel incredibly angry or sad and may result in an argument or attack by the victim. At the end of this argument or attack the manipulator will find some sort of "proof" that their infidelity did not happen. If they manage to convince their victim of their innocence then this will result in a feeling of incredible emotional vulnerability and insecurities within the victim. Because of this the victim will not feel as though they can trust their own instincts, I will not be able to fight back against the manipulator. This can also pop up in platonic relationships with the use of backhanded compliments. By giving a compliment to somebody that seems like a compliment at face value but in reality, is an insult the person being given the backhanded compliment becomes uncomfortable because they aren't quite sure how to respond. They can't get angry at the person complimenting them because to the surrounding people it appears to be a complement however they also do not want to Simply accept the compliment because it isn't a compliment but an insult. The resulting confusion and unsteadiness within the victim give manipulate a room to sweep in and further control their victim. When checking for a manipulative relationship you want to see if there is a history or consistency of backhanded compliments amongst the two people. You may also want to check and see if there is seemingly too obvious evidence towards some type of negative action of one of the individuals. If either or both of these signs are apparent in a relationship, then you may be looking at or in your own manipulative relationship.

The third sign of manipulation that you need to look for in a relationship that we are going to discuss is the act of breaking or damaging things that are important to the victim. This is a very obvious and physical form of manipulation but pops up quite often amongst both platonic and romantic relationships. This type of manipulation can oftentimes be explained away by blaming the victim and saying that they were in an argument or that the victim made them very angry. These are not excusing. Manipulators are often very in tune with what is important to the victims of their manipulations. They typically know what some of the most important and prized possessions of their victims is. They use this to their advantage because if In the Heat of the Moment they get too angry then they may be able to destroy one of those very important items of the victim. They will do this for a variety of reasons.

The first reason is they may wish to leave you in a sad or depressed state wish they could achieve by destroying something very close to you. If this item has any kind of emotional or nostalgic value than it may serve a second purpose of making you feel as though you and your emotions are not safe. This is a very powerful feeling an emotion work very dangerously in the hands of the manipulator. A manipulator makes a victim feel as though they need a person to protect them from the world. This is a dangerous feeling because it leaves room for the manipulator to come in and convince them they are the ones to protect them from the world. In their emotional state a victim will not realize the irony behind this as the person trying to protect them also destroy the things they love. In checking for a manipulative relationship, you will always want to watch out for this type of behavior. In either a platonic or romantic relationship somebody destroying something that is important to another person is very manipulative and cannot be ignored.

The fourth type of warning sign that we will discuss but you need to keep an eye out for when looking for a manipulative relationship is the encouraging of jealousy within a relationship. This type of manipulation is most common in romantic relationships but can also pop up in the tonic relationships under the correct circumstances. Jealousy is a hugely damaging emotion for a person because it tends to encourage a lack of trust in a relationship which is very beneficial to a manipulator. Manipulators are very conscious of this and know that they need their victims to trust them, but they also know that they themselves cannot trust their victims. Manipulators feel as though their victims could turn on them at any moment and because of this incite a huge amount of jealousy within themselves.

Most people understand the concept that when a person is jealous of somebody else and incite a feeling of uneasiness and sadness within themselves. This may lead a manipulator to try and insight jealousy within their victim. You may do this by flirting very obviously with others in front of their romantic partner or may even try to compare their victims to strangers. Doing this puts their victim the sense of unease and makes them feel as though they are not good enough. Because of this feeling of not being good enough it will feel as though they need to constantly be gratified and assured by the person that is manipulating them. This is very powerful for the manipulator and very dangerous for the Victim Because by giving the manipulator the power to decide whether or not the victim feels gratified and safe with the manipulator who can then choose how the victim feels at any given point. If you are checking for manipulation in a relationship and it is important to check for this clear warning sign. If you're looking from the outside-in and you happen to be in public with a couple and one of them is very clearly flirting with people around you seeming to make the victim uncomfortable and you may be witnessing a manipulative relationship. If you are inside your own relationship and you notice that your partner is consistently putting you down and comparing you to those around you then you may be in your own manipulative relationship. It's important to keep an eye out for these obvious warning signs when checking for a Manipulative relationship.

The fifth warning sign that you may be in a manipulative relationship is that manipulative individuals will often act as though they are the victim of manipulation. This may seem confusing and it can be somewhat difficult to understand if you are in the situation yourself. In order to fully understand and be able to pinpoint this warning sign you have to be able to logically take a step back and look at the relationship from the outside in. This may seem difficult to do but it is possible if you look at it from a logical standpoint. A person manipulating you in a manipulative relationship will often act as though they are the victims of a manipulative relationship. They may outright accuse you of being manipulative and will twist your words to make you feel guilty about something you did even if that thing you did wasn't actually wrong. They will try to convince you to apologize even when you don't feel you've done anything wrong. If you fall into this trap, then you will become more and more prone to their manipulation and find it harder and harder to see their manipulation from an outside stance.

The six-warning sign that you may be in a minute later relationship is an individual may try to make you feel guilty for a mistake that they made out of their own accord. Emotional manipulators are very good at finding ways to place blame on to those around them. Let's say for instance that your significant other forgets something at home. This might be something very important to them or it might be something very small. Either way they may try to convince you that they forgot to bring whatever it was because you do not remember to remind them. If that person happens to be late for an event it's because you didn't tell him the correct time even if you do remember telling them the proper time they should have shown up. Every time this person makes a mistake or are out of their own accord, they will find a way to make it your mistake before you've even realized what is happening. The easiest way to pinpoint this is to look at things that have gone wrong in your relationship and try to see if your significant other has ever taken the blame for anything that has happened. If the answer is no then they may be manipulating, you. This is very important to remember when checking for manipulation in a relationship. This is not only possible in a romantic relationship that also possible in business relationships as well. Within a business standpoint you may be able to see this form of manipulation most common amongst people of high standing and their assistance. A manipulator with an assistant is often very easy to go unnoticed by those around them because people may view it as simply the person doing their job. This is not always the case. If a person finds every reason to get angry at their assistant for doing things that really shouldn't even be in their job description, then you may be looking at a manipulative relationship.

The 7th warning sign that you or somebody you know maybe in a manipulative relationship is that the person doing the manipulating may rush the victim to make decisions. The act of doing this makes it more difficult for the person being manipulated to make rational and informed decisions in an instant. If somebody is rushing or pushing a person to make a decision very, very quickly then they are putting that person under a certain level of stress that makes them feel helpless and doesn't allow them to make a good decision. Because of this a victim may make decisions that they will later regret or that will have some underlying consequences. If this person is in a manipulative relationship, then the manipulator will refuse to admit that they are the reason that the person made these negative decisions. And while the manipulator is not directly the reason that the person made these decisions, they are the reason why the person wasn't able to think through their decisions before making them entirely. The manipulator will try to claim that the person made the decision on their own and should just try to live with their decision even if they are not happy with it later. This is not to be confused with somebody refusing to accept responsibility for their own actions. A manipulator may use this as a tactic because when a victim is given less time to think through their choices, they're more likely to go with the decisions of another person. This puts the manipulator into a place of control because they can more easily decide what the victim wants to do next. The victim may have a hard time even noticing that this is happening.

If you are on the inside of this relationship and you notice that your significant other never gives you more than a few seconds to make a decision before calling you an indecisive person you may be in a manipulative relationship. On the flip side if you are on the outside of a relationship and you notice that an individual is rushing their significant other to make a decision then you may be looking at a manipulative relationship. We have mostly discussed this happening in romantic circumstances it is also very common in business settings. It is less of a negative action in a business setting and more of a strategy to gain the upper hand. Within the business discussions and negotiations having a time constraint can often lead to a person making a decision in favor of a product that they normally would not have chosen. A skillful negotiator and manipulator will be able to use this fact well and Rush the person making the decision without them realizing or feeling as though they're being rushed. They might do very subtle things like ask them what time it is or look at a clock and know how late it has gotten. They may even remind the person making the decision of something that they previously said that they need to do before they leave for that day.

The 8th warning sign that you should look for when checking for a manipulative relationship is when the actions of a person do not match their words. As we have discussed deeply within this text emotional manipulators tend to use language to control people through a variety of methods. Because they were using this language does not always mean that they are going to act on whatever this language is promising to the other person. They may use flattering language and make certain promises in order to make you trust them or feel comfortable with them. The idea of keeping these promises for meaning these flatteries is only an afterthought to a manipulator. Because of this these individuals very rarely will actually act out on these phrases that they make. If you were to call them out one of their promises, they would blame you for it in some way. This is one of the few ways that manipulators and to be behind other people and their manipulations. In other words, while manipulators tend to be very logical and intelligent this is one of the few ways that they tend to come up short. By not following through with their word they often can label themselves as liars without meaning to. If you are on the outside looking at a relationship and you notice that one person is consistently making outrageous Promises to the other person then you may be looking at a manipulative relationship. On the flip side if you are within a relationship that a person makes lots of promises to you in the beginning of your relationship and have not yet gone through with any of those promises, depending on the amount of time that has passed and the nature of his promises you may be in a manipulative relationship.

the 9th warning sign that you may be in a manipulative relationship is the feeling that manipulators make you feel as though you're always negotiating. This goes along with the way that manipulators use language to control their victims. Manipulators will twist your words and constantly make you feel as though you are attacking or attempting to negotiate everyday things with the manipulate. Manipulators will twist your words and constantly make you feel as though you are attacking or attempting to negotiate everyday things with the manipulator. By constantly feeling as though you are in the act of negotiation you're constantly being kept on your toes and made to feel unsafe and unsteady in your own relationship. An added bonus of this for the manipulator is that once you reach the end of your negotiation even if it is about something completely nonsensical, you'll feel as though you've reached a middle ground with your manipulator. In reality you will most likely have given the manipulator what they wanted in the first place. Because of a manipulator's prowess with the language they will be able to convince you that you have gotten something out of the negotiation when in reality it wasn't a negotiation to begin with it was just manipulation. This is very beneficial to the manipulator because by convincing the victim that they are getting something out of a negotiation they are keeping the victim happy. Or at least make them believe that they are happy. And a victim that believes that they are happy is one that will not try to fight back against their manipulator. If you are on the outside of relationship looking in, you may be able to spot this Telltale sign by an individual turning every single decision into a negotiation and not simply agreeing to do one or the other thing at any point. If you spot this you may be looking at a manipulative relationship. If you are inside a relationship and you begin to notice that your significant other refuses to ever simply agree with you and has to argue with you over every single decision that you make you may be in a manipulative relationship yourself.

the 10th warning sign that you may be in a manipulative relationship is that manipulative people tend to lie on a constant basis. Over years of manipulating those around them this has probably become part of the daily routine of an emotional manipulator. These are not always big crazy lies about exceptional situations. Sometimes they can be about tiny little insignificant details. These small details may not always have anything to do with the end goal of a manipulator, but in fact may simply be a form of practice for the manipulator. Lying is a very baseline tactic for a manipulator, and so it is important for a manipulator to practice this skill constantly in order to stay good at it. By lying to their victims, a manipulator can basically make a victim believe whatever they want as long as they are good at lying. If a manipulator gives way that they are lying it can still benefit them because the victim can feel as though they are unsafe and unsteady within their relationship and not really know how to trust anyone. Having a lack of trust within a victim is good for a manipulator because in order for a victim to get out of a manipulative relationship they need the support of those around them. And if a victim is having trouble trusting those around them then they will not be able to accept that support. If you are outside of a relationship and you begin to notice that an individual is making outrageous claims that do not consistently line up with previous claims made by the same person and you may be looking at a manipulative relationship.

Now that we have discussed some common signs that you may be in or looking at a manipulative relationship, we will discuss some ways to avoid a manipulative relationship. A good way to avoid finding yourself in a manipulative relationship Is to keep a steady eye and watch out for these types of interactions that we have previously discussed. If you find that a person is exhibiting some of these characteristics it would be in your best interest to stay away from them. Find excuses to not have to be near them. If for some reason you're incapable of staying away from a manipulative person you simply have to avoid becoming a part of their manipulations by not falling into their traps. With all of the methods we have discussed it should be fairly easy for you to spot and avoid these circumstances.

Practice

Everybody knows that. The learning of a new skill practices it in order to better. Exactly what we're going to do here. Within this section of this text I will give the reader A series of examples and the reader will try to decide whether or not the individuals in the example Are participants of a manipulative relationship. I will follow up each of these examples with whether or not the relationship truly was manipulative and the reasoning why.

Scenario A)
John is known around the office as being the jokester. Not everybody in the office understands or even enjoys his jokes. People Oftentimes find themselves feeling attacked or insulted by John's jokes. Nobody dares to bring this up to John of course because everybody else believes that everyone around them is having a good time. One day George decides he has had enough. After a particularly scathing comment from John around the water cooler, George speaks up to give John some of his mind.
"You're being very insensitive and just downright mean. I really wish you wouldn't make such insensitive and damaging jokes John. You're a nice guy most of the time but your jokes just go too far." Everybody in the group is taken aback for a moment. After a second people in the group seem to begin to agree with George, they start nodding their heads and one of them seems as though they are about to say something. Before anyone can speak up however John response back in a minimizing tone.
"Geez George I was only joking I didn't know you were so sensitive. Can you take a joke?" Everybody in the group immediately shuts their mouths and feels uncomfortable for calling out John's joke. Everyone in the surrounding group begins to feel like they don't have a sense of humor and just overall start to feel negative about themselves. As a result, John begins to take the stage once more continuing on with his jokes.

is this manipulation?
If you answered yes you would be correct. This example is a form of minimization on the part of John. John is clearly making inappropriate or damaging remarks towards the other people in his office. When called out on his behavior John chooses instead of taking responsibility for his actions to minimize what he is done by calling it a joke and making everyone around him feel uncomfortable and as though they have done something wrong. There are other examples of this that have nothing to do with jokes of course. Similar examples are if somebody tries to vent and

explain that they are feeling stressed on a certain day a manipulator might respond with "you don't know what stress is!" in this situation the manipulator minimizes a person feeling by claiming that they are invalid and that they don't know what they're talking about.

Scenario B)
John and Erica have been dating for some time. John finds that soon after beginning his relationship with air he has a lot of trouble locating items that he normally would have no trouble locating. These are items such as keys, pens, or even his wallet. He's also begun to notice that when it comes to information, he seems to be wrong about everything. Every time he tries to remember a situation that Erica was involved in, he remembers it incorrectly. Thankfully for him Erica is always there to tell him what properly happened. John is also eternally thankful that he always has Erica there to show him where his keys are. I always make jokes about how awful his memory is and how is his head wasn't screwed on to him he would lose it as well. It's funny because when John thinks about it, he never had any of these issues before he started dating Erica. But then again how can John trust what he remembers when he has so much trouble remembering where his keys are and basic information like what he did at the last party. Recently it's begun to get so bad that John doesn't even like to bring up fun stories that he remembers because he knows he'll most likely get them wrong. Thankfully for him Erica is always there to tell the story, people usually like it better from her anyway. One day John began to wonder if maybe Erica was being a negative influence on him. But then he began to wonder if he was being too sensitive. Other people don't seem to have these issues with their relationships oh, it must be me He had decided. He always finds himself apologizing to Erica. He's not even quite sure what he's done wrong most of the time. But with how awful his memory is he doesn't even take a moment to second-guess whether or not he's done something wrong, he simply assumes he has and doesn't remember it. One time one of John's friends noticed that Erica had his keys in her pocket. When he brought this up to John, he laughed and waved his friend away saying that Erica was most likely just saving them for him because she knew that he would lose them otherwise. John has also begun to notice that he tends to withhold information from his family because he's tired of their concerned questions. Making excuses or trying to explain Erica's actions towards him is just too exhausting. After a few weeks of all of this happening john Begins to realize that there might be something wrong with their relationship. John doesn't want to face up to the idea that their relationship might be toxic and as a result he decides to ignore this feeling and just move on. Besides John decides if there is a problem with a relationship if probably has something to do with him, he's probably not good enough for Erica anyway.

Is this emotional manipulation?

Yes absolutely. This is a type of emotional manipulation known as gaslighting. In Gaslighting a manipulator will try to find ways to make victims doubt their own thoughts memories or actions. At some point the victim becomes too frightened to bring up a topic or story for fear they'll be wrong about it or not remember it correctly. And in extreme cases gas lighters will even create situations that will lead to the victim doubting themselves. In this example we can see that Erica has been hiding John's Keys wallets and other important objects so that he begins to feel as though he cannot trust himself to locate his own things. She also goes out of her way to make him feel as though he can't remember stories properly.

Erica has put it into John's mind that he needs her to remember these things for him. Don't even goes on to point out that there may be something wrong with their relationship but doesn't want to face the fact that Erica might be manipulating him. It's more comfortable and he would rather just believe that he's the problem and that Erica really is good for him. This will damage him in the long run, but it would be more emotionally taxing for him to have to deal with it now which is probably why he is not breaking up with Erica. Scenario C) Ben is a director of sales at a local paper company. He has an assistant named Karen. Ben and Karen and have a very good relationship for a boss and his assistant. They're not perfect of course, Karen has on occasion given him the wrong information and ben isn't always the most understanding of bosses. Ben always apologizes if he snaps at Karen and Karen always corrects it if she gives him the wrong information.

Is this emotional manipulation?

No. This is not a sign of being in a manipulative relationship. It is within an assistant's job to do what their boss tells them to do, it is within the boss's job to receive that information understandably kindly. The relationship isn't perfect, but it is not intentionally manipulative.

Chapter Eight: Manipulation in the Workplace

Within this chapter we will be discussing common signs of manipulation within the workplace.

Sarcasm and offensive jokes

The use of thinly veiled sarcasm is often a form of manipulation that goes unnoticed in the workplace. Sarcasm in the workplace Works to make an individual feel very uncomfortable and uncentered because it makes it hard to tell if an individual is being serious or not. In an area such as workplace where it is exposed it can be hard to tell if someone is being legitimate when they're using sarcasm. In addition to this people will often use defensive or scarring jokes to subconsciously harm the person they're trying to manipulate Within the workplace. An offense of joke at another person's expense can make them feel uncomfortable, and unsafe in their own work environment. By doing this a manipulator is able to take away the public work environment may bring to a victim.

Devaluing the achievement of others

Another method of a manipulator in the world is the act of devaluing the achievement of those around them. By making individuals around them feel as though their achievements are not impressive or important in any way, do they make the victims in the workplace your words about themselves as well as making the manipulators seem better than them by insinuating that their achievements are not as impressive as the manipulators. By doing this they develop a sort of respect from other people and make themselves appear to be more important than they truly are. In addition to this, the insecurities and self-consciousness that devaluing the achievement of the victim can bring opens up room for the manipulator to then come in and push their agenda on to the person.

Putting down the opinions of others

Another method of a manipulator within the workplace is the putting down or an appreciation of the opinion of those around them. By making an individual feel that their opinion doesn't matter or has no real meaning in the world makes an individual feel undervalued and unappreciated. This is helpful to the manipulator because it may lead to the victim coming to them hoping for some level of value or appreciation. This will leave the victim in a vulnerable state in which all they want is to feel valued or appreciated and they won't care about who it comes from. This leaves room for the manipulator to come in and push their agenda on to the victim.

Not appreciating the work of others

refusing to appreciate the work of those around you is another common method of a manipulator in the workforce. If an individual refuses to appreciate the work that people put in to make their everyday lives easier than they can put the people around them down, but it can also make it easier for them to do their work. This makes their act of manipulating others easier and less difficult.

Chapter Nine: Manipulation and Defending yourself Against It

Within this chapter we are going to go through how you can defend yourself against each of the manipulation tactics that we have discussed. Most of our methods of Defending ourselves against manipulation have to do with using positive self-esteem. Positive self-esteem is often used to overcome manipulation emotionally. Within this chapter we will also cover several skills you can use to improve your self-esteem to help protect yourself against manipulators.

Raising the Voice

previously in this text we discussed how the act of raising one's voice can bring about panic in a victim and as such give a manipulator more power in a situation. If you find yourself in a situation in which you believe you are being manipulated by a person raising their voice against you one of the best things that you can do in order to fight back against this form of manipulation maintain a sense of calm. If you can stay calm you can very easily rationalize with the person trying to manipulate you. You can do this by taking a deep breath and pausing for a moment before giving a response to the person raising their voice at you. If you can give a calm and rational response to a person raising their voice at you, you take away the power that comes with shouting at another person. By showing the manipulator that you are not frightened or panicked by their loud actions they themselves will become panicked. Please be warned and remember that in this moment of panic you cannot be sure of what the manipulator is going to do. They make shout more and may become physically aggressive or they may simply concede and leave. Either way the best way to stand your ground and not succumb to the manipulation is to stay calm and collected and only give back to the person shouting at you rational and logical responses. You want to be careful with these responses because you want to make sure that you're not giving them any kind of ammo that they can use at you later. What I mean by this is you don't want to say anything accusatory or make it sound like you're insulting them in any way you want to simply state facts and make sure that they understand that you're only stating what is actually happening.

Acting Superior

the best way to respond to somebody that tends to act Superior to you is, if you can do it, simply to stay away from them. The problem with this form of manipulation is that over time it becomes an instinctual have it with a manipulator may not know how to break by themselves. Because of this as the victim it is within your best self-interest to Simply separate yourself from that person and to not try and be a part of their life anymore. If that is simply not an option for you then the second-best method to try and get past somebody acting Superior to you is completely ignore their superiority complex. By not giving them the satisfaction of feeling second to them you are robbing them of the entire reason they act this way in the first place. This will probably make the manipulator very frustrated and angry with you. In fact, there's a very good chance that if you do this consistently for a long. Of time that the manipulator will choose to not even concern themselves with you and will move on to a different victim entirely. The trick to this is not to take their attempts at acting Superior seriously. Treated as though a small child is trying to tell you how to do something that you know how to do. Ignore them belittle them basically throw the manipulation back into their face.

Victimization

the best way to handle a manipulator acting like they are being victimized in their everyday life is not to give in to their want of sympathy. You can tell them "I'm sorry that must be really hard I can't really help you" and that is fine. You cannot allow them to pull you into this idea that you need to fix them. That is when you fall into their manipulative trap. To avoid this, you have to let them know that you are not somebody that is going to fix them. Do not offer them suggestions Because they will not want or take them. Do not try to make them feel better because it will not work. Simply accept that they feel that way and let them know that there is nothing you can do. This may be hard for some people to do because the feeling of empathy is very strongly encouraging within us from the time that we were small children. But if you really focus and put your mind to it, it is quite easy to logically understand why you cannot help every single person who tries to make you feel like they need your sympathy.

Lying

the best way to deal with a manipulator that is constantly lying on a daily basis is quite simple but quite difficult to do. The best way to deal with this type of person is simply to cut them out of your life completely. While I understand completely that this is not always possible and not super realistic for everyday life it truly is the only way to completely and entirely stop somebody from lying to you. If someone can't speak to you in the first place, then they cannot lie to you that is just a fact. Obviously since this isn't something that we can just go out and do every single day here's a couple of methods for dealing with liars that you simply cannot get rid of.

The first thing to remember is that you need to always take what they say with a grain of salt. Always second-guess the things that they tell you and don't take what they said you at face value. This can be very exhausting. Second guessing everything that someone tells you can quickly get old, but you have to be Vigilant if you would like to be aware of this person's manipulations. You may have to fact-check things they say to you either literally through the internet or locally with some friends. Another method is to always have somebody around you when this person is speaking to you. It may be easier to pick up on this person's Lies when the other person is not directly connected to them. So, if you have a friend who maybe doesn't like this person very much or simply doesn't know them that well it would be in your best interest to keep that person around when you know you're going to be having long-winded conversations with this individual. If you use these tactics you may be able to fight off a compulsive liar that is trying to manipulate you. It will however be very difficult, and I would strongly recommend simply cutting this person out of your life begin with. It would be very difficult at the moment but be very beneficial in the long run.

Control

In order to counteract somebody that is trying to have complete and utter control over you have to simply not give in to their controlling Tendencies. What I mean by this is that you cannot allow a person that makes you feel as though you have no control to know that they are making you feel like you have no control. If you give them that satisfaction, then they will know that what they are doing is working and will continue to do it. Instead you need to keep a constant Mantra in your brain telling yourself over and over again that you have the power in your life. That you can make decisions for your own and that the person who's trying to control you in reality has no control over your actions. It may be difficult to do this, and it may be beneficial to keep strong support of friends around you at all times. If you ever feel yourself beginning to doubt whether or not you have control over your life or your actions, you can consult one of your friends and I guarantee you that as long as they are not a manipulator themselves, they will assure you that you make your own decisions. Other ways of keeping somebody from using their control to manipulate you is by going to somebody that has control over them. In a business setting this can mean somebody that is the boss of your boss. If there someone above person that is supposed to be your boss and you feel as though your boss is using unfair or inappropriate tactics to try and control you and your co-workers it may be in your best interest to go to the person above your boss to discuss some kind of consequences or reprimands. As with all of these tactics there's one more method you can use to avoid somebody who's trying to use their control over you to manipulate you. That is of course to stay away from or cut that person out of your life. Once again, I know that this is a very difficult thing to do and is not always possible in the situation at hand but if you can manage to do this it would greatly benefit you in the long run. Somebody that has control over you may have an undying thirst to use that control to manipulate you.

That is not necessarily something that you can change, it's similar to Greed or addiction to power. This person simply wants to be in control at all times and that's not necessarily something that you can fix. Coming to this conclusion is very difficult for some people and sometimes can put you into a state of depression. Try to work through this in order to avoid staying with or near the person that is trying to control you. You will be happier in the long run.

Projection

A person that is projecting their problems onto you to manipulate you it's not really looking for any kind of help. There's a chance that they need it though. These individuals do not always know that they are projecting onto other people. Sometimes it is a subconscious action that they don't mean to do but find themselves doing without realizing it. A good way to help or change a person that is doing this is to contact their mental physician if they have one and if they do not contact a professional that you know yourself. Internal mental discrepancy such as these are not ones that average people should concern themselves with. These are things that professionals need to look into within an individual. As a normal person it is not your responsibility to help somebody who is projecting themselves onto you. Finding them professional who can help them discover why they tend to do this will be far more beneficial to you and them in the long run.

Denial

To defend yourself against the manipulation tactic of denial you have to first understand what a person who is doing the denying is trying to prevent by denying that thing. Let's say for instance that somebody denies about an action is their fault. Listen to try to blame you for that action. What do you think they are trying to prevent from happening here? If they were to admit that is their fault that they did a certain action what would they be admitting to themselves? Once you understand the answers to these questions you can begin to break down this person's wall of denial. This will be a very painful and difficult process for the person that has been doing the manipulation. But unless you want to try and cut this person out of your life entirely this is the way to go. You have to break down this person's wall of denial by making several statements towards them that prove that their actions are of their own choices.

These are statements that primarily consists of explaining how nobody else can control that person's actions and how they are fully grown adults who can control their own decision-making. If you can succeed in doing this, you may be able to change the manipulator in your life. Be careful with this because if you get too stuck into this mindset of trying to change a person who is manipulative in your life you may begin to be manipulated by them again. So, keep a safe distance while also tearing down their wall of denial.

Intimidation

To fight back against a manipulator that's trying to use intimidation as a form of manipulation against you, you have to understand that you have nothing to be intimidated about. Please note that we are not discussing any form of physical intimidation within this section just yet. Intimidation within the economic or social sphere is a very powerful tool that a manipulator can use. You can take away this power by turning to those that are closest to you and that you believe would properly support you in the case that A manipulator tries to act on their threats. These are typically family members or very close friends. To stop intimidation from working on you as a form of manipulation you have to stop yourself from allowing yourself to be intimidated. What I mean by this is you need to understand that most of the threats of somebody trying to intimidate are empty. This means that you can realistically Act of your own accord and ignore these threats without facing any damaging repercussions. If you are afraid this may not be the case, then it is important to keep that support group around you at all times. If you are not able to physically fight back against this intimidation it may be within your best interest to cut this person out of your life entirely. Once again this is very difficult to do and follow through with but once it is completed it will greatly benefit you in your life. A person whose main form of manipulation is intimidation typically is secretly afraid of something. Typically, this is something that you have the power to wield over them. Once you can discover what this is you can usually manage to convince that person stop trying to intimidate you by wielding this power.

The reason that the majority of people manipulate through intimidation is that they are scared of the person they're trying to intimidate. It's an interesting sort of irony how these two works together. The fear that one has of another Austin convinces themselves to try and scare that person. In order to fight back against this all that you have to do is not be intimidated. Do not back down if they try to intimidate you or scare you. Stand up to them and be ready and willing to disagree with them. Obviously in the case of physical intimidation this is not the same advice that I would give. If you are scared of someone because they are physically intimidating it may be in your best interest to get somebody in law enforcement involved. Or somebody that can protect you in some way. It may be best to go to the route of a restraining order in this situation.

Restraining orders are very useful for these types of situations because they prevent the manipulator from getting close to you and you are able to stand up to them without risk of harm. In the world of intimidation as a form of manipulation it can be very difficult to stand up the Intimidator. If you stand strong and continuously have about social support. Love you too and stand up your Intimidator in life. You may even find that your Intimidator was intimidated by you to begin with.

Conditioning

There are two main types of conditioning that we have discussed within this text that is often used for manipulation. These two types are known as classical and operant conditioning. These types of manipulation are hard to protect yourself against because they can be hard to pinpoint. The good thing is that they are very easy to stop or change once you have realized that they are happening. If you start to notice that someone is conveniently doing nice things for you for no apparent reason and you're beginning to feel unconsciously happy whenever you see them, you may be the subject of classical conditioning. The bad part about this is that it's somewhat already too late. You've already been conditioned to feel happy when this person enters the room. The good part about this is that we as humans are smarter than dogs and so are able to change these traits within ourselves. You can begin to fight back against this by starting to refuse the nice actions of these individuals, you don't have to be mean about it just say no thank you. You can continue by not acting on the operant conditioning that you may want to act on.

Self-esteem is a very important factor in the world of manipulative relationships. The majority of manipulation tactics rely very heavily on the low self-esteem of the victim. Because of this, if an individual begins to gain higher self-esteem the manipulator may become hostile or start fighting to lower the self-esteem of the individual. Do not let this deter you because that is what the manipulator wants. Having positive self-esteem about yourself can help you in manipulative relationships because you will be less at risk for falling for the traditional manipulative traps. With higher self-esteem you will not fall for degrading comments or let yourself be put down the way that somebody with lower self-esteem would. If you find that you already have pretty low self-esteem here are some tips and tricks on how you can improve your self-esteem in the hopes of helping yourself in a manipulative relationship.

1) Being Mindful
That is pretty simple in the world of improving your self-esteem. This is simply becoming aware of the idea that you have low self-esteem. Is important to understand and accept the fact that you are having negative feelings about yourself if you would like to feel better about yourself. Helpful things to remember when you are trying to be more mindful is to remind yourself that the negative thoughts you have about yourself are only thoughts and not facts.

2) Changing your story
every person in this world has an internal Narrative of what they believe are their core ideals and who they are. Is also connect to our main self-image of ourselves. People with low self-esteem often have a negative self-image and if they want to change that ideal, they have to understand where it is coming from what voices are being internalized within us. Some negative ideas are repeated so often in our lives that we begin to believe that they are true. The first step to understanding that these are not facts or to unlearn these phrases is to understand where they come from and to know what you wish you believed about yourself.

3) Don't Compare yourself
Comparisons amongst people are never good. If you find yourself comparing yourself to other people and feeling bad about yourself as a result you may have low self-esteem. You need to remind yourself that nobody is perfect and the person you were comparing yourself to isn't either. This may be difficult to understand but you need to understand that the person you're comparing yourself to has their own issues and problems and even if you had what you like about them you wouldn't be perfect either.

4) Think about your positive skills

Every person in this world has their own set of special skills or weaknesses. Someone who is good at one thing is not going to be good at everything. If you wish to increase your self-esteem you need to try your best to focus on some of your positive skills and things that you know you are very good about. feeling confidence in things that you enjoy will increase your self-esteem and help you to fight back against manipulators in your life.

Conclusion

Within this text we've covered a lot of information regarding manipulation and the psychology behind manipulative tendencies. In the very first chapter I gave a brief explanation of manipulation psychology and the history of Psychology of manipulation. I traced back the roots of manipulation to Aristotle's beliefs of persuasion in the ancient Greeks while also giving some examples of manipulation in history. After doing this I gave a brief explanation on why people choose to manipulate others and where manipulation tends to pop up the most in the average person's life. This is greatly helpful to a person who feels that they may be being manipulated in their life. This chapter can help you see where you should look to check for manipulation.

In the next chapter I listed some of the common expressions of manipulation. In the next part of this chapter explain some of the most common tactics used by emotional manipulators. I went through the acts of raising your voice, acting Superior to others, victimization, lying, and control over those around you. Explain how these tactics work and how manipulators may use them in context. This would be helpful to a person in pinpointing these types of manipulation in their lives. In the next chapter I gave some in-depth techniques of manipulation. Are techniques for more complicated and had more difficult explanations than the last. These techniques were known as projection, denial, intimidation, conditioning, stalking, and much more.

I went into detail on how these techniques of manipulation worked and how they can be used against others. I explained how words contribute to emotional manipulation due to our connection to language as a species. Within the next chapter I began to go into the power of persuasion. I explained the origins of persuasion going all the way back to the ancient Greeks with famous philosopher Aristotle explaining his three proofs of the art of persuasion. I also explained how persuasion could be used in everyday life and everyday scenarios. Moving on to the next chapter I gave an in-depth explanation of a form of psychology known as neuro-linguistic programming. I explained the background of neuro linguistic programming and how it could be used to manipulate those around you. Within the next chapter I went into how we could use our learned skills to gain new friends in this world. I went through each of the skills that I taught during this text and explain how they could be used to win friends. In the next chapter I began to discuss how we can avoid manipulation in a relationship. Explain how you can spot manipulation in a relationship that you are in or that friends of yours are in and how you can avoid said manipulative relationship. I also gave some practice examples to help you pinpoint manipulative tendencies. These consisted of both scenarios in which somebody was manipulating somebody and in which someone was not manipulating somebody.

I explained whether or not someone was being manipulated in each situation and also gave an explanation on the type of manipulation that was being used and the tactics that were being implemented. This can serve as practice so that you can help yourself in trying to pinpoint manipulative Tendencies and try not to fall into a manipulative trap in the future. The following chapter I explained how you can defend yourself against manipulation in a relationship.

I went through each tactic that we discussed within this text and explain how you can properly defend yourself against it. I also spoke briefly about self-esteem and how the use of positive self-esteem can help you overcome manipulation in your life. I also gave a list of tips and tricks on how to improve your self-esteem.

I have greatly enjoyed opening up your world to the possibility of manipulation psychology and hope that you find a use for the information within this text. Make sure to check out my other book "How to analyze people-Robert Leary", thanks!

Stoicism

Scoticisim

Representatives of a philosophical doctrine that emerged at the end of the 4th-century B.N.E. based on Hellenistic culture, under the spread of cosmopolitan and individualistic ideas and the development of technology-based on mathematical knowledge. The main figures of the stoic school of the 4-3 centuries A.N.E. were Zeno and Crispo. The latter determined the place and role of the sciences that the stoics were dealing with using the following comparison: logic is the fence, physics, fertile soil, and ethics, its fruits. The main task of philosophy is contained in ethics; knowledge is but a necessary means of becoming wise and knowing how to live. You have to live in line with nature. This is the ideal of the true sage. Happiness consists of getting rid of passions, peace of mind, and indifference. Fate predetermines everything in life. The one who wants it, fate takes him with him, and the one who opposes it takes him violently. In understanding nature, stoics were materialistic, but their materialism was geared with nominalism. Unlike the logic of the predicates (Aristotle), the Stoics created the sense of the statements as a doctrine of the formation of complex statements from the simple ones and developed on this basis the propositional theory of the conclusion. The stoics established the types of connection of judgments, which modern logic calls conjunction, disjunction, and material involvement. In the early centuries of our age, stoicism began to develop on the Roman ground, mainly studying the moral and religious ideas of ethical doctrine.

History

If there is a philosophy that has managed to charm people of all conditions and times, that is stoicism. This branch of thought, whose foundation we owe to Zeno of Citio, would remain at the front row of philosophical culture for no less than half a millennium (from the 3rd century BC to the 2nd century AD) and maintain influence over the following centuries as history has rarely seen. Let's take a look here at its most outstanding features that may explain why such success.

As we have said, the founder of stoicism was Zeno de Citio, a disciple of Crates of Thebes. The latter developed his thought from the cynical thesis of his master (hence the clear harmony between the two philosophies in various aspects).

However, the one who turned stoicism into a doctrine of relevance was Crispo de Solos, who led the Stoa (the stoic school, located in the painted portico of Athens) from 232 a. C. in 204 BC Thanks to his enormous dialectical talent and gigantic production - no less than about 700 works, of which only fragments have come to us - Crispo managed not only to make stoicism a philosophy of great relevance, but the Stoa came to pass to the Academy of Plato and the Lyceum of Aristotle.

While there were other renowned philosophers in this school - such as Cleanthes, Panecio, Posidonia, and his most famous disciple, Cicero - we would have to wait for the Roman Empire to arrive at the new consign of philosophers of enormous fame, with Seneca, Epictetus, and the philosopher emperor Marcus Aurelius.

Man, And His Morals, Main Concern

The center of the study of stoics is very clear: the human being. His whole philosophy is intended for man, and more specifically, for his morals. Logic, physics, and ethics are presented at the service of the person with a goal that never seems to lose course: to teach us to live according to our nature.

A Sensualist Theory

The theory of knowledge of stoics is part, such as that of Aristotle, empiricists, or positivists, of sensory experience. I mean, the senses. For stoics, it is a process that goes through different stages. First of all, what comes to us by the purposes leaves a representation (an impression, Zeno says) in our reason, which, as we have already said, is the part of "divinity" that we possess, and that connects us to the rationality of nature. However, these representations are not yet knowledge. If we just accepted that as a sign of reality, we would not be faced with experience, but in the face of an opinion. For it to become knowledge, such representation must possess evidence that invites intelligence to accept it. Hegemonic, the Self must give that consent. Wisdom comes when the data offered to us by the senses pass through the sieve of rationality.

Cosmopolitan

Stoics, unlike cynics, did not despise their fellowmen or society. To the pessimist, all those who lived wrongly were nothing more than minds, who deserved to be insulted and ridiculed for their stupidity. One architect of this was Diogenes, famous for his raffirrafes with subjects of all fur. However, the cynic's scathing critique did not try to correct or set an example for his fellowmen but was content to belittle them.

Stoics, for their part, have that critical vision, but they don't share the form. In fact, for them, the idea of community is extremely important. However, true to their thinking and their belief that the fine thread of rationality unites the world, they considered themselves citizens of the world. They didn't believe in being here or there for reasons of birth or culture. They were of reason and virtue wherever they reigned.

What is stoicism, the 2,000year-old philosophy used to survive the chaos? In 1965, during the war between the United States and Vietnam, U.S. Navy pilot James Stockdale was shot while flying over the enemy country.

The young man didn't know he'd spend seven years as a prisoner of war for the Vietnamese. And that a philosopher who had lived in Greece in the 1st century AD would become his great teacher and friend, helping him endure unimaginable suffering.

The philosopher was called Epictetus, and his philosophy, stoicism what the philosopher Michael Sandel teaches, considered "the most popular professor in the world" at Harvard. In the book "Stockdale Talks Stoicism," the pilot says how the teachings of this philosophical school comforted him during his long years of captivity.

"Everything I know about Epicteto I've practiced over the years," Stockdale wrote.

"He taught me that it is necessary to maintain control of my moral purpose. In fact, (he taught me) that I am my moral purpose."

"That I am completely responsible for everything I do and say. And that I decide and control my destruction and my liberation."

Three specialists in this philosophical current who spoke in the BBC World Service Forum program present - in plain language - some of the central ideas of stoic thinking. They also provide us with a practical guide to stay calm amid the chaos.

Stoicism: Calm During Chaos

How can we do our best while accepting what is beyond our control?

These are the central issues of stoicism and philosophy created more than 2,000 years ago in which more and more people are seeking antidotes against the difficulties of contemporary life.

Stoicism preached the value of reason by proposing that destructive emotions are the result of errors in our way of seeing the world and offered practical guidance to remain resolved, strong, and in control of the situation.

The Stoic school had a profound influence on Greco-Roman civilization and, consequently, on Western thought in general. And it went further.

It is present in Christianity, Buddhism, and the thinking of several modern philosophers, such as the German Immanuel Kant, in addition to having influenced the contemporary technique of psychotherapy called cognitive-behavioral therapy.

How to Shield Us Against Misfortune?

After surviving a shipwreck in which he lost everything he had, Zeno went to Athens. There he met the philosophies of Socrates, Plato, Aristotle, and his followers.

The early Stoics created a philosophy that offered a unified view of the world and the place that man occupied in it. Thought was composed of three parts: ethics, logic, and physics.

For the Stoics, the universe was governed by reason or logos, a divine principle that dominated everything. Therefore, being in harmony with the universe meant living in communion with God.

Stoic philosophy also proposed that men live with virtue, a concept that for them was intimately associated with reason, as the philosopher Donald Robertson explains.

"If we can live wisely, guided by reason, we will flourish and develop our potential as human beings. God has given us this ability. It is up to us to use it properly," he paraphrases.

Stoicism flourished for two centuries in ancient Greece, and around 100 BC, its popularity came to Rome.

One of the best-known thinkers of the time is Seneca, advisor to the infamous Roman emperor Nero.

In a letter to his friend Lucilio, the philosopher speaks of one of the central components of virtue: the ability to arm ourselves against misfortune.

"For that reason, make life in general pleasurable to you, eliminating all concerns about it."

The central idea of this letter is that we must not only prepare ourselves to meet the needs of life but also prepare for the worst, explains the Italian Massimo Pigliucci, contemporary and stoic philosopher.

How to Deal with Our Emotions?
Stoics also had a particular vision of emotions, called passions, which were divided into three categories: good, bad, and indifferent emotions. They proposed that we should focus on bad or unhealthy emotions, learning to deal with them.

Admired by philosophers over the centuries, Seneca's famous essay "On Anger" proposes ways to deal with this feeling.

"Seneca suggests the following: you have a vision of something bad that happened, but you can change your mind about it. (You can tell yourself that) it wasn't so bad, it was an accident, it didn't mean it, or it's not important to you," Nancy Sherman explains. In the following excerpt from his manual, Epitecto reflects on the same topic: passions and how to treat them:

"Men are not disturbed by things, but by their opinions on them."

Therefore, when we are ashamed or disturbed, we do not attribute it to another but to ourselves. I mean, according to our own opinions. These words have been a revelation to many people over the centuries, and to this day, Robertson says.

"He's saying it's our opinions on things that will determine whether or not they're going to bother us."

"But instead of trying to suppress (emotions), we need to confront the beliefs that will lead us to turn them into healthy emotions," he explains.

About the third category, that of indifferent emotions, the idea is simply to ignore them.

Prioritize and Understand What's Under Our Control
The pursuit of self-control is fundamental to stoic philosophy. But for this, it is important to be able to distinguish what is under our control.

In response to this question, Epitecto created two lists.

"The things that are under our control are our judgments, opinions, and values that we decided to adopt, and what is not under our control is everything else besides everything external," explains Italian philosopher Massimo Pigliucci.

"You can influence your body, maintain a healthy diet, exercise, but in the end, your body isn't under your control, because you can get a virus or have an accident and break your leg."

According to Pigliucci, this distinction makes it possible to realize that if the only things that are under our control are judgments, opinions, and values, it is in them that we must maintain our approach.

Cold and Conformist

The importance that stoics attach to the use of rationality in daily life ended up creating an image of the stoic as a cold person, disconnected from his feelings. For Robertson, this is a superficial interpretation of this thought.

"In modern English, the stoic eventually became synonymous with a repressed, emotionless person. But stoicism, the philosophical school of antiquity, is much more sophisticated and has a much more complex psychological theory."

What is "absurdity" and what it has to do with a casserole full of chickpeas. What is sought, explains the philosopher is not the absence of emotions, but the control of them.

Critics say that by proposing that we set aside and accept everything external, that is beyond our control, this philosophy generates politically apathetic and conformist people. In a column in the British magazine The New Statesman, the philosopher Jules Evans refutes this idea.

"Stoicism creates individuals who cannot be intimidated by the powerful because they are not afraid to abandon everything or die," Evans says

"Their philosophy trains them to give up life without fear or sorrow, to defend their rational principles above any threat or bribery."

How the Stoic Philosophy Works

Stoicism sits on a handful of fundamental teachings, from which all others derive. To give just a few examples: it tells us how fleeting our passage through life is, how unpredictable each of our days can be, how to prepare ourselves for possible surprises, and how to control our impulses through logical reasoning, among others.

Being stoic also has to do with ethics and morals, doing the right thing whenever it is within our reach. With being the best people, we can be and doing the work we need to do.

Being stoic can't be achieved overnight. It requires work, effort, patience, perseverance, lucidity. But the reward is infinite: a better life.

How Is It Different from Epicureanism?

Although they are often confused, the school of Stoicism has nothing to do with that of epicurism. The latter was founded by Epicurus of Samos and is based on the search for happiness through sexual pleasures, ataraxia, and friendship.

Instead, Stoicism believes that happiness is in virtue and not pleasure. This is the main difference between the two schools.

Later we will talk more about epicurism and its characteristics and delve de more into what differs from Stoicism with everyday examples. Still, for now, we will leave it here.

Who Are the Main Stoic Examples?

The names that always arise when we talk about Stoicism are three: Marcus Aurelius, Seneca, and Epictetus.

But this is not to say that there are no more global and historically well-known stoic people. To give just a few examples, Frederick the Great, George Washington, Thomas Jefferson, Adam Smith, or Michel de Montaigne are some of the most recognized stoics over the centuries.

What do they all have in common? Who are figures who held positions of vital importance for the future of history?

Three Basic Stoic Exercises to Apply in Our Daily Lives

Once this brief introduction to what Stoicism is and what its meaning is, we will see a series of basic exercises that we can apply from this very moment to improve our daily life. We reiterate that Stoicism is a practical philosophy; only in this way can we learn its basic precepts.

Is This Under My Control Area?

"The main task in life is simply this: to identify and separate issues so that you can tell me which ones are external and not under my control and which ones have to do with the choices I control. Where, then, do I seek good and evil? Not in uncontrollable externals, but within myself and in the elections that are mine."

Let's look at some examples:

We go out on the street, it's raining, and it's cold. Our first thought is, "what a bad day it is, what the desired summer will come." The problem comes when this thought puts us in a bad mood for a few hours. Here the stoic exercise (habit) to be performed is to ask yourself: "Can I control that it is bad weather? If it's something I can't control, am I going to let it affect me?" It is extremely difficult to ask yourself this question when such situations arise, and our negative emotions "kidnap us." The secret is to do it little by little, thinking about the long term and without being overwhelmed.

An employee in customer service is rude to us, and we get angry because we think, "How can it be so unpleasant if your job is to help people?" Once again, Stoicism proposes that we ask ourselves, "Is the way I speak of this person under my control?" And then choose how we're going to react to that situation, something that's under our control. For example, being patient and kind to that employee.

271

We're at the airport, and they just announced that the plane leaves at least an hour late. Our first reaction is to get angry and say, "Again late? This company is always the same!" Again, we know that this is not under our control, so we can react stoically and think, "Well, so I have one more hour to read/see the chapter I was so eager to see/etc."

Although the first impression is that Stoicism may seem that we must settle for everything we don't like, it's not really like that. What he proposes is that if we can't control what's going on outside of us, what practicality does it make for us to get angry?

If you manage to make this exercise a habit, you will have managed to improve the quality of your thoughts and your life significantly.

Remember You're Going to Die
"Let us prepare our minds as if we had reached the end of life. Let's not postpone anything. Let's balance the books of life every day. He who gives the last touches to his life every day will never be short of time." – Seneca

Right now, you're thinking, "What a macabre all this, I don't want to think about my death." No one likes to do it, but stoics argue that it is better to do so to be more aware of the gift that life is, and how to keep in mind that we are going to die will help us make small daily decisions about how to live our lives better.

Stoicism, A Timeless Philosophy of Life

The loss of someone close, an incurable disease, a traumatizing experience. There are so many unfortunate hazards that can happen to us in life, and they seem to be obstacles to the achievement of happiness. This supreme value, very often considered the ultimate goal of human life, is it a sweet utopia or an accessible state? Many philosophies opt for the second option. If Buddhism has more and more adherents throughout the world, however, it is not the only model that has the tranquility of the soul, also called "ataraxia," as its goal. From Ancient Greece, we inherit from "schools of happiness" such as Epicureanism, Aristotelianism, or also Stoicism. This system gives rational and reasonable answers to explain the unfortunate chances of our existence. And what we can learn from that increases year after year.

Stoicism was born in Ancient Greece and spread for almost six centuries in three main currents: Old Stoicism, Middle Stoicism, and New or Imperial Stoicism, especially with Seneca, Epithet, or Marcus-Aurelius (1st and 2nd centuries BC). In this vast philosophical current, happiness is defined as follows: it consists of ataraxia, that is, the absence of disorders of the soul and serenity. It is a eudaemonic philosophy that makes happiness the natural purpose of human existence and wisdom the condition to achieve it.

Although Buddhism is one of the most popular life philosophies in the world today, there is a discreet Stoic community. This community was formed in October 2012 in the UK, during a seminar organized at the University of Exeter. The founders, who run the website, are seven university students and psychotherapists who passionately study this ancient philosophy together. They will organize in 2015, and for the fourth time, the Stoic Week (stoic week), an international event open to all Internet users. For seven days, the participants are invited to follow the Stoic practices adapting them to the modern world. Throughout the week, online courses allow you to understand the basic principles of Stoicism. The challenge is to see the potential benefits of such a way of life on our own lives and to measure its usefulness in everyday life.

The Utility of Stoicism

Whatever the unfortunate chances of our existence, Stoicism helps us to accept and overcome them. So, it is a real therapeutic philosophy. Never does a stoic complain about his situation or let his feelings overcome his reason. The example of Epicteto freed slave and patient constitutes a real model. One day his teacher amused himself by twisting his limp leg with an instrument of torture. While the philosopher calmly warned him of the risks and that he could break his leg, what had to happen happened. "I already told you that you would break my leg, there it is broken," Epicteto said coldly after the drama. As a stoic, he was not disturbed by his misfortune. A Stoic remains serene in all circumstances, whether the wound is moral or physical.

Stoic ethics follows simple precepts that today have lost none of their effectiveness. Epicteto explained the importance of distinguishing what depends on us and what does not depend on us: "There are certain things that rely on ourselves, such as our judgments, our tendencies, our desires and aversions and, in a word, all our operations. Others do not depend, such as the body, wealth, reputation, power, in a comment, everything that is not our operation. " - Manual of Epicteto. As long as something does not depend on us, lamentations are useless. On the contrary, according to Stoic logic, we have to overcome this sadness.

All Stoic ethics is articulated with the good use of reason, which should allow us to control our representations, in all circumstances.

Stoicism: A Response to The Crisis?

But to take a more modern example, the economic crisis is an external event that does not depend on us, but that can bring us misfortunes such as layoffs, lower purchasing power, or additional stress. Two other great principles of Stoicism are the formula "Suffer and abstain" and indifference to the outside world. In the role of a victim of the economic crisis, a Stoic should admit poverty, endure external misfortunes, and finally accept his fate. If it is not your responsibility to get out of your misery, then why wish for happiness that is as vain as it is utopian? Like Camus's Sisyphus in the Sisyphus Myth, it is precise because you live in the present, without looking for an impossible way out of your tragic destiny, that you become happy.

In any case, Stoicism is not the only answer to the crisis, but to all the unfortunate chances of our existence in general, which makes it a universal and timeless philosophy.

Stoicism and Loving Passion

Faced with the problem of love sentiment, which has not ceased to be topical, Stoicism considers this passion like any other. What is a force? A perverted natural inclination under the influence of the social environment and disturbing the soul. The Stoics believe that custom and education persuade us of some things; for example, that pain is evil. The reason must act as a filter that accepts or not passion, and that regulates it. Only then is it possible to be in love and stoic, only if this love is kept under control?

The following speech by Epicteto in his Manual has not lost its modernity. "In everything that happens to you, consider in yourself the means you have to defend yourself. For example: if you see a beautiful woman, notice that you have temperance, which is a powerful means to oppose beauty. If you are forced to undertake some hard work, use patience. If you have been injured, arm yourself with perseverance. And if you get always used to do this, the objects will never have power over you. Never say that you have lost something, but still, say that you have restored it. When your son or your wife dies, do not say that you have lost your son or your wife, but that you have converted them to the one who gave them to you. " In this way, stoicism finds applications even in seduction, with the control of too strong drives, or in the death of someone close, with the acceptance of things.

Prejudices About Stoicism

Despite being clear teachings, the term Stoic as well as the Epicurean today, suffer from numerous prejudices. If the Epicurean does not correspond to the original definition of the living Man, the Stoic does not define a man without emotions. Next, we will see the most common prejudices.

A Stoic is insensitive, emotionless, and numb. The Stoic does have emotions but hears them only if he does not lose his clarity. Rationalize your passions. It is possible to want and be stoic, provided you control your representation of love. This means that a Stoic will not be affected by the death of his wife because he has already considered her loss in some way. Again, you do not control destiny, but the vision you have about things. It is the same for physical pain: you feel the pain. Still, you have a different perception from common opinion, you do not associate it with something bad.

A stoic lets things get done, lets himself die if he is sick. Once again, this is a misconception of Stoicism. If he is sick, the stoic calls a doctor to cure him because it is in his power (up to him) to call a doctor to fix him: health is preferable to disorders of the body.

Stoicism is a selfish philosophy, not concerned with the common good. The Stoic indeed seeks his balance first and foremost, and love, as love for others, does not have the most important place in this philosophy. But this egoism is relative, because the Stoic does not stop being a Man, and Man is naturally pleasant. It will be "lucid" philanthropy and not an abandonment of oneself to the other. But no one would need generosity if they were stoic.

The 5 Principles of Stoicism

Already in a previous post, we introduced the theme. Still, here it is our turn to know why it is so beneficial, in fact, even evolutionarily necessary. And the first thing you need to know is what are the fundamentals of this philosophy of life that have worked very well for influential leaders and people.

1. He lives every day like he's the last. The reality is that you don't have all the time in the world to leave the right thing (usually what makes you uncomfortable) for later. In modernity, most people do not grow personally or succeed precisely because they reject many things for later and for the wrong reasons, and that after never arrives or when they do, it no longer gives them enough time. This does not mean uncontrolled YOLO, nor do you misunderstand.
2. Food is the best test of self-control and temperance. The key to too many accomplishments in your life lies in your ability to self-control and stability and learning to control your desires in something you find daily as food is key to developing this ability. Also, in passing, it will help you live longer and better.

3. Wrong is natural; lamenting is silly. Solving life's problems and trying different approaches exposes you to making mistakes and failing in your attempts. Accept, and instead of repenting or complaining, learn from the mistake and move on. Lamenting (or worse, blaming someone else) will only keep you in the hole you fell and prevent you from getting better. Also, sorry to complain about the benefits you.

4. Focus on small things. The reality of life is that happiness is not even in what you achieve or achieve but in the process of solving life's problems. If you learn to focus and enjoy the small (as in those habits that over time make a difference), you will not only enjoy the greatest, but you will avoid self-destructive trends such as addictions or depression.

5. Eliminate vanity. And not only vanity as we normally know it: the need to "look good" with others through our external appearance or the number of "friends." This principle also includes the fact that when you think you already don't allow you to learn more or get out of your mistake. Eliminate unnecessary pride. He seeks to understand by assuming you can always be wrong, and you never know enough.

Ethics of Stoicism

For Seneca, a late stoic thinker, philosophy is the science of behavior; and happiness is synonymous with virtue, a concept that for stoicism means to live according to nature. Advice and exhortation are his primary concern in the education of moral values, principles that benefit man's mental state and behavior.

Seneca's stoicism is a practical ethical doctrine. According to stoic principles, there are no evil acts in themselves but the moral evil that represents the absence of moral order in the human will.

In both physics and morality, opponents act with each other. One could not understand what it is to have courage if one does not know fear, justice without injustice, courage without cowardice, which means pleasure if the pain is not known.

Living according to nature and its laws means for stoicism to adhere to the principles that operate in it, of which the human soul also participates. Diogenes Laercio points out that virtue is to live according to righteous reason, according to nature.

Man is the only one who can know these laws and consciously accept them and is free to change his attitude according to his will and responsibility because no action is good or bad in a determined way.

Therefore, some things will be preferable, others rejectable, and others indifferent, and pleasure can never be an end in itself.

The essential virtues are prudence, strength, temperance, and justice that complement each other. Still, the truly virtuous behavior is that of the sage, who has freed himself from passions, has self-control, and accepts his finitude.

Late stoics emphasize the idea of progress and divide humanity into two groups, that of the foolish and those who progress toward virtue or wisdom.

A characteristic of stoic ethical doctrine deals with passions and moods such as sadness, depression, desire, and fear. But in practice, it refers more to the struggle to achieve one's dominance and moral freedom.

For stoicism, every man is a social being by nature, and the reason is the essential nature that is common to all men. The stoic ethical ideal is achieved when we manage to love all humanity as ourselves.

Stoics speak of the divine providence that governs the universe in a foolproof way and allows it to achieve all the objectives that it has envisaged. For this reason, they participate in esoteric and divinatory doctrines.

For stoicism, nothing is coincidental, and each one is necessarily produced in the only way it should be and necessarily goes towards fulfilling what has been assigned to it.

The true freedom of the wise man is to confirm his desire to the divine Fact, that is to desire what the Done wants, what is given to him.

Freedom is not about aiming for the fulfillment of our projects because these projects will be upset by the Fact of which we are hopelessly slaves.

For the Stoics, there are no evil acts in themselves, but the moral sea lies in deprivation of moral order in the human will. Opponents are involved: justice cannot be understood without injustice.

Stoics paid great attention to behavioral problems. The end of life, happiness, is to attain virtue in its stoic sense (living according to the Law of Nature). For man, since the universe is governed by a Natural Law, conforming to the laws of the universe in a broad sense and adapting his conduct to its essential nature to reason, form a unity. For the early Stoic philosophers, it is, therefore, a "Nature." Later, they would conceive of it from an anthropological point of view. But in any case, living according to nature meant sticking to the principle that operates in it from which the human soul was not excluded.

Seneca already observes a practical moral doctrine. Stoicism is valued for the benefits that its principles can confer on a man's mental state and the conduct of his life.

For Diogenes, Laerecio, virtue means living according to the nature that, in the case of man, is understood as life according to reason since man is a rational being who has the privilege of knowing natural laws and accepting them consciously. Man is, therefore, free to change his inner attitude.

No action is good or bad in itself; determinism leaves no room for this differentiation. Only virtue is good. What is not virtue or vice cannot be considered good or bad but indifferent. They are for the stoic cardinal virtues:

- Prudence
- Temperance
- Fortress
- Justice

But the virtuous behavior only day be attained by the wise, absolutely free of passions. Pleasure could not be considered an end in itself but an outcome or accompanying certain activities. Thus, a rigorous moral idealism characterizes the first stoicism. At the same time, later, the notion of progress would be emphasized, encouraging the man to walk the path of virtue to stay on it.

Virtue, Reason, Passions, And Happiness

The ethics of the stoics are consequential to the deterministic physical conception: virtue consists in living according to nature and the second reason, two things that coincide since the natural, divine order is intrinsically rational and man can participate with his rationality to divine rationality. This results in giving consent to the course of events, to follow him willingly, since the alternative is to be dragged maliciously.

Error is generated when an individual logos judges as a good something that a good is not or as an evil something that evil is not; a false opinion arises, the consequence of which will be a passion: passion is always a wrong judgment. Forces for stoics are of four types: desire, fear, pleasure, and pain, understood as moods.

Passions are contrasted with states of health, rational mental states proper to the wise: desire is contrasted with a will, fear, prudence, pleasure, and joy; pain is not opposed to anything, because the problem is the idea of a lack, and the wise are not missing anything.

For the Stoics, virtue is enough for happiness. All virtues are a single virtue declined by different names depending on the field in which it is applied, and since integrity is knowledge, being virtuous will consist of the awareness of stoic physics. To live according to reason means to serve the universal logos, the usefulness of the cosmos, even against one's survival. Only well is a virtue; vice is the opposite of virtue; everything else is indifferent; that is, it has no moral relevance.

However, some "indifferent" such as life, health, beauty, wealth, are "according to nature," have a value, and are called "preferable." They are not relevant to morality, but they can be chosen rationally: the stoic thus introduces the concept of katechon, often translated as "duty" or "convenient," but it is always a relatively good, while virtue is an absolute good.

Focus on What You Control
When people say that a person is stoic, we usually mean that he is passive, he tolerates everything without asking questions and without emotions.

The Focus of Stoicism Is Another: To Have A Better Life.
And it's not being passive or suppressing the emotions that you reach it.

Indeed.

Let's start with three stoic disciplines

- Desire – That is, what we should or should not aim for
- Action – How we should behave
- Consensus – How we should react to actions

hence a long series of inspirations.

Not everything is under your control. Focus your strength on the things you can handle, and don't worry about the rest.

Example 1: The Airplane
Get on the plane and suffer all the way. What is the point of all this? Unless you are the pilot of the aircraft, your concern to avoid disasters does not affect the flight but makes you consume energy preventing you from enjoying the trip (a few hours reading/watching a movie without anyone calling you and needing you)

What was in your power: choosing the airline, the schedules, the stopovers, the books to read in-flight was done, and now you have to rely on the pilots, who do their job.

Example 2: Sport
Let me give you an example with something more personal: as someone who has been reading me for a bit practical Brazilian jiu-jitsu (a kind of judo). My age, my physical conformity, and other life decisions prevent me from training so much that I aspire to become a champion.

But they do not prevent me from going to training every day, studying my techniques, taking notes, being careful not to hurt any of my training partners, and give my best in the gym. I'm certainly sorry not to go to the World/European/Italian Championships to win medals. Still, I think I'm doing everything (or at least a lot of) what I can in my field of maneuvering.

At this point, it is easy for me to accept the results with happiness. I'm less happy when I skip workouts, eat badly, go to bed late when I have to go to the gym the next day. These things are under my control.

Theoretical Part on The Classical Stoic Philosophy
Classical Philosophy
The classical philosophy is based on its three main pillars:

- Logic (i.e., as we know it)
- Physics (the object of knowledge)
- Ethics (conduct)

They bear a similarity: the reason is the fence that delimits the ground, the physics the tree, and ethics is the fruit

Stoic Logic in Detail

The stoics have brought important contributions both in nosology and in the actual logic. The stoic, although he had in mind the image of the Wise who knew everything, was aware that in practice, the improvements were progressive. This very modern concept will be one of the cards that will help this reboot of stoicism to sell in these ten years.

Gnoseology

- The stoicism distinguished "knowledge" in
- Opinions (weak or even false).
- Understanding (intermediate epistemological value).
- Knowledge (strong impressions that cannot be altered by reason).

Logic

The stoicism used five basic cyclability and four rules that serve to bring each syllogism back to one of the five bases. They introduced the modal (necessity, possibilities) that they used to protect the fruit of their work, that is, ethics.

Physical

Physics means both the natural sciences, as well as metaphysics and theology.

The stoicism had the goal calibrated on nature, implying that they had to do everything they needed to understand it as best they could. This also means that the study of nature is not the end, but the means to live at best in this environment. Now it would be called a holistic approach, a few decades ago, "cybernetic."

Ethics

As I have already written the Stoic philosophy, it is not a theoretical topic, but a practical one. Ethics as the study of how to live one's life was the point of doing philosophy.

For the stoics, the human being is, by its nature, a being with a propensity for moral development. Moral development as:

- Acting to achieve our goalsIdentize with people's interests
- Being able to extricate yourself between the various vicissitudes of life

4 Cardinal Virtues of Stoic Ethics

This is explicit by four cardinal virtues:

- Practical wisdom
- Temperance
- Courage
- Justice

The 3 Related Disciplines

from the three fields linked to the virtues just mentioned

- Desire (Acceptance) (related to courage to follow nature's plans and temperance to control one's impulses)
- Action (philanthropy) – the human being is a social being (this is linked to justice)
- Absence – accept that past experiences are part of the experience and reject them before making judgments

Value or Disvalue

Zenone, in his writing dises between things that have value (hello, money, education) and things that take away their value (illness, poverty, ignorance). These are called "indifferent": they do not count in achieving ethics.

Stoic Wisdom

Wisdom is what you see from outside stoicism, but it's also the most easily sellable thing, and it's, in fact, the thing that they're pushing into America at the moment.

Stoic wisdom consists of the ability to achieve happiness and is therefore centered on ataraxia, or ireflwerability of the soul, a concept derived largely from the cynical school. First of all, it comes to it by becoming a master of oneself. According to the stoicism, the will of the wise man adheres perfectly to his duty (kathekon), obeying a force that does not act outwardly on him, but from within. He wants what he owes, and he owes what his reason dictates to him. Stoicism is, therefore, not a kind of forced exercise of life, because everything, in the existence of the wise, flows peacefully.

In the money: We cannot control or rely on external events, only ourselves and the answers we give very modern as discourse.

Teachings of stoicism:

- The world acts in its way
- Our lives have the duration of a spark in history.
- So, learn to be strong and control yourself.
- The source of the lack of happiness depends on our impulsive dependence on the senses instead of logic.

Stoicism, therefore, aims not to talk about a thousand theories about the origin of the world but to act on destructive emotions. Action instead of chatting

Although the three most famous people were the Marcus as mentioned earlier, Aurelius (emperor of the Roman Empire), Epitteto, who as a freed slave founded his school, and Seneca, the list of kings, presidents, artists, and entrepreneurs who like to practice stoicism is incredibly long and varied

Famous Stoicism Scholars
- Frederick the Great (King of Prussia)
- Michel de Montaigne (written and political French)
- George Washington (US founding father)
- Thomas Jefferson (U.S. Founding Father)
- Adam Smith (economist)
- John Stuart Mill
- Wen Jiabao, (Chinese Prime Minister)
- Elle MacPherson (model)
- Tom Wolfe (American writer)

Train Perception to Avoid Good and Evil
If you are afflicted with something external, the pain is not due to the thing itself, but to the evaluation that you make of it, an assessment that you have the power to revoke at any time. Marcus Aurelius

The stoicism were masters of finding good even in the worst things. If you're a fan of NDP and reframes, these are a great exercise in training this ability

In Ryan Holiday's book Obstacle is the Way, he makes his phrase (also by Marcus Aurelius):

"Obstruction of action advances action. What is on the road becomes the road."

For the practitioner of stoicism, there is no right or bad. It is all and only perception. But you can control this perception and the way you react: "Can you learn or reason to jump down?"

Everything Is Ephemeral
Alessandro the Macedonian and his dying mule passed to the same condition: in fact, either they were summarized in the same seminal reasons of the cosmos or were dispersed, in the same way, in the atoms – Marcus Aurelius

And it goes on:

What annoys you? The nastiness of men? Given the terms of the problem, namely that rational beings exist for one another, that tolerance is part of justice, who make mistakes unintentionally and considered how many already, after feeding hostility, suspicion, hatred, lie pierced, reduced to ashes, stop it, finally!

To return to the context of the exercise. Remember that we are small in front of the world and that our lives last nothing, your successes are temporary, and you own them for a single moment.

But if we're small and everything is temporary, what matters?

The present matters! Being a good person and doing the right thing at the moment is what matters (Here's ethics, one of the three pillars of stoic philosophy I mentioned above).

Stoicism and Fitness
I recovered what Epitteto said, which disdained exercise to improve the physical appearance. Since this sentence was at odds with other points (progressive personal improvement), I investigated more: I found comments but no specific quotes. If you have any, please write to me.

The sentence of Epitteto mentioned above must be completed. Exercise to improve the physical appearance is indeed disdained, but for the stoic, fitness is much more than this: it is mastery, discipline improvement, and body and a healthy mind.

Exercise creates people with more energy and more likely to endure any challenges that life brings you together.

Marcus Aurelius talks about how to get up in the morning and abandon the warm embrace of the bed is an important exercise to fortify yourself. Later, there will be an exercise based on just that.

Why Stoicism Is Perfect for The Modern World
The stoicism was honest and critical of themselves. They sought a way of improvement and calmness.

In this world of Social Network with the gratification of the instant, of reality shows shouted, and the tractate of already knowing everything, stoicism could be a world-changing discipline, one person at a time.

Obstacles to The Spread of Stoicism 2.0
If it is true that stoicism can be the cure for some things, the biggest obstacle will be the potential lack of empathy that degeneration of the same could create.

It is very easy that those who look only at the patina above things put on the same level the stoicism to the slamming of all and everything, with the excuse of philosophy.

The Two Principles for Training Stoicism
stoic texts are used to move the wheels in the brain: they are therefore not treated with tritamagrons as one might expect.

The exercises are based on two fundamental principles:

- Car Discomfort
- Auto Control

Get Good from Yourself

Identifying your goals can be difficult and tedious in the modern world. Thousands of distractions compete to get your attention and prevent you from thinking about your life. Stoicism can help you move in the right direction because it teaches a moderate lifestyle.

It shows us what is worth pursuing, such as tranquillity, and what is not, like outdoor pleasure. As such, it is a way to simplify our lives immensely.

There are two central themes in stoicism, values that all Stoics strive to integrate as much as possible into their lives. These two goals are virtue and tranquillity.

For example, I am committed to the values of goodness, honesty, righteousness, dignity, integrity, loyalty, decency, and merit. I do what I can to apply these values in what I say and do.

If you can see that your actions can benefit you and those around you, you should take that into account. Living a virtuous life could be about making your loved ones happy, sharing your knowledge to help people live better.

Seneca explains how to pursue tranquillity better. Use your reasoning ability to drive away from anything that excites or frightens you. If you can do that, there will be uninterrupted tranquility and lasting freedom.

A quiet person shows great self-control and will not let his emotions dominate his intellect, for example, by staying calm in a traffic jam, because he knows that getting angry with traffic or pestering against delays of public transport is useless.

Enjoy What You Already Have Using Negative Viewing

"The easiest way to earn happiness is to want the things you already have." — William Irvine

One of the worst vicious circles we face, especially in the Western world, is the trap of consumerism.

According to this theory, when a person earns more money, expectations and desires increase in tandem, resulting in no permanent gain in happiness.

When you were a student, you could enjoy a pasta dish and a glass of water, but later on, your appetite might be satisfied with an expensive risotto and wine or frequent outings to restaurants.

A quiet and virtuous person knows that he must get out of this cycle, and the Stoics do so by learning to want the things they already have and to appreciate things in their lives. The more you like what you have, compared to what you want, the happier you will be.

The Exercise of Negative Visualization

Take the time to imagine that you have lost the things you enjoy. That your wife has left you that your car has been stolen, that you have lost your job. This will allow you to value your wife, your car, and your work more than you would otherwise.

Several advantages:

- We are learning to take steps to avoid this loss
- We reduce the emotional impact of loss if this happens
- We develop greater gratitude for what we have

This will make you feel bad for a moment because the thought of loss is painful, but at the same time, it will give you a wave of instant appreciation and show you how lucky you are always to have them in your life. This will encourage you to appreciate better and treat your loved ones.

Minimize Any Negative Emotion

In old age, however, waking up every morning can be a cause for celebration.

If that were the case for you, a Stoic would say that you should learn to cherish your life. An octogenarian who is aware of the value of his life and time could derive more joy from life than their grandchildren who take any aspect of their lives for granted.

When people experience personal disasters, it is only natural to feel grief. After this period of reflexive grief, however, a Stoic will try to dispel all that is left of his misery by trying to reason with him out of existence.

He will invoke the kind of arguments Seneca used in his consolations: "Is this what the dying person would want me to do? Of course not, she would like me to be happy. The best way to honor one's memory is to cry and continue to live.

Voluntary Discomfort to Better Appreciate Its Comfort

A more advanced variant is to imagine the loss of things that make our lives enjoyable and to choose to occasionally abstain from certain pleasures, as this will help you control your desires.

What's the point? First, you harden in case you were facing a harrowing situation. Second, you might want to enjoy your comfort best when you return, since you no longer take it for granted.

You can start using this tactic little by little. For example, you can walk barefoot in the snow, take your bike instead of your car, become thirsty or hungry, even if water and food are within your reach. In this way, you will increase the pleasure of regaining comfort.

If you experience minor discomfort periodically, you will feel more comfortable coping with significant pain. So, you won't be afraid of such misery in the future.

Such abstinence can be very beneficial, as it promotes strong will and personal freedom. By feeling unsuited, you train yourself to be brave and vaccinate yourself against future discomfort. You know you can handle all the obstacles that life presents to you.

Voluntarily Accept What Is Outside Your Control Zone

The biggest step towards greater tranquility that you can take is to change your attitude towards things you can't control.

Separate that you can control what is beyond your influence. You will then abandon the pursuit of uncontrollable things, and you will focus on finding happiness through what is your power.

Anger is an emotional trap. Often, we react angrily not because people have not helped us, but because they have not allowed us enough.

A simple exercise to dispel anger is to relax your face, soften your voice, and slow down your walk to regain some control.

Internalize Goals to Do Your Best

For example, you want to get good grades or win when you compete, but other people also have a say. So instead of thinking about winning, focus on doing your best to maximize your chances of success.

Even if your efforts are ineffective, you can rest knowing that you have accomplished your goal: you have done what you can do.

Not only will you get better results, but you won't feel crushed if you don't reach your goal — because it wasn't up to you to achieve it.

Knowing this, it is better to avoid seeking the approval of others and to practice indifference to their opinion. To strive for the admiration of others is to give them power over us because we are forced to do things that will hold us in their favor.

Another advantage of being Stoic is that decision-making becomes easier. All you have to do is determine whether a decision helps or hinders your peace of mind, and whether or not it enables you to achieve the goals you have set for yourself.

This simple step decreases the chances of taking a wrong turn in your life and doing something you might regret later.

Hence the value of being self-disciplined to be able to determine your life according to your will and not according to what others expect of you.

How to Be Happy

For many, improving the way we work mentally has become a goal that has become part of the plan. Some tips and tools can help us. In this article, we propose several stoic strategies to be happier.

Although centuries have passed, this current, whose origin dates back to Ancient Greece, continues to be present. An obvious example is a mindfulness. Today they present this therapy to us as if it were a modern invention, but it appeared in Asian cultures already several decades ago. The same applies to the following stoic strategies to be happier.

Stoic Strategies to Be Happier

To implement one of these stoic strategies to be happier, one will have to join a philosophical current that boasts great thinkers. Figures such as Cicero, Seneca, or Marcus Aurelius stand out.

We focused on the theories of the Spanish coach Alberto Blisquez to introduce you to these strategies that once used stoics to seek happiness. Take notes.

There Are No Obstacles, Only Paths

The first strategy, which, at first analysis, may seem complicated, is straightforward. When you encounter an obstacle, turn it into an opportunity to learn, progress, become stronger, and use it as a basis for continued growth.

So, if something happens that you consider an obstacle, avoid the spiral of toxic thoughts. That is, try not to lose control of your inner world. You may not be able to govern what goes on outside, but what happens inside you does.

Recovering Balance as A Challenge

According to experts, this was a strategy widely used by Marcus Aurelius. What does it consist of? Whenever a situation threatens or breaks our balance, one of our most immediate goals will be to protect it or recover it.

How to regain balance? Simple, taking it as a challenge. In this way, our brains exploit the competitive disposition that we have towards ourselves to achieve a goal. Once reached, the reward mechanisms will be activated, so we will probably search for it unconsciously in the future to replicate the feeling of strengthening and well-being

Practicing Stoicism Everyday
Have A Plan (Own)

Seneca said that a life without a design behind it is erratic, because to which you have something deliberate, then the principles take over.

Those without plans are more likely to feel stress and get overwhelmed by situations. Probably because of the uncertainty or lack of control we may have.

If first, our parents wanted to have everything settled with a house, a car, and a family at 30, today, what is sold mostly seems to be spontaneity. Something that may be fine during a few weeks of mental rest, but that after a while, one realizes that one cannot achieve goals in life without organization.

But is the first example synonymous with "having a plan" to be the case?

I don't think so. Maybe the people in question ended up with a job they hated. Perhaps they didn't want the car or even kids. But they ended all this because that's what society was asking for.

By March 28, the idea of stoic philosophy was how having a plan can save me from ending screaming with a conversation that began as a debate. Or how my sports team lost because I didn't have in my head what I had to do.

To which I add: to have my plan and not that of others.

What My Need Is to Impress Others

Today's idea is quite straightforward and leaves no room for doubt: is there anything sadder than how far we are willing to go to impress someone?

And the irony of life is that the people we're trying to get attention to aren't that cool.

I guess we need to be accepted somehow, but why do we usually want to impress the wrong people?

Just yesterday, I saw The Choir Boys. The children's director is passionate about music and loves what he does. However, Pepinot counts as his adoptive father never tried to be famous.

He did what he did because it was his nature.

Like heroes almost.

Then I thought we could try to impress by buying a 12,000-euro sweatshirt, or going to Africa to volunteer to hang it on Instagram.

Within these two ways of wanting to get the approval of others, at least in the second, the world changes for the better.

The Reason I Give You

Good Friday, and I guess I couldn't go any better to think about the reason for things, and because something like this is still being celebrated, but I guess we need a vacation all the time.

Today the book of stoic philosophy speaks as in the past. Many times, we have been carried away by deliberate impulses and actions without going through our subconscious mind. Doing things by the hand of forces, we've let them control us.

I think although it is essential to let a few seconds pass before doing any subconscious action, so that reason (and consciousness) take place, I believe that after all, we are animals but also humans.

We are different, and I know people who are unable to resist certain impulses that tend to be, unfortunately, angry.

I'm not quite sure if this can be trained, but I like to think that reason is something I've been working on for a long time, and I try to catch all the problems calmly and calmly.

That everything I do has to be dominated by reason? I agree with 90%. We should always take at least a couple of seconds to think about what we are going to do. Still, if I see a puppy being run over or a person drowning, in situations of stress and maximum intensity, I do not think that consciousness can take the reins of subconsciousness, which would help (or at least do something) in situations like these.

Hypocrisy Pays Expensive

In today's daily stoic philosophy, the idea is clear. A mind without knowledge or discipline will be manipulated by external factors easily. He'll want to go everywhere at once without understanding anything.

An investor without discipline or knowledge only plays. A child without discipline is just a spoiled brat.

I know several people who have not had an education or involuntary (school), or volunteer (read or learn). Aware of this, these people consume mass media and focus on spitting facts as if they were their ideas.

On the other hand, others contrast sources, constantly read the topics that interest them, and come to conclusions based on their experiences and knowledge.

Although everyone has the right to have an opinion, I'm not quite sure if two ideas are worth the same.

You have no idea or information about what you're talking about, but let go of the first thing that goes through your head. The other is based on proven facts, information, knowledge, and experience.

I would put my life and direction in the hands of the second opinion. Still, luckily, I have enough power to regulate my mind, consider both people and all information, and generate my way of seeing things.

What Color Is My Mind?

In today's stoic philosophy, what is conveyed by Marcus Aurelius's phrase is that our minds will take the form of constant thoughts.

If I think of negative things always, almost like snowballs, I will end up feeling wrong more often and more dramatically.

Ryan says the same goes for fitness. If I sit for 10 hours a day in front of a computer, my body will end up with a different shape than you spend 10 hours in the field.

The conclusion that I can draw in addition to the typical "I agree" is the fact that perhaps. However, on today's page, they massacre pessimism a little. It would also not be a good idea to try to think positively always.

What preaches stoic philosophy and what I think could be implemented here is precisely neutrality because it is critical thinking and objectivity.

I think it's much more useful to the checklist when I'm in front of a situation:

- How it makes me feel
- Is it my fault?
- Can I change it now or in the future?

Like this. Taken off the sideburn. But you understand the idea. If I train my mind in this way, my thoughts will no longer be negative or positive and will (in my opinion) be more critical.

It is up to us, then, the "form" our minds take.

Boredom Leads to Drama

Every day we are exposed to hundreds of news containing drama or some kind of information that "stains" our principles.

Similarly, it is also more challenging to do the right thing, being surrounded by people with principles that do not come close to my morals.

The idea of this stoic philosophy is powerful, and it's something I've started to ponder since I read Walden de Thoreau's book. All the news that doesn't feed the mind is a drama that only serves to inflate this drama further.

And from my humble, I think it's the fault of boredom, to have nothing else to do. A person with projects won't have time to surround himself with the pink press. You'll want to learn more about what you're working on or grow as a person.

Someone without any ambition will be swept away by the easiest and most irrelevant information that goes through his face.

Stop and Think for Two Seconds

Inside all of us, there's a little "civil war." Our plans and desires are contradicted on many occasions, and then we do not understand how we may not have succeeded.

Stopping for a second and thinking, "OK, what do I want to achieve with this?" could save me a lot of headaches and wasting time.

I can relate him to complaining without doing anything about it. The other day my sister was crying over a hypothetical case that had never happened.

We divide our thoughts and what's worse is that we get used to clinging to the negative parts. Maybe because they cause more drama, and our subconscious needs a little pepper to take purpose.

Here's yesterday's thought. And with this, I realize that many of the ideas of stoic philosophy so far make me think that many of the problems that we have as humans could be mitigated if we stopped for a second before acting.

If we ironically used the reason, we've been able to develop for thousands of years and realize that the ego has taken a privileged position in our lives without it being deserved.

But this is for another day.

Reason Has to Reign Over Fortune

I love the message of humility today. Marcus Aurelius ended up being, without eating or drinking it, emperor. The richest and most influential man in the world at the time, and still wrote messages in his book "Meditations" that reminded him of keeping his feet on Earth.

Staying good, simple, pure, healthy, a friend of justice, affective, and strong in my work, regardless of my successes. Since my online story began, and a few months, I entered sums that I had never imagined would end up in my bank, the reason was one of the first things I wanted to keep.

Fortune is passing. There will be better periods than others, but it's not about not changing for what others will say, but about staying true to my values. If these changes according to the time of life I am going through, it will be that my morals should not be ingrained and, therefore, not work.

From my point of view, if I have worked on myself as a person, I am clear about the justice and values to which I cling.

Stoic philosophy refers to this. One of Marcus Aurelius's quotes leave no room for doubt.

Impassive and motionless as the rock, to which the angry waves of the ocean frequently strike. Until they back off.

They Have to Prove Who They Are. Not My Mind

Our brain has an incredible ability to make decisions in a second based on years of knowledge on a particular topic.

Unfortunately, it's just as quick to judge people we don't know or to reinforce stereotypes. In today's stoic philosophy, it's time to re-examine because to let the subconscious take power. The importance of styling to ask questions such as, "What do I know about this person?" or "why do you feel this feeling so strong suddenly?" help to use reason at times when prejudices and stereotypes, controlled by the subconscious, take over.

Maybe in the past, I was overweight and hated myself as a person, and my great mind to see a fat man immediately jumps to look at him with bad eyes.

I must "re-teach" and use reason not to jump into the wrong conclusions. You can relate to today's press: I can see a news story, but if it's shocking, it would be my turn to check it out first.

It would be the responsibility of the medium, but in today's world, speed matters more than the sources for this, before jumping to hate for a headline, better to stop to think and check if it is necessary.

Deal with Problems as A Stoic
Practicing Hard Times

"Even in quiet times, the soul prepares for difficult times, and when everything goes well, it strengthens against the blows of fate. The soldier does the drills in peacetime, builds trenches when there are no enemies and undergoes unnecessary fatigues to be able to support the necessary ones"

Seneca, Nero's counselor, before he forced him to commit suicide, suggested training to poverty one day a month. Little food, ruined clothes, away from the comforts

So, ask yourself: Is this what I'm afraid of? Am I a slave to these comforts? Is it so tragic if I were left without it?

This exercise in shrinkage is not a metaphor, but something to live and feel on your skin. Comfort is one of the worst types of slavery because you live in constant fear that someone or something will take you away. If you practice the path of narrowness, this fear is dispelled.

There's a saying that says. Money is a great servant and a bad master. It applies to money, but also many other things. The exercise below serves precisely this: breaking the chains of slavery from a bad master and appreciating what we have

Exercise

Get a pen and paper mark 5 things you usually do but could avoid without your life-changing (I don't know: use dishwashers when you can wash dishes by hand, iron your clothes instead of you, take the car to make 200 meters, prepare food instead of taking pre-packaged ones)

Mark 5 things that you could do in another way but that are heavy/ a despondency (pretending not to have the car, living with 50% of the money you usually use, don't use the ethtricity for a day, do the smaller portions of 25%, get off a bus stop first and walk a few miles to get home). Write your expectations of when the fulfillment of an immediate need fails.

From the first list, you mark one thing and get into the habit of doing it differently / don't make it your own, at least until you become indifferent, which of the two ways you use.

From the second list marks something, you can do a fly the month to train the muscle of the narrowness. Practice it at least six months - Reread your expectations in step 3. How do you feel after six months of feeling good?

Tips to Insert into Our Routines
Waking Up Caught

We have already talked about it several times on the blog and also a few lines above. Do not stay in bed to glorify unnecessarily, not every day, at least. Your dreams don't come true on their own, but they need you.

"Those days, you struggle to get up, keep this in mind – I'm waking up to do the job of being human. So why am I disturbed by this thing, for which I was created, the something for which I was put into this world? Or I was made to stay under the covers all the time and stay warm. She's so good. But were you made just to be pampered or to grow up?

Exercise

get into the habit of going to bed "soon" (whatever it means for you) and at the same time. Bed at the same time for six days in a row and wake up at the same time. On day 7, you set the alarm before 45 minutes. There are many but not so many to destroy you (if you always went to bed early) – use them to write in your diary what you will do with the time gained the next day woke up only 10 minutes earlier than usual. Continue for a week. On the seventh day, you wake up 45 minutes compared to the standard (i.e., 55 minutes compared to the one set in step 2) keep repeating from 2 to 6 until you've found enough time in your morning habits.

They had noticed the power of habits 2000 years ago and have also written a lot about it. Even on cocoa, we got busy (with the review of the book "The Dictatorship of Habits" and with various articles on installing habits).

If you don't want to be irascible, don't feed the habit. First, keep calm and count the days when you didn't get irritated. I got angry every day, then one yes and one no, then one every three or four If you continue for 30 days. Thank goodness! At first, the habit is weakened and then obliterated. When you can tell yourself, "I have not lost my patience today, and not even yesterday, and so I will continue for months, to remain impassive to provocations, you will know that you are more forceful. " Epitetto, Speeches.

We talked a lot about it here about cocoa, and every 2 February (the famous day of the marmot), I pull out a series of articles about it.

Am I Getting Closer or Away from My Goal?

take your calendar, notebook, or whatever you want, and at the end of the day, ask yourself:

- What habit did I get out of the way today?
- Have I improved since yesterday?
- Did I act righteously?
- How can I improve?

Stoicism to Deal with Pain

Difficulties are an integral part of everyone's life. Regardless of ethnicity, class, or gender, all human beings suffer: it is something inevitable.

But how can we deal with suffering from lawlessness, that is, by exercising virtue, remaining impassive and balanced? How can you turn suffering in your favor, to better understand yourself? The stoicism of the Roman philosopher and statesman Lucius Anneo Seneca can provide some food for thought.

Born at the beginning of the first century, Seneca was attracted from an early age by rhetoric, literature, and stoic philosophy. Stoicism is a philosophical one that emphasizes virtuous behavior, control of emotions, and rational use of the mind.

Seneca's stoicism is based on the thought that destructive emotions such as pain and anger should be weakened until they are removed; wealth should go hand in hand with virtue; friendship and kindness are essential, and difficulties should be positively accepted, rather than avoided.

Seneca has tried to live precisely following these stoic principles whenever he has encountered difficulties.

Difficulties offer an opportunity to apply virtue and self-control. Seneca says: "Every night we should ask ourselves: what difficulty have I been able to master today? What passions did I have opposed? What temptations have I resisted? What virtues have I acquired? Our vices will disappear if they are weakened every day."

Seneca tried every day to abandon vices, to resist temptations, to embody virtue, and, in a nutshell, to become a better person.

In his early career, the well-known Latin author was elected as a public official and Roman senator. His success in the Senate due to his oratory skills made Emperor Caligula jealous, who ordered Seneca to commit suicide.

Later, Caligula withdrew his order, convinced that Seneca, already seriously ill, would soon die of natural causes.

Within four years, around 41 A.D., Claudius became the new emperor, and Seneca was still alive. But Claudio's third wife, Messalina, accused Seneca of adultery of political purposes, so the philosopher was sentenced to exile in Corsica.

In Rome, Seneca was appointed teacher of Agrippina's son, Nero. At first, Nero was strongly influenced by his master Seneca. The first five years of his domination of Rome were a success thanks to the stoic reminiscences of Seneca's teaching.

Later, Nero moved further and further away from his master. In 59 A.D., the emperor ordered that his mother be executed, and Seneca was forced to write a letter justifying his execution in the Senate. Lucius Anneo Seneca was also charged with other crimes, but he always abided by his stoic principles.

Exhausted, Seneca twice attempted to withdraw from his position, but Nero rejected his request both times. At this point, the well-known Roman philosopher began to move away from the Senate and lead a quiet and study life.

Nero, however, accused Seneca of being involved in Pisone's Conspiracy, a conspiracy to assassinate the emperor. He was sentenced to death by suicide, but historians doubt Seneca's involvement in that conspiracy.

The wise Seneca calmly accepted this sentence and followed the Roman tradition by receiving the order to commit suicide. It caused a cut, but since it was bleeding slowly, it also took poison and was placed in a hot bath to speed up the process.

The 19th-century Spanish painter Manuel Donguez Sanchez depicts the moment of Seneca's death in his painting The Suicide of Seneca. Senchez shows lifeless Seneca, in the bathtub, with other figures surrounding it.

The composition follows the pattern of the classic horizontal frieze in the wall on the back. A figure leans against the column on the right of the painting and looks at Seneca's lifeless body, preventing the observer's eyes from moving from the plane of the image.

Thus, the author communicates that Seneca is the central figure of his painting. Another model, closer to the tub and punching in the chest, is also looking at Seneca. He seems to beg not to look away so that one can contemplate Seneca's stoic sacrifice.

Although the figures surrounding the wise philosopher are mourning his death, most of them appear to stand, standing upright and still, like the columns around them. Their poses refer to the practice of stoicism: they stand up and accept the situation of pain and difficulty due to Seneca's death. This is their way of honoring the philosopher's life, instead of mourning his death.

However, there is a limit to the endure of pain, and in fact, one of Seneca's friends' cries lying on the tub.

Seneca's stoicism had a profound influence on the culture of subsequent generations. His thoughts, over the centuries, have also helped to influence the Italian Renaissance and the return of classical content and morality in the French and Spanish art. This painting is just one example of his influence, and he won the award at the National Exhibition of Fine Arts in 1871.

Recovery of Stoic Vision

Seneca had to endure tremendous hardships and suffering: he was exiled by one emperor and sentenced to death by two others. Fellow senators tried to defame him, and he dealt with the disease so many times that his colleagues came to think he was on the verge of death.

Despite everything, what Seneca was interested in was just being a good person, and stoicism was the way he followed to accomplish this.

His stoicism has affected the people next to him, however. He had directed Nero on the right path, but when this helium renounced the stoic principles, he made his emotions and desires to determine his actions. Seneca's death also symbolizes the end of that stoicism that had accompanied Nero to a certain point in his life; stoicism has passed away, Rome has fallen into misfortune, pain, and suffering.

How then can stoicism help the individual to take responsibility for his actions and endure the suffering so as not to let emotions determine his actions, thus causing pain and suffering for himself and others? To answer this question, for example, one might ask, for example, first of all: how often do you allow a bad day to work to affect not only yourself but also your colleagues and family?

It becomes easy to lose your temper and have a negative attitude when things don't go as you would like. Those who are involved in these conflicts are the ones who inevitably feel and experience their negativity, despite all attempts to blame others and, usually, not being able to control their emotions, ends up spreading the negativity due to his bad behavior.

Managing difficulties with temperance and lawfulness simply means accepting the suffering as they come and reflecting on yourself while you are experiencing that suffering. Stoically speaking, it can be useful then to control emotions (including fear), resist temptations, and align with one's understanding of virtue, as Seneca did.

At the very least, when you endure difficulties and deepen your understanding of the meaning of suffering, you can come to understand the sufferings of others better, treating it with compassion instead of unnecessary negativity.

Start from The Worst So You Can Not Be Disappointed

The ancient emperor Roman Marcus Aurelius was one of the famous Stoics, just like Seneca and Cicero. Aurelius wrote a journal to create a dossier intended to help him become a better leader. There could be things like every morning expecting to face idiots for a whole day, which prepared him mentally for trials. Maybe his day wasn't half as bad as he anticipated, and that's a bit of the point of stoicism – starting from the worst, you can't be disappointed.

Moldy Bread Worse in Mind Than in Reality

Stoicism was very much about preparing for the worst, training the psyche for trials. One example is Seneca, who, despite his wealth, sometimes dressed in sacks and ashes and ate paupers. Why? Because he was worried about losing his wealth. By practically exploring what he was afraid of, he was able to ease his concerns. Moldy bread and broken clothes were, in reality, not as bad as in mind.

Self-Control Is Masculine

I'm sure you've heard expressions like "stoic calm." This is since the Stoics are trained continuously to control themselves, not to be dragged by impulses and emotional outbursts. This is close to masculinity. For a while, the female power is the hustle and bustle, wind in the trees and emotional storms, the male energy is calm and stability – self-control is somewhat masculine.

There are questions that men and women at some point in their lives cannot refrain from asking themselves. How to lead your own life? According to what codes of conduct, according to what moral? How to respond to difficulties, how to deal with pain?

In a secularized and relativist era, the tremendous ethical-religious designs seem less and less able to provide useful indications for all. Each of us answers these questions as we can, drawing on different codes of reference, family tradition, or sometimes (re)discovering millennial and distant cultures. Sometimes, simply, these questions are ignored as long as you can.

Among all the philosophies that have traveled this world and many eras, stoicism offers teachings that can still be as simple as powerful to live a good life and, why not, a good death.

Acting Following the Nature of The World in The 21st Century

So, what can stoicism tell us today? Perhaps we do not believe that the universe is entirely rational, maybe we do not think that there is a destiny, we do not feel that we are sparks of God and let alone to contain in us all the existing. Despite this, however, stoicism can still be useful to us.

It is true, perhaps a destiny does not exist, nor is there something like providence. But even if it is true that nothing happens because it has to happen, what happens indeed happens. In other words, whatever the reason, if there is one, you cannot change the fact in itself that things happen. Many of these things lie beyond our control. The only thing we can control, as men are our thoughts, the way we react to the things that happen to us.

"You have power over your mind, not on external events. Do this, and you will find your strength." It was Marcus Aurelius, who, as emperor, perhaps had power over external events that many of us can only dream of. Yet, like all men, he had to face what chance, or in his case, fate, put before him. And like everyone else, he had the goal of feeling good even during a thousand difficulties.

This, after all, means for a stoic to live well: to reach the tranquility of the soul. In other words, atarassia – which is not the absence of passions but, rather, the domination over desires.

The stoics, therefore, distinguish between the spontaneous and involuntary reaction to events and the rational and detached judgment on events. The first is natural, and it rushes into all men. The second is a virtue, and as such, it must be cultivated.

Epictetus tells us: "It is not the facts that baffle human beings, but their judgments around the facts."

292

To observe events with detachment and judge them properly, a tremendous mental presence is needed, which can only be acquired through constant practice. In Buddhism, which is in these aspects very similar to stoicism, such a cognitive company is achieved through "mindfulness" meditation. Stoic philosophers, on the other hand, often had daily rituals.

Marcus Aurelius, for example, prepared to meet horrible people during the day and not to lose his temper for this, repeating these words every morning: "I will meet vain people, ungrateful, violent, fraudulent, envious, unsocial; all this happens to them because of ignorance of good and evil. I, on the other hand, which I understood, having pondered the nature of good, that it is beautiful, and the nature of the evil that it is bad and the nature of those who are wrong that he is my relative, not because he is of the same blood and seed, but because he is, like me, mentally and participating in the divine, and that any of they cannot harm me, because no one can involve me in his turpitude, well, I can neither be angry with him."

Seneca used to remember the brevity of his life (and he writes, not surprisingly, the De Brevitate Vitae). In the Letters to Lucilio, he says to his friend and disciple: "Here is our mistake: we see death before us, and instead much of it is already behind us: past life belongs to death. So, Lucilio dear, do what you write to me: put to good use every minute; you will be less enslaved to the future if you seize the present. Between postponements, life goes away."

From this and similar reflections arises, for example, the exercise of the Praemeditatio Malorum (or negative visualization), that is the practice of imagining that something dear to us, if we also want our own life, is taken away from us, or that something that awaits us goes wrong. Not only should this theoretically help us to be more prepared when unpleasant things happen and to be more ingrained in the present moment, knowing that everything can end at all times, but it is the stoic belief that difficulties should be avoided. It is, in fact, in the problems that the true nature of man is revealed, and it is in the situations that man can grow and advance in self-understanding. It is the task of the stoic to exploit the issues, instead of suffering them. As Marcus Aurelius reminds us in his Meditations, "Our actions can be hindered, but there cannot impede our intentions or our disposition of mind. Because we can change and adapt. Obstruction of action advances action.

What Is on The Road Becomes the Road
Epitteto finally ended his days with three questions addressed to himself. What did I do right? What did I do wrong? What duty have I left aside? Reflecting on the day just passed was useful for him to observe with the detachment given by time his reactions and realize his mistakes. In this way, he could approach the next day with more clarity and awareness.

Well, why would a person remember in the morning that the world is full of horrible people, in the afternoon that he will have to die, and in the evening to reflect on what is wrong all day?

The constant exercise of these practices is aimed at clearing the mind of one's emotions and judging what happens with clarity and rationality and allows us to achieve a state of lucidity and inner peace that is necessary to act in a correct and just way. Just think of how often we say things we don't want to say, we hurt people we don't want to break, and we indulge in habits that we know are harmful to us. All this happens because we are not entirely mastering of ourselves. We let our instinctive emotions guide our actions, and although this is human and normal, led to excess can sometimes have even disastrous consequences. Knowing yourself deeply, being self-masters, and being happy with yourself beyond all external circumstances are the basic requirements to be able to treat others and the world with respect due to them, carry out one's duty and act as a "righteous men." For the Stoics, human nature is essentially altruistic, and we are not in the world for ourselves, but others, and to this awareness must be directed our daily work.

All this can be as true as it is today. Almost at the end, we can briefly list five crucial lessons that stoicism offers us to "live a good life":

We live in the present moment, aware that everything has an end and that, therefore, everything around us is also of extreme value.

Let's act on what we can control, and don't worry about what doesn't matter.

Nothing that happens is good or bad in itself and what makes us suffer is not the events itself, but the interpretation we give to these events. Difficulties help to grow and are not, therefore, to be avoided at any cost.

We are selfless, bearing in mind that we are all part of something greater than ourselves and that we are but a small amount of it.

Exercising one's mind is the only way to live fully since we act rationally only when our instinctive emotions do not drive us.

And in the moments when you are working, studying, talking to someone – whatever you are doing, remember the words of the ever-wise Marco Aurelius: "Concentrate every minute as a Roman – as a man – on doing what is in front of you with precise and genuine seriousness, tenderly, willingly, with justice. And about getting rid of any other distractions. Yes, you can do it – if you do everything as if it's the last thing you'd do on earth, stop wandering and let your emotions take over what your mind tells you, and stop being hypocritical, self-centered, and irritable. If you can do them, there is nothing more than the gods can ask you."

This, in essence, means acting according to nature.

Stoic View on Death

Stoics are not afraid of death. Marc Aurelius tells in "Meditations" that people should not be scared of dying. What for? What is fearful of death will no longer exist in the presence of it.

The brain that stresses out the idea of disappearing will no longer exist when it is dead. So why be afraid of something you'll never know?

Stoics imagine themselves losing a loved one or disappearing. So, the little things in life get back to color. Maybe every meal is your last. Every discussion may be the last.

Some people see this as the best way to be always anxious, but it's more interesting to put yourself in the shoes of a meteorologist who observes a hurricane. He keeps this one, but because the storm is far away, he remains calm.

Visualizing the end of your life more often allows you to live with more infatuation. This will enable us to anchor in ourselves that we are only here for a brief period and that we have every interest in taking advantage of this time that is available to us.

No one knows precisely what to do with the fear of death. No one. We are all afraid because no one knows what it is like to die. Death is terrifying and paralyzing. If at night it does not interfere with sleep, then at least gives nightmares. In the daytime, it forces you to move forward to do something to be proud of. It will surely come to everyone. But when and what will follow? This issue has plagued humanity for thousands of years. And it's a great mystery. The Great Unknown. Great inevitability. And for most people, great fear.

The death has been reflected throughout the documented history, from the Schumers to the Incas, and good philosophical and practical advice has been left on how to overcome this fear. In all the books of stoic philosophers, there is one valuable advice - to lead a good life. Stoics did not like empty words, as it is now fashionable for coaches to "help yourself." To help guide a good life, they developed a whole concept that consists of three disciplines: perception, action, and will. Each is followed by an in-depth analysis and lived experiences. Perception - how we see things and events, story - how we react, and will - how we tolerate. These three disciplines constitute a common approach to life that answers all questions of death.

The Power of Ancient Tradition

"Look at what life takes, calculate how much time we spend on short calculations, how much intrigue, how much fear takes, how much to treat those who need, and how much - the pleasure of those who need, how much time is spent on going to court on their own or other people's affairs, how much on feasting, which is responsibilities. You will see that this whole nightmare - or happiness, from which side to look - does not allow us to translate our spirits."

Paradoxically, what we are so desperately fleeing in life is the truth. We run away from anything that reminds us of reality, in fantasies to live safely and pleasantly, though not useful. But there is a straightforward fact that most of us avoid so skillfully that we do not think about it at all, pretend that it is not at all: the fact of mortality. Man is mortal, and as if he did not want to avoid the end - he will overtake him.

The stoic philosophy in realizing this fact has progressed so far that Socrates described the purpose of studying philosophy as "to learn to die and be dead." Early Buddhist texts used the term maranasati, which translates to "remember death." Sufi was called "people of graves" because they often went to cemeteries to reflect on death. For the modern man, all this seems frightening and strange. Who wants to think about dying of their own free will?

Why, instead of being afraid, do the opposite - accept it? What if thinking about death is the easy key to a fulfilling life? What if that is the key to our freedom, as Michel de Montaigne said: "To practice death is to practice freedom. A man who has learned to die has forgotten to be a slave."

There was a tradition in ancient Rome. When the commander returned from the victorious battle, the inhabitants of Rome greeted him with jubilation, laid a wreath on his head, in every way extolled flattering words. The feast could last for several days. The commander was considered almost a god in the flesh. And at the same time, according to the rules, one slave had to continually follow him and, from time to time, whisper in his ear!

"Look back. Remember, you're mortal. Remember, you must die!"

The slave reminded the victor at the height of his fame that this adoration would soon end, glory would end, and eventually, life would end. All are mortal - nothing lasts forever.

Thinking about your death is depressing only if you miss its essence. Death is a tool that helps to create priorities in life and gain meaning. It is a tool that has been used by hundreds of generations to understand what to do in life, when and most importantly, why. For example, treat time as a gift, and do not spend it on trifles and fuss. Death does not make life meaningless but rather purposeful and meaningful.

Fortunately, we don't need to die to understand this physically. A simple reminder can bring us closer to life, which we desperately want to prolong. No matter who you are or how many things still have to be done, and the car can crash into you at an intersection. That's it. It could be over today, tomorrow, or sometime soon.

In death, there is only one eternal truth on which one can rely on whether you are rich or not, successful or not, religious, philosophical, or scholar - it does not matter - death awaits everyone. From the beginning of time to the end, death is one that unites all people. Kings, peasants, smart, stupid - all die or die. People try not to think about it. Unfortunately, the safer the world becomes, the more willing we are to believe that we will live forever, and everything will be as we want. Stoics would say that death is what gives life meaning - it is the inevitable end that helps us make the most of the time we have.

Three Disciplines of Stoics Philosophy That Aim to Realize Death
Perception

Perception is how we think about what we see. Our thoughts. Thoughts form actions because perception always leads to activity (and the decision to do nothing is also an action). Perception is generally one of the main ideas on which the theory of cognition in stoicism is based. Marcus Aurelius, Epictetus, Seneca, Caton, and other fathers of stoicism wrote about it.

Only a person has the cognitive ability to use perception to assess an event as either "good" or "evil." At the same time, it is based solely on the interpretation imposed by the initial impression. Stoics called it "the ability of the mind" or "the ability to choose." At the same time, they argued that there is neither good nor evil - it is merely a product of personal judgment.

Stoics have spent a considerable amount of time and effort on reflection and trying to master their perception because perception forms behavior. If our perception is clouded, colored by ephemerality, nonsense, or if it has simply been subjected to pressure, fused with our circumstances and surroundings, things such as fear, anxiety, uncertainty, and a sense of unhappiness have complete control over life. This perception process can be presented as a habit. Habits are formed from listening, practicing, repeating the same thing from day today. In many ways, the same thing happens with perceptions rooted in repetitive thoughts.

"People are tormented not by things, but by ideas about them."

Thus, perception can be a powerful source of strength and determination or a powerful source of weakness and horror. It's the truth that should be comforting. We can control our thoughts. We have to make a choice. Thoughts, interpretations, impressions that you are now carrying can be turned upside down with attention and resilience. Then they will serve you, not feed the fear of death.

The Epictetus said of this through life situations: "Never say you lost something, but say you gave it away. Is your son dead? He was given back. Is your wife dead? It was given back. Have you been robbed of a piece of land?

Consequently, and he was given back. However, the one who takes away is dishonest. But what do you care whose hands the giver claimed back? And for how long he will give you this to use, take care of it as guests take care of the hotel."

Action

Perception is what we think about death. Action is what we do base on our thoughts. How do we feel about fear? Do we allow him to torture us? Do we push out of ideas with all our might and try to avoid it? Remember that the opposite of "fear" is "to conquer fear." Win! So there has to be a battle, and a war is an action.

If you treat death passively, the fear becomes excruciating, and its shadow is darker. Death can polarize life and paralyze. We don't want to think about it. We don't want to talk about her. We tend to avoid even thinking that we will die one day. Faced with the death of loved ones, we strive as quickly as possible to "get back in line" and do not let in thoughts because they paralyze. But this one is precisely what we have to do - let death in, they say stoics! We do not allow thoughts of death to live their lives, to come and go when they are comfortable. We do not let reviews be a dream of inattention, but we always look at them from top to bottom, treat them as a wound, and remember that this is our future. We use death to gain strength, not to be paralyzed. Then we can live accordingly.

Memento Mori is a reminder that time is fleeting, and we have only the present moment at our disposal. The memory of death is a jolt of happiness when you realize that you can let go of all the trivial and questionable. Marcus Aurelius said: "Focus on living what you can live (which means the present), then you can spend the rest of your time in peace. And in kindness. And in a world with a spirit within you." This is what we all want to get - meaningful living, freedom from the stresses and anxieties that are too often so quickly let in. Take action. Start your battle. Think of death.

Will

The third discipline, to which stoics have devoted a considerable amount of time, is the will. Stoics divided everything into two categories: internal and external. The inner is simply what we control, things like perception and action. External factors are the exact opposite. The outside is something we have no power over. Will determines our attitude to what is beyond our control, to what is happening to us under the influence of external forces.

We are powerless in the face of external events, except in how we will react to them. Will has power - it can grow indifference to what is beyond our control correctly. Cicero also said that it was foolish to be afraid of death. Even regardless of religious views or scientific atheism, this ancient power of stoic philosophy is sobering and soothing:

"A man who has not realized in his long life that there is nothing to be afraid of is a miserable person. For death either destroys the human soul, in which case it is insignificant or takes the soul to where it can live forever, which makes it desirable. There is no third option."

The last thoughts of this article I want to give to Marcus Aurelius, who carefully described how to think about life and death: "You lived as a citizen in a big city. Five years or a hundred, what difference does it make? And being banished from it is not a tyrant or a dishonest judge, but the nature that first invited you to enter the city - why is it so awful? As the impresario lowering the curtain in front of the actor: "But I only played three acts!" Then it will be a drama in three acts, the duration of which is determined by the force that directed your creation and now requires your disintegration. And it's not for you to decide. So leave with grace, the same class that has been shown to you."

Stoicism is primarily focused on teaching how to deal with emotions. But it is essential to understand that stoics do not encourage us to suppress our feelings or ignore grief and fear. It would be disconcerting if we never felt grief. In stoicism, suffering is seen as one of the prominent examples of the universal human urge to care for others. In short, our emotional responses to death are part of what makes us human.

What Is The Essence Of Stoicism's Attitude To Death?

The basic message of stoicism philosophy about death is that death is not something to be afraid of. Any game is meaningless without completion. Books and movies will be boring without denouement. Sport is enjoyable because there are an end and a winner. We're running around with the clock. Stoics advise every day to ask me what I did today and whether I have lived the day as I see fit? If not, I live in a fantasy world where I don't die and have an infinite amount of time. It's a stupid position.

Death scares us by not knowing anything about it. What happens after we die? Is there an afterlife, or will we simply disappear into oblivion? Countless philosophers have focused on this issue, but no one will ever be able to say what is going on for sure. But in fact, it does not matter what happens there - we have little choice. With a 100% guarantee, our lives are limited to the disappearance. Our desires don't matter. After all, whatever happens after death is beyond our control and our control.

Reaping the Benefits of Stoicism

Some of the great leaders in history were stoic: Cicero, Epictetus, Seneca, Marcus Aurelius. It's no surprise considering the emphasis of stoicism on self-control. Success and leadership come out of reflection in the mirror. The key is not to react or respond to external circumstances. The Stoics taught us that while we cannot control what happens to us in life, we can control our perception. That makes all the difference.

To respond, you need to be aware and be in control so as not to let yourself be dominated by emotions. We can choose to perceive events productively or destructively. The stoics decided to see the glass half full. They saw the bright side in every single thing. These seven lessons from stoicism will undoubtedly bring a positive change to your life.

1. Meditate on Thought
"If you are distressed by something external, the pain is not due to the thing itself, but to your estimation of it, and you have the power to avoid it at any time," Marcus Aurelius

Only an attentive mind can filter and reverse evil thoughts. Stoicism taught the clear distinction between your thoughts and behaviors. It's like that adage, think before you act. The meaningless person acts without thinking.

The next time you face someone in a frustrating conversation or if your schedule is out of control, stop for a moment to process what happened, then ask yourself: what's the best way to respond? The simple act provokes self-reflection. You need to put an end to hostile and impulsive responses.

2. New Day, New Beginning
"Start living and count every day as a new life."

Stoics saw every day as a new opportunity. Remember, you only need one event, one conversation, to change the trajectory of your life completely. A bad day doesn't mean it must be a bad week. If you don't deliver a job on time, it can cause you to be rejected in certain positions. When they find cancer, it is necessary to remove it before it spreads throughout the body. Put an end to the domino effect before your little mistakes turn into big crises.

3. Proposed Action
A stoic wakes up and knows what he wants to do in his day. His goals and destiny are clear. If you start your day writing down your goals, you'll create a previous psychological commitment that will increase the likelihood of them being met. Any action must be connected to the target. Otherwise, you can browse all day and end where you started.

4. There Is A Season for Everything
"The best is not created out of nowhere, as well as a bunch of grapes or a fig. If you tell me you want a fig, I'll tell you have to give him time. Let it bloom first, bear fruit and then mature".

Ambitious people live ten years into the future. Patience is not our virtue. Stoicism emphasized living according to our internal flow and the external flow of life. Patience is not an enemy of productivity. Trying to find shortcuts frequently will make you move in circles. Quality is sacrificed if products are developed quickly. Emotion causes us not to know how to do the necessary procedures.

5. You Are Already There
"True happiness is to enjoy the present without anxiously relying on the future, not to have fun, whether with hopes or fears, but to rest satisfied with what we have, which is enough," Seneca

We all believe that achievement and success will lead us to happiness, but surprisingly the equation may be different. Joy brings us success and accomplishments. Modern science has discovered what stoics knew for centuries.

6. Authenticity
"If I were a nightingale, I would like to play the role of a nightingale; if I were a swan, the swan part.

It is imperative to have mentors and models to admire. But emulation can become imitation, and all you're going to produce is copies. Stoicism emphasized the harmony between acceptance and change, the perfect balance of destiny and free will. Find out what your talents are and explain them. We always look for external sources to be inspired when the answer is more profound.

7. Accept Death
It's not something we like to talk about, but death is the only thing in our lives. Confronting that is liberating. You realize it or not, and death anxiety is the root of our fears. Our fighting/flight

mechanism serves to preserve life, escape death. But it is activated long before death enters the painting, paralyzing us not to leave our comfort zone to pursue our passions and creations.

Stoics looked death in the eye and accepted it as a natural part of life. Steve Jobs said very well: "Remembering that you're going to die the best way I know to avoid the trap of thinking you have something to lose. You're already naked. There's no reason not to follow your heart."

Conclusion

In theory, Stoicism is a philosophical system that considers reason as a remedy for disorders in life. It is thanks to this reason, specific to the human species, that Man can achieve happiness (defined as ataraxia), whatever the circumstances of his life. Slave or teacher, working-class or wealthy, the Stoic is master of his representations, that is, of his vision of things. See things as they are and are aware of their temporality. He dedicates himself only with reason to his passions.

Does applying Stoic principles allow for a better life? According to statistics collected by the Stoic Week 2013 team, among the 2,400 participants, 56% of them say they have gotten wiser and better. Among these same 2,400 people, 14% saw an increase in their life satisfaction, 9% an increase in positive emotions (joy or optimism), and 11% a decrease in negative emotions. The results may seem weak, but they are significant in such a short period. You don't get stoic in a week. It takes several years to come close to the ideal of wisdom supported by this philosophy. But the fact is, in seven days, we get results with some people. In several months or several years, the positive effects will probably be more consistent.

Be that as it may, the incredibly modern works of Seneca, Epicteto or Marco-Aurelio constitute a perfect continuation of this article for the most interested.

Goes very well to use stoicism to learn how to manage anger and disappointment, to increase resilience, or as a technique to introduce healthier habits. Roberson and Pigliucci do this. What convinces less, however, is the branding of stoicism and the storage of its brand for exclusive use. Also, because, as we have seen, the attribution of labels does not work, since, in the last twenty-three centuries, stoicism has been more or less recovered continuously, but it has done so by changing skin and re-presenting under a false name.

The discourse of the philosophers' saints is similar. Seen in a more authentic light, the stoics themselves were imperfect men, obliged as much as anyone to approach, within their limits, the relative perfection of their teaching.

But above all, it is the spirit with which to look at the advice of the stoic that needs to change. We have said this: stoicism is one of the great ethical traditions of universal history, which has crossed Western thought by grafting into other very fruitful strands of thought.

As Epictetus put it, if you expect the universe to deliver what you want, you will be disappointed, but if you surround what the universe provides, life becomes much softer. Again, this is easier said than done, but more and more people are taking note of this Stoic Council and working hard to incorporate it into their daily lives

NLP Secrets

What Is NLP

Many times, in our lives, we happen to want to say one thing, and another comes out of our mouths. Alternatively, we happen to think about ourselves something contrary to what we present to others and yet to collect from them as a treatment, what we truly believe in ourselves. What's going on?

Are we the curious, the deficit, the troubled? I guess not all of us have imprinted in our unconscious mind specific "programs" that define the way we perceive reality, that guide our thinking, emotions, action, and behaviors in our daily lives, our reaction to external stimuli, and which almost pre-define our emotional, logical and practical response to everything. In other words, we are perfect beings who perform perfectly the programs that others have uploaded to our "hard drive." Although we prefer to consider ourselves a carrier of free will, rather than an instrument of mechanical behavior, many of our daily reactions - especially negative ones - have been formed years ago, in our childhood, i.e., from 0 years to 6, from previous similar experiences we have experienced in our family environment—either the direct or the broader. The reactions we chose to have at the time created an impression within us and continue to reproduce in a change in every new situation reminiscent of the old, riveting us. And while we have many options, we don't take advantage of them, since our behavior has been locked in a certain way of reacting. Any pathological, psychological behavior can be reduced to such mechanisms, resulting in disparaging situations and dead ends and, of course, become practically ineffective.

So, one rightly wonders, are we doomed to carry out for life the unconscious education we received in our childhood? A kind of robot that simply tries, without success, to avoid unpleasant experiences by continually reproducing destructive behaviors? No, of course not. There are various means (one of them, and the NLP) by which one can change the original programming and find his true identity, his values, his "wants."

The goal of NLP, both in its therapeutic and other applications, is to quickly change the way we understand and act, to change the approach of life and behaviors, through the disappearance of these unconscious programs and their replacement with the programs that we wish to define our lives.

Because ultimately, what differentiates a "successful" from an "unsuccessful" in any field of man is his ability to live his life within the framework that he determines based on his personal needs and balances and to bring the result that satisfies him and not his environment. The disappearance of our restrictive beliefs brings us back to a state of freedom, flowing, effortless and in-depth communication, and sincere interest in others, free from the heavy shackles of chronic compulsive behavior.

How Can It Help?

What is NLP, and how can this help me?

NLP is a potent "tool" used to enhance personal growth and pushed towards personal transformation. The unconscious mind is a powerful part of yourself "located where your thoughts, your behaviors, your memories, your habits are. The whole model of your world lives off this magical and mystical place! He has received in every piece of information and detail everything you've ever seen, done, heard, decided, hesitated, tried. Isn't that amazing?

NLP therapy is beneficial because, in addition to discussing a topic and other techniques can be used to help you change your behavior and thinking. This allows you to free yourself from the negative memories, thoughts, or feelings that hold you back from making progress.

There are many names for the techniques used in the NLP process; however, most of the time, it is the therapist/coach who will be creative in the way that will help you redefine the damaging patterns of thought and behaviors of the past and give you a way to create new ones.

A little analysis of what the words mean:

Nerve: Each of us has created our unique system of spiritual "filtering" to process the massive amount of information absorbed through our senses. All the information we receive daily through our senses is filtered through our "personal sieve" (beliefs, values, etc.). Therefore, our perception of what we see, hear, taste, or smell turns into a unique understanding and experience of the world around us. It looks a bit like when you make a cake: you pour all the ingredients into a bowl, but how you mix them - the ingredients you put in it - and the temperature you bake it will affect it in taste, appearance, and smell. No cake is the same as the other. There's always a personal footprint.

Linguistic: You can then put your personal and unique interpretation of the information you received from the world around you.

Notice when someone describes a situation to you. The language he uses can be very different from the way you would describe the same problem. We've deleted, spoiled and exaggerated when we talk most of the time without realizing it! We delete, distort, exaggerate most of the time without even realizing it.

Programming: Your behaviors, habits, and mentalities have been shaped according to the information you receive throughout your life and the influence of those around you.

Your brain creates "neural pathways" when you do something repeatedly, such as a new way of functioning your body, eating habits, and even the way you say something.

These neural impulses can either be to your advantage or detrimental, resulting in a negative effect on your life. The important thing is that the mind can train it, learn it, and know it as well!

Your mind and body are connected; your feelings will always be manifested and expressed through your body language. Sometimes, you don't even have a conscious awareness of how you express yourself. However, 90 percent of your communication is externalized through body language so that you can say something to someone linguistically. Still, your body language can say something completely different!

So, How Can the NLP Help Me?

- You can find yourself in your present, and in the way you see your past.
- You can work with your procrastination and all the things that continuously procrastinate when you need to complete a project.
- You can find out why you feel depressed, depressed, upset, and you're not sure why.
- You can increase your performance to improve work to become more productive and increase your income.
- You can figure out how to adopt a new habit that you try every week, month to achieve, but you don't make it, and you feel frustrated with yourself.
- You can get out of a rut that you feel you've fallen into through a situation or a relationship, and you don't know how to get out.
- You can regain the confidence that prevents you from taking the initiative.
- You can increase your sales if you're a salesman.
- You can improve your mental and physical performance.
- You can find and reveal the obstacles that keep you locked in your place, that hold you back from your freedom and independence.

Neuro-linguistic Programming

Neuro-Linguistic-Programming is a systematic collection of scientific information, observational knowledge, and experience, as well as mental techniques that together work to improve thinking, behavior, and emotional response – as well as methods of supporting other people to achieve the same goal. By being familiar with NLP, even its fundamental principles, we can:

- We make the things we already do even better.
- We have the skills and attitudes to do what we cannot do now, but we would like to be able to do so.
- We communicate more effectively with others.
- We think and express ourselves more clearly and systematically.
- We manage our thoughts, behaviors, and moods based on our real goals.

The Study of Success

NLP (Neuro-Language-Programming) has been variously described as the technology of the mind, as the science of achievements, and as the study of success. It is based on the research and analysis of those factors that bring about either the success or failure of human performance.

For more than 30 years, NLP researchers around the world have been studying and "modeling" the behavior and thinking of highly successful and efficient executives in business, education, sales and marketing, therapeutics, sports, and personal development. The results of this work are presented today in educational workshops and seminars, as well as in NLP long-term studies programs. In essence, this knowledge skills answer the question: how in practice and in life itself is structured optimal and successful performance and how the elements and skills that create success for me personally, professionally, and socially become my property.

NLP What A Name!

The term "Neuro-Language-Programming" is considered to be the result of an attempt to define in a relatively precise way the scope of this complicated subject matter:

- "Neuro": indicates how the mind interacts and synchronizes with the body through the functioning of the human nervous system.
- "Language" refers to knowledge of the way of thinking of man taken from careful observation of the use of language.
- "Programming" refers not to the action of programming, but to the study of patterns of thought and behavior or "programs" that people use in their daily lives and relationships with each other.

Many who come into the first contact with the sound of the term NLP are repelled, as the word "programming" brings about associations restrictive or automatic of human behavior. But it is not so, neither in its depth nor in its substance. The name NLP has spread around the world and is used with the abbreviation of three letters.

And so, thanks, we can say that the NLP has achieved so much of its mission not because of its title, but because of its code! And this is precisely the value revealed to the private student or professional: that "by unlocking our mental codes, we can recreate the reality of our lives."

How They Refer to the NLP

The reputable scientific publication "Science Digest" states for the NLP that "it may be the most important synthesis of knowledge about human communication that has occurred since the 1960s".

The international magazine "Time Magazine" announces that "NLP has countless possibilities for dealing with and handling individual problems."

The Professional Review "Training & Development Journal" states that the NLP "enables us to bring about change without the known anguish and pain that accompanies these phenomena" and that it "allows for the increase and expansion of our choices, flexibility, creativity and, for this reason, greater freedom of action and will for most of us."

An internationally acclaimed speaker and personal development writer Anthony Robbins have said that "NLP is an incredibly effective and enjoyable way to gain access to the more and more real potential of your mind."

- NLP and Sales: the use of NLP inadequate customer satisfaction and satisfaction – and in the development of long-term mutual benefit relationships (win-win), results in us being the preferred supplier of services and products to our customers.
- NLP and Career: the implementation of NLP perfects the unique technical skills we already possess as professionals and significantly develops the skills of influencing, consulting, trading, communication, motivation and motivation, staff training.
- NLP in Management: NLP is an almost irreplaceable tool to be used by the manager to implement the planned changes in the professional exercise or business landscape.
- NLP in Relationships: the use of NLP in close relationships deepens the bond through a clear understanding and understanding between the parties while allowing the maintenance of personal autonomy and power.
- NLP and Personal Development: the application of NLP in all areas of personal development is one of the most useful and impressive applications of science and art of this subject.
- NLP and Counselling: the application of NLP to the exercise of all kinds of advisory services to individuals and professionals, such as business consulting, coaching & mentoring, or to the practice of related professions such as social worker or psychologist, dramatically enriches the know-how and enhances the result. This is achieved, in particular, through the study and practical experience through the NLP of Systemic Thought across the web of human relations and the collective phenomena of life.
- NLP and Sport: regardless of whether we are athletes, coaches, or coordinators of sports and sports, NLP provides an excellent set of techniques and methods of superior performance and strengthening of our internal attitude during sports activity, thus enhancing performance in quality and duration.

You teach neurolinguistic programming. What should someone know before starting this method? And what is it?

Neurolinguistic Programming (NLP) is a broad method of self-awareness and self-evolution, created about 50 years ago at the University of Santa Cruz, California, by a Gestalt psychologist, Richard Bandler, and a linguist, John Grinder.

With NLP, what one manages is to discover his restrictive beliefs, that is, those that prevent him from creating the results he dreams of in all areas of his life, driving them easily and quickly, with lasting results and having secured the knowledge and tools he will use whenever he needs them in later life.

Because ultimately, what differentiates a "successful" from an "unsuccessful" in any field of man is his ability to live his life within the framework that he determines based on his personal needs and balances and to bring the result that satisfies him and not his environment. The disappearance of our restrictive beliefs brings us back to a state of freedom, flowing, effortless and in-depth communication, and sincere interest in others, now free from the heavy shackles of chronic compulsive behavior.

What Can He Help Us With? And Who Is It Addressed To?

It is addressed to all people who want to change some areas of their lives, work, finances, relationships, or some part of their personality, e.g., cowardice, indecision, low self-esteem, anxiety, fear, and so on.

What difference does it make from classical psychotherapy?

First of all, it's not psychotherapy. We don't deal with trauma and the past here. Here we learn techniques and ways to bring results, and through this path, we heal the wound.

How does it apply in practice? Can he help us in our careers?

NLP is something you learn, committing yourself to actively taking part in your change through specific speech exercises and particular action. This is done either through groups or through personal sessions.

You recently held a daily experiential seminar entitled "Your Best Year." You talked about a method. What makes her stand out and how she can help us.

Your best years is a specialized, targeted system within the framework of NLP that guides you through creating a plan of professional success either independently as a professional or as a company. It cultivates group consciousness and boosts the company's results in all areas. I represent this method exclusively in Greece and Cyprus.

How many years have you been involved in neurolinguistic programming, and why did you decide to engage?

I've been involved in neurolinguistic programming for 14 years. I've worked with over 1500 people so far. Through the NLP, I was able to change my life and achieve goals in a way I never imagined. Seeing my results, I decided that this method is valuable for all people who ask to make a new life with their own beliefs, desires, and needs. So, I got on this magical journey called NLP.

The people who have been and are with me on this journey bring their results and experience their lives in a new creative way. They connect with themselves better and create the conditions they wish to have in every area of their lives.

Can Someone Heal Their Childhood Traumas with Neurolinguistic Programming?

Of course, I do. But if you don't heal your childhood traumas, you'll always find them in front of you. I have a two-day seminar, called children's injury an old history with a happy end, which is specially designed to lead us to the identification of our childhood traumas and the lousy past while creating the possibility of a liberated life from the emotional burdens of the past and thus the creation of a new beautiful relationship with ourselves and our environment. At the same time, it gives us valuable information - knowledge of how to play our role as parents successfully.

What are the most common requests that most people visit you?

Work, finances, relationships, children, relationship with oneself. If we told you to give us some advice to apply it to our daily lives, what would it be?

Whatever fits in my imagination, I can achieve. I have all the talent I need. All I have to do is find out how. Everything I know, I can do easily. My only competitor is the restrictive – deficit programming that lurks within me.

The most valuable tool is to remember how much I have achieved so far!

NLP 3rd Generation
NLP is now in its third decade as a field of education and has evolved significantly since its inception in the mid-1970s. Through all these years, it has spread around the world and has touched, affected the lives of millions of people. The people who develop NLP and those who implement it continue to expand the boundaries of NLP applications, creating what we call "the new generation of NLP models and applications."

- This new generation of NLP works with the interaction between three different intelligent or "minds."
- the cognitive intelligence that emerges from the brain
- physical intelligence that is focused on the body
- in the "intelligent field" that comes from our contact and our relationship with larger systems around us

1st Generation Of NLP
But to change, one needs:

The first generation of NLP was the original NLP model created by Grinder & Bandler from their work with successful psychotherapists. These initial techniques were applied mainly on an individual level and focused almost exclusively on the individual. NLP was considered a method that one (mostly therapists) used to another person. NLP techniques in these first steps focused on working at the level of the individual's behavior and abilities.

2nd Generation Of NLP

The second generation of NLP began to emerge in the mid-1980s. At the time, NLP was expanding to include other fields besides psychotherapy. Although it continued to focus on the individual, the 2nd generation of NLP emphasized the relationship between the individual and others. It thus included other areas of NLP application such as negotiation, sales, education, and health. NLP techniques and tools have been extended to include higher-level topics related to an individual's beliefs and values.

3rd Generation Of NLP

3rd Generation NLP has been in development since the 1990s. 3rd Generation NLP applications are productive, systemic, and focus on even higher levels of learning, interaction, and evolution - including stories of identity, vision, and destination. The 3rd generation NLP focuses on changing the whole system and can be applied to societies as effectively as it is used to smaller groups and individuals. 3rd generation NLP techniques are "field" based on principles of self-organization, archetypes, and what is known as 4th place: a holistic concept. The tools of the 3rd generation NLP are focused on internal harmonization and like-mindedness, multi-level perception, and the skills of support. The premise of 3rd generation NLP is that the wisdom needed for change to occur is already within the system and can be discovered and emerged by creating the right circumstances and conditions.

NLP Training Strong Minds

NLP is about identifying patterns in thinking, beliefs, and behavior and knowing how to choose the designs to keep consciously and which to change. NLP has helped many people improve their communication skills and achieve their business and personal goals.

Neuro-Linguistic Programming (NLP) is the study of how we think and perceive the world around us. The nature of our brain and our consciousness are not a specific science yet, so the primary method used by the NLP is to form models of how they work. These models are then used to create techniques to change thoughts, beliefs rapidly, and behaviors that one may not want to have, need not have, or not know that one has.

The idea behind NLP is to offer several tools that anyone can use to monitor themselves so that they can operate more efficiently. When seemingly invisible forces no longer push one, one's self-confidence and energy can increase sharply as he has greater control over the circumstances. In this way, he will always have more options available in each situation, rather than being limited to one or two that the conditions in the past allowed him to.

Neuro-Language programming operates on the fundamental premise that reality is subjective. Instead of assuming that there is only one objective reality in which everyone participates, it focuses on how each person perceives and experiences reality from within. Therefore, instead of "facts," the NLP studies personal beliefs and perceptions.

Each of us perceives reality through a vast collection of perceptions, thoughts, beliefs, and, which has a structure and organization, even if it is too complex to understand on our own.

This is no different from the prevailing principles of psychology, according to which the roots of a problem in the patient's childhood are sought, in the belief that there is a connection. The NLP examines these links in much more detail, arguing that even the smallest verbal or non-verbal communication or behavior can reveal some of the necessary internal structural processes and that is trained in observing these signals can "work" to change these behaviors.

Instead of being a rigidly disciplined theory, this method uses tools having freely, and discriminably borrowed data from various ideas and disciplines. Experimentation is encouraged to find the appropriate means that the person will use. Since we are all different, a specific approach that will apply to everyone is less effective. As a result of this perception, the NLP is more of an ever-evolving process than philosophy and focuses more on what "works" than what is "true."

The Essence of The Relevant Education

Unlike various methods of psychotherapy, the NLP does not "examine" people and then decide for them what problems they have and how they should be "cured." In essence, it helps individuals decide for themselves what their "problems" are and then helps them in trying to solve them. In other words, everyone is allowed to determine what they do not like about themselves or in their life. A vital element of the method is that the NLP does not make judgments about its problems, nor does it try to highlight issues that the person himself does not detect.

Any "region" that one decides subjectively that he wants to change or improve in his life is considered valid and acceptable. The person himself decides what material could be useful for the "therapist" to hear. Diagnosis determines what the treatment should be, but this, at every step, can change if it turns out that another direction or dimension would be more constructive for the individual.

"With NLP, you can discover your spiritual map and how it affects what you do. Interesting, isn't it? What NLP education offers is one of the most reasonable questions one can ask when one wants to know more about NLP."

"For many people, NLP applications are still unknown and certainly not so clear. But it's quite interesting that with the same process, you can develop your professional flexibility and performance, have a better relationship with the people around you. Of course, the sooner you discover and become familiar with this art, you'll realize that there are limits only where you want to put it for its use. You learn specific step-by-step methodologies to improve the way you think, the way you receive information through the five senses, to understand people, to socialize more effectively, to look for new and more creative approaches, for the challenges of life."

"Due to the dual nature of NLP training, it can be described as the most penetrating, the most direct and the most effective. In particular, throughout the training, each individual has the opportunity to imagine and create, first conceivable, and then practically, his professional - personal success. At the end of this, the sense of the learner is of complete spiritual integration."

"The most important benefit that NLP offers is the excellent nation thorough knowledge of how the human mind works and how we can harness its unlimited power."

Stresses John Stockdale, Master Coach & Trainer of NLP, Stockdale & Associates, and Performance Partnership. He points out that through specific methods, techniques, and communication tools, the NLP allows each of us to create immediate and lasting change.

"Therefore, you learn to change the way you communicate and behave, set and achieve goals consistently, and change your attitude to life. In short, I would say it is the ultimate "manual" of the human mind!" he concludes.

"NLP training offers recognition of our way of thinking and, at the same time, acquiring techniques for self-improvement. As a result of this training, the person concerned can create the future he deserves and has dreamed of".

"It offers us several tools and techniques for how the human brain works. It gives us a manual for using the mechanism of what we do and how to find out what keeps us away from what we are capable of achieving. It also offers us the science of communication. Our success in any field, personal or professional, has to do with how effectively we communicate."

Structure and Content

One of the basics that one who is interested in training in NLP must understand are the 4 points, also known as its pillars. These four 'bases' are summarized as follows:

Rapport: How to build a relationship with others and with yourself is probably the essential gift offered by NLP. Because of the pace at which most people live and work, a great lesson from rapport is how one can say "no" to all demands that require time and, at the same time, continue to maintain friendly or professional relationships.

- Sensory Awareness: When one uses all his senses to recruit stimuli from the environment, discoveries about the world around him are truly unique.
- Outcome Thinking: The term is associated with starting to think about what it is that they want instead of sticking to a negative situation or negative thoughts. The principles of such an approach can result in better decision-making and choice, whether it is personal life or something about the workplace. At its maximum use, outcome thinking can lead even to the real purpose of man in his life.
- Behavioral Flexibility: The term means finding out how one can do something different when one realizes that the way it does to date does not work-performs.

"The topic of NLP Training is quite broad and, at the same time, focused on issues faced by the person concerned every day. Issues related to solving stress management and targeting issues to canceling restrictive beliefs and phobias. The only sure thing is that the learner will be able to cope with his daily life with a dynamic and effective set of techniques".

In the same vein, J. Stockdale, "The NLP moves in the field of personal improvement and performance that draws from a wide range of themes. Therefore, the trunk of NLP Training, at the introductory certification level of NLP Practitioner,

1. effective communication internally and externally - applying in a verbal and non-verbal field.
2. It is changing perception and behavior, 3. techniques of an effective response to negative emotions such as stress, and 4. a unique method of shaping and achieving any objective".

"The ultimate goal of NLP training is to discover our inner strengths and abilities to achieve better harmonization with the environment around us. This is why objects such as representation systems, strategies, reframe emotions and behaviors, anchoring words and actions, metamodellas, and Milton models are taught. Equally important topics taught are metaphors, categories of emotions, and positions of perception. The theme also includes sales, negotiation techniques, as well as the creation of harmonious relations and targeting."

According to M. Kankel, the thematic body is quite large and, for example, includes the following sections of education:

- Change Strategies - How to create change in yourself and others.
- Language and Communication.
- Understanding how to develop your auditory attention so you can see what's happening to others.
- 5 Step Model for Successful Sales.
- Object Management.
- We are negotiating and persuasion techniques.
- Techniques for successful presentations.

Practice - the training is designed so that all participants can practice the techniques enough, so that they leave with a series of techniques directly applicable and not with theoretical approaches, as is usually the case.

Not Just Coaching

With coaching gaining ground and responding to the needs of executives, the reasonable question arises as to what the relationship of coaching is with the NLP. "The NLP is, to a large extent, the background for what we now call coaching. It is also taught in many coaching schools as a module in "communication" and "rapport," two of the essential elements that a good coach must possess" argues J. Stockdale and continues, "NLP coaching differs from the more traditional methods in how it approaches the issues that the customer wishes to improve and at the same time offers the customer analytics tools and specialized methodology that he can use and become, in part, the coach himself."

"Neuro-Language Programming was born by studying man and more specifically by studying how some people were "perfect" in what they did. They then found a way to model these "perfect" behaviors so that they could reproduce them to themselves or others. If we take into account the way the N.G.A. was born and how much it focuses on change and achieving goals, we would say with certainty that it is a form of coaching. The most crucial advantage is time; the techniques are designed so that changes are made immediately and quickly."

"It is like the carpenter who has his case full of tools and uses the appropriate tool for the corresponding work. The most important advantage of coaching with NLP over more "traditional" methods is the speed in achieving the desired result," he points out.

"Once we handle the N.G.A., we develop the knowledge and skills for the success of our goals, and we improve the quality of our personal and professional lives, I can state with certainty that it is the most authoritative and comprehensive coaching."

Regarding the comparative advantage of NLP, he says that the mind, body, and soul combine for complete assimilation. It is not only the changes that are caused for the better but also the continuous development of life that it offers.

"NLP techniques are necessary for the context of the broader concept of Coaching" stresses N. Francis and argues: "Robert Dilts, when asked what NLP is, replied: "The NLP gives us tools and skills to study and manage the psychological situations that govern us. It is also a system of strengthened beliefs with several discoveries about what people are, about what communication is.

On another level, the PPA is about self-awareness, the discovery of our identity, and our purpose." It also provides the framework of understanding and correlation with our spirituality, which is part of human experience or existence and explores beyond us as units, society, and a more general system. It's not just about skill and perfection; it's about vision and travel beyond the comfort zone we live in."

On the other hand, according to him, the NLP under Coaching or Counselling, which is a vast umbrella that includes many techniques, can be joined with big claims. A Consultant/Coach can train as an NLP Coach using NLP techniques or can already be a Consultant/Coach and use THE NLP's tools as extra knowledge in his toolbox depending on the challenges he faces. We learn to learn all the time.

For the Record

The NLP started in California and, more specifically, at the University of Santa Cruz in the early 1970s. Richard Bandler, a master's degree, and Dr. John Grinder, a professor of linguistics, studied people who were considered gifted in communication and excellent at helping their clients change. They were fascinated by how some people defied the odds of accomplishing something that was theoretically difficult or how others failed to connect.

Since its inset, Neuro-Language Programming has included many specialties from all over the world. The NLP authorities have certainly come a long way from the 1970s to the present day. Many pioneers relied on the first steps of Neuro-Language Programming and advanced the methods by making it practical and helping many people change their lives. Today, NLP applications are found in many professions, such as doctors, nurses, salespeople, coaches, teachers, etc.

Concerning NLP, you may hear several things related to integrity, ethics, and manipulation. The truth is that we can all more or less influential people in our narrow or broader environment. But when one does so consciously and possibly fraudulently, then the question of moral integrity indeed arises. The point is to have ethical safeguards that do not allow people to exploit their partner, colleague, client, etc. Because NLP can provide tools to convince others, but you can preserve your integrity by asking a simple question: Do I intend to deceive, to do something at the expense of my interlocutor?

The situation can be cleared up with the following example: Think of a salesperson attempting to close a deal with a customer-company. If his intention is good, and he has the required integrity, he

309

will take care to secure a win/win deal. If not, then it's heading for the manipulation of the other side. But when his goal is the win/win agreement, he is on his way to success.

NLP Training: Interpreting the World

"Every man is different." "Every man perceives things differently." "Every man communicates differently." I had used the above proposals many times in personal and professional discussions, listened to them from third parties, and taught them in communication seminars. But there came a time in my life when I began to wonder what makes each person different and behave in a certain way? How can I understand the way I act and think? Starting the search for answers, I discovered the NLP. NLP has helped me better and more methodically understand everything we experience in our daily lives. The way we think, express ourselves and feel. After all, for someone to accept an event, a feeling, an idea, or communication more efficiently, they must first have understood how it came about - why. Through NLP, one can find interpretation in everything that happens in and around us.

This helps to understand the "model of the world" that every person has built. This understanding finds application in the early stages of getting to know someone and helps to achieve an excellent first impression, which is catalytic for a successful future relationship. But to build a meaningful relationship, it is crucial to learn to adapt the way one communicates according to the priorities of one's interlocutor and not to his own. What is impressive is that THE NLP's practices are multidimensional, applying not only on a professional but also on an interpersonal level. These practices have helped me, as HR Professional, to identify workers' needs more quickly, as a Trainer in passing, during training, messages in a way that is understood by everyone, and as a human being in handling difficult situations better.

The truth is that we live in an ever-changing environment, where everything around us changes, just like we do ourselves, whether it is done consciously or not. So, for those interested in "listening to the music behind the words," I would highly recommend their acquaintance with NLP! In conclusion, it is essential to know that the certificate in NLP is the standard certification of knowledge. Its essence is based on everyday application.

NLP - In Which Domains Does It Apply

NLP was developed in the early 1970s. Its conception and evolution into structured theory and methodology were first made by Dr. Richard Bandler and Dr. John Grinder to discover ways to help people have a better and more complete life. It is an innovative system of techniques and a methodology that helps us understand how the human mind operates, communicates, and processes information. Each person perceives the world differently, developing his model according to the information he receives.

It is a question of noticing and reflecting how everyone thinks and acts, intending to align with them and enhance the effectiveness of communication. While initially used as a therapeutic tool, NLP techniques have also been adopted for the development of personal communication skills. They are an excellent tool for every professional, with applications in various fields. In particular, in terms of negotiation, sales, and customer service, NLP techniques help overcome obstacles and create a climate of acceptance. In the field of Management and Leadership, they act as techniques for identifying the elements that affect people's thinking and the way they work.

We have all met people who left their mark and admired them for the way they inspired others. Also, at the human resources development level, NLP techniques provide knowledge of how the employee is mobilized to make full use of his potential. In Education, they allow the cultivation of a willingness to learn and the development of alternative forms of thinking. In Marketing and Advertising, they help shape the right messages. In the context of personal change, NLP techniques enhance energy and self-confidence, turning undesirable behaviors into practical actions, and eliminating habits that create internal conflicts and limit us. In practice, there are no restrictions. NLP is applied in almost every area of human activity. It allows us to know how we think, reacts, and behave and what impact this has on others, with the ultimate goal of creating the right conditions for better communication with our environment.

NLP Techniques

NLP neurolinguistic programming is not magic. It's a psychological approach to personal development and communication. It was created from ideas that emerged from the study of the habits of successful people in the 1970s. Scientists then realized that there is a link between the neurological processes, language, and patterns of behavior that we learn through experiences (programming), and these can change to achieve specific goals in our lives.

NLP neurolinguistic programming is a tool for change and evolution. It redefines restrictive beliefs and behaviors, facilitates growth, enhances self-confidence and self-esteem, and gives the impetus that man needs to achieve his goals in life, professional and personal.

There is not a single NLP neurolinguistic programming technique, and it does not fit a method in each case. NLP neurolinguistic programming is a method of identifying, modeling, and copying successful strategies pursued by other people. The neurolinguistic programming techniques known today are the result of the optimization of skills and processes followed by successful professional people and psychotherapists. Plans are not neurolinguistic NLP programming per itself, but the development of the application of neurolinguistic programming. Methods used by a successful person in the field we are interested in can become role models and be implemented in any situation we want. In this way, we find solutions/techniques/strategies for the problems we face. If we focus only on neurolinguistic programming techniques, we lose the essence of NLP. We turn into robots that apply NLP techniques. On the other hand, if we turn our attention and energy towards optimizing skills and behaviors, then we will soon create our unique methods.

The mind is everything. It becomes what you think. Buddha, concerning the definition of neurolinguistic programming, the "nerve" refers to the way of thinking or the various (conscious and unconscious) ways of processing information coming from the outside world. We experience the world in which we live uniquely and subjectively. NLP neurolinguistic programming concerns these personal experiences. Whether a day will be good or bad depends mainly on what happens to us and how we feel about them that day. Often, if we think about the good things that will happen, we may feel good even on the rainiest day, or it can happen the other way around. The challenge lies in the fact that we think that what we believe (our subjective experience that is) is not under our control. That emotions come and go on their own. Among other things, neurolinguistic programming is about influence and power over what we feel.

"Language" refers to the words. People describe their experiences in words. But in addition to representing an experience, comments hide other meanings, as well as an attitude towards things. Neurolinguistic programming explains how words affect our thinking, mood, and behavior.

"Programming" refers to habits. People create patterns all the time. Sometimes, these habits are useful and desirable, but others are undesirable or negative. Neurolinguistic programming uses simple (but instrumental) methods of changing the way we think, according to our values and goals, and results in desired changes in behavior.

NLP Techniques That Can Change Your Life
1. Distancing

Have you experienced a situation that has left you with a bitter experience? You may have experienced something that, whenever you remember it, or something reminds you of it, discourages you, or gives you confidence. Or you may become nervous in various situations where you have to talk in front of others. You may be ashamed when it comes to talking to someone you care about personally! Although these feelings of sadness, nervousness, or shame seem automatic or unstoppable, the technique of distancing can help you a lot.

- Recognize the feeling (e.g., fear, anger, discomfort) from which you want to get rid
- Imagine that you hover outside your body, and how you look at yourself, watching it evolve as an observer.
- Notice how the feeling changes completely
- For even greater empowerment, you can imagine observing your observer, observing yourself. This double distancing will change even the smallest traces of emotion.

2. Reframe

You can use this technique when you feel that a situation is hostile or deadlocked. Re-development can empower you to deal with any situation by changing the meaning of the experience to something positive.

For example, let's take the breakup. It may sound horrible that you broke up, but let's reframe it. What can be the positives of this situation? For example, you are open to new relationships! You have the freedom to do whatever you want, whenever you wish, without explanation. And you've learned important lessons from the previous relationship that will allow you to have a better relationship in the future and make a wiser choice of partner.

By changing the meaning of separation, you change your life and your feeling.

This technique allows you to clear your mind and make responsible choices for your good, without panic and fear.

The NLP neurolinguistic programming methodology uses the skills and habits of successful people as a model. It aims to allow everyone to acquire these skills. Neurolinguistic programming is used in addition to the treatment of specific problems such as phobias, depression, psychosomatic disorders, and learning difficulties.

3. Anchor

Anchoring creates a neurological connection between a behavior and an emotion. It allows you to link any positive feeling/thinking to a specific movement. So, when you want to bring that feeling to your mind, you can make that move, and the surface will immediately change.

Recognize how you want to feel (confidence, joy, tranquility, etc.)

Decide in which movement and at what point in the body you would like to make this anchoring, for example, by pulling your ear, clenching your fist, pressing a finger or elbow. This natural stimulus (touch) will allow you to bring the feeling you want at will. It doesn't matter what you choose, as long as it's a unique touch you don't use for something else.

Think of a moment in the past when you felt that way (e.g., self-confidence). Bring that memory to your mind, where you were, what you saw, what you heard, and mostly how you felt. As you relive this moment, you will find that you will relive the feeling. It's like telling the story to a friend, and reviving the moment!

As you look back at this memory, start touching (touching, pulling, pushing, etc.) with the part of your body you have chosen. Leave this point after the feeling peaks and begins to decrease.

This creates a neurological connection, a stimulus-reaction that will bring that feeling when you make this move. That is, to feel confident, make the same move when you want to feel that way.

To further enhance this connection, think of a second moment where you felt that way, revive it, and connect the same feeling to the same place as before. Each time you add one more memory, the anchor becomes more vigorous and will bring a more powerful effect. Use this technique whenever you need to change your mood.

4. Connection

Or, in other words: synchronization, coordination, how to like your others in the first acquaintance (rapport). This is a set of NLP techniques that have the power to help you have a good connection with anyone. There are many techniques, but perhaps the most important is the imitation of the interlocutor's movements, tone of voice, rhythm, and words. People like people who look like them, and when the brain unconsciously records these similarities (through "mirror neurons," it creates a feeling of familiarity and friendliness towards the interlocutor.

The technique is simple: imitate your interlocutor's posture, similarly shake your head, smile when they smile, imitate facial expressions.

But all this must be done very gently and calmly, do not be in a hurry and not intense changes and movements. Otherwise, it will be perceived that you are doing and will have the opposite effects.

NLP neurolinguistic programming deals with various aspects of human existence. It is a process that develops our skills and flexibility, strategic thinking, and understanding of the mental and mental processes behind our behavior. Neurolinguistic programming provides tools for individual excellence.

NLP Basic Techniques

It all started during the 70s when Richard Bandler and John Grinder decided to consume a significant part of their time analyzing how the brains of people considered geniuses and highly successful in their fieldwork. The basis of this strategy was the thought that the behavior of a genius could be copied by the average person and lead him to miraculous results.

Neuro-linguistic programming is an area characterized by a curiosity about what it is that uniquely affects every person in their life and what we need to start to change our experiences for the better. He argues that all human behavior can be analyzed, organized, and copied by a third party.

But let's look at what the words that make up the name of this particular school of psychology represent.

- Neuro: Our nervous system, which accepts experiences through the five senses and transports them for processing in the brain
- Linguistic: communication systems - verbal and non-verbal - with which the neutral stimuli of the environment are organized and become meaningful.
- Programming: The ability of each person to organize his communication and his neurological experience to achieve the goals in his life.

The NLP thus organizes the human experience so that its structures positively affect the individual. In other words, it changes the process by which the person experiences reality. The simplistic and effectiveness that distinguishes his techniques made him resonate in the advertising space, in sales as well as in the new age and occult scene.

Both Californian Bandler and Grinder worked at the beginning. They copied the methods of modern psychology as Fritz Perl's, founder of Gestalt psychology, Virginia Satir, leading family therapist, and charismatic hypnotherapist Milton Erickson, who, for many, is the most gifted hypnotist of all time.

The two of them from the beginning rejected treatment as ineffective and time-consuming through discussions and counseling. They turned to faster and more effective methods.

Neurolinguistic programming, as a natural evolution of hypnotherapy, is interested in bypassing consciousness and installing new connections - anchors to the unconscious of the subject.

He argues that he can install submissions even through simple spoken words, only by skillfully placing the phrase within the sentence.

Several therapists characterize neuro-linguistic programming as pseudoscience.

However, the effectiveness of his techniques soon made Bandler rich, and several controversies broke out over who has the right to deliver NLP seminars. CIA officials, company directors rushed to apprentice to Richard Bandler. Self-help gurus like Tony Robbins using NLP techniques became multimillionaires in the 80s.

If we try to overspill organize a relatively complex field of knowledge, we would say that the first mission of the experienced NLP is to find out what sensation dominates the interlocutor's brain.

A pivotal key to helping someone optimize their way of thinking is to understand how they use their senses and in what layout they follow internal processing.

There are three categories: the visual type, the auditory type, and the kinesthetic type.

The visual type mentions information in images, doesn't easily remember speeches and gets bored of prolonged lectures, prefers to read or see information, uses more expressions of style, " are you watching me? "See what I'm saying?" "I formed/made a picture."

The acoustic guy converses with himself and is easily disturbed by noise; they find math and writing more complicated than the auditory learning of a foreign language. The kinesthetic type: he likes to touch people and be generally close. "I'm holding what you said "

Thus, NLP understands from the verbs used by the interlocutor his sensory preference as well as the sequence he uses to motivate himself to action - his strategy -.

NLP Gets Information Through Eye Movements

Every movement of the eye is also related to a specific way of brain function. For example: When a right-handed person creates mental images of memories, his eyes tend to turn up and to the left. When he develops mental pictures of things he has never seen before (i.e., the imagination is involved and probably the lie), his eyes go up and to the right. When he speaks to himself, his eyes go down and left, and when he feels deep emotions, his eyes go down and right. The sentimentality with the movement of the eyes downwards is something that, indeed, all of us have dozens of examples.

Several psychologists disagree vertically with the model of eye movements, but as Bandler says, it is complicated to escape you when you are on stage. You ask four hundred people to remember something that has happened to them, and you see four hundred pairs of eyes moving up and left as they think hmm to see. It's just as hard to escape that when someone suffering from depression looks down, their eyes play right to the left as he talks to himself about how bad he feels. Actors follow this pattern even in silent movies.

So, the NLP manages to penetrate the speaker's way of thinking. What are the next steps?

It uses the mirroring technique. This technique is about copying the physiology of the interlocutor. When two interlocutors communicate with similar body movements, their bodies send subliminal messages that they match. Communication is improved, and verbal statements are more readily accepted. NLP tries to copy both the tone as well as the tone of the voice. He also starts using keywords used by the interlocutor depending, of course, on what sense he has discovered that dominates his brain.

He's even trying to mimic the rhythm of breathing. Knowing how the brain works and having the "favor" of the unconscious, NLP is now ready to proceed to the deep rapport stage in establishing in-depth communication where submissions and anchors are much easier to achieve.

NLP Persuasion Techniques

You may be wondering how NLP persuasion techniques can change your life, first, what NLP (Neuro-Linguistic Programming) means. It involves procedures for changes in yourself and other people from the inside out, i.e., from the mind to the behaviors.

These techniques have gained tremendous success over the last few decades. They are now used in many self-development techniques and therapeutic sessions.

Recognize What Makes People React

Knowing what people like and what they don't like is an essential aspect of NLP's technical persuasion. Since this type of technique is distinctive, they also have a greater chance of success.

For example, if you want to make a wealthy older man donate money to a charity, you won't make him do it just by asking him (unless he's a vast philanthropist).

Ask one of your most beautiful volunteers to talk to him and frivolously notice that women are going crazy by the rich who do charity work.

Invest in Sympathy (Rapport)
The word rapport is essential in the field of NLP. If you are the kind of person who has no problem chatting with strangers on a train, on the bus, anywhere, then you probably have excellent persuasion skills. It is also known that building rapport, camaraderie with people gives a free, even temporary, entry into their circle of trust.

Cancel (Angor) Your Feelings
The great thing about persuasion and the NLP is that most of the tactics involved are not complicated at all. An example of this is anchoring. An anchor connects a particular emotion with a movement, sound, vision, etc.

Case: Maria, an introverted girl who always feels terrible (anxiety, nerves, fear) before a presentation. To help her subside her nervousness, she sings a particular song because it makes her feel safe and carefree.

You can also link certain emotions to specific anchors. Just make sure to strengthen the connection multiple times to establish the relationship.

Persuasion techniques are essential in personal development. They will help you become better people and, in turn, help others.

NLP - Neurolinguistic Programming Applications
There is enormous confusion regarding neuro-linguistic programming (NLP), and this makes people not understand what it is, as well as its importance. Neurolinguistic programming describes the relationship between the mind (nerve), language (linguistic), and how their interaction affects our body and behavior (programming). Our nervous system regulates the functioning of our bodies; language determines how we connect and communicate with other people and ourselves. Programming determines the patterns we create for the world.

NLP neurolinguistic programming is known for its techniques, and this is the primary source of confusion. Although these techniques are instrumental, they are not the most important. Neurolinguistic programming is a communication model that deals with:

The study of the connection between communication, thinking, and behavior.

Techniques to improve communication, change in behavior, and achieve goals.

Neurolinguistic programming is based on two essential conditions:

"The map is not the area." As human beings, we are finite. We cannot perceive the whole reality. We can only speculate on fact. We experience things and respond to the world around us based on our senses and beliefs, the way they sign with things. These are the "neurolinguistic" maps of reality as we perceive it, which determines how we behave and react. It is usually not this reality that limits or encourages us, but our map of reality and what is happening.

Life and mind are systemic processes. The processes that happen within us, but also between people and the environment, are systemic. Our bodies, societies, and the world form a cluster of systems and subsystems, all of which interact with each other. Not every part of this system can be isolated from other systems.

All neurolinguistic programming models and techniques are based on a combination of these principles. The aim is to create a rich and flexible "map" as possible. The people who are most effective in life are those who have a "map" for the world that allows them to perceive the largest number of options available and apply them.

The Main Elements of NLP Neurolinguistic Programming
The pillars on which NLP neurolinguistic programming is based include:

Nerve: NLP studies the way the mind works, the way we think and how we store past experiences, and how we can use all of this whenever we want to achieve a goal. It's about how the brain works and how it interacts with the body.

Linguistics: the use of language (verbal and body) affects us, and the neurolinguistic programming NLP creates models and techniques on it, i.e., it uses vocabulary and ways of expression to help achieve personal goals.

Programming: the way we organize our actions, thoughts, and past process experiences can be reprogrammed so that we have the best possible strategy to achieve our goals. The habits of our way of thinking lead to patterns of behavior. By discovering these habits, you can then decide whether they help you or put obstacles in your way. NLP gives you a choice if you want to change behavior and thinking habits.

NLP neurolinguistic programming was created based on the patterns of behavior and habits of successful people. It concerns the use of techniques and strategies to effectively make changes in thinking and communication to achieve better results. In essence, NLP neurolinguistic programming involves patterns of behavior, which means that any skill that is well (or exceptionally) done by someone can be decoded and copied so that other people can learn the same skill and use it to achieve goals.

1. Business: neurolinguistic programming enhances a multitude of business actions. It applies to sales, advertising, and teamwork. It helps people communicate more effectively and convincingly, speak publicly, train employees effectively, acquire practical tools to achieve maximum performance, and enhance motivation and values in the workplace. Improves communication, trading capabilities, and goal achievement.
2. Education: provides models of how we can communicate with ourselves and others. NLP neurolinguistic programming is used to help the ability to recruit information and memory to facilitate learning. It also helps to communicate clearly with students.
3. Sports: used by coaches to help athletes reach and maintain their maximum performance. NLP techniques enable performance to be maximized by overcoming limits and psychological barriers.
4. Health: it concerns a cognitive model and practical tools that can help people improve their health. NLP can help with the quality of life and the satisfaction one gets from experience by helping to change restrictive beliefs, habits, and behaviors, overcome fears. It makes it easier for people to manage situations and emotions and to find meaning in their lives by setting realistic, well-defined goals.
5. Personal relationships: NLP neurolinguistic programming sessions help communicate with other people. Therefore, neurolinguistic programming techniques help you live in harmony with your family members and friends. Neurolinguistic programming helps to maintain a balance between family members and your career and to set boundaries so that you don't let work interfere with the family and vice versa.
6. Personal evolution: helps to deal with obstacles, unpleasant feelings, and patterns. NLP can boost self-confidence and self-esteem. It is used in addition to psychotherapy, counseling, and life coaching to achieve changes by looking at the processes that form the basis of a particular pattern, emotion, or habit. It is stressed that NLP is not a form of psychotherapy.

The Many Applications Of NLP
What most people who learn NLP discover is that they come into contact with a whole new "technology" of thinking and behavior reconstruction, where there are no limits to its application. NLP is not just a method. It is not only a technique. It does not propose a specific model of "our life and function as humans." It's the other way around. Since NLP is a scientific field of knowledge that is continually being developed through research into the phenomena of human action, just as all humanities develop, it cannot self-restrict itself for commercial purposes, offering "rosettes" and "easy solutions" through, e.g., a short seminar.

The learner in the Principles and the various applications of NLP acquire new personal skills and skills of perception and communication.

It then has the responsibility to adopt, implement and further develop the NLP in its own space, in its professional field, with its particular requirements, and in its directions.

Therefore, NLP, since it is a behavioral process, is a cognitive object for experiential learning and personalized application. We can excellently read about NLP, but not act on the principles of NLP.

Neurolinguistic Programming: How to Use Your State of Mind
Neurolinguistic programming is an approach that is interested in exploring and enhancing each individual's ability to reach excellent performance.

Neurolinguistic programming (NLP) is a model of interpersonal communication that is applied to psychotherapy as well as to organizations/enterprises and focuses mainly on the study of successful patterns of behavior as well as the way of thinking from which these shapes are motivated.

Put merely. Neurolinguistic programming is an approach that is interested in exploring and enhancing each individual's ability to reach excellent performance, have more effective interpersonal communication, and improve their completeness and quality of life.

9 Keys to Achieving Your Goals
Through the various techniques of neurolinguistic programming, the maximum cultivation of the individual's ability to achieve his goals and achieve is encouraged. The keys to the process of setting successful objectives are, therefore, the following:

Know what it is you want accurately. So, first of all, ask yourself, 'What exactly do I want?'. Then express what you want in an affirmative/positive way. For example, it wouldn't make sense to say, 'What I want is not to be in such a bad financial situation anymore.' What he hears is: 'I want poor financial situation.'

A classic example of this process is:

Try not to think of a blue horse. Don't think of a blue horse. Repeat this sentence in your mind. What are you thinking?

Most people tend to take a picture of what they were asked not to think. Because your unconscious mind has great power, always focus on what you want, not what you don't want. To formulate your goal in the affirmative, in the present time, as if you have already acquired it.

For example, 'I have an excellent financial condition, and I buy what I want.'

Ask yourself where you are now concerning getting your goal. How long do you think it will take to reach your goal?

As mentioned above, our thoughts have the power to determine how we feel and act. So imagine that day when you have already managed to achieve your goal.

- What do you see around you?
- What are you listening to?
- How are you feeling?
- What do you say to yourself?

When you invite the senses to participate in the vision of your goal, do so by paying attention to the details that exist around you. Make the image alive, attractive, and see yourself in it. Feel how you'd feel. Here's what you'd hear if your dream had come true.

How will you know you've reached your goal? What details will indicate to you that you have succeeded?

If, for example, your goal is professional success, how will you know you've reached it? What does professional success mean to you? Think of all the details and aspects of this goal that will be for your indications that you have achieved what you wanted.

When we change a factor in our lives, other changes tend to follow. The result you wish to bring into your life is linked to different desires, values, or other goals that you may have. To be the change you want to achieve significant and lasting, you need your plan to blend harmoniously with the different aspects of your life.

Do you want to achieve this goal just for yourself or others?

The change you want to achieve is essential to start because you want it first of all. If, for example, you want to lose weight or quit smoking, do you want to do so because your family is urging you or because you want to? Who do you want to change for? Of course, wanting to achieve a goal for others may be a factor that motivates you, as long as it's not just for others.

Have you set the framework within which this objective will be achieved?

Consider: Where will this goal be achieved?

- I'm sorry.
- I don't know.
- With who?

Where will you focus your weight loss effort more? At home, at work, or both? Set an exact date. How do you plan to lose weight? Diet, exercise, or both? Who are you going to make this effort with?

- What resources do you need to achieve your goal?
- Have you ever done, or have you ever had anything like this before?
- Do you know anyone who's done it?
- Can you behave as if you had already succeeded?
- The goal here is to discover successful patterns of behavior of your own that have helped you reach your goals in the past or get ideas from another person's strategy that accomplished something similar to what you're targeting now.
- How does this goal bind to your worldview? In other words,
- What do you want this for?
- What if you get it?
- What won't happen if you get it?
- What if you don't get it?
- What won't happen if you don't get it?

One adage says that 'a goal that has been set in the right way is already half-achieved.' That's why, according to neurolinguistic programming, having clear and carefully defined goals increases the likelihood of making them happen.

That, after all, is the difference between dreams and goals. The former is based more on the hope that one day we will get what we want, while the latter is based on the formation of an action plan to achieve them.

NLP To Improve Communication
Every person experiences perceive and give meaning to their experiences in a unique way.

External stimuli captured through the senses are filtered by adding, subtracting, and altering elements based on our values, beliefs, memories, past decisions, and post - programs.

Thus, we shape our model of the world, which we express by communicating and acting in our environment.

Neurolinguistic Programming (NLP) helps us to recognize the way someone thinks and acts so that then we can coordinate with him and improve the effectiveness of our communication. It also allows us to identify our way of thinking and to behave to intervene if necessary, utilizing our existing strengths.

At a professional level, first, through Neurolinguistic Programming (NLP), we can immediately and quickly create a positive climate of acceptance with the people we come in contact with. We will also gain more flexibility in handling issues, expanding the scope of our choices while at the same time, we will be able to set and plan our goals, ensuring their achievement.

We can increase our self-confidence but also overcome situations that create embarrassment for us.

Also, by understanding the way our colleagues, associates, or clients think, we can identify their way of thinking, their values, their limitations, their selection criteria, and decisions. Once we understand how they act, we will be able to predict their behavior, motivate and motivate them, strengthening our influence.

Finally, through Neuro-linguistic Programming, we will be able to develop methods for the effective handling of difficult situations, to settle differences of opinion, but also to reach agreements.

Neurolinguistic Programming In Education

Neurolinguistic Programming in education is based on:

- In learning types,
- In multisensory learning,
- In focus and attention,
- In goal setting and self-motivation
- In communication and sociability.

Neurolinguistic Programming further enhances our ability to help children develop and improve their thinking organization, responsibility, expression, and sociability.

NLP In the Classroom

From the teachers' point of view, the use of NLP helps in:

- How to gain students' interest
- How to better understand those around them and their behavior
- How to have good chemistry with them
- How to influence them
- How to change their behavior
- How to change their perspective
- How to listen properly to what they say
- How to read their eyes
- How to help them in a difficult situation they are experiencing
- What types of students are there, and what are their motivations?
- How do students manage their time, and what can we conclude from this?
- The systems in which we learn and their characteristics
- Phrases/words we can use to influence and guide our students or learners, based on NLP models.
- Is the NLP the method that suits you?

Neuro-linguistic Programming is a series of techniques that will teach you to use an NLP special advisor to change desirable and entrenched behaviors that keep you away from the life you dream of. Replacing unwanted behaviors with new that support your goals, new conditions are created that will lead you to the future you want and deserve.

What changes if you say something different than you said?

Think about it! What's better to say to yourself, "I'm fat" or "I have to lose some weight"?

If you decide to say differently the phrases that make up your inner voice and therefore shape your everyday life, then a lot of things can change.

If you decide to say differently the phrases that make up your inner voice and therefore shape your everyday life, then a lot of things can change. It's like the brain is reprogrammed. For example, if you're used to saying "I have to go to work today" and replace it with "I can go to work today" or "I'm lucky to have a job," this small and simple change in the way you choose to talk to yourself is the point that connects the language part with the conscious and the unconscious and can drastically affect the way you operate every day.

How Can Replace A Negative Phrase with A Positive Change?

All the techniques and procedures of Neuro-Language Programming are designed to make the change in the unconscious mind, which controls all our behaviors, but in cooperation with the full conscious participation of the individual. Working with the cold and the aware at the same time, changes become faster and more effective. In short, through NLP, you learn how to use the language of your mind and build direct and better communication with the unconscious, which, scientifically proven, has more and more severe influence on your life than you think.

Where Do the Inner Voices Come From?

From your experiences, memories, experiences, how you have grown up, and what you have learned from your close family and broader social environment. But the truth is, NLP consultants don't care much about who's to blame and why. They don't waste time looking for where to lay their responsibilities. They're not looking for excuses. The first thing they do is help you recognize those problematic "I didn't make it again" voices. Then they look for where they come from, i.e., the nucleus that has "given birth" them and that in some cases may be the parents or some other significant person in your life. The ultimate goal is to replace each negative voice with a favorable vote to get rid of complicated feelings, phobias, inhibitions, and all kinds of restrictive beliefs that hinder your personal development.

Can the NLP Help You?

The cases that Neuro-Language Programming can help are numerous and include techniques of memorizing or improving spelling to significant efficiency in the professional, personal, or even athletic field. Neuro-Language Programming can also help you get out of stagnant situations, immediately mobilize, and increase your self-esteem, while helping to combat stress and phobias. Finally, it can also help in problems of all kinds of relationships, in the achievement of professional goals, in smoking cessation, in weight loss, but also the elimination of some tics.

Why Would You Prefer It?

Because it is a fast and useful tool for someone who wants immediate positive changes in their life, the changes are evident from the very first sessions. Usually, they do not take more than 8 to 10 sessions to resolve the issue that concerns you.

Mind Reading Using NLP

We'll see what "read the mind" means for the NLP. We have sometimes analyzed an essential aspect for Neurolinguistic Programming: the power of language, effective communication, to make sure that what you say is what you mean, reconnecting language with experience.

The NLP Precision Model or Metamodel covers these aspects for quality information. So, before you go any further, I propose to read the following >>Report- PNL Metamodel<< to better understand what follows

As you may have seen in the previous report (in the Distortion part), there are processes by which representations of a person's mental model have been distorted, so they limit their ability to act and generate a particular dysfunctional emotionality.

But it also makes artistic creations possible or anticipates and imagine something, for example, rehearsing a speech, preparing us for what will come.

One type of distortion in NLP is "read the mind." It is when one person is chatting with another, presumes to know without having any direct evidence, what his interlocutor is thinking or feeling at the time.

Sometimes we read someone else's mind as an intuitive response to specific non-verbal keys that we detected from our interlocutor, and which we unconsciously realized.

Although they are often hallucinations, fantasies, or what we would think or feel in that situation and we project our unconscious thoughts and feelings and experience them as if they came from the other person.

People who "read the mind" usually think they're always right. But this doesn't guarantee they will have it.

That's why with the NLP Metamodel, you get quality of information, asking the other person in a certain way. Why guess when you can ask?

There are two great ways to "read the mind":

Way 1- In this case, one person assumes knowing what the other thinks. For example:

- "Daniel is unhappy."
- "I knew you'd like it!"
- "I know what's best for you."

Way 2- This second case is a mirror of the first and gives other people the power to "read our minds" what can be used to blame them for not understanding us when we think they should! For example:

- "If you loved me, you should have known what I wanted"
- "Can't you see how I feel?"

A person using these models will not communicate to others what he wants; it's the others who are supposed to know. And this can lead to varied and even intense fights and litigation.

Instead, what the NLP proposes with its Precision Model is to ask appropriate questions to obtain accurate information and clarify the situation.

I mean, the way to question the reading of the mind is to ask, "How do you know?"

For example, applied to Mind Reading Way 1, you might ask:

- "How do you know specifically that Daniel is unhappy?"
- "How do you know what's best for me?"

Other examples:

- "How do you specifically know what I'm thinking/feeling?"
- "How do you realize I'm okay/bad, etc.?"
- The key is to ask, "as you know it."

Applied to Mind Reading Way 2, you might ask:

- "How am I supposed to know on time what you wanted/how you felt?"
- "How could you know better that you don't like that?"
- Another example of mind-reading:
- "Marcela no longer cares about me in the least."

In this case, you have to extract quality information by asking:

- "How do you know that Marcella no longer cares about you in the least?"

To which the person may answer with a generalization (which also has ways to analyze it in the metamodel):

- "Because he never does what I say."
- And this, in turn, could detect a limiting belief: "it never does what I say."

Reading the mind – and others – is an aspect that can be analyzed and overcome through the NLP Metamodel, to collect accurate information, clarify meanings, identify limitations and beliefs, open new options.

The "linguistic" part of Neurolinguistic Programming is exciting. It has powerful tools, such as the metamodel, for improvement in communication and quality of life.

NLP To Connect with Others

At NLP, we do something very similar using the concept of "rapport" when we want to talk about empathy.

In every interaction with each other, it is essential to establish "rapport" to achieve genuine contact.

What Is Rapport?

A phenomenon in which two or more people feel they are in "tune" psychologically and emotionally(sympathy) because they feel similar or relate well to each other.

How to Establish Rapport

The rapport theory tells us that there are three pillars, coordination (or mirroring), reciprocity, and the search for familiar places.

Coordination or Mirroring

The "mirroring" technique consists of acting as a mirror of the other person, adapting to their rhythm both gesturally capturing the general whole of their nonverbal language and replicating it similarly, as well as orally managing to adapt to the tone of voice and the rhythm of the other person's speech. Above all, approaching emotionally, reflecting oneself the emotional state of the other person, to empathize and at the same time make manifests that empathy.

Reciprocity

To show reciprocity, we must find ways to correspond to each other's contributions, either with actions or with prayers.

Reciprocity is embodied by active listening, whereby, despite remaining quieter than the other, we give clear signs of listening and react to what the other says.

Common

places Commonplace search is based on focusing the focus of messages and actions on topics that are of interest to the person we're interacting with.

Representative systems

If you ever had the feeling of being incapable of being able to communicate with a particular person and couldn't understand why the next few lines are going to answer that mystery.

The NLP postulates that all human beings have three representative systems through which we know, learn, and think. That is, they are the filters by which we perceive the world:

The three representative systems are:

- Visual
- Auditory
- Kinesthetic

All three are present in each of us, although there is always one that is dominant over the others. This determines how we relate to the world.

Knowing and learning to recognize the dominant system of the people with whom we interact is one of the keys to good communication because it will allow us to establish rapport more quickly.

How to Recognize the Dominant Representative System?

There are specific keys to being able to recognize the dominant representative structure of the person with whom we are interacting. Let's see what they are:

Visual

People whose dominant system is visualization prioritize the sense of sight over the rest can see images in their head of what they are thinking; are characterized by:

- Speaking very fast, loud, and without pauses
- His voice is sharp and with high tones
- They are usually well upright, shoulders back and chin up
- Their conversations often jump from one topic to another, as their heads process at a faster rate than their mouths
- They move their arms a lot when they talk
- They speak in little detail
- Your breathing is brief, high, and chest
- When sitting, they do it on the edge of the chair
- They use many words that refer to images
- They remember people's faces, not names
- They capture information quickly and with minimal detail
- To learn, they need visual aids
- It is common for them to get bored during speeches and to remember little of them
- They are more interested in the appearance of the product than how it sounds or the feeling it gives them
- When they attend events, they mainly go to see that they see
- Noise often distracts them
- When talking about a feeling, they have an image inside instead of a feeling

Auditory

For hearing aids, the world is perceived through the sense of hearing, and they need to listen to assimilate information. Among its main characteristics we can name:

- When speaking, they use a calm and harmonious tone, they say cautiously
- His voice the most serious
- They breathe regularly and rhythmically from the middle of the chest, and they sigh frequently
- Their conversations are always sequential and one topic at a time
- They use a lot of detail when talking
- They maintain a medium posture, with shoulders and chin in the middle
- They move fewer arms than visuals and keep forearms attached to the body
- They use many words that refer to the sense of hearing
- They're usually good at listening
- They remember words, and they have a remarkable ability to remember what they heard
- They remember people's names
- The raucous, high-pitched noises put them in a bad mood and distract them
- They use many expressions like "uh," "um," "ah," etc. when speaking
- They tend to dominate the conversation by the abundance of words they use

Kinesthetics

When the dominant system is kinesthetic, the rest of the senses that are not the sight or the ear are enhanced. For them, the world is perceived by the experiences that include touch, smell, and taste, i.e., anything they may feel is characterized by:

- They speak slowly and slowly
- His voice is grave
- His shoulders are low and drooping
- They make slow movements
- They are dead in their answers
- His breathing is low and deep
- They tend to be in deconstructed postures and embrace themselves
- When sitting, they do so use the whole chair in poses that are comfortable for them
- They are very connected to their emotions and sensations
- They are guided a lot by their intuition
- They like to be very close to people and touch or hug when greeting
- They use many words that refer to emotions and feelings
- Enjoy activities where you can touch, taste, or feel some aroma
- They are always looking for their comfort and that of others

Digital Hearing

There are also digital hearing people, which has to do with internal dialogue. Digital auditors will often exhibit characteristics of some of the significant representative systems so that they may differ significantly from the description below; Among its features, we can cite:

- They talk with long, complicated phrases
- Breathe in a leisurely and regular way
- His posture, in general, is upright, with his shoulders back and arms folded
- They're always in dialogue with themselves
- They won't give any clues they understood unless we ask them
- His tone of voice for the approach is thoughtful, considerate, and slightly above the monotonous
- They'll want to know if what the caller says "makes sense."

Preaches from Each System

"Predicates" or "verbal predicates" is what the NLP calls the way we talk about each of the representative systems, phrases, and words that we usually use when communicating with others. Through "verbal predicates," we can understand what each person's network of preference is. Let's see how the predicted ones for each system manifest:

Visuals: the phrases that characterize them are:

- Bird's eye view
- Having a good perspective
- He appears before me
- I don't see it.
- In light of the facts
- Because of that

Words they usually use:

Look, appear, reveal, see, imagine, illuminated, bright, show, and focus, among others.

Auditoria's: the phrases that characterize them are:

- I'm all ears
- Hidden message
- Low and clear
- Describe in detail
- Sounds weird to me.
- Frivolous dialogue

Words they usually use:

Silence, being heard, harmony, resonant, silence and hearing among others

Kinestesicos: those of the phrases that characterize them are:

- Connected with
- Floating in the air
- Trapitos in the sun
- It smells terrible to me.
- Hand-to-hand
- Hothead
- Put the cards on the table
- Fall into account

Words they usually use:

Holding, hard, thinking, touching, feeling, pulling out, grabbing, tempering, and impressing are some of them.

Digital Auditoria's: the phrases that characterize them are:

- This increases my chances
- Get an explanation
- I'm in the middle of the process.
- I need to understand.
- Keep that in mind
- In short
- I need to reason it.
- I know what you think.

Words they usually use:

Experience, decision, motivation, change, be conscious, attend, perceive, coherent, process, and meaningless.

We all use visual, kinesisk, and auditory "verbal predicates" all the time, although some contexts mean that we only use one of them; for example, if we ask someone to describe a photo, they may do so on visual terms. In other cases, when we have the option to choose, we will tend always to use the predicaments of our central representative system; let's look at an example for each plan:

- A visual person would say: You
- showed me a brilliant idea about it, and I'd like to see more about it.
- Instead
- A hearing person would say: You
- told me an idea that sounds good, and I'd like to hear more about it.
- While
- A kinesthetic person would say:
- You offered me an idea that makes me feel good, and I would like to get down to business.
- And finally:
- A digital aviation person would express it if:
- You provided me with a way of proceeding that makes sense, and I would like to know more details.

Eye Access Keys

Have you ever noticed that people move their eyes when they talk? These eye patterns have a meaning for NLP, are directly related, and are called keys or eye access tracks.

Eye access allows us to almost infallibly identify a person's dominant representative system as these eye movements are involuntary and, therefore, impossible to control.

Studies were conducted where it was shown that depending on where the eyes move, the person uses different senses and hemispheres of the brain to process the information.

Visual Processing

system People whose dominant representative system is visible move their eyes to the top right when they are building an image, while if they look to the top right, it is because they remember an idea.

Hearing Processing

system Hearing people will look sideways, i.e., towards their ears, this movement will be left when they remember a sound and to the right when they are building it. It is common to accompany it with a slight movement of the head, similar to when we talk on the phone.

Kinesthetic Processing

system In the case of kinesthetic people going to look down and to the right, this is because they are having access to their feelings; an example of this is when we are sad and tend to look down.

Hearing-Digital Processing

system Finally, auditory-digital people are going to look down, and to the left, this means they're talking to themselves.

Optimal Distance

The optimal distance, or also called a comfort bubble, is the patio perceived as ideal when we establish an interpersonal relationship as being a conversation.

This distance is different for each person and, as it could not be otherwise, also depends on its dominant representative system.

It is imperative to take this distance into account to prevent the other person from feeling uncomfortable or invaded or, on the contrary, feel a lot of remotenesses. Whatever the case may be, the result will be that communication between the two will not be successful.

While the optimal distance will depend on each person, standard features are relying on the representative system of preference; visuals, for example, have to prefer to be further away from other people during a conversation, especially if they are not people from their close social circle.

Hearing people, on the other hand, are characterized by preferring a distance a little closer to people. This distance is comfortable for them to be able to hear clearly from others.

Kinesthetic people otherwise are characterized by enjoying an almost non-existent distance between them and each other, and they like to always be in contact with each other. They often touch and hug people by greeting them, even if they know them.

Is it clearer now what to do when we feel uncomfortable in a conversation where people are too far away or too close?

To understand what the optimal distance of each person is, we must listen to their body language, so we will have clues about when the other person is comfortable or not. For example, some people may change the tone of their skin when they are at a distance that generates discomfort.

Now that we have been going through some of the main concepts of NLP, they will understand why we often have this feeling of not being able to understand each other; this happens when the person with whom we try to have a dialogue has a different dominant system than ours. It is common for a visual person to be difficult to interact with an auditory and much more so with a kinesthetic. However, now they know it is all due to representative systems!

How to Implement These Tools?
So far, everything is adorable, although I'm sure you're wondering how to put all this into practice, aren't you? Well, not to despair, let's look at an efficient example.

Let's take a typical situation from user research practice: an interview.

We may know some data about the person we are interviewing even if we probably don't know what their dominant representative system is, which is key to being able to generate rapport. To quickly detect its dominant system, we can design some ice-breaking questions that allow us to recognize it so that we can accommodate it.

The questions we design will depend on which footprint is more straightforward and faster for us to read. For example, if we find it easy to read eye access, we can ask a question that refers you to a situation of the past, for example:

How's the weather outside? Or did it cost you a hard time getting here?

The way he inadvertently moves his eyes will give us the first indication of his dominant representative system.

Its optimal distance can obtain another key. It is essential to choose a comfortable place where we will conduct the interview; when I say pleased, I mean propitious to be able to generate rapport. If we make the person sit behind a desk and we sit on the opposite side, we will hardly succeed in developing rapport since that space will prevent us from connecting with the other.

It is essential to let the interviewee choose where to sit, and then locate us; be attentive to the distance in which we sit so that he or she feels comfortable. If we observe their body language, we will notice some changes in their bodies when it is uncomfortable.

It's also important to look at other features like the ones we saw before, the tone of your voice, the speed you're talking to, the way you move your hands, or how you feel in a chair.

The only thing I never recommend you ever do is give you a test of those on the internet to recognize the dominant system.

I've already misgendered the dominant representative system of the person I'm going to interview, and now what do I do?

Once we are clear about the dominant system of the person with whom we are going to engage in conversation, we must "put ourselves in the mode of their dominant system" this means that we must behave as closely as possible to it, replicate their tone of voice, cadence when speaking, the way we move, etc., in this way we will communicate with him in the way he perceives the world around him.

It is also time to implement the techniques that allow us to generate rapport, such as coordination, reciprocity, and the search for familiar places. In this way, we can be in complete harmony with each other, and he will feel confident to talk with us.

It is almost enough to say that all this requires training, surely it will not come out at the first attempt, although I risk saying that by putting into practice these tools, we will be able to obtain excellent results in our work and our personal lives in a short time.

Conflict and Congruence in NLP

This space is intended for those who want to make changes in their lives, improving communication, and discovering their resources. In this way, it is possible to know and recognize each other, creating the bridges that lead to the best understanding among people, becoming aware that change is possible always! I propose to be open to new learning, to accept the challenges, motivated, committed, and confident in their strengths.

The NLP studies the structure of subjective experience. With NLP tools, people can understand their internal states and change them if needed.

The world we create in our minds as a result of sensory perception and its internal representation is our real world as well, and that's where we act from.

Changes can be made to our experience by modifying our representations. This ability to change, making our behavior more flexible, generates changes in our internal states, causing an excellent capacity for choice and control.

Ecological check is essential because it allows us to connect with what we want, with the resources to achieve it while maintaining the internal balance and that of the environment.

NLP tools work to achieve internal unity, self-awareness, improve interpersonal relationships and our internal conversations, change beliefs, and set enriching goals.

Our beliefs, values, styles of choice generate our internal states if there is unity, harmony, and the inner state is of well-being.

We are consistent when verbal and body language (gestures, tone of voice, breathing, body posture) are aligned.

Let us remember everything we express with our bodies, beyond words.

Consistency in communication is an indispensable requirement for us to appreciate that the message issued is received, which was understood.

When we transmit consistent messages, we are credible.

If we communicate incongruously, we will transmit confusing messages to our environment and ourselves, limiting statements, justifications, self-buttoning, self-deception.

We can detect signs of inconsistency in our interlocutor by sharpening our sensory, calibrating their behavior, verbal and body language.

If we recognize internal conflicts internally as a result of inconsistency, it is time to integrate our parties in search of balance, to generate agreements.

If internal incongruity persists over time, physical symptoms will appear, making the internal imbalance conscious.

With NLP tools, people can understand their internal states and change them if needed. The world we create in our minds as a result of sensory perception and its representation.

The NLP Studies the Structure of Subjective Experience

With NLP tools, people can understand their internal states and change them if needed. The world we create in our minds as a result of sensory perception and its internal representation is our real world as well, and that's where we act from.

Changes can be made to our experience by modifying our representations. This ability to change, making our behavior more flexible, generates changes in our internal states, causing an excellent capacity for choice and control.

Ecological check is essential because it allows us to connect with what we want, with the resources to achieve it while maintaining the internal balance and that of the environment.

NLP tools work to achieve internal unity, self-awareness, improve interpersonal relationships and our internal conversations, change beliefs, and set enriching goals.

Our beliefs, values, styles of choice generate our internal states. If there is unity, harmony, the inner form is of well-being.

We are consistent when verbal and body language (gestures, tone of voice, breathing, body posture) are aligned.

Let us remember everything we express with our bodies, beyond words.

- Consistency in communication is an indispensable requirement for us to appreciate that the message issued is received, which was understood.
- When we transmit consistent messages, we are credible.
- If we communicate incongruously, we will transmit confusing messages to our environment and ourselves, limiting statements, justifications, self-buttoning, self-deception.
- We can detect signs of inconsistency in our interlocutor by sharpening our sensory, calibrating their behavior, verbal and body language.
- If we recognize internal conflicts internally as a result of inconsistency, it is time to integrate our parties in search of balance, to generate agreements.
- If internal incongruity persists over time, physical symptoms will appear, making the internal imbalance conscious.

NLP In Therapy

There are a large number of published researches on the use of Hypnotherapy and Neurolinguistic Programming as complementary therapeutic approaches to anxiety, fears, and phobias.

In several cases, direct submissions to relieve anxiety or phobias have proven effective. When direct recommendations are ineffective, many other hypnotic techniques can be useful. The process of introduction alone and deepening into a hypnotic state relieves stress in general.

Hypnotically given, systematic desensitization (a process of Nerve Language Programming) is very useful. The person learns to acquire a sense of internal control over stimuli that produce fear or anxiety. Advantages of hypnotic desensitization, compared to traditional behavior desensitization therapies, include enhanced urbanization of incentives and the ability to give Post–Hypnotic submissions to encourage behavioral responses to situations they had imagined.

Mental rehearsal in a hypnotic state, so that the person can cope with tense situations, is another method for dealing with anxiety and phobic disorders.

When low self-esteem is one aspect of the problem, ego enhancement techniques can be used; because hypnosis exploits the close connection between mind and body, it provides relief through improved self-regulation and also beneficially affects the experience of self-sufficiency.

Hypnosis age regression techniques can be used to help clients experience experiences immediately before they start to feel anxious. This can help identify the situations that cause stress, as well as internal dialogue and images that cause problematic reactions.

Age regression in times before the development of phobia, when the client successfully encountered phobic stimuli, provides a state of empowerment that can be established and lead the person to manage negative emotions in times of high stress. Age regression techniques with hypnotherapy provide access to identify conflicts or experiences of the past that are beyond conscious awareness. When traumatic events related to phobic reactions are found, you facilitate a release by psycho-correcting the emotions associated with the experience.

Hypnotherapy is effective in managing pre-operative and postoperative anxiety, including situations in which the patient is in a period of crisis. This may also apply to the treatment of fears about dental treatments. Examples that hypnotherapy can be used as a supplement to treat anxiety in medical conditions and treatments that typically cause significant stress may include dental procedures, surgical and postoperative conditions, lumbar punctures and bone marrow aspiration, chronic headaches, cancer, pain from burns, gastrointestinal disorders, nausea, respiratory disorders, tinnitus, and obstetrics/gynecology.

One example is the reduction of stress caused by the Magnetic Tomography (MRI). This medical diagnostic procedure requires the patient to lie down in an enclosed space for about an hour. This immobility and confinement cause panic and claustrophobic reactions in up to 10% of patients undergoing the MRI procedure. Hypnotherapy has been successfully used to alleviate these reactions.

Interestingly, it has been shown that phobic patients are, on average, more subject than others. The essence of the phobic experience is not unlike that of the manifestation of the hypnotic state, since the phobic incident occurs spontaneously - as do the cross-country experiences. Hypnotherapy helps patients learn more about their cross-abilities and learn to control them.

NLP For Trauma Healing
Individual Therapy

Realizing at times in our lives that we need to seek the help of a mental health professional is not an easy task. The same criteria apply to hypnotherapy as to any treatment method. When we have exhausted our stamina and are tired of seeing the same repetitive pattern of behavior, either from others or ourselves, then we need help. Friends and family are not always the right people to help us change our perspective, perhaps because they do not have the proper training, although they may be in a good mood. So instead of watching our lives steadily lose their quality, suffer and feel like we are at a dead-end, let's do something about it. This decision is the first step to taking responsibility for ourselves. Our problem is not others but ourselves. He is responsible for our procrastination, our malicious behavior, our evil thoughts that become physical problems, the neglect of ourselves, the unhealthy foods we eat, the lack of joy, and creativity. But there is a solution to everything, and we have to start somewhere.

Individual Hypnotherapy

What it takes for individual hypnotherapy to work:

The first thing that needs to exist to start a beneficial therapeutic relationship between the therapist and the patient is trust.

There is a need for honesty when taking the history so that the therapist can have a complete picture of the condition. Honesty is also present on the part of the therapist, who always points out the points that need to be worked on with the appropriate priority.

The therapist distinguishes the most vital healthy part of each person, his healthy identity, and, at the same time, those points that need to be strengthened so that the person regains his limits and the correct view of the situation. At the same time, he chooses the most appropriate technique depending on the person and the occasion.

Personal motivation, the will to live, and the individual's promise to himself for self-love are discussed and reinforced in each session.

During these six sessions, the patient:

- He comes into contact with emotions that he was afraid to unlock in a field of security and calm without emotional outbursts.
- He composes all the parts of himself, faces his image with love, and feels fullness and acceptance.
- He places himself at the center, sets his healthy boundaries, and then places every person in his life at the right distance, outside his center at the right space at which he feels comfortable.
- He observes his behavior as a third person. He examines his behavior and his relationships with his environment objectively by solving entanglements.
- It composes the most useful image and behavior through a series of experiential exercises, time-shifting, visionary ideas, and dialogue. Revises old behaviors, unhealthy beliefs, and bad planning. He accepts the past and learns to respect and love himself in the present. He overcomes the problem because now he can see and believe that he deserves to be healed.

Conference Program

An indicative treatment number is a cycle of six sessions, always depending on the topic. This framework is agreed between the therapist and the patient after receiving a history. After that, the sessions begin, which take place every 7-10 days, so that there is the required period after each hypnotherapy to test the person alone the beneficial result of the procedure. This result is built and made permanent from the first to the sixth session. This period has been characterized by those who have completed it as a beautiful journey of rapid personal development and inner change in which they calm down, understand the area of their mistakes, stop sweating and take their lives in their hands. More than six sessions are needed for skin problems and depression. After the first round of sessions and having achieved good victories, the person can consider who he wants to be his next step. The sessions that make up this core cycle continue to work in the long run, according to clients.

What Neurolinguistic Programming Helps
They were decoding the function of the mind concerning the nervous system, physiology, and communication and gave us the method with steps, instructions, and infinite techniques.

The NLP process leads each person to find the right solutions on his own by bringing him into contact with his inner wisdom, which knows better than anyone what is best for him. Through the techniques and steps that one gives us, one can overcome obstacles and create a new self and a new life.

It is a simple but, at the same time, resourceful system that effectively addresses most of the issues that modern man has to deal with.

Some of them are:

1. Trains the Mind to Think Differently
To see things from another angle that frees you up so that you can take your strength and move forward. A lot of times, people block and think they're at a dead-end because they've learned to believe in a certain way that repeats over and over again like a single tape in their minds, bringing the same unwanted results to their daily lives.

Conscious and Subconscious: Why don't we control our lives?

The NLP, through various techniques as well as the method of "reframe," gives a new interpretation to events, creates a space of different internal representations, and gives new suggestions and solutions to life.

2. Improving Self-Confidence And Increasing Self-Esteem
Self-confidence and self-esteem are the qualities that make a difference in all areas. Without these two, there is no inner driving force that takes the helm of life. There is no satisfaction, no pleasure, no evolution.

What reduces our self-confidence, and how do we enhance it?

This can change when someone starts using their brain in the right way to create a different self-image, different internal dialogue, and further interpretations of themselves by pressing the corresponding psychological buttons.

3. Creating A New Behavior
This also involves eliminating old behaviors and habits that are harmful or unhealthy. There are several ways and strategies to create new synapses in the brain. These new neuro-associations will support the desired behavior.

4. Tackling Phobias
The NLP argues that as a phobia of an event was created conscious or unconscious by installing a specific fear program in the brain, so it can be created by changing and replacing the program by changing the internal representations that feed it.

5. Excellent Methodology of Personal Development and Success
And since we have already said that it helps to deal with phobias, it is next to have the strength to assist in the evolution of man, since usually what prevents someone from moving forward is his phobias.

It also helps to end decisions, to clarify internally, to set objectives, and to take steps to achieve them. It can also provide significant help to people who are already good in some areas and want to get even better at increasing performance, expanding skills, and excellence.

6. Helps Man Dare to Dream

People are often even afraid to think about the future they would like to live for many different reasons. Sometimes they think it's impossible to happen, that they don't deserve it, that they're helpless, sometimes they've forgotten how to dream, or they don't know-how.

But if the man himself does not envision his future, then he will simply follow the future envisaged by others. With special techniques, he is called to see his future, to take action, to dare to dream but also to enjoy it!

Further NLP Training Strategies

The NLP has been an important place among the disciplines that assist in achieving objectives so that many psychologists, doctors, and coaches apply it in the field of personal development individually or in a group way.

One of the foundations of NLP is evidence that each of us builds different representations of the reality to which we add our emotions and language processes.

By modifying our beliefs and emotions, the way we express ourselves, we can also change the perception of reality and self-image that we have of ourselves.

On the other hand, Neurolinguistic Programming ensures that memory and imagination use the same neurological circuits and the same impact on humans. Next, 8 NLP transformative strategies were collected by psychologist Jasmine Zambrano in her book PNL for All.

1. Sub Modalities or Learning Styles

Sub Modalities are variants of representation systems, that is, the way our brain encodes and classifies an experience. There are three types: visual (color, distance, depth, clarity, contrast, and luminosity), auditory (volume, tone, rhythm, and pauses), and kinesthetic (temperature, vibration, texture, pressure, movement, and weight).

All these nuances would serve us, through imagination, to be able to change the characteristics of the memories that we have edited as a film of our life and thus modify, for example, the memory of an unhappy childhood

Another way to apply them would be through "dissociation." We move to the moment when we live an unpleasant experience, feel the touch that an object had or see what was happening, and then dissociate ourselves, get out of the situation and look at it as if we were out of it, observing ourselves.

For NLP, the goal of dissociating is to take emotional power away from the experience we have experienced. Thus, experience loses strength, disassociates from suffering, and can even be associated with a pleasant moment.

2. Anchoring Technique

In the process of anchoring technique, an external stimulus or "anchor" is associated with positive behavior that you want to acquire. Anchors can be words, gestures, smells, or colors that lead us to a positive state of mind.

An example of this anchor would be to associate the gesture of touching one's ear with feeling good so that, in times of crisis or difficulty, with that small gesture, we could regain well-being and feel better.

3. Reframe

Reframe, in NLP, is to modify the frame of reference in which a person lives the situation to change its meaning and, therefore, the emotional state and behavior that, in principle, accompanied it. It is to see the glass half full instead of half empty, find an unexpected edge in the situation that manages to reverse its impact and positivize it.

4. Calibration

This strategy is to recognize the mental state of the individual through his verbal and nonverbal behavior, that is, whether he is sad, angry, or even if he is lying. By looking at their behavior, we will be able to get to know each other better and help them in their process of change.

5. Modeling

Modeling helps determine how other people acted to achieve success in some area of their lives and to be able to imitate them. With the modeling technique, what is being attempted is to create as faithful a representation as possible of another person, especially their behaviors, to achieve something.

6. Induction

With the induction technique, people are guided to specific emotional states to modify painful situations. Whether it is inducing feelings of discomfort that match the experience they lived or pleasant sensations to be able to face their fears and concerns about such cases.

7. Synchronization

Synchronization would be like deep empathy, through which other people's feelings are understood until a strong link between the conscious and unconscious level of the interlocutor is created. This technique is used to optimize interpersonal communications.

8. Relaxation

Finally, the NLP considers relaxation a useful tool for relieving tensions, expanding awareness, and freeing the spirit. Relaxing always comes in a good to face our day today.

Conclusion

You've probably already found that functional relationships are vital to the success of work and personal life. Very often, people do not know that the language they use significantly affects their professional associations, how the people they communicate with the feel and react.

Moreover, if you study the NLP communication model, you will find that every time an event occurs, everyone will perceive it differently and react to it differently as well. So, whatever's going on around you, your brain processes it, using your own "personal filters," e.g., your beliefs, past experiences, your way of thinking. These personal filters that you use to process every experience you experience make you perceive things in your way, which can be very different from how others perceive them. That is why each of us often has a different attitude towards the same event. If you understand this, you will be able to develop more mutual understanding, as well as better communication and harmony with yourself and those around you.

In this way, NLP contributes to more effective communication, better understanding, and mutual understanding. As relationships regain a sense of meaningful dialogue and a new kind of perception develops, interacting with others is more effective and significantly broadens your horizons.

Because NLP is so extensive, anyone can benefit from it. Ideally, it would have it with you in education right from primary school. An important part is communication, so you are a leader, entrepreneur, teacher, salesperson, or work with people in one way or another so that NLP can facilitate communication with other people. Maybe you have habits or behavior patterns you would like to change or become better at managing your state of mind? Perhaps you are practicing sports or doing something where goal management and motivation are important factors? Or maybe you are interested in working with your personal development and learning more about yourself and others around you? Whatever the reason, NLP can be a tool for you.

NLP allows us to understand how we perceive the world. This helps us to know ourselves more and to understand others. If we provide the tools provided by the NLP, we can achieve more effective communications as well as better relationships and links, in my particular case, in addition to using these tools for my personal life.

NLP (Neuro-Linguistic Programming) has discovered and released the enormous hidden potential of people to heal and solve their problems permanently and quickly. It has evolved into a dynamic system of development and improvement of personality. It is the most impressive knowledge discovered in the last 40 years to radically change man's perceptions and behaviors, transforming his weaknesses into abilities and perspectives.

CPSIA information can be obtained
at www.ICGtesting.com
Printed in the USA
LVHW050712271220
675069LV00010B/231

9 781914 176807